Microsoft®

Visual Basic 2010

for Windows Applications
Introductory

Gary B. Shelly

Corinne Hoisington
Central Virginia Community College

COURSE TECHNOLOGY
CENGAGE Learning™

Australia • Brazil • Japan • Korea • Mexico • Singapore • Spain • United Kingdom • United States

COURSE TECHNOLOGY
CENGAGE Learning

Microsoft® Visual Basic 2010 for Windows Applications: Introductory
Gary B. Shelly
Corinne Hoisington

Vice President, Publisher: Nicole Pinard

Executive Editor: Kathleen McMahon

Product Manager: Crystal Parenteau

Associate Product Manager: Aimee Poirier

Editorial Assistant: Lauren Brody

Director of Marketing: Cheryl Costantini

Marketing Manager: Tristen Kendall

Marketing Coordinator: Stacey Leasca

Print Buyer: Julio Esperas

Production Director: Patty Stephan

Content Project Manager: Heather Hopkins

Development Editor: Lisa Ruffolo

Copyeditor: Michael Beckett

Proofreader: Andrew Therriault

Indexer: Sharon Hilgenberg

QA Manuscript Reviewers: Serge Palladino
and Danielle Shaw

Art Director: Marissa Falco

Cover Designer: Lisa Kuhn, Curio Press, LLC

Cover Photo: Tom Kates Photography

Text Designer: Joel Sadagursky

Compositor: PreMediaGlobal

For product information and technology assistance, contact us at
Cengage Learning Customer & Sales Support, 1-800-354-9706

For permission to use material from this text or product, submit all requests online at **cengage.com/permissions**
Further permissions questions can be emailed to
permissionrequest@cengage.com

Library of Congress Control Number: 2010929659

ISBN-13: 978-0-538-46845-9

ISBN-10: 0-538-46845-9

Course Technology
20 Channel Center Street
Boston, MA 02210
USA

Cengage Learning is a leading provider of customized learning solutions with office locations around the globe, including Singapore, the United Kingdom, Australia, Mexico, Brazil, and Japan. Locate your local office at: **international.cengage.com/region**

Cengage Learning products are represented in Canada by Nelson Education, Ltd.

To learn more about Course Technology, visit **www.cengage.com/ coursetechnology**

To learn more about Cengage Learning, visit **www.cengage.com**

Purchase any of our products at your local college store or at our preferred online store **www.cengagebrain.com**

Microsoft is a registered trademark of Microsoft Corporation in the United States and/or other countries. Course Technology, a part of Cengage Learning, is an independent entity from the Microsoft Corporation, and not affiliated with Microsoft in any manner.

Printed in the United States of America
1 2 3 4 5 6 7 16 15 14 13 12 11 10

CHAPTER 4
Variables and Arithmetic Operations

INTRODUCTION 196
USER INTERFACE 197
TextBox Objects 197
Label Objects 208
Accept Button in Form Properties 210
Cancel Button in Form Properties 211
Visual Studio Preparation for Code Entry 211
INTRODUCTION TO DATA ENTRY AND DATA TYPES 212
String Data Type 213
Assignment Statements 214
Numeric Data Types 219
Other Data Types 222
Literals 224
Forced Literal Types 225
Constants 225
Referencing a Variable 227
Scope of Variables 227
Converting Variable Data 228
Option Strict On 231
ARITHMETIC OPERATIONS 232
Arithmetic Operators 233
Displaying Numeric Output Data 239
Clearing the Form — Clear Procedure and Focus Procedure 242
Form Load Event 244
Class Scope 247
Debugging Your Program 248
PROGRAM DESIGN 250
Event Planning Document 252
Code the Program 253
GUIDED PROGRAM DEVELOPMENT 253
CODE LISTING 271
SUMMARY 272
LEARN IT ONLINE 274
KNOWLEDGE CHECK 274
DEBUGGING EXERCISES 276
PROGRAM ANALYSIS 277
CASE PROGRAMMING ASSIGNMENTS 279

CHAPTER 5
Decision Structures

INTRODUCTION 292
CHAPTER PROJECT 292
User Interface Design 294
Using the GroupBox Object 294
Adding the RadioButton Objects 298
Using the Checked Property of RadioButton Objects 300
Windows Application Container Objects 302
Displaying a Message Box 303
String Concatenation 311
MAKING DECISIONS WITH CONDITIONAL STATEMENTS 312
Using an If . . . Then Statement 312
Relational Operators 313
Comparing Different Data Types 317
Using the If . . . Then . . . Else Statement 318
Using the If . . . Then . . . Elseif Statement 320
Nested If Statements 322
Testing the Status of a RadioButton Object in Code 326
Block-Level Scope 327

Using Logical Operators 328
Select Case Statement 332
Code Snippets 337
Validating Data 339
PROGRAM DESIGN 342
Event Planning Document 343
Design and Code the Program 344
GUIDED PROGRAM DEVELOPMENT 344
CODE LISTING 355
SUMMARY 356
LEARN IT ONLINE 358
KNOWLEDGE CHECK 358
DEBUGGING EXERCISES 359
PROGRAM ANALYSIS 361
CASE PROGRAMMING ASSIGNMENTS 364

CHAPTER 6
Loop Structures

INTRODUCTION 378
CHAPTER PROJECT 378
USER INTERFACE DESIGN 380
MenuStrip Object 380
InputBox Function 387
Displaying Data Using the ListBox Object 390
Accumulators, Counters, and Compound Operators 396
USING LOOPS TO PERFORM REPETITIVE TASKS 399
Repeating a Process Using the For...Next Loop 399
Repeating a Process Using a Do Loop 405
Do Until Loops 410
Avoiding Infinite Loops 412
Priming the Loop 413
Validating Data 414
Creating a Nested Loop 416
Selecting the Best Loop 417
USING A DATATIP WITH BREAKPOINTS 417
PUBLISHING AN APPLICATION WITH CLICKONCE
DEPLOYMENT 425
PROGRAM DESIGN 430
Event Planning Document 432
Design and Code the Program 433
GUIDED PROGRAM DEVELOPMENT 433
CODE LISTING 452
SUMMARY 454
LEARN IT ONLINE 455
KNOWLEDGE CHECK 455
DEBUGGING EXERCISES 457
PROGRAM ANALYSIS 459
CASE PROGRAMMING ASSIGNMENTS 462

APPENDIX A   UNICODE ....APP 1
APPENDIX B   THE MY NAMESPACE ....APP 5
APPENDIX C   NAMING CONVENTIONS ....APP 11
Index ....IND 1
Photo Credits ....IND 20

PREFACE

The Shelly Cashman Series® offers the finest textbooks in computer education. This *Microsoft Visual Basic 2010* book utilizes an innovative step-by-step pedagogy, which integrates demonstrations of professional-quality programs with in-depth discussions of programming concepts and techniques and opportunities for hands-on practice and reinforcement. The popular Guided Program Development section supports students as they work independently to create useful, realistic, and appealing applications, building their confidence and skills while guiding them to select appropriate Visual Basic 2010 programming methods. Online Reinforcement boxes direct students to online videos that show how to perform a series of steps. Other marginal elements, such as In the Real World boxes, provide expert tips to add interest and depth to topics. A robust and varied collection of exercises, including a series of practical case-based programming projects, ensures students gain the knowledge and expertise they need to succeed when developing professional programs.

Visual Basic 2010 builds on the features of Visual Basic 2008, which introduced coding once and deploying on multiple devices. Some of the major enhancements to Visual Basic 2010 include rapid application development tools, a redesigned interface that support Windows Presentation Foundation, dual-monitor support, improved IntelliSense features to increase productivity, and a more helpful debugging experience. Using Visual Basic 2010, you can design, create, and deploy Windows, Mobile, Web, Database, and Office applications. Visual Studio 2010 includes several productivity enhancements including IntelliSense tools, new and updated project types, and includes Silverlight expanded sample applications, and more.

Objectives of this Textbook

Microsoft Visual Basic 2010 for Windows Applications: Introductory is intended for a one-credit course that introduces students to the correct ways to design and write programs using Visual Basic 2010. The goal of this text is to provide an introductory-level course in computer programming for students with little or no previous programming experience. The objectives of this book are:

- To teach the fundamentals of the Microsoft Visual Basic 2010 programming language
- To understand and apply graphical user interface design principles
- To emphasize the development cycle when creating applications, which mirrors the same approach that professional developers use
- To illustrate well-written and readable programs using a disciplined coding style, including documentation and indentation standards
- To create Visual Basic applications that deploy on multiple platforms such as handheld computers, cell phones, Web pages, Windows, and Office environments
- To demonstrate how to implement logic involving sequence, selection, and repetition using Visual Basic 2010

- To write useful, well-designed programs for personal computers and handheld computers that solve practical business problems
- To encourage independent study and help those who are working on their own in a distance education environment

The Shelly Cashman Approach

Features of this *Microsoft Visual Basic 2010* book include:

- **Realistic, Up-to-Date Applications** Each programming chapter focuses on building a sample project, a complete, useful application that showcases Visual Basic 2010 features and the latest technology.
- **Guided Steps to Encourage Independence** After observing how a professional developer would build the chapter project and exploring related programming concepts and Visual Basic 2010 techniques, students create the sample application on their own in the Guided Program Development section. This step-by-step section provides enough guidance for students to work independently, with Hint Screens that verify students are performing the tasks correctly.
- **More Than Step-By-Step** Each chapter offers clear, thorough discussions of the programming concepts students need to understand to build the sample application. Important Visual Basic 2010 design and programming features are also highlighted, including time-saving techniques such as using IntelliSense, code snippets, and the Toolbox. As appropriate, students design and prepare for applications the way professional developers do — by creating or analyzing requirements documents, use case definitions, and event planning documents.
- **Online Reinforcement Boxes** The Online Reinforcement boxes send students to the Online Companion at scsite.com/vb2010 to watch videos illustrating each step in the chapter project. Students can refer to the Online Reinforcement boxes when they work through or review the chapter, watching videos as they prepare to create the chapter application on their own.
- **Heads Up Boxes** Heads Up boxes appear in the margin to give advice for following best programming practices and tips about alternative ways of completing the same task.
- **In the Real World Boxes** This marginal feature provides insight into how developers use Visual Basic tools or programming techniques to save time or enhance professional development projects.
- **Watch Out For Boxes** These boxes explain how to avoid common pitfalls when using a particular command, programming structure, or technique.

Organization of this Textbook

Microsoft Visual Basic 2010 for Windows Applications: Introductory provides detailed instructions on how to use Visual Basic 2010 to build authentic, effective, and appealing applications for Microsoft Windows personal computers and mobile devices. The material is divided into six chapters and three appendices as follows:

Chapter 1 — Introduction to Visual Basic 2010 Programming   Chapter 1 provides an overview of programming with Visual Basic 2010. The chapter defines a computer program, describes the role of a developer in creating computer programs, and discusses event-driven programs that have a graphical user interface (GUI). The chapter also explains the roles of input, processing, output, and data when running a program on a computer; examines the basic arithmetic and logical operations a program can perform; and explores the use of databases and computer programming languages in general. Finally, the chapter introduces Visual Studio 2010 and the .NET 3.5 Framework, including the .NET class libraries and related features, and surveys the types of Visual Basic 2010 applications.

Chapter 2 — Program and Graphical User Interface Design   Chapter 2 introduces students to the major elements of the Visual Studio 2010 integrated development environment (IDE) while designing a graphical user interface mock-up. Topics include opening Visual Studio 2010, creating a Windows Forms Application project, adding objects to a Windows form, assigning properties to objects, aligning objects on the Windows form, and saving Visual Basic projects. The chapter also discusses how to apply GUI design principles and examines the first two phases of the program development life cycle (PDLC).

Chapter 3 — Program Design and Coding   Chapter 3 provides students with the skills and knowledge necessary to complete phases 2, 3, and 4 of the PDLC by enhancing a GUI mock-up, designing program processing objects, and coding a program. Topics include using IntelliSense when writing code and enhancing a Visual Basic 2010 form by changing the BackColor property of an object and displaying images. This chapter also explains how to enter Visual Basic 2010 code, correct errors, and run a completed program. Finally, the chapter discusses the value of creating an event planning document.

Chapter 4 — Variables and Arithmetic Operations   Chapter 4 introduces variables and arithmetic operations used in the coding of a Visual Basic application. The chapter provides in-depth coverage of declaring variables, gathering input for an application, differentiating data types, performing mathematical calculations, and understanding the proper scope of variables. The chapter also shows how to use various types of TextBox objects.

Chapter 5 — Decision Structures   Chapter 5 begins how to create a Visual Basic 2010 Windows application. This application uses decision structures to take different actions depending on the user's input. Topics include using If...Then statements, If...Then...Else statements, nested If statements, logical operators, and Case statements. The chapter also explores how to use the Panel object, place RadioButton objects, display a message box, insert code snippets, and test input to ensure it is valid.

Chapter 6 — Loop Structures   Chapter 6 presents another type of fundamental programming structure — the repetition structure, including Do While, Do Until, For...Next, For Each...Next, and While...End While loops. Topics include repeating a process using the For...Next and Do loops; priming a loop; creating a nested loop;

selecting the best type of loop; avoiding infinite loops; validating data; and understanding compound operators, counters, and accumulators. The chapter also shows how to insert a MenuStrip object, use the InputBox function, display data using the ListBox object, debug programs using DataTips at breakpoints, and publish a finished application using ClickOnce technology.

Appendices   This book concludes with three appendices. Appendix A explains the purpose of Unicode and provides a table listing Unicode characters and their equivalents. Appendix B examines the My namespace element of Visual Basic 2010 in detail. Appendix C lists the common data types used in Visual Basic 2010, including the recommended naming convention for the three-character prefix preceding variable names.

End-of-Chapter Activities

A notable strength of this *Microsoft Visual Basic 2010* book is the extensive student activities at the end of each chapter. Well-structured student activities can make the difference between students merely participating in a class and retaining the information they learn. These end-of-chapter activities include the following:

- **Learn It Online**   The Learn It Online section directs students to Web-based exercises, which are fun, interactive activities that include chapter reinforcement (true/false, multiple choice, and short answer questions), practice tests, and a crossword puzzle challenge to augment concepts, key terms, techniques, and other material in the chapter.

- **Knowledge Check**   The Knowledge Check section includes short exercises and review questions that reinforce concepts and provide opportunities to practice skills.

- **Debugging Exercises**   In these exercises, students examine short code samples to identify errors and solve programming problems.

- **Program Analysis**   The Program Analysis exercises let students apply their knowledge of Visual Basic 2010 and programming techniques. In some exercises, students write programming statements that meet a practical goal or solve a problem. In other exercises, students analyze code samples and identify the output.

- **Case Programming Assignments**   Nine programming assignments for each chapter challenge students to create applications using the skills learned in the chapter. Each assignment presents a realistic business scenario and requires students to create programs of varying difficulty.

  - Easiest: The first three assignments provide most of the program design information, such as a requirements document and use case definition, for a business application. Students design an application, create an event planning document, and write the code for the application.

  - Intermediate: The next three assignments provide some of the program design information, such as a requirements document. Students create other design documents, such as a use case definition and event planning document, and then build the user interface and code the application.

  - Challenging: The final three assignments provide only a description of a business problem, and students create all the design documents, design the user interface, and code the application.

To the Instructor

Each chapter in this book focuses on a realistic, appealing Visual Basic 2010 application. A chapter begins with a completed application, which you can run to demonstrate how it works, the tasks it performs, and the problems it solves. The chapter introduction also identifies the application's users and their requirements, such as running the program on a handheld computer or validating input data.

The steps in the next section of a chapter show how to create the user interface for the application. You can perform these steps in class — each step clearly explains an action, describes the results, and includes a figure showing the results, with callouts directing your attention to key elements on the screen. Some marginal features, such as the Heads Up boxes, provide additional tips for completing the steps. The Online Reinforcement boxes direct students to videos that replay the steps, which is especially helpful for review and for distance learning students.

This section also explains the Visual Basic 2010 tools and properties needed to understand and create the user interface. For example, while placing a text box in an application, the chapter describes the purpose of a text box and why you should set its maximum and minimum size. You can discuss these ideas and strategies, and then continue your demonstration to show students how to apply them to the chapter application.

After completing the user interface, the chapter explores the programming concepts students should understand to create the application, such as proper syntax, variables, data types, conditional statements, and loops. This section uses the same types of steps, figures, and marginal features to demonstrate how to enter code to complete and test the application.

To prepare students for building the application on their own, the chapter next considers the program design and logic by examining planning documents:

- *Requirements document* — The requirements document identifies the purpose, procedures, and calculations of the program, and specifies details such as the application title, restrictions, and comments that help to explain the program.
- *Use case definition* — The use case definition describes what the user does and how the program responds to each action.
- *Event planning document* — The event planning document lists each object in the user interface that causes an event, the action the user takes to trigger the event, and the event processing that must occur.

You can discuss these documents in class and encourage students to review them as they create a program, reinforcing how professional developers create applications in the modern workplace.

In the innovative Guided Program Development section students work on their own to create the chapter application. They complete the tasks within each numbered step, referring to Hint Screens when they need a reminder about how to perform a step or which method to use. Many tasks reference figures shown earlier in the chapter. Students can refer to these figures for further help — they show exactly how to use a particular technique for completing a task. Steps end with a results figure, which illustrates how the application should look if students performed the tasks correctly. To reinforce how students learned the chapter material, the Guided Program Development section also focuses first on designing the user interface and then on coding the application. A complete program listing appears at the end of this section, which students can use to check their work.

At the end of each chapter, you'll find plenty of activities that provide review, practice, and challenge for your students, including a summary table that lists skills and corresponding figures and videos, descriptions of online learning opportunities, and exercises ranging from short, focused review questions to assignments requiring complete programs and related planning documents. You can assign the Learn It Online, Knowledge Check, Debugging Exercises, and Program Analysis activities as necessary to reinforce and assess learning. Depending on the expertise of your class, you can assign the Case Programming Assignments as independent projects, selecting one from each level of difficulty (easiest, intermediate, and challenging) or concentrating on the level that is most appropriate for your class.

Important to Note: In previous editions of Visual Basic we covered mobile applications. However, Microsoft has not yet included this in Visual Basic 2010. They are currently developing a new mobile application platform for Visual Studio 2010 called Microsoft® Phone 7. When this feature becomes available for Visual Basic 2010, online updates to Chapter 5 and Chapter 12 will be available at scsite.com/vb2010/mobile.

INSTRUCTOR RESOURCES CD-ROM

The Instructor Resources includes teaching and testing aids.

- **Instructor's Manual** The Instructor's Manual consists of Microsoft Word files, which include chapter objectives, lecture notes, teaching tips, classroom activities, lab activities, quick quizzes, figures and boxed elements summarized in the chapters, and a glossary page.

- **Syllabus** Sample syllabi, which can be customized easily to a course, cover policies, assignments, exams, and procedural information.

- **Figure Files** Illustrations for every figure in the textbook are available in electronic form. Figures are provided both with and without callouts.

- **PowerPoint Presentation** PowerPoint Presentations is a multimedia lecture presentation system that provides slides for each chapter. Presentations are based on chapter objectives. Use this presentation system to present well-organized lectures that are both interesting and knowledge based. PowerPoint Presentations provides consistent coverage at schools that use multiple lecturers.

- **Solutions to Exercises** Solutions are included for all end-of-chapter and chapter reinforcement exercises.

- **Test Bank & Test Engine** Test Banks include 112 questions for every chapter, featuring objective-based and critical-thinking question types, and include page number references and figure references, when appropriate. Also included is the test engine, ExamView, the ultimate tool for your objective-based testing needs.

- **Printed Test Bank** A version of the test bank you can print also is included.
- **Data Files for Students** Includes all the files that are required by students to complete the exercises.
- **Additional Activities for Students** These additional activities consist of Chapter Reinforcement Exercises, which are true/false, multiple-choice, and short answer questions that help students gain confidence in the material learned.

About Our Covers

The Shelly Cashman Series® is continually updating our approach and content to reflect the way today's students learn and experience new technology. This focus on student success is reflected on our covers, which feature real students from University of Rhode Island using the Shelly Cashman Series in their courses, and reflect the varied ages and backgrounds of the students learning with our books. When you use the Shelly Cashman Series®, you can be assured that you are learning computer skills using the most effective courseware available.

To the Student

Getting the Most Out of Your Book

Welcome to *Microsoft Visual Basic 2010 for Windows Applications: Introductory*. To save yourself time and gain a better understanding of the elements in this text, spend a few minutes reviewing the descriptions and figures in this section.

Introduction and Initial Chapter Figures
Each chapter presents a programming project and shows the solution in the first figure of the chapter. The introduction and initial chapter figure let you see first-hand how your finished product will look and illustrate your programming goals.

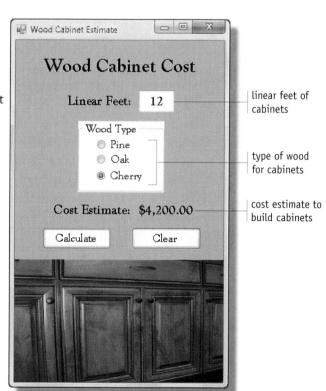

Guided Program Development   After reading through the chapter and observing how to create the chapter application, the Guided Program Development section takes you through building the chapter project step by step. As you perform each task, you can refer to Hint Screens that remind you how to complete a step or use a particular technique. If you need further help, some steps include references to figures shown earlier in the chapter — you can revisit these figures to review exactly how to perform a task. Each step ends with a results figure, so you can make sure your application is on the right track. A complete program listing also appears at the end of the Guided Program Development section, which you can use to check your work.

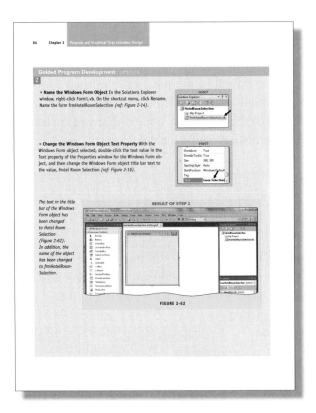

Visual Basic 2010 Online Reinforcement Videos   The first of their kind, the Shelly Cashman Online Companion provides video reenactments of every new Visual Basic process that is introduced in each chapter. These animated tutorials provide a Web-based visual instruction on how to complete a Visual Basic task. You can watch these videos to learn how to perform the steps shown in the book or to review the steps and techniques.

To access the Online Reinforcement videos, you need only a computer with an Internet connection. Use your Web browser to visit scsite.com/vb2010, click the link to the appropriate chapter, and then click the link to a figure to play a video.

Marginal Boxes   Marginal elements include Heads Up boxes, which offer tips and programming advice, In the Real World boxes, which indicate how professional developers use Visual Basic 2010 tools, and Watch Out For boxes, which identify common errors and explain how to avoid them.

HEADS UP

During the development of the program, periodically you should save the program so you do not lose your work.

IN THE REAL WORLD

Program names can contain spaces and some special characters, but by convention most developers use a name with capital letters at the beginning of each word in the name. This naming convention is called camel case.

WATCH OUT FOR

If you make an error while typing a property, such as the Name, you can press the BACKSPACE key to erase your mistake, and then type the correct data. You also can double-click the property you want to change and start all over again.

Learn It Online   Reinforcing what you're learning is a snap with the Chapter Reinforcement exercises, Practice Test, and other learning games on the Learn It Online page of the Online Companion. Visit scsite.com/vb2010 to access these fun, interactive exercises.

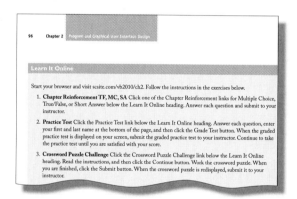

Knowledge Check   To verify you've learned the essential information in the chapter, you can work through the Knowledge Check exercises. Use these short exercises to test your knowledge of concepts and tools and to prepare for longer programming assignments.

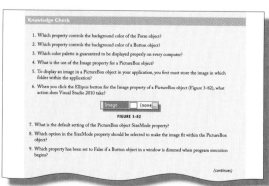

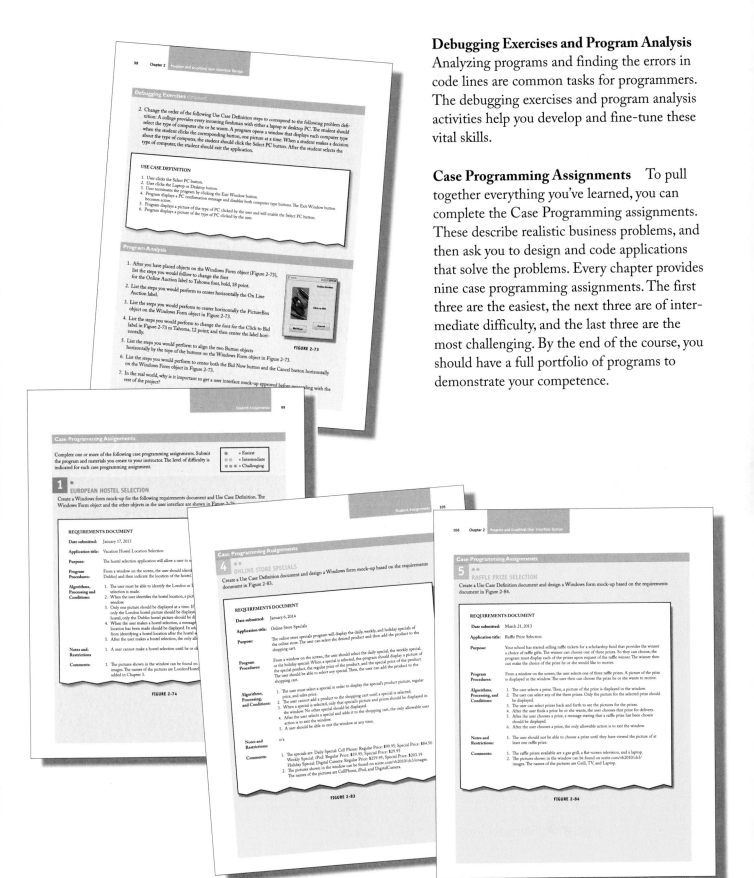

Debugging Exercises and Program Analysis
Analyzing programs and finding the errors in code lines are common tasks for programmers. The debugging exercises and program analysis activities help you develop and fine-tune these vital skills.

Case Programming Assignments   To pull together everything you've learned, you can complete the Case Programming assignments. These describe realistic business problems, and then ask you to design and code applications that solve the problems. Every chapter provides nine case programming assignments. The first three are the easiest, the next three are of intermediate difficulty, and the last three are the most challenging. By the end of the course, you should have a full portfolio of programs to demonstrate your competence.

CHAPTER 1

Introduction to Visual Basic 2010 Programming

OBJECTIVES

You will have mastered the material in this chapter when you can:

- Understand software and computer programs

- State the role of a developer in creating computer programs

- Specify the use of a graphical user interface and describe an event-driven program

- Specify the roles of input, processing, output, and data when running a program on a computer

- Describe the arithmetic operations a computer program can perform

- Explain the logical operations a computer program can perform

- Define and describe the use of a database

- Identify the use of a computer programming language in general, and Visual Basic 2010 in particular

- Explain the use of Visual Studio 2010 when developing Visual Basic 2010 programs

- Specify the programming languages available for use with Visual Studio 2010

- Explain the .NET 4.0 Framework

- Explain RAD

- Describe classes, objects, and the .NET Framework 4.0 class libraries

- Explain ADO.NET 4.0, ASP.NET 4.0, MSIL, and CLR

- Specify the types of Visual Basic 2010 applications

Introduction

A computer is an electronic device that completes tasks, under the direction of a sequence of instructions, to produce useful results for people. The set of instructions that directs a computer to perform tasks is called **computer software**, or a **computer program**.

When controlled by programs, computers can accomplish a wide variety of activities. For example, computers can interpret and display a page from the World Wide Web, compute and write payroll checks for millions of employees, display video and play audio from the Web or from digital video discs (DVDs), create messages on mobile phones, and be used to write a book (Figure 1-1).

FIGURE 1-1

internal hard drive
(storage)

monitor
(output device)

system unit
(processing)

DVD
(storage)

RAM
(storage)

printer
(output device)

keyboard
(input device)

mouse
(input device)

speakers
(output device)

scanner
(input device)

digital camera
(input device)

FIGURE 1-2

Two vital components of a computer must interact with one another for any activity to be performed. These components are computer hardware and computer software. **Computer hardware** is the physical equipment associated with a computer. This includes the keyboard, mouse, monitor, central processing unit (CPU), random access memory (RAM), hard disk, DVD drive, printer, and other devices (Figure 1-2).

Computer software, or a computer program, is a set of electronic instructions that directs the computer hardware to perform tasks such as displaying a character on the monitor when a key on the keyboard is pressed, adding an employee's regular time pay and overtime pay to calculate the total pay for that employee, or displaying a picture from an attached digital camera on the monitor. Computer hardware cannot perform any activity unless an instruction directs that hardware to act. In most cases, the instruction is part of a computer program a developer has created to carry out the desired activity.

A third component required is data. **Data** includes words, numbers, videos, graphics, and sound that programs manipulate, display, and otherwise process. The basic function of many programs is to accept some form of data (sometimes called **input data**), manipulate the data in some manner (sometimes called **processing**), and

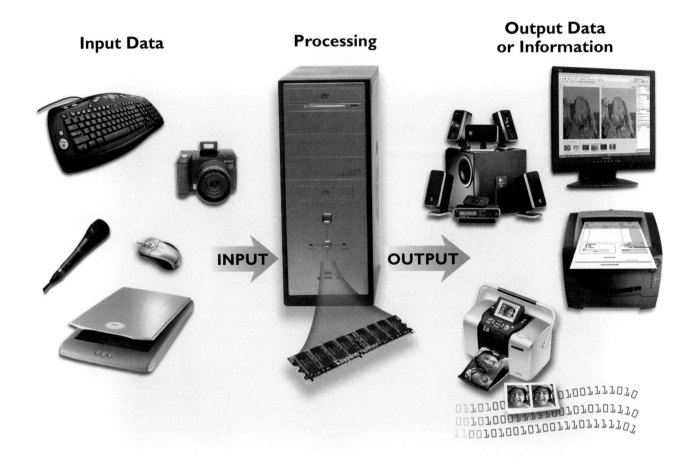

Input Data　　**Processing**　　**Output Data or Information**

INPUT　　OUTPUT

FIGURE 1-3

create some form of data usable by people or other computers (sometimes called **output data**, or **information**) (Figure 1-3). In short, many computer programs perform the following general steps: accept input data, process the data, and create output data. The data that acts as input to a program, the processing that occurs, and the output that is created varies with the requirements of the program.

In order for the computer to execute a program, both the program and the data must be placed in the computer's **random access memory (RAM)** (Figure 1-4). Once the program is stored in RAM, the **central processing unit (CPU)** of the computer can access the instructions in the program and the data in RAM to perform activities as directed by the program.

One other activity that hardware and software typically carry out is saving both the data and other software. **Saving**, or **storing**, data refers to placing the data or software electronically on a storage medium such as hard disk or Universal Serial Bus (USB) drive. The software and data are stored so they can be accessed and retrieved at a later time. Stored data is said to be **persistent** because it remains available even after the computer power is turned off.

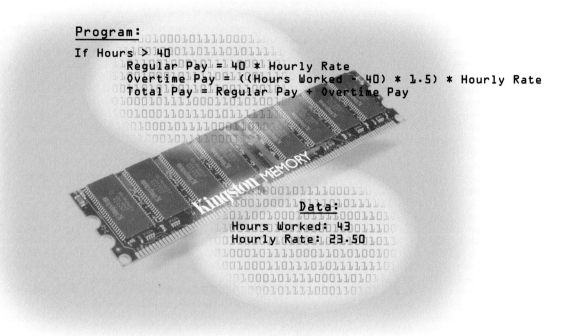

```
Program:
If Hours > 40
        Regular Pay = 40 * Hourly Rate
        Overtime Pay = ((Hours Worked - 40) * 1.5) * Hourly Rate
        Total Pay = Regular Pay + Overtime Pay



                                              Data:
                                    Hours Worked: 43
                                    Hourly Rate: 23.50
```

FIGURE 1-4

Computer Programmers and Developers

A computer program is designed and developed by people known as **computer programmers**, or developers. **Developers** are people skilled in designing computer programs and creating them using programming languages. Some computer programs are small and relatively simple, but often a problem to be solved on a computer requires more than one program. Thus, you will find that developers speak of developing an **application**, which can mean several computer programs working together to solve a problem.

When designing a program, developers analyze the problem and determine how to solve it. Once a computer program or an application is designed, the developer must create it so it can be executed on a computer. In most cases, the developer creates the program by writing the code for the program(s) using a **programming language**, which is a set of words and symbols that can be interpreted by special computer software and eventually executed as instructions by a computer. In this book, you will learn the skills required to both design and create computer programs using the Visual Basic 2010 programming language (Figure 1-5).

Event-Driven Computer Programs with a Graphical User Interface

Most Visual Basic 2010 programs are **event-driven programs** that communicate with the user through a **graphical user interface (GUI)**. The GUI usually consists of a window, containing a variety of objects, that can be displayed on various devices

```
24      Private Sub btnSelectRoom_Click(ByVal sender As System.Object, ByVal e As System.Ev
25          ' This code is executed when the user
26          ' clicks the Select Room button. It
27          ' disables the Standard Room button,
28          ' the Select Room button, and the
29          ' Deluxe Room button. It hides the
30          ' Instructions label, displays the
31          ' Confirmation Message label, and
32          ' enables the Exit Window button.
33
34          btnStandardRoom.Enabled = False
35          btnSelectRoom.Enabled = False
36          btnDeluxeRoom.Enabled = False
37          lblInstructions.Visible = False
38          lblConfirmationMessage.Visible = True
39          btnExitWindow.Enabled = True
40
41      End Sub
42
43      Private Sub btnDeluxeRoom_Click(ByVal sender As System.Object, ByVal e As System.Eve
44          ' This code is executed when the user
45          ' clicks the Deluxe Room button. It
46          ' displays the Deluxe Room picture,
47          ' hides the Standard Room picture, and
48          ' enables the Select Room button.
49
50          picDeluxeRoom.Visible = True
51          picStandardRoom.Visible = False
52          btnSelectRoom.Enabled = True
53
54      End Sub
```

FIGURE 1-5

such as a computer monitor or a mobile phone screen. Users employ the GUI objects
to select options, enter data, and cause events to occur. An **event** means the user has
initiated an action that causes the program to perform the type of processing called
for by the user's action. For example, a user might enter data into the program, and
then click a button. Clicking the button triggers an event, resulting in the program
performing the processing called for by clicking the button.

To illustrate the process of entering data when using a graphical user interface
and then triggering an event, consider the window shown in Figure 1-6.

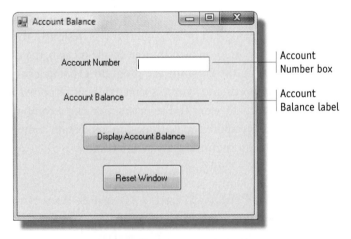

FIGURE 1-6

This window is part of a banking application. When it is displayed, the teller at the bank or a user on the Web can enter an account number. Then the user can click the Display Account Balance button (that is, trigger an event) and the program displays the account balance. The following steps illustrate the dynamics of the interaction with the program:

STEP 1   The user enters the account number in the Account Number box.

The account number the user entered is displayed in the Account Number text box (Figure 1-7). The Account Balance label displays no information.

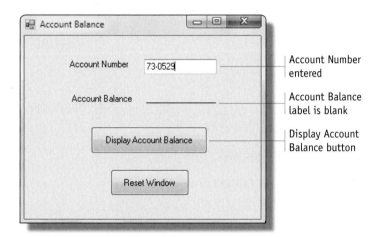

FIGURE 1-7

STEP 2   The user clicks the Display Account Balance button.

The account balance is displayed in the Account Balance label (Figure 1-8). Clicking the Display Account Balance button triggered the event that caused the program to determine and display the account balance based on data that the program accessed.

FIGURE 1-8

STEP 3   The user clicks the Reset Window button to clear the text box and the label and prepare the user interface for the next account number.

Clicking the Reset Window button triggers another event. The text box and the label are cleared and the insertion point is placed in the Account Number text box (Figure 1-9). The user now can enter a new account number to determine the account balance.

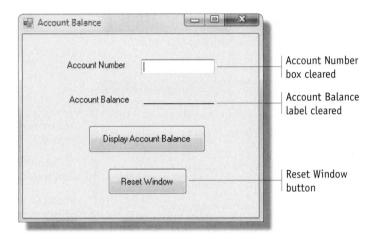

FIGURE 1-9

The events in the previous example consist of clicking the Display Account Balance button and clicking the Reset Window button. The program reacts to the events by performing specific actions (showing the account balance and resetting the text box and label). This is an example of an event-driven program. The Visual Basic developer designs the user interface and writes the program code that performs these event-triggered actions.

Basic Program Operations

All programs, regardless of their size and complexity, execute only a few fundamental operations: input, output, basic arithmetic operations, and logical operations. These operations can be combined in countless different ways to accomplish the tasks required of the program. The following pages describe these basic program operations.

Input Operation

As noted previously, a fundamental operation in most computer programs is the user entering data. For instance, in Figure 1-7 on page 7, the user entered the account number. The steps that occurred when the user typed the account number are shown in Figure 1-10.

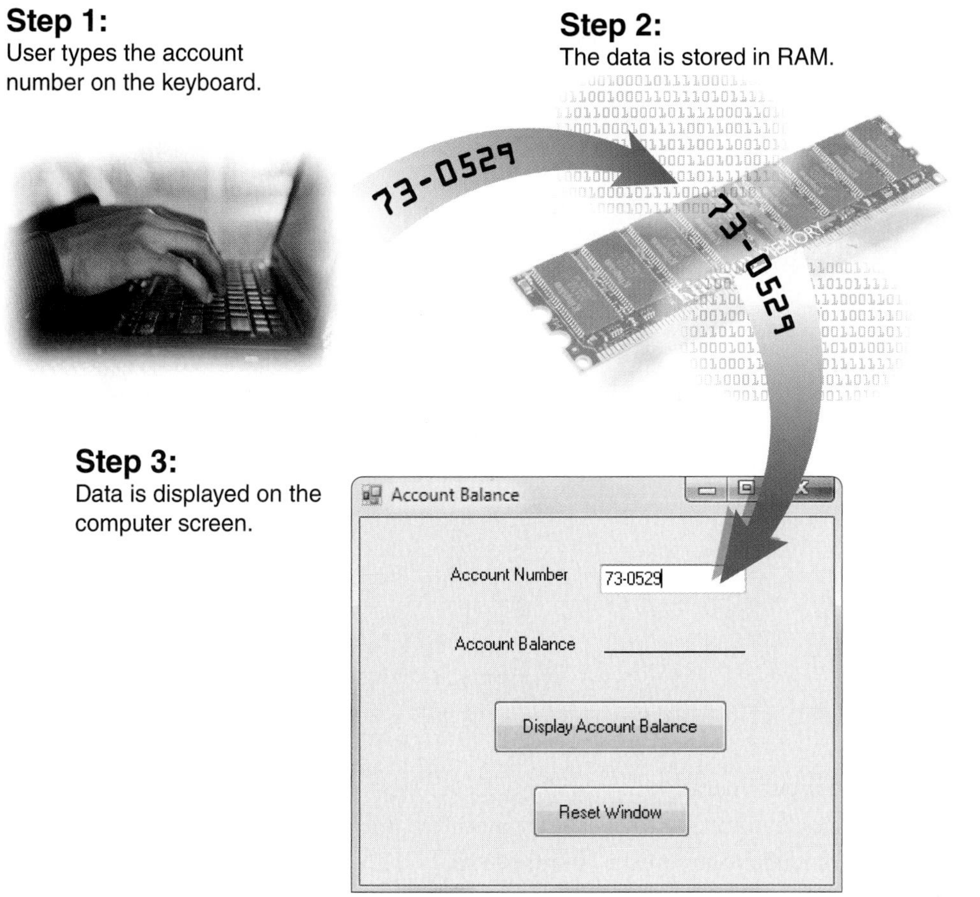

Step 1:
User types the account
number on the keyboard.

Step 2:
The data is stored in RAM.

73-0529

73-0529

Step 3:
Data is displayed on the
computer screen.

Account Balance

Account Number   73-0529

Account Balance

Display Account Balance

Reset Window

FIGURE 1-10

In Figure 1-10, the banking computer program that processes the user's request
is stored in RAM. The data entered by the user also is stored in RAM. Depending on
the input device, data entered might also be displayed on the computer screen. The
input device used to enter data depends on the application. In Figure 1-10, the user
typed the account number on a keyboard. Other applications might allow data to be
entered with a scanner, digital camera, video camera, mouse, or other device. In each
instance, the data is stored in the computer's RAM. When the data is in RAM,
instructions in the program can operate on the data.

Output Operation

The second basic program operation is creating output, or information. As you
learned previously, a major goal of most computer programs is to create output data,
or information, that is useful to people. In Figure 1-8 on page 7, the information
requested of the program is the account balance. The process of creating output is
shown in Figure 1-11.

As always, the program must be stored in RAM to control the operations of the
computer. In the example, the program sets the text of the Account Balance label
equal to the account balance, and then displays it on the screen.

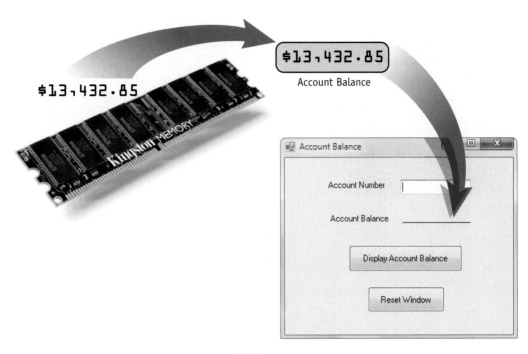

$13,432.85

$13,432.85
Account Balance

Account Balance

Account Number

Account Balance

Display Account Balance

Reset Window

FIGURE 1-11

As with input operations, a variety of devices can present output. Common output devices, in addition to computer monitors, include printers, gaming console screens and smartphone screens (Figure 1-12).

Input and output operations are basic to all computers and most computer programs. It is the ability to enter data, process it in some manner, and create output in the form of useful information that makes a computer valuable. Understanding input/output operations is essential because they provide the foundation for many of the programs you will write in this text.

Basic Arithmetic Operations

Once data is stored in main computer memory as a result of an input operation, the program can process it in some manner. In many programs, arithmetic operations (addition, subtraction, multiplication, and division) are performed on numeric data to produce useful output.

Prior to performing arithmetic operations, the numeric data used in calculations must be stored in RAM. Then, program instructions that also are stored in RAM can direct the computer to add, subtract, multiply, or divide the numbers. The answers from arithmetic operations can be used in additional calculations and processing, stored for future use, and used as output from the program.

The example in Figure 1-13 illustrates the steps an application performs to calculate an average test score. The average test score is calculated from the three test scores a user enters.

In the example in Figure 1-13, the program adds the three test scores the user enters, and then divides the total by 3 to obtain the average score. As always, both

smartphones

printer

FIGURE 1-12

the program and the data required to calculate the average test score must be stored in the computer's RAM. As you can see, when the user enters data in a text box, the data is stored in RAM and is available for arithmetic and other operations.

This example demonstrates the three fundamental operations of input (entering the three test scores), processing (calculating the average test score), and output (displaying the average test score). Although most applications are more complex than the one illustrated, the input, process, and output operations are used; and arithmetic operations commonly part of the processing step.

Logical Operations

It is the ability of a computer to perform logical operations that separates it from other types of calculating devices. Computers, through the use of computer programs, can compare numbers, letters of the alphabet, and special characters. Based on the result of these comparisons, the program can perform one processing task if the

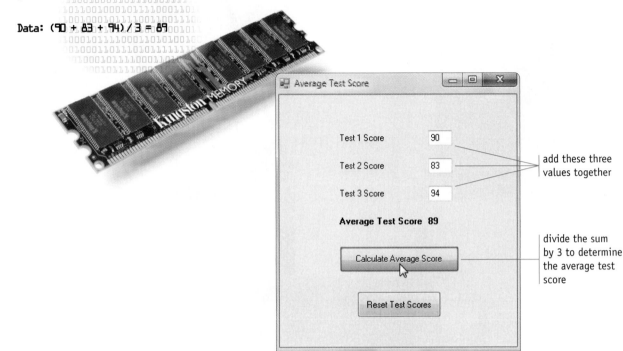

Program: (Test 1 Score + Test 2 Score + Test 3 Score) / 3 = Average Test Score

Data: (90 + 83 + 94) / 3 = 89

add these three values together

divide the sum by 3 to determine the average test score

FIGURE 1-13

condition tested for is true and another processing task if the condition is not true. Using a program to compare data and perform alternative operations allows the computer to complete sophisticated tasks such as predicting weather, formatting and altering digital photographs, editing digital video, and running high-speed games.

A program can perform the following types of logical operations:

- Comparing to determine if two values are equal.
- Comparing to determine if one value is greater than another value.
- Comparing to determine if one value is less than another value.

Based on the results of these comparisons, the program can direct the computer to take alternative actions.

Comparing — Equal Condition

A program can compare two values stored in RAM to determine whether they are equal. If the values are equal, one set of instructions will be executed; if they are not equal, another set of instructions will be executed.

Comparing to determine if two values are equal requires comparing one value to another. In an application for calculating student tuition, different rates might apply based on the student's residence. If the school is located in Texas, and the student resides in Texas, the tuition per unit is one value; if the student does not reside in Texas, the tuition per unit is another value (Figure 1-14).

BEFORE:

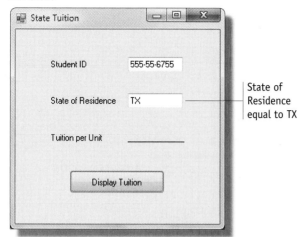

State of Residence equal to TX

AFTER:

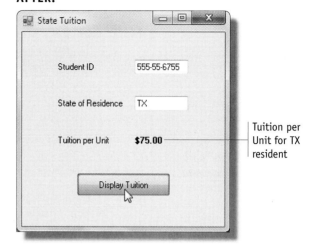

Tuition per Unit for TX resident

BEFORE:

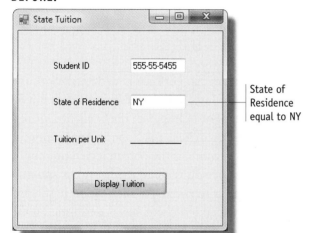

State of Residence equal to NY

AFTER:

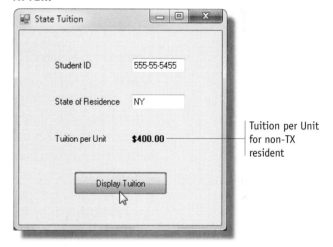

Tuition per Unit for non-TX resident

FIGURE 1-14

When the Display Tuition button is clicked and the state is equal to TX, the program displays the in-state tuition per unit. If the state is not equal to TX, the program displays the out-of-state tuition per unit.

Comparing can be used to determine if a condition is selected. For example, in Figure 1-15, the Campus Parking Fees window contains a Student Name text box that provides space for the student name On-Campus Housing and Off-Campus Housing option buttons, or radio buttons, that allow the user to select either on-campus housing or off-campus housing. When the user clicks the Calculate Parking Fees button, the program displays the appropriate parking fee.

In Example 1, the user name is Phyllis Gomez and the On-Campus Housing option button is selected. When the user clicks the Calculate Parking Fees button, by comparing, the program determines that the On-Campus Housing button is selected. Because it is selected, the result of the comparison is true and the program displays the parking fee for on-campus housing. In Example 2, the Off-Campus Housing button is selected, so the program displays the parking fee for off-campus housing.

EXAMPLE 1:
On-Campus
Housing selected

Parking fee for
On-Campus Housing

EXAMPLE 2:
Off-Campus
Housing selected

Parking fee for
Off-Campus Housing

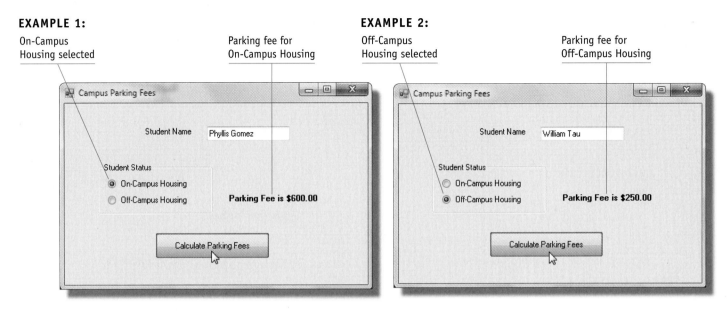

FIGURE 1-15

Comparing — Less Than Condition

A second type of comparison a computer program can perform is to determine if one value is less than another value. If it is, one set of instructions will be executed; if it is not, another set of instructions will be executed. For example, in the Student Dorm Assignment program in Figure 1-16, when the user clicks the Submit Application button, the program makes a comparison to determine if the person registering for a dorm room is less than 18 years old. If so, the person is considered a minor and a parent signature is required. If not, no signature is required. An instruction in the program to place a check in the Parent Signature Required check box is performed if the age is less than 18, and the instruction is not executed if the age is 18 or more.

BEFORE:

AFTER:

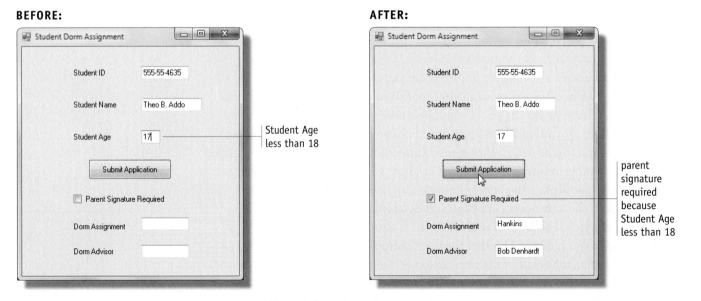

FIGURE 1-16 (*continues*)

BEFORE:

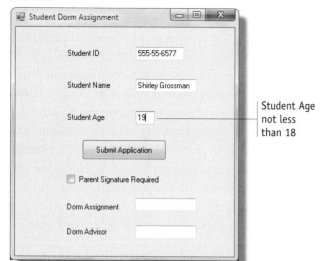

Student Age
not less
than 18

AFTER:

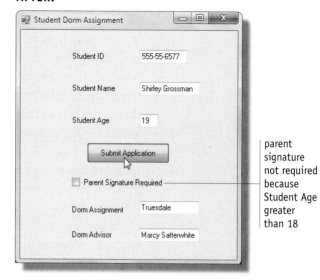

parent
signature
not required
because
Student Age
greater
than 18

FIGURE 1-16 (*continued*)

Comparing — Greater Than Condition

The other condition a computer program can determine is whether one value is greater than another value. For example, in a payroll application, the hours worked by an employee can be compared to the value 40. If the hours worked are greater than 40, then overtime pay (1.5 times the hourly rate) is calculated for the hours over 40 worked by the employee. If the employee worked 40 hours or less, no overtime pay is calculated. This comparing operation is shown in Figure 1-17.

In Figure 1-17a, the Hours Worked box contains 42, so the program calculates overtime pay for employee Anna Junga. In Figure 1-17b, George Ortega worked 30 hours, so no overtime pay is calculated. When the Hours Worked value is greater than 40, the program executes one set of instructions; if the Hours Worked value is not greater than 40, the program executes another set of instructions.

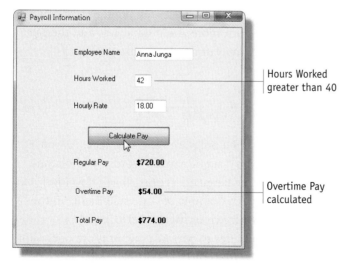

Hours Worked
greater than 40

Overtime Pay
calculated

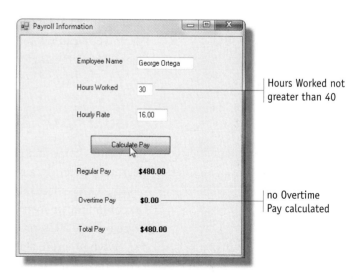

Hours Worked not
greater than 40

no Overtime
Pay calculated

FIGURE 1-17a   FIGURE 1-17b

Logical Operations Summary

While the logical operations shown in the previous examples might seem simple, it is the ability of a computer running under the control of a program to perform millions of these comparisons in a single second that provides the processing power of a computer. For example, if you are participating in a road race computer game, the game program uses comparisons to determine where your car is located on the screen, which graphic road elements should be displayed on the screen, where the car you are racing is located, whether your car has collided with your competitor, and so on. All of the many decisions that are required to display your game on the screen and respond to your actions as you participate in the game are made based on comparisons to determine if one value is equal to, greater than, or less than another value. As you can imagine, millions of these decisions must be made every second in order for your high-speed road race game to provide you with an enjoyable experience.

Saving Software and Data

When you develop and write a program, the code you write and the other features of the program you create, such as the graphical user interface, must be saved on disk. Then, when you want the program to run, you can cause the program to load into RAM and execute. By saving the program on disk, you can execute the same program many times without rewriting it each time you want to run it.

The program you write, however, also can save data. This data, which can be generated from the processing in the program, can be saved on disk for future use. For example, in a banking application, a customer might open an account. The computer program that is used to open the account saves the customer's information, such as name, address, account number, and account balance, on disk. Later, when the customer makes a deposit or withdrawal, the customer information will be retrieved and modified to reflect the deposit or withdrawal.

In most cases, data such as a customer's name and address is saved in a database. A **database** is a collection of data organized in a manner that allows access, retrieval, and use of that data. Once the data is saved in the database, any programs with permission can reference the data. You will learn more about databases and their use when programming using Visual Basic 2010 later in this textbook.

Visual Basic 2010 and Visual Studio 2010

To write a computer program, a developer uses a programming language. As you learned previously, a programming language is a set of written words, symbols, and codes, with a strict set of usage rules called the language **syntax,** that a developer uses to communicate instructions to a computer. An example of code statements in the Visual Basic 2010 programming language is shown in Figure 1-18.

Each program statement causes the computer to perform one or more operations. When written, these instructions must conform to the rules of the Visual Basic

```
42          Do Until intNumberOfEntries > intMaximumNumberOfEntries _
43              Or strVehicleSpeed = strCancelButtonClicked
44
45          If IsNumeric(strVehicleSpeed) Then
46              decVehicleSpeed = Convert.ToDecimal(strVehicleSpeed)
47              If decVehicleSpeed > 0 Then
48                  lstRadarSpeed.Items.Add(decVehicleSpeed)
49                  decTotalOfAllSpeeds += decVehicleSpeed
50                  intNumberOfEntries += 1
51                  strInputBoxMessage = strNormalBoxMessage
52              Else
53                  strInputBoxMessage = strNegativeNumberErrorMessage
54              End If
55          Else
56              strInputBoxMessage = strNonNumericErrorMessage
57          End If
58
59          If intNumberOfEntries <= intMaximumNumberOfEntries Then
60              strVehicleSpeed = InputBox(strInputBoxMessage & intNumberOfEntries, _
61                                  strInputBoxHeading, " ")
62          End If
63
64      Loop
65
66      ' Makes label visible
67      Me.lblAverageSpeed.Visible = True
```

FIGURE 1-18

2010 language. Coding a program is a precise skill. The developer must follow the syntax, or **programming rules**, of the programming language precisely. Even a single coding error can cause a program to execute improperly. Therefore, the developer must pay strict attention to coding an error-free program.

When writing Visual Basic 2010 programs, most developers use a tool called Visual Studio 2010. **Visual Studio 2010** is a software application that allows you, as the developer, to create Visual Basic 2010 programs using code you write, code prewritten by others that can be incorporated into your program, and sophisticated tools that speed up the programming process significantly while resulting in better executing and more reliable programs. In this book, you will be using Visual Studio 2010 to write Visual Basic 2010 programs.

Visual Studio 2010 is a type of **integrated development environment (IDE)**, which provides services and tools that enable a developer to code, test, and implement a single program, or sometimes the series of programs that comprise an application. Visual Studio 2010, which was developed by Microsoft Corporation, works specifically with Visual Basic 2010 as well as other programming languages to develop program code.

After you start the Visual Studio 2010 application, the Visual Studio 2010 window is displayed. In this window, you can develop and write your Visual Basic 2010 program, as shown in Figure 1-19.

The following are general guidelines for using this window. In subsequent chapters, you will learn to use each of the elements found in the Visual Studio 2010 window.

Title Bar: The title bar identifies the window and the application open in the window. In Figure 1-19, the open application is Payroll.

HEADS UP

Various versions of Visual Studio 2010 are available, including Visual Studio Standard Edition, Visual Studio Professional Edition, Visual Studio Express Edition, and Visual Studio Team System. The MSDN Academic Alliance allows students to get a free copy of Microsoft Visual Studio Professional 2010 if the school is part of the Academic Alliance. For more information, see the MSDN link at http://msdn2.microsoft.com/en-us/academic/bb676724.aspx.

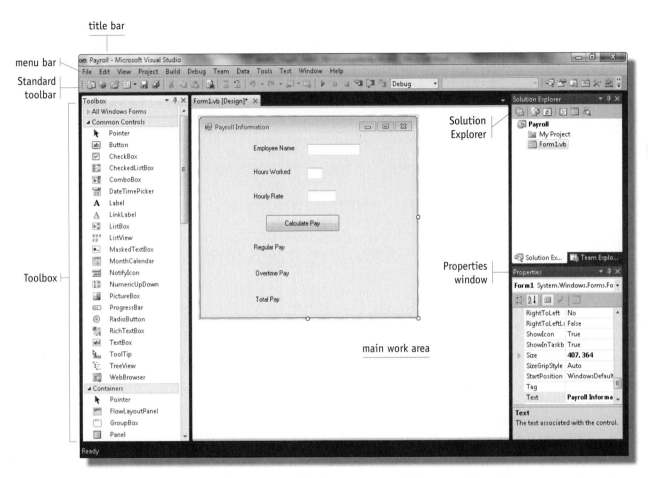

FIGURE 1-19

Menu Bar: The menu bar displays the Visual Studio 2010 menu names, each representing a list of commands that allow you to create, edit, save, print, test, and run a Visual Basic program, as well as perform other functions that are critical to the development of Visual Basic programs.

Standard Toolbar: The Standard toolbar contains buttons that execute frequently used commands such as Open Project, New Project, Save, Cut, Copy, Paste, and Undo.

Toolbox: The Toolbox contains **.NET components** that you can use to develop the graphical user interface for the program. For example, through the use of the Toolbox, you can place buttons, picture boxes, labels, radio buttons, and other Windows GUI objects in the window you develop for your program.

Main Work Area: The main work area is used to contain the item on which you are working. In Figure 1-19, it contains the Payroll Information window, which has been developed in the Payroll program.

Solution Explorer: The Solution Explorer window displays the elements of the **Visual Basic solution**, which is the name given to the Visual Basic program and other items that are generated by Visual Studio so the program will execute properly. You will learn about these items and how to use the Solution Explorer window throughout this book.

Properties Window: An item that is a visible part of a graphical user interface, such as the Calculate Pay button in Figure 1-19, is called an **object**, or **control**. Each object in a Visual Basic program has a set of characteristics called the **properties** of the object. These properties, such as the size of the button and the text that displays within the button, can be set in the Properties window within Visual Studio. You will learn about the properties of many objects throughout this book.

To code a Visual Basic program, the developer starts the Visual Studio program, identifies the kind of program to be developed, and then uses the tools and features of Visual Studio to actually create the program.

Programming Languages

Several thousand programming languages exist today. Each language has its own rules and syntax for writing instructions. Languages often are designed for specific purposes, such as scientific applications, business solutions, or Web page development.

Visual Studio can be used to write programs in four languages: Visual Basic, Visual C++ (pronounced Cee Plus Plus and called C++ for short), Visual C# (pronounced Cee Sharp and called C# for short), and Visual F# (pronounced F Sharp and called F# for short). Each of these languages is described in the following sections.

Visual Basic

Visual Basic 2010 is a programming language that allows developers to easily build complex Windows and Web programs, as well as other software tools. Visual Basic 2010 is based on the Visual Basic programming language that Microsoft developed in the early 1990s. Visual Basic, in turn, was the BASIC (Beginner's All-purpose Symbolic Instructional Code) language, which was developed in the 1960s.

Visual Basic's popularity evolved from the wide range of productivity features that enabled developers to quickly generate high-quality software applications for Windows. Today, Visual Basic is the most widely used programming language in the world because it is English-like and is considered one of the easier enterprise-level programming languages to learn. Visual Basic is the only language in Visual Studio that is not case sensitive, which makes it easy for entry-level programmers. It is as powerful as the other programming languages in the Visual Studio suite such as C++ or C#. An example of Visual Basic 2010 code is shown in Figure 1-18 on page 17.

In this book, you will learn to become a proficient Visual Basic developer.

C++

C++ is a derivative of the programming language C, which originally was developed at Bell Labs in the 1970s. It gives developers exacting control of their applications through optimized code and access to system-provided services. It contains powerful language constructs, though at the price of added complexity. C++ provides unrivaled performance and precision for applications that require a high degree of control.

Visual C#

Introduced in 2001 by Microsoft, Visual C# offers a synthesis of the elegance and syntax of C++ with many of the productivity benefits enjoyed in Visual Basic. Visual C# can be used to create both Windows and Web applications, as well as other types of software tools. Microsoft designed Visual C# to overcome some of the limitations of C++ while still providing the depth of control C++ developers demand. The C# language includes aspects of several other programming languages, such as C++, Java, and Delphi, with a strong emphasis on code simplification.

Visual F#

A new Microsoft .NET object-oriented language that debuts with Visual Studio 2010 is called F#. A multipurpose language similar to Visual Basic and C#, the F# language is known for its math-intensive focus, making it perfect for heavy-duty scientific programming applications. The language is brand new and it is just beginning to gain popularity in the business and science environments.

.NET Framework 4.0

In the year 2000, Microsoft announced a set of software technologies and products under the umbrella name of .NET. The .NET technologies and products were designed to work together to allow businesses to connect information, people, systems, and devices through software. Much of this connection occurs over the Internet.

The software environment in which programs and applications can be developed for .NET is called the **.NET Framework**, which provides tools and processes developers can use to produce and run programs. The most recent version is called **.NET Framework 4.0**. Visual Studio 2010 provides the development environment for the developer to have access to the .NET Framework 4.0 tools and processes. This version of the .NET Framework provides better computer performance, faster application startup, and smoother animations.

Four major features of .NET Framework 4.0 are the .NET class library, ADO.NET 4.0 (provides the ability to read and write data in databases), ASP.NET 4.0 (provides the ability to develop Web applications), and the Common Language Runtime (allows programs to run on different computers under different operating systems). Each of these features is explained in the following sections.

.NET Class Library

As you have learned, most programs written using Visual Basic 2010 are event-driven programs where a user performs an action, such as clicking a button, and the program executes the appropriate instructions. The instructions a program executes when a user clicks a button are normally are written by the Visual Basic developer and are unique to the processing required by the program. For example, when a user clicks a button in one program, the overtime pay for an employee is calculated, whereas in another program parking fees are calculated. Each program responds to the events triggered by users with unique processing based on the requirements of the program.

In many programs, however, much of the programming code that must be developed is common for all the programs. For example, in all the programs you have seen in this chapter, a button was used to trigger an event in the program. The button appears in a window on a screen and senses when it has been clicked through the use of program instructions.

When certain code is common to multiple programs, the best approach is to write the code one time and then reuse it wherever its use is appropriate. For example, whenever a button is required in the graphical user interface of a program, it is more efficient to use common programming code that can place the button in the user interface than to require a developer to write all the code for a button each time one is required. When a common task must be performed or a new object such as a button is required, a developer can write the code one time and save it as a class. That class can then be referenced by all other programs when the task or object is required.

In short, the coding required for a button can be placed in a class. A **class** is a named group of program code. Once the class is coded, it can be stored in a **class library**, which makes the class available to all developers who need to use it. For example, when you as a developer need to place a button in the user interface, you can use the Button class stored in a class library to create the button without writing all the programming code associated with the button (Figure 1-20).

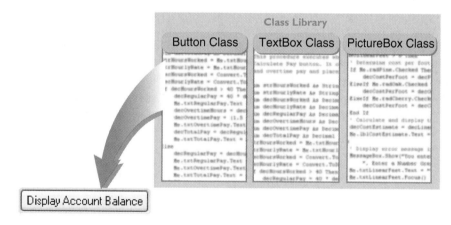

FIGURE 1-20

A button created from a class is called an **object**, or sometimes an **instance** of a class. In programming terminology, the process of creating a Button object from the Button class is called **instantiation**. In other words, a class acts as a general template, while an object is a specific item generated based on the class template. Thus, all buttons can be generated, or instantiated, from the Button class. The Display Account Balance button in Figure 1-20 is a specific Button object instantiated from the Button class.

In Visual Studio 2010, to create a Button object from the Button class, all you must do is drag the Button .NET component from the Toolbox to a Windows Form object, as you will learn in Chapter 2.

A button in a graphical user interface is only a single example of using classes and class libraries. The .NET Framework 4.0 class library contains thousands of classes and many class libraries that can be used by Visual Basic developers who use Visual Studio to create programs.

With so many classes available in .NET Framework 4.0, developers use a method of program development called rapid application development. **Rapid application development (RAD)** refers to the process of using prebuilt classes to make application development faster, easier, and more reliable. Throughout this book, you will gain a further understanding of classes and their use in modern computer programming, and will see how the classes in the .NET Framework 4.0 class libraries can be used for RAD.

ADO.NET 4.0

Often, programs you write must access data stored in a database. A set of prewritten classes called ADO.NET 4.0 (ADO stands for ActiveX Data Objects) provides the functionality for a program to perform the four primary tasks required when working with a database: getting the data, examining the data, editing the data, and updating the data.

Getting the data refers to retrieving the data from the database and making it available to the program. Once the data is retrieved from the database, ADO.NET 4.0 provides the tools for the program to examine the data and determine how to use it. For example, a program might retrieve data from a database to create a printed report. The program can examine the data to determine its use for the report.

In other applications, the program might examine the data to determine if it is appropriate data to display for a user. Thus, in a banking application such as in Figure 1-21, the program might require the user enter a special value, such as her mother's maiden name, to verify the identity of the person requesting the information. The program, using ADO.NET 4.0 classes, can compare the special value to the data retrieved from the database to determine if the user is permitted to access the data.

A third facility provided by ADO.NET 4.0 is the ability to edit the data, which means make changes to the data. For example, if you change your address or telephone

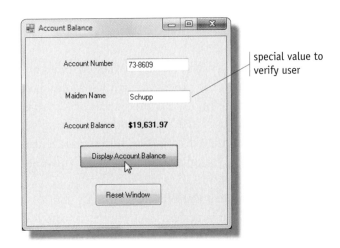

FIGURE 1-21

number, those values in your account database information should be changed. ADO.NET 4.0 supports the ability to make those changes.

Finally, once changes to data have been made, ADO.NET 4.0 enables a program to update the database with the new information by writing the data into the database.

ADO.NET 4.0 is a powerful and necessary part of the .NET Framework 4.0. The developer uses Visual Studio 2010 to access the ADO.NET 4.0 classes.

ASP.NET 4.0

The Internet and World Wide Web are integral technological resources. Modern Web sites provide services from selling products to sharing the latest medical research on any known disease. The development and maintenance of these Web sites is a constant requirement and consumes many developer hours.

Recognizing the importance of the Web, Microsoft included in .NET Framework 4.0 a programming framework called ASP.NET 4.0 that developers can use, through Visual Studio 2010, to build powerful and sophisticated Web applications on a Web server. Using ASP.NET 4.0 classes, the Visual Basic 2010 programmer can create Web sites that are able to perform any function available on the Web today.

ASP.NET 4.0 offers several advantages for developers. First, almost all the objects available in the .NET framework, such as buttons, text boxes, and picture boxes, are available in ASP.NET 4.0. So, developers can use the same techniques to create a Web application that they use to create Windows applications such as those shown in this chapter. In addition, deploying the Web application on a Web server almost is automatic. Visual Studio 2010 now incorporates a new Web designer interface into ASP.NET 4.0 that uses the design engine of a popular Web page designing program named Microsoft Expression Web. This design engine greatly improves moving between HTML (Hypertext Markup Language) source code, cascading style sheets that assist in layout, and Visual Basic code.

Important Web requirements such as performance and security are enhanced and maximized through the use of the tools offered with ASP.NET 4.0. In short, ASP.NET 4.0 offers a complete solution for developing modern Web applications.

Microsoft Intermediate Language (MSIL) and Common Language Runtime (CLR)

After a developer writes a program in a programming language such as Visual Basic 2010 using Visual Studio 2010, the programming statements must be translated into a collection of instructions that eventually can be understood by the electronics of the computer. These electronic instructions then are executed by the computer to carry out the tasks of the program. This process of translation is called **program compilation**.

Program compilation for a Visual Basic 2010 program creates a set of electronic code expressed in an intermediate language called the **Microsoft Intermediate Language (MSIL)**. When the program is executed, a portion of .NET 4.0 called the **Common Language Runtime (CLR)** reads the MSIL and causes the actual instructions within the program to be executed (Figure 1-22).

In Figure 1-22, the Visual Basic program written by a developer is compiled, which translates the human-readable statements in Visual Basic into MSIL, which is the set of

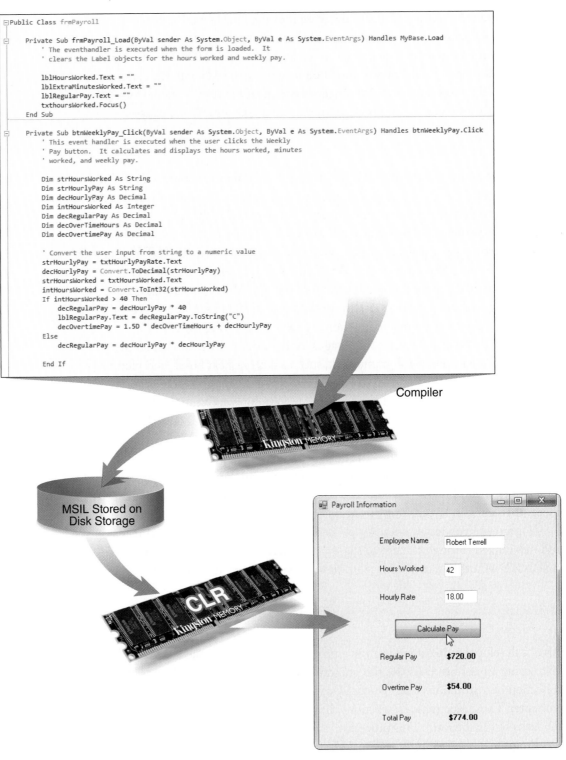

```
Public Class frmPayroll

    Private Sub frmPayroll_Load(ByVal sender As System.Object, ByVal e As System.EventArgs) Handles MyBase.Load
        ' The eventhandler is executed when the form is loaded.  It
        ' clears the Label objects for the hours worked and weekly pay.

        lblHoursWorked.Text = ""
        lblExtraMinutesWorked.Text = ""
        lblRegularPay.Text = ""
        txthoursWorked.Focus()
    End Sub

    Private Sub btnWeeklyPay_Click(ByVal sender As System.Object, ByVal e As System.EventArgs) Handles btnWeeklyPay.Click
        ' This event handler is executed when the user clicks the Weekly
        ' Pay button.  It calculates and displays the hours worked, minutes
        ' worked, and weekly pay.

        Dim strHoursWorked As String
        Dim strHourlyPay As String
        Dim decHourlyPay As Decimal
        Dim intHoursWorked As Integer
        Dim decRegularPay As Decimal
        Dim decOverTimeHours As Decimal
        Dim decOvertimePay As Decimal

        ' Convert the user input from string to a numeric value
        strHourlyPay = txtHourlyPayRate.Text
        decHourlyPay = Convert.ToDecimal(strHourlyPay)
        strHoursWorked = txtHoursWorked.Text
        intHoursWorked = Convert.ToInt32(strHoursWorked)
        If intHoursWorked > 40 Then
            decRegularPay = decHourlyPay * 40
            lblRegularPay.Text = decRegularPay.ToString("C")
            decOvertimePay = 1.5D * decOverTimeHours + decHourlyPay
        Else
            decRegularPay = decHourlyPay * decHourlyPay

        End If
```

Compiler

MSIL Stored on
Disk Storage

CLR

Payroll Information

Employee Name   Robert Terrell

Hours Worked   42

Hourly Rate   18.00

Calculate Pay

Regular Pay $720.00

Overtime Pay $54.00

Total Pay $774.00

FIGURE 1-22

electronic code that forms the input to CLR. Then, when the program is ready for execution, the CLR reads the MSIL and places the MSIL in RAM in a form that allows the computer's CPU to actually execute the instructions in the program.

The use of MSIL and CLR offers multiple benefits that provide speed and flexibility for both the development and execution environments of a program. Utmost in these benefits is the fact that a program written using Visual Studio 2010 and compiled into MSIL can be executed on any computer using any operating system, so long as .NET Framework 4.0 is available on the computer. So, with no changes to a program you write, the program could be executed on a Dell computer running Windows 7 or on an IBM computer using the Linux operating system. This flexibility in being able to execute programs on different computers running different operating systems is a primary benefit of using .NET Framework 4.0.

Types of Visual Basic 2010 Applications

When you begin creating a new Visual Basic 2010 program in Visual Studio 2010, you must choose the type of application you will be developing. Based on your choice, Visual Studio 2010 provides the classes, tools, and features required for that type of application.

Five major types of applications are: Windows applications, mobile applications, Web site applications, Office applications, and database applications. A **Windows application** means the program will run on a computer or other device that supports the Windows GUI. You can run Windows applications on a variety of computers.

You can create **mobile applications** that are designed to run on mobile devices such as smartphones, Pocket PCs, and computers running the Windows CE operating system.

You create a **Web site application** using ASP.NET 4.0. The application runs on a Web server. It produces Hypertext Markup Language (HTML) code that is downloaded to the client computer where the browser on the client computer interprets the HTML and displays the contents of a Web page. In a Web application created with ASP.NET 4.0, the developer can include items such as security and forms processing to provide all the services required of a modern Web site.

An **Office application** includes writing Visual Basic 2010 code to automate and manipulate documents created using Microsoft Office 2003, Office 2007, and Office 2010.

A **database application** is written using ADO.NET 4.0 to reference, access, display, and update data stored in a database. The Visual Basic 2010 developer writes the code to process the data.

Other types of applications Visual Basic 2010 developers can create include console applications, classes for class libraries, certain controls to use in Windows applications, Web services, and device-specific applications. For more information regarding the types of applications that you can create, visit *msdn.microsoft.com/vbasic*.

> **HEADS UP**
>
> When Visual Studio 2010 was released, the mobile applications portion of Visual Basic was not included because Microsoft Phone 7 is still being developed. When the VB 2010 portion is added to Visual Studio, a digital chapter for this book will be added online to show a mobile application.

Summary

In this chapter, you have learned the fundamentals of computer programming and have been introduced to the Visual Studio 2010 and Visual Basic 2010 program development environments. In subsequent chapters, you will learn to use Visual Studio 2010 and Visual Basic 2010 to create Windows applications, database applications, Web applications, and Office applications.

Knowledge Check

1. Explain the differences between computer hardware and computer software.

2. The basic functions of many programs are: a) _____ ; b) _____ ;
   c) _____ .

3. Match the following terms and their definitions:

   a) Developer

   b) Persistent data

   c) Programming language

   d) Graphical user interface

   e) Database

   f) Class library

   g) Rapid application development (RAD)

   1. A collection of classes that are available for use in programs

   2. Someone skilled in designing computer programs and implementing them in programming languages

   3. A window with a variety of objects that can be displayed on a variety of devices

   4. Data that is stored on a storage medium

   5. The process of using prebuilt classes to make application development faster, easier, and more reliable

   6. A collection of data organized in a manner that allows access, retrieval, and use of that data

   7. A set of words and symbols that can be interpreted by special computer software and eventually can be executed as instructions by a computer

4. Explain what an event is in the context of event-driven programs. Give two examples.

5. Give examples of the differences between an input operation and an output operation.

6. What are the four primary arithmetic operations a computer program can perform? Give an example of each.

7. In the following examples, identify the condition a program would detect (the first exercise is solved for you):

   a. 4 is _____ 3   a. greater than

   b. 8 is _____ 8   b. _____

   c. 17 is _____ 17.8   c. _____

   d. 75 is _____ 85   d. _____

   e. "Microsoft" is _____ "Microsoft"   e. _____

8. Describe three different databases where you think information about yourself might be stored.

9. What is programming language syntax? Why is it important?

10. Visual Studio 2010 is a type of _____ developed by _____ .

11. What is a Toolbox in Visual Studio 2010? Why is it valuable?

12. Name two properties that a Button object can possess.

13. What are the four programming languages you can use with Visual Studio 2010?

14. State three reasons that Visual Basic is the most widely used programming language in the world.

15. What are four major features of .NET Framework 4.0?

16. Why is a class developed? How are classes organized and stored?

17. Differentiate between a class and an object. Give three examples each of classes and objects.

18. What is the primary use of ADO.NET 4.0?

19. What is the process of translating statements written by a developer called? What is the result of this process?

20. What are five types of applications you can create in Visual Basic 2010?

CHAPTER 2

Program and Graphical User Interface Design

OBJECTIVES

You will have mastered the material in this chapter when you can:

- Open and close Visual Studio 2010

- Create a Visual Basic 2010 Windows Application project

- Name and set the title bar text in a Windows Form object; resize a Windows Form object

- Add a Label object to a Windows Form object; name the Label object; set the text in the Label object; change the Font

- properties of the text in the Label object

- Add a PictureBox object to the Windows Form object; name the PictureBox object; resize the PictureBox object

- Add a Button object to the Windows Form object; name the Button object; set the text in the Button object; change the Button object size

- Align objects on the Windows Form object

- Save and open Visual Basic projects

- Understand and implement graphical user interface design principles

- Understand and implement the first two phases of the program development life cycle

Introduction

Before a program actually can be coded using Visual Basic 2010, it must be designed. Designing a program can be compared to constructing a building. Before cement slabs are poured, steel beams are put in place, and walls are built, architects and engineers must design a building to ensure it will perform as required and be safe and reliable. The same holds true for a computer program. Once the program is designed, it can be implemented through the use of the Visual Basic 2010 programming language to perform the functions for which it was designed.

To illustrate the process of designing and implementing a computer program in the Visual Basic 2010 programming language using **Visual Studio 2010** as the integrated development environment, the application shown in Figure 2-1 will be designed and implemented in this chapter and in Chapter 3.

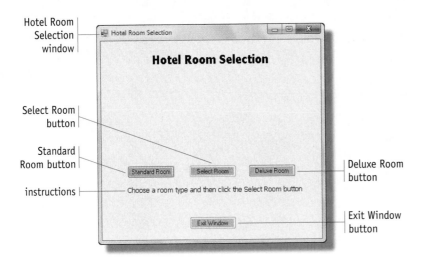

FIGURE 2-1a

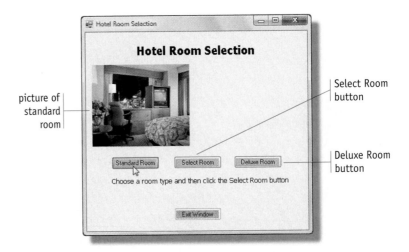

FIGURE 2-1b

The application in Figure 2-1 could be part of a larger computer application that is used to make hotel reservations. The program that creates the window in Figure 2-1 will run on a personal computer using the Windows operating system and will allow a reservation clerk or a customer to select the room type for a hotel reservation.

In Figure 2-1a, the program begins by displaying the Hotel Room Selection window on a PC monitor. The program provides instructions that tell the user to choose the room type (by clicking the Standard Room or Deluxe Room button), and then click the Select Room button to make a room selection. If the user clicks the Standard Room button, a picture of a standard room is displayed (Figure 2-1b). If the user clicks the Deluxe Room button, a picture of a deluxe room is displayed (Figure 2-1c). After choosing a room type, the user can click the Select Room button and the program informs the user the room selection has been completed (Figure 2-1d). To close the window and exit the program, the user can click the Exit Window button after making a room selection.

By the end of Chapter 3, you will have completed the design and implementation of this program.

ONLINE REINFORCEMENT

To view a video of the program execution shown in Figure 2-1, visit scsite.com/vb2010/ch2 and then click Figure 2-1. Turn on your speakers to listen to the audio walkthrough of the steps.

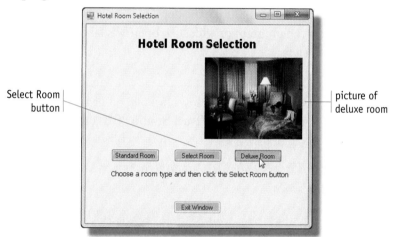

FIGURE 2-1c

FIGURE 2-1d

Using Visual Studio 2010

When designing an event-driven program that uses a graphical user interface (GUI), such as the program in this chapter, one of the first steps is to design the user interface itself. Recall that the user interface is the window that is displayed on the screen when the program is running, together with the variety of objects such as buttons that are displayed in the window. Before beginning to design the user interface, however, the developer should know how to use certain Visual Studio and Visual Basic **rapid application development** (**RAD**) tools because these tools are used in the design process. For example, you use the Visual Studio tools to place a button on the window. So, before starting the design of the user interface for the program in this chapter, you should know how to accomplish the Visual Studio tasks described in the following pages.

Open Visual Studio 2010

To design a user interface using Visual Studio, the developer must open Visual Studio 2010 and then use the tools the program provides. To open Visual Studio 2010, you can complete the following steps:

STEP 1 Click the Start button on the Windows taskbar, point to All Programs on the Start menu, and then point to Microsoft Visual Studio 2010 on the All Programs submenu.

The program name, Microsoft Visual Studio 2010, is displayed on the Microsoft Visual Studio 2010 submenu (Figure 2-2).

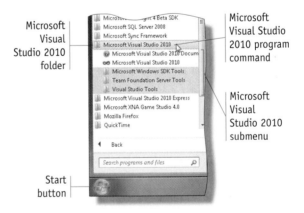

FIGURE 2-2

STEP 2 Click Microsoft Visual Studio 2010 on the submenu.

For a short time, a Visual Studio splash screen appears, and then Microsoft Visual Studio 2010 opens (Figure 2–3). The title of the window is Microsoft Visual Studio. The menu bar and the Standard toolbar are displayed at the top of the window. The Start Page contains information regarding Visual Basic. To close the Start Page, click the Close button on the Start Page title bar. You will learn the other elements of this window as you progress through this book.

menu bar   New Project button   Start Page Close button   Standard toolbar

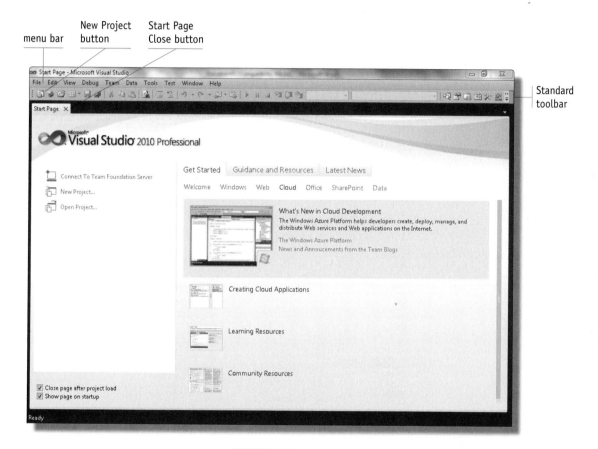

FIGURE 2-3

ONLINE REINFORCEMENT

To view a video of the process in the previous steps, visit scsite.com/vb2010/ch2 and then click Figure 2-2.

Create a New Visual Basic 2010 Windows Application Project

A **project** is equivalent to a single program created using Visual Studio. A **Windows Application project** is a program that will include, as the user interface, a window on the screen of a computer using the Windows operating system. When the program is executed, the user will interact with the program by using the window and its components (the user interface).

To create a new project using Visual Studio, you must specify the programming language you want to use and the type of program, or application, you will create. To create a new Visual Basic Windows Application project, you can take the following steps:

STEP 1 Click the New Project button on the Standard toolbar.

Visual Studio opens the New Project window (Figure 2–4). The New Project window on your computer might be displayed differently, depending on selections made at the time Visual Studio was installed on your computer. The left pane contains the programming languages and other types of templates available in Visual Studio. The middle pane contains the types of applications you can create within each programming language. The right pane displays a description of the selected application. At this time, you want to create a Windows Application using Visual Basic.

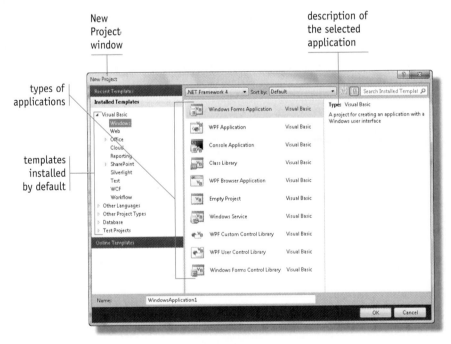

FIGURE 2-4

STEP 2 If necessary, in the left pane, click Windows so it is selected.

Windows is highlighted in the left pane and the types of Windows projects you can create using Visual Basic are listed in the middle pane (Figure 2-5).

Visual Basic
expanded

Windows Forms Application

Windows selected

FIGURE 2-5

STEP 3 If necessary, click Windows Forms Application in the middle pane.

Windows Forms Application is selected in the middle pane (Figure 2-6). By making this selection, you have specified you want to create a program that will run under the Windows operating system using the Windows graphical user interface.

Windows Forms
Application selected

Name
text box

FIGURE 2-6

STEP 4   Double-click the text, WindowsApplication1, in the Name text box to select the text. Type the project name. For this example, you could type `HotelRoomSelection` as the name.

The project name appears in the Name text box (Figure 2-7).

project name

OK button

FIGURE 2-7

STEP 5   Click the OK button in the New Project window.

Visual Studio creates a new project (Figure 2-8). The project name is displayed in the title bar of the window.

project name

Form1.vb [Design] tabbed page

Toolbox button

title bar

Windows Form object

Close button

Maximize button

Minimize button

work area

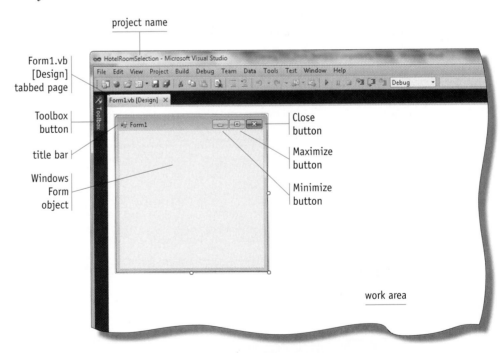

FIGURE 2-8

The Visual Studio window contains several important features of which you should be aware. First, in the portion of the window known as the **work area**, a tabbed page named Form1.vb [Design] contains a Windows Form object called Form1. A **Windows Form object** is the window you will use to build the program and is the window that will be displayed on your screen when you execute the program. The Windows Form object is the fundamental object in the graphical user interface you will create using Visual Studio tools. Notice in Figure 2-8 that the Windows Form object contains a blue title bar, a window title (Form1), a Minimize button, a Maximize button, and a Close button.

A second important element is displayed on the left of the window. Depending on the settings within Visual Studio, the left portion of the window will appear as shown in Figure 2-8 or as shown in Figure 2-9. In Figure 2-8, the left margin contains the Toolbox button. The Toolbox button also appears on the Standard toolbar.

Display the Toolbox

You can use the **Toolbox button** to display the Toolbox. The **Toolbox** is the primary tool you will use to place objects such as buttons on the Windows Form object. To display the Toolbox, you can take the following steps:

STEP 1   If the window does not already display the Toolbox, point to the Toolbox button in the left margin of the window.

When you point to the Toolbox button, the Toolbox is displayed on the window (Figure 2-9). Notice that the Toolbox hides part of the Form1 Windows Form object.

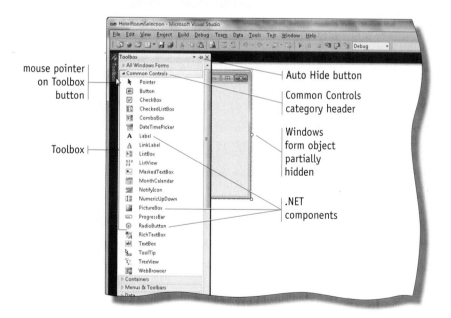

FIGURE 2-9

The Toolbox contains, among other things, many graphical elements called **.NET components** that you can place on the Windows Form object as graphical user interface objects. For example, it contains buttons that can be placed on the Windows Form object. You will learn how to perform this activity in the next section of this chapter.

Permanently Display the Toolbox

As long as the mouse pointer is within the Toolbox, the Toolbox is displayed. If, however, you move the mouse pointer off the Toolbox, it no longer is displayed.

When you are designing the graphical user interface, normally it is advantageous to display the Toolbox at all times. To keep the Toolbox on the window at all times, you can complete the following step:

STEP 1   If necessary, point to the Toolbox button in the left margin of the window to display the Toolbox. Then, click the **Auto Hide button** on the Toolbox title bar.

When you click the Auto Hide button, the Pushpin icon on the Auto Hide button on the Toolbox title bar changes from being horizontal, which indicates Auto Hide, to vertical, which indicates the Toolbox has been "pinned" to the window and will remain there (Figure 2-10). Form1 is moved to the right so you can see both the Toolbox and all of Form1.

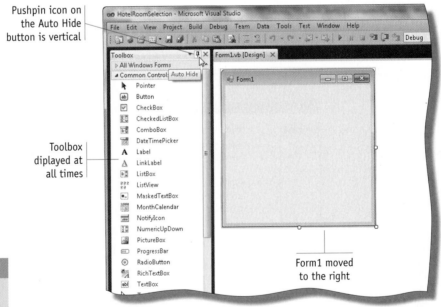

Pushpin icon on the Auto Hide button is vertical

Toolbox diplayed at all times

Form1 moved to the right

FIGURE 2-10

When the Pushpin icon is vertical, the Toolbox is said to be in Dockable mode, which means it can be dragged around and placed anywhere within the Visual Studio window. In most applications, it should remain on the left of the window as shown in Figure 2-10. Later, you can change the Toolbox back to Auto Hide mode by clicking the Auto Hide button again.

View Object Properties

Every object you create in the user interface, including the Windows Form object, has properties. **Properties** can describe a multitude of characteristics about the object, including its color, size, name, and position on the screen. You will learn about the properties of all the objects you create using the Toolbox.

To view the properties for an object in Visual Studio, you use the Properties window. By default, the Properties window is displayed in the lower-right section of the Visual Studio window (Figure 2-11).

HEADS UP

If the Solution Explorer window is not displayed on your screen, you can display the window by taking the following steps: 1) Click View on the menu bar; 2) Click Solution Explorer on the View menu. The Solution Explorer window will be displayed in the location shown in Figure 2-11.

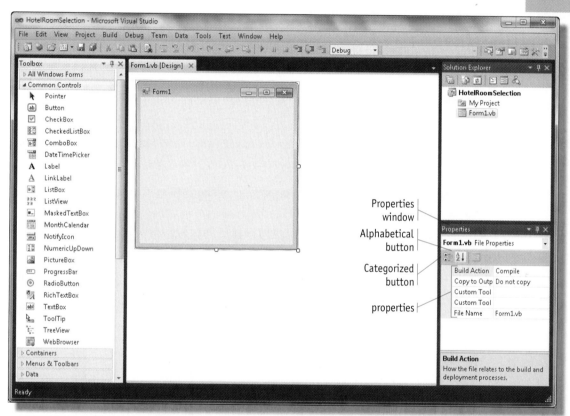

FIGURE 2-11

In the **Properties window** shown in Figure 2-11, the property names in the left list appear in Alphabetical view. Many developers find the Alphabetical view the easiest to use when searching for properties. Some developers, however, prefer the Categorized view, where properties are organized according to type. You can change the order of the properties into Categorized if you click the Categorized button on the Properties window toolbar (see Figure 2-11). In this book, the properties are shown in Alphabetical view, which is achieved by clicking the Alphabetical button on the Properties window toolbar.

HEADS UP

If the Properties window is not displayed on your screen, you can display the window by taking the following steps: 1) Click View on the menu bar; 2) Click Properties Window on the View menu. The Properties window will be displayed in the location shown in Figure 2-11.

Name the Windows Form Object

Visual Studio gives every object in a Visual Basic graphical user interface a default name. For example, the name for the first Windows Form object in a project is Form1. In virtually every instance, a developer should assign a meaningful name to

HEADS UP

If the properties in the Properties window do not appear in alphabetical order, click the Alphabetical button to place them in alphabetic order.

an object so the program can reference it if required. The name for an object should reflect the object's use. For example, a good name for the Hotel Room Selection window might be HotelRoomSelection. Notice in the name that each word is capitalized and the remaining letters are lowercase. You should always follow this naming method when naming objects.

No spaces or other special characters are allowed in the object name. Also, by convention, each object name should begin with a prefix that identifies the type of object. For Windows Form objects, the prefix is frm. Therefore, the complete name for the Windows Form object would be frmHotelRoomSelection. The form name should be changed in the Solution Explorer.

To give the name, frmHotelRoomSelection, to the form in Figure 2-11, you can complete the following steps:

STEP 1 Click anywhere in the Windows Form object to select it.

When you click within any object, including a Windows Form object, that object is selected (Figure 2-12). Sizing handles and a heavier border surround the selected object. In addition, the Properties window displays the properties of the selected object.

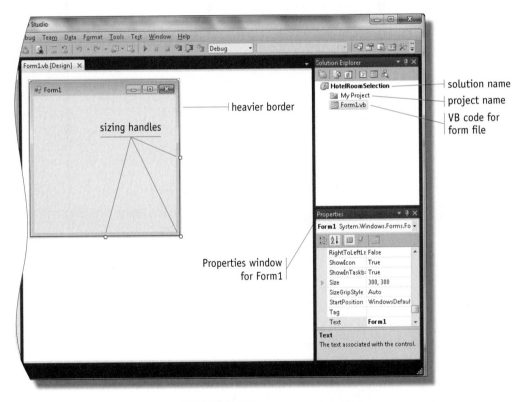

FIGURE 2-12

STEP 2 In the Solution Explorer window, right-click the Form1.vb filename. On the shortcut menu, point to Rename.

The name, Form1, is right-clicked in the Solution Explorer window. The shortcut menu for the Form1.vb file appears. Rename is highlighted (Figure 2-13).

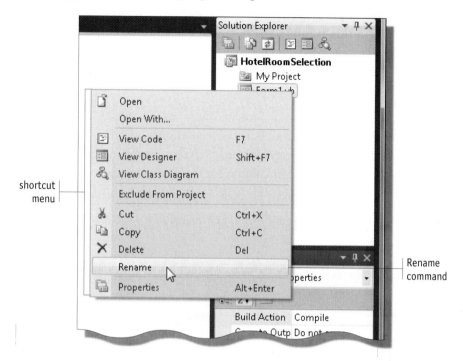

FIGURE 2-13

STEP 3 Click Rename. Type `frmHotelRoomSelection.vb` and press the ENTER key.

The Form1.vb form file is given the new name frmHotelRoomSelection.vb in the Solution Explorer window (Figure 2-14).

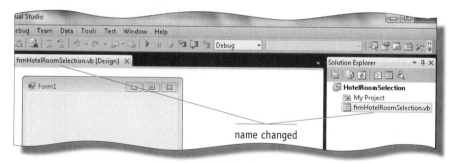

FIGURE 2-14

Set the Title Bar Text in a Windows Form Object

After you name the Windows Form object, often the next step in the graphical user interface design is to change the title bar text so it reflects the function of the program. In this example, the name used is Hotel Room Selection. The **Text property** in the Windows Form object Properties window contains the value that is displayed in the title bar of the window. You can set the Text property using the following steps:

STEP 1   With the Windows Form object selected, scroll in the Properties window until you find the Text property. (Remember: The properties are in alphabetic order.) Then, double-click in the right column for the Text property.

The text, Form1, is selected in the Properties window (Figure 2-15). Form1 is the default text value for the first Windows Form object created in a project. Whenever a property is selected, you can change the property.

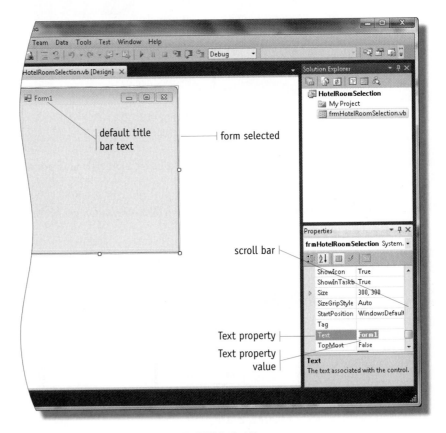

FIGURE 2-15

STEP 2 Type Hotel Room Selection and then press the ENTER key.

The value, Hotel Room Selection, is displayed for the Text property in the Properties window and also is displayed in the title bar of the Windows Form object (Figure 2-16). You can enter any value you like for the Text property of the Windows Form object.

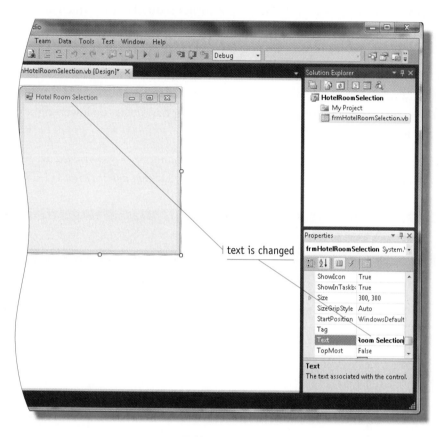

text is changed

FIGURE 2-16

ONLINE REINFORCEMENT

To view a video of the process in the previous steps, visit scsite.com/vb2010/ch2 and then click Figure 2-15.

You can change many of the properties for any object in the graphical user interface using the techniques just illustrated.

Resize a Form

To resize a Windows Form object, you can change the **Size property** in the Properties window to the exact number of horizontal and vertical pixels you desire. You also can change the Windows Form object size by dragging the vertical border to change the width of the window or the horizontal border to change the height. Another way to change the size is to drag a corner sizing handle, which allows you to change both the width and the height at the same time.

The following steps illustrate using the sizing handles to change the size of the Windows Form object shown in Figure 2-17:

STEP 1 Place the mouse pointer over the sizing handle in the lower-right corner of the Windows Form object.

When the mouse pointer is over the sizing handle, it changes to a two-headed arrow that indicates you can drag to change the size of the Windows Form object (Figure 2-17).

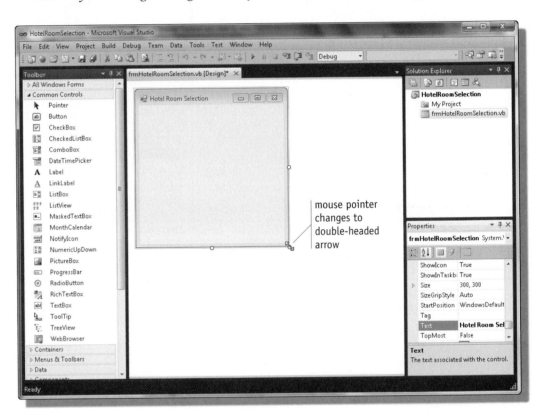

FIGURE 2-17

STEP 2 Drag the sizing handle to the right and down until the window is the size you want. Then, release the left mouse button.

The Windows Form object has been resized (Figure 2-18). The exact size of the Windows Form object is shown on the Status bar as (number of horizontal pixels, number of vertical pixels). In Figure 2-18, the size of the Windows Form object is 430 pixels horizontally by 395 pixels vertically.

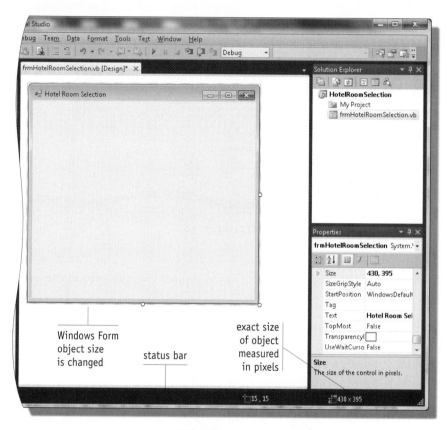

FIGURE 2-18

ONLINE REINFORCEMENT

To view a video of the process in the previous steps, visit scsite.com/vb2010/ch2 and then click Figure 2-17.

Add a Label Object

After sizing the Windows Form object, you can use the Toolbox to add other GUI objects as required. For example, a graphical user interface often displays a message or labels an item in the window. To accomplish this, you can use the **Label .NET component** in the Toolbox to place a **Label object** on the Windows Form object. To add a Label object to a Windows Form object, you can complete the steps on the next page.

STEP 1   Drag the Label .NET component button from the Common Controls category in the Toolbox over the Windows Form object to the approximate location where you want to place the Label object.

The mouse pointer changes to a crosshair and small rectangle when you place it over the Windows Form object (Figure 2-19). The Label object will be placed on the form at the location of the small rectangle in the mouse pointer.

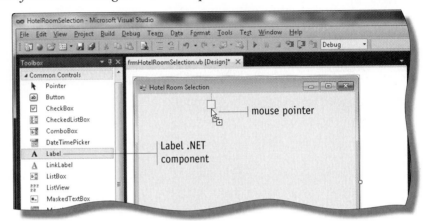

FIGURE 2-19

In addition to dragging a .NET component from the Toolbox to the Windows Form object, you can place an object on the Windows Form object by double-clicking the .NET component in the Toolbox. You can move and resize the object after it has been placed on the Windows Form object. You also can click the .NET component in the Toolbox and then click the Windows Form object at the desired location for the object. The object will be placed where you clicked. Developers use the technique they find most convenient.

STEP 2   When the mouse pointer is in the correct location, release the left mouse button.

The Label object is placed on the Windows Form object at the location you selected (Figure 2-20). The label is selected, as identified by the dotted border surrounding it. The default text within the label is Label1. In virtually all cases, you must change the label text to reflect the needs of the interface.

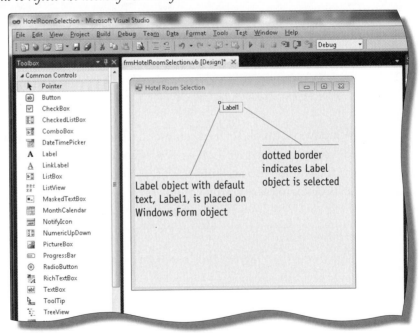

ONLINE REINFORCEMENT

To view a video of the process in the previous steps, visit scsite.com/vb2010/ch2 and then click Figure 2-19.

FIGURE 2-20

Name the Label Object

As with most objects you place on the Windows Form object, the first step after creating the object should be to name the object. To give the Label object the name, Heading, together with the Label prefix, lbl, complete the following steps:

STEP 1   With the Label object selected, scroll in the Properties window until you find the (Name) property. Then double-click in the right column for the (Name) property.

The default name, Label1, is selected (Figure 2-21). When a property is selected, you can change the property.

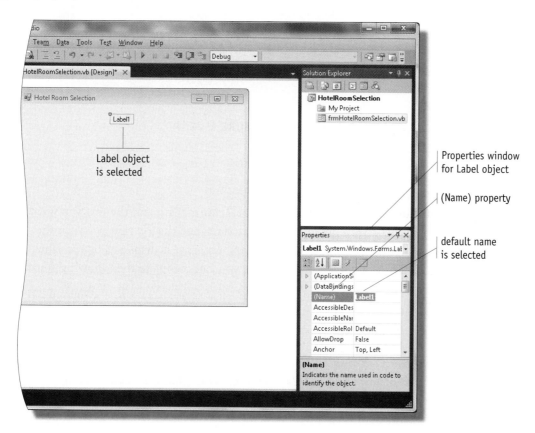

Properties window for Label object

(Name) property

default name is selected

FIGURE 2-21

STEP 2   Type the new name, lblHeading and then press the ENTER key.

The name you entered is displayed in the Name property in the Properties window (Figure 2-22). You now can reference the Label object by its name in other parts of the program.

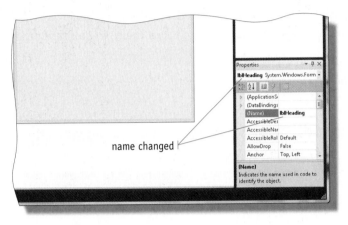

name changed

FIGURE 2-22

Change the Text in a Label Object

The default text in a Label object, Label1, normally is not the text you want to display in the label. Therefore, you should change the Text property for the Label object to the desired value. To change the text that is displayed on the label in Figure 2-21 to Hotel Room Selection, you can complete the following steps:

STEP 1   With the Label object selected, scroll in the Properties dialog box until you find the Text property. Then, double-click the Text value in the right column.

The text value in the right column of the Text property, which is the text that is displayed in the label, is selected (Figure 2-23). When the Text value is selected, you can change it.

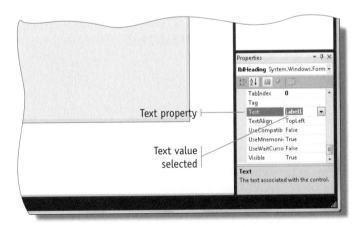

Text property

Text value selected

FIGURE 2-23

STEP 2 Type `Hotel Room Selection` for the Text property.

The text you typed, Hotel Room Selection, is displayed in the Text property for the Label object (Figure 2-24).

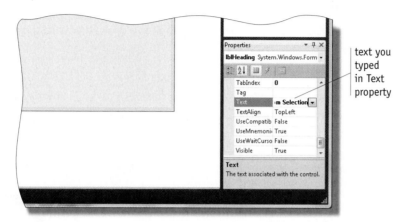

text you typed in Text property

FIGURE 2-24

STEP 3 To enter the Text property, press the ENTER key.

The text you entered, Hotel Room Selection, is displayed in the Text property and also in the label itself (Figure 2-25). The text is, by default, 8 points in size. The Label object automatically expanded horizontally to accommodate the text you typed. By default, Label objects change size so they are just the right size for the text in the Text property.

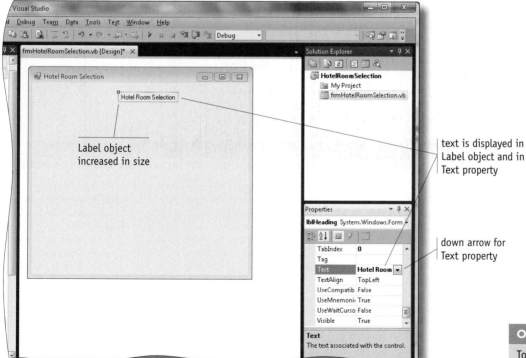

text is displayed in Label object and in Text property

down arrow for Text property

FIGURE 2-25

ONLINE REINFORCEMENT

To view a video of the process in the previous steps, visit scsite.com/vb2010/ch2 and then click Figure 2-23.

The text in a Label object can be multiple lines. To enter multiple lines for a Label object, you can complete the following steps:

STEP 1 With the Label object selected, click the Text property name in the left column of the Properties window. Then, click the down arrow in the right column of the Text property.

A box opens in which you can enter multiple lines (Figure 2-26). As you type, you can move the insertion point to the next line by pressing the ENTER key. To accept the text for the label, press CTRL + ENTER (this nomenclature means you hold down the CTRL key, press the ENTER key, and then release both keys).

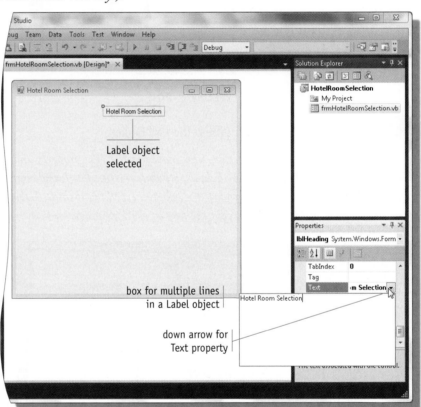

FIGURE 2-26

Change Label Font, Font Style, and Font Size

Many times, the default font, font style, and font size of the text in a Label object must be changed to reflect the purpose of the label. For example, in a label that is used as a heading for a window, the text should be larger than the default 8-point font used for Label objects, and should be bold so it stands out as a heading. To change the font, font style, and font size of a label, you can select the label and then use the **Font property** to make the change. To change the text that appears in the lblHeading label to Tahoma font, make the font bold, and increase the font size to 16 point, you can complete the following steps:

> **STEP 1**   Click the Label object to select it. Scroll until you find the Font property in the Properties window. Click the Font property in the left column of the Label property window.

The Label object is selected as shown by the dotted border surrounding it (Figure 2-27). When you click the Font property in the Properties window, an ellipsis button (a button with three dots) is displayed in the right column. In the Properties window, an ellipsis button indicates multiple choices for the property will be made available when you click the button.

WATCH OUT FOR

When you click an object to select it, you might double-click it accidentally. If you do, a tabbed page with programming code opens. To return to the form and continue developing the user interface, click the [Design] tab for your form, such as the frmHotelRoomSelection.vb [Design] tab.

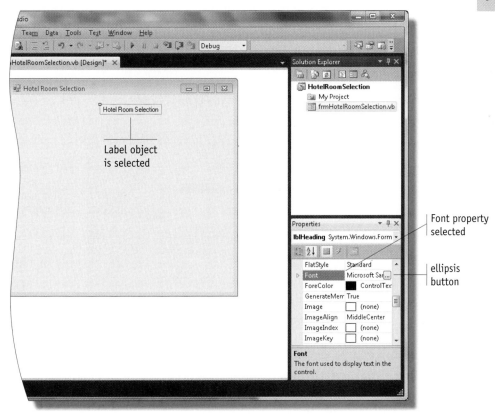

FIGURE 2-27

STEP 2 Click the ellipsis button for the Font property.

The Font dialog box is displayed (Figure 2-28). Using the Font dialog box, you can change the Font, Font style, and Size of the text in the Label object.

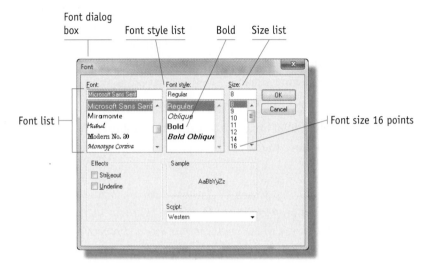

FIGURE 2-28

STEP 3 In the Font dialog box, scroll to find Tahoma in the Font list and then click Tahoma in the Font list. Click Bold in the Font style list. Click 16 in the Size list.

The selections are highlighted in the Font dialog box (Figure 2-29).

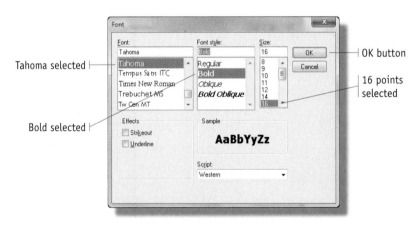

FIGURE 2-29

STEP 4 Click the OK button.

The font, font style, and font size in the Label object are changed as specified in the Font dialog box (Figure 2-30). The Label object automatically expands to accommodate the changed font. The changes also are made for the Font property in the Properties window.

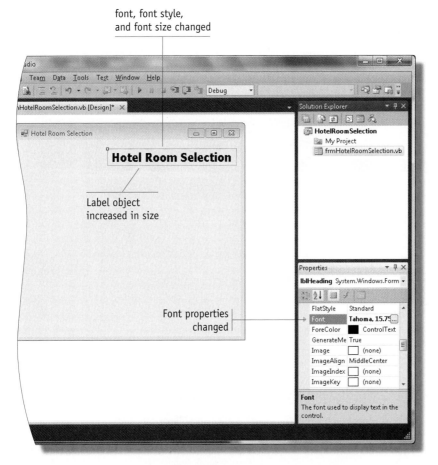

FIGURE 2-30

ONLINE REINFORCEMENT

To view a video of the process in the previous steps, visit scsite.com/vb2010/ch2 and then click Figure 2-27.

Center a Label Object in the Windows Form Object

When you place an object on the Windows Form object, the object you place may not be located in precisely the correct position. So, you must align the object in the window. A single label often is centered horizontally in the window; that is, the distance from the left frame of the window to the beginning of the text should be the same as the distance from the end of the text to the right frame of the window. To horizontally center the label containing the heading, you can complete the following steps:

STEP 1 With the Label object selected, click Format on the menu bar and then point to Center in Form on the Format menu.

The Format menu is displayed and the mouse pointer is located on the Center in Form command (Figure 2-31). The Center in Form submenu also is displayed. The two choices on the Center in Form submenu are Horizontally and Vertically. Horizontally means the label will be centered between the left and right edges of the window. Vertically means the label will be centered between the top edge and the bottom edge of the window.

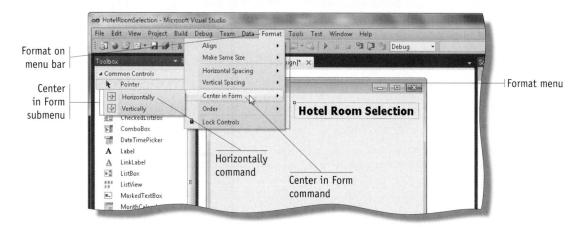

FIGURE 2-31

STEP 2 Click Horizontally on the Center in Form submenu.

The label is centered horizontally in the window (Figure 2-32).

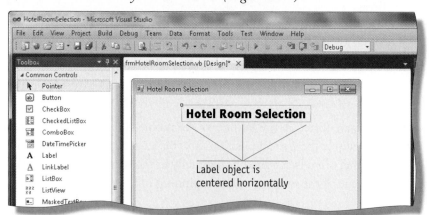

FIGURE 2-32

Object alignment is an important aspect of user interface design because carefully aligned objects in an interface make them and the interface easy to use. Centering within the Windows Form object is the first of several alignment requirements you will encounter in this chapter.

Delete GUI Objects

In some instances, you might find that you add an object to the Windows Form object and later discover you do not want or need the object in the user interface. When this occurs, you should delete the object from the Windows Form object. Visual Studio provides two primary ways to delete an object from the Windows Form object: the keyboard and a shortcut menu. To delete an object using the keyboard, perform the following steps:

STEP 1   Select the object to be deleted by clicking it.

When you click an object, such as the label in Figure 2-33, the object is selected. When a label is selected, it is surrounded by a dotted border. As you saw with the Windows Form object (Figure 2-12), other objects are surrounded by a heavier border and sizing handles.

FIGURE 2-33

STEP 2   Press the DELETE key on the keyboard.

When you press the DELETE key, Visual Studio removes the object from the screen (Figure 2-34).

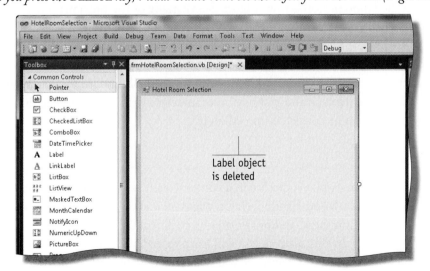

FIGURE 2-34

ONLINE REINFORCEMENT

To view a video of the process in the previous steps, visit scsite.com/vb2010/ch2 and then click Figure 2-33.

A second way to delete an object is to use a shortcut menu. To use a shortcut menu, right-click the object to be deleted and then select Delete on the shortcut menu.

Use the Undo Button on the Standard Toolbar

As you work in Visual Studio to create a graphical user interface, you might delete an object or perform another activity that you realize was an error. You can undo an action you just performed by clicking the Undo button on the Standard toolbar. To undo the action of deleting the heading label, you can perform the following step:

STEP 1 Click the Undo button on the Standard toolbar.

When you click the Undo button, the last action performed in Visual Studio is "undone." In Figure 2-35, the action that deleted the label (Figure 2-34) is undone and the Label object now appears on the Windows Form object again.

Undo button

Undo button arrow

Redo button

Label object appears

FIGURE 2-35

ONLINE REINFORCEMENT
To view a video of the process in the previous step, visit scsite.com/vb2010/ch2 and then click Figure 2-35.

You can use the Undo button to undo more than just the last action performed. If you click the Undo button arrow (Figure 2-35), many of the previous activities are shown in a list. You can undo a number of activities by clicking an activity in the list.

When you use the Undo button, you might undo something you do not want to undo. You can click the Redo button on the Standard toolbar to redo an action.

Learning to use the Undo and Redo buttons on the Standard toolbar means you can add or delete items in the graphical user interface with the assurance that any error you make can be corrected immediately.

Add a PictureBox Object

When you want to display a picture in a window, such as the hotel room pictures shown in Figure 2-1b and Figure 2-1c on pages 30 and 31, you must place a PictureBox object on the Windows Form object. Then, the picture is placed in the PictureBox object. In this section, you will learn to add a PictureBox object to the Windows Form object. In Chapter 3, you will learn how to place a picture in the PictureBox object.

A **PictureBox** is an object much like a label. To add a PictureBox object to the window, you can use the Toolbox, as shown in the following steps:

STEP 1   With the Toolbox visible, drag the PictureBox .NET component on the Toolbox over the Windows Form object to the approximate location where you want the PictureBox object to be displayed.

The mouse pointer changes when you place it over the Windows Form object (Figure 2-36). The upper-left corner of the PictureBox object will be placed on the form at the location of the small square in the mouse pointer.

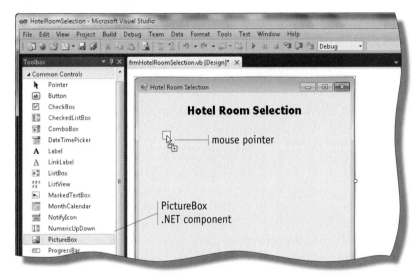

FIGURE 2-36

STEP 2   When the mouse pointer is in the correct location, release the left mouse button.

A PictureBox object is placed on the Windows Form object in the default size (Figure 2-37). The PictureBox object is selected as indicated by the sizing handles and the heavier border. Notice that when the mouse pointer is inside the PictureBox object, it changes to a crosshair with four arrowheads. This indicates you can drag the PictureBox object anywhere on the Windows Form object.

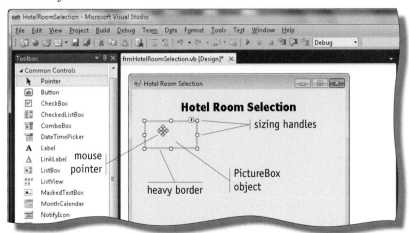

FIGURE 2-37

ONLINE REINFORCEMENT

To view a video of the process in the previous steps, visit scsite.com/vb2010/ch2 and then click Figure 2-36.

As you can see, placing a PictureBox object on the Windows Form object is similar to placing a Label object on the Windows Form object. You will find you can use the same technique for most objects within the Toolbox.

Name a PictureBox Object

When you add an object to the Windows Form object, the first action you should take is to name the object. The technique for naming a PictureBox object is identical to that used for naming a Label object except that the prefix for a PictureBox object is pic. For example, to give the name, picStandardRoom, to the PictureBox object just added to the form, you can complete the following steps:

1. Select the PictureBox object.
2. Locate the (Name) property in the Properties window for the PictureBox object.
3. Double-click the value in the right column for the (Name) property, type picStandardRoom as the name, and then press the ENTER key.

Resize a PictureBox Object

When you place a PictureBox object on the Windows Form object, it often is not the size required for the application. You can resize a PictureBox object using the same technique you used to resize the Windows Form object. The step on the next page will resize the Picture Box object:

HEADS UP

The Size property will change to the new size in the Properties dialog box. If you know an exact size, you can also enter that size directly in the Size property for that object.

STEP 1   Place the mouse pointer over the sizing handle at the lower-right corner of the PictureBox object, and then drag the handle to the size 185 × 150.

When you drag the sizing handle, both the width and the height of the PictureBox object can be changed. In Figure 2-38, the width and the height of the PictureBox object are increased. The actual size of the PictureBox object in pixels (185 horizontal pixels, 150 vertical pixels) is shown on the Status bar.

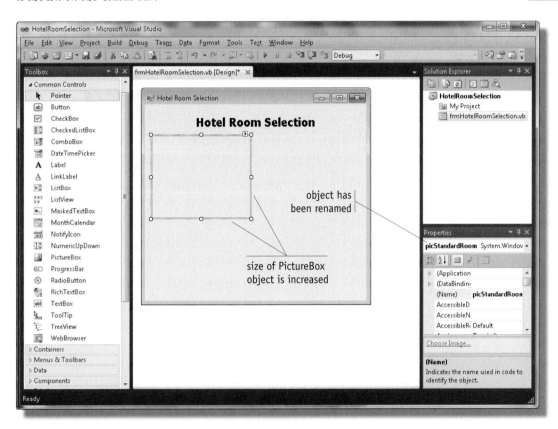

FIGURE 2-38

ONLINE REINFORCEMENT

To view a video of the process in the previous step, visit scsite.com/vb2010/ch2 and then click Figure 2-38.

Add a Second PictureBox Object

You can add a second PictureBox object to the Windows Form object by performing the same technique you have seen previously, as in the following step:

STEP 1 Drag the PictureBox .NET component in the Toolbox to any location in the Windows Form object, and then release the left mouse button.

The PictureBox object is placed on the Windows Form object (Figure 2-39). Notice that the PictureBox objects in Figure 2-39 are different sizes. If you see a blue line as you drag the PictureBox object onto the Windows Form object, ignore it. You will learn about these lines later in this chapter.

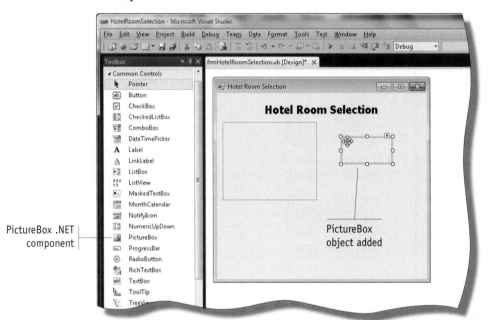

PictureBox .NET component

PictureBox object added

FIGURE 2-39

ONLINE REINFORCEMENT

To view a video of the process in the previous step, visit scsite.com/vb2010/ch2 and then click Figure 2-39.

As with all objects added to the Windows Form object, you should name the PictureBox object immediately after adding it. A good name for the second PictureBox object is picDeluxeRoom.

Make Objects the Same Size

Often you will want Picture Boxes and other GUI elements in your user interface to be the same size. You can use the Format menu to make GUI objects the same size, as shown in the steps on the next page:

STEP 1   Select the object whose size you want to duplicate (in this example, the left PictureBox object in the window), and then hold down the CTRL key and click the object you want to resize (the right PictureBox object in the window).

Both the left PictureBox object and the right PictureBox object are selected (Figure 2-40). The left PictureBox object is surrounded by white sizing handles and the right PictureBox object is surrounded by black sizing handles, which indicates the left PictureBox object is the "controlling" object when sizing or alignment commands are executed. The first object selected always is the controlling object.

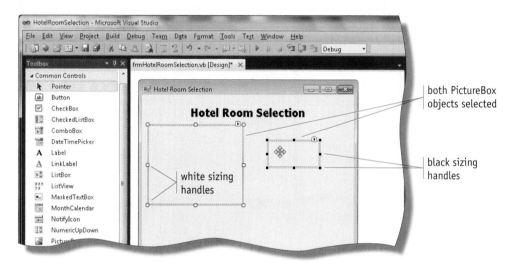

FIGURE 2-40

STEP 2   Click Format on the menu bar and then point to the Make Same Size command on the Format menu.

The Format menu and the Make Same Size submenu are displayed (Figure 2-41). The Make Same Size submenu provides commands to make the width, the height, or both dimensions the same as the controlling object.

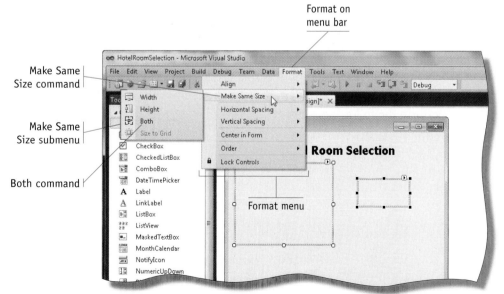

FIGURE 2-41

STEP 3   Click Both on the Make Same Size submenu.

Visual Studio changes the size of the right PictureBox object to match the size of the left PictureBox object (Figure 2-42). Both the width and the height of the right PictureBox object are changed.

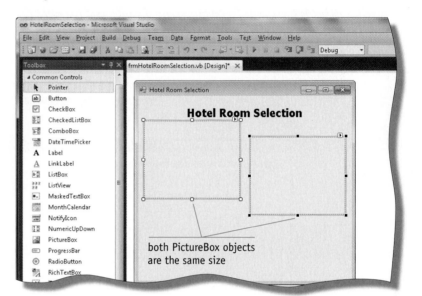

ONLINE REINFORCEMENT

To view a video of the process in the previous steps, visit scsite.com/vb2010/ch2 and then click Figure 2-40.

FIGURE 2-42

Align the PictureBox Objects

Notice in Figure 2-42 that the left PictureBox object is higher in the form than the right PictureBox object. When designing a graphical user interface, you should consider aligning the elements to create a clean, uncluttered look for the user. **Alignment** means one element in the GUI is lined up horizontally (left and right) or vertically (up and down) with another element in the window. For example, in Figure 2-42 the GUI would be better if the PictureBox objects were aligned horizontally so their tops and bottoms were even across the window.

When you want to align objects already on the Windows Form object, select the objects to align, and then specify the alignment you want. As you have seen when changing the object size, the first object selected is the controlling object; when aligning, this means the other objects that are selected will be aligned on the first object selected. To horizontally align the two PictureBox objects in Figure 2-42, you can perform the following steps:

STEP 1 With the left and right PictureBox objects selected as shown in Figure 2-42, click Format on the menu bar and then point to Align on the Format menu.

The Format menu and the Align submenu are displayed (Figure 2-43). The left PictureBox object is the "controlling" object as indicated by the white sizing handles, so the right PictureBox object will be aligned horizontally with the left PictureBox object.

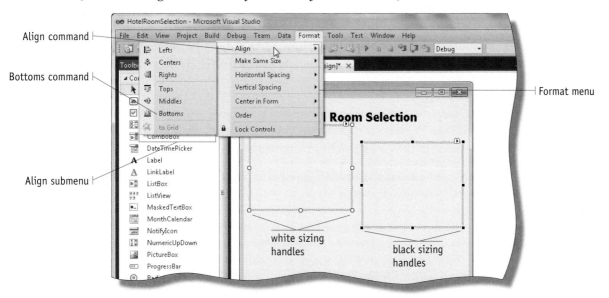

FIGURE 2-43

STEP 2 Click Bottoms on the Align submenu.

The bottom of the right PictureBox object is aligned horizontally with the bottom of the left PictureBox object (Figure 2-44). In addition, because the PictureBox objects are the same size, the tops also are aligned.

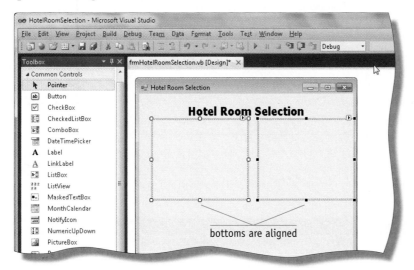

FIGURE 2-44

ONLINE REINFORCEMENT

To view a video of the process in the previous steps, visit scsite.com/vb2010/ch2 and then click Figure 2-43.

Notice on the Align submenu in Figure 2-43 that Visual Studio offers seven choices for alignment. When you are aligning objects horizontally, you should choose from the Tops, Middles, and Bottoms group. When you are aligning objects vertically, you should choose from the Lefts, Centers, and Rights group. Aligning to a grid will be covered later in this book.

Center Multiple Objects Horizontally in the Window

From Figure 2-44 on page 63 you can see that the PictureBox objects are not centered horizontally in the Windows Form object. As you learned, you can center one or more objects horizontally within the Windows Form object by using a command from the Format menu. To center the two PictureBox objects as a unit, you can complete the following steps:

STEP 1 With both PictureBox objects selected, click Format on the menu bar and then point to the Center in Form command.

The Format menu is displayed (Figure 2-45). The Center in Form submenu also is displayed.

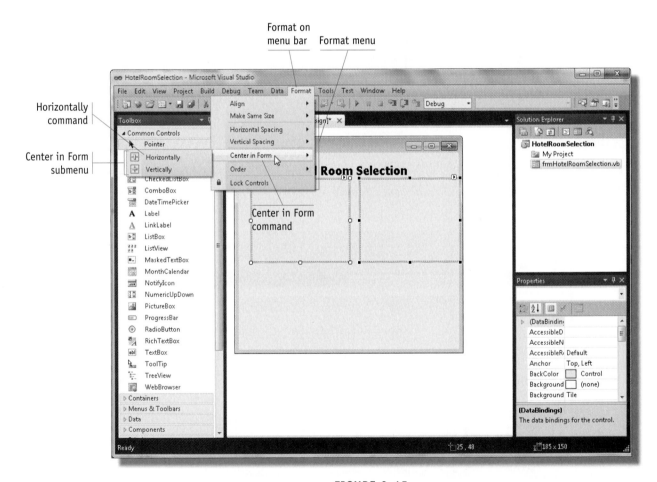

FIGURE 2-45

STEP 2   Click Horizontally on the Center in Form submenu.

The two PictureBox objects, as a unit, are centered horizontally in the Windows Form object (Figure 2–46). The left border for the left PictureBox object is the same distance from the window frame as the right border for the right PictureBox object.

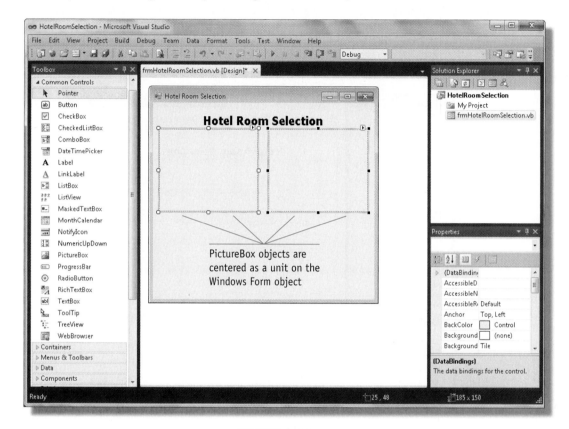

FIGURE 2-46

Adding an object, naming it, sizing it, and aligning it are basic to all graphical user interface design.

Add a Button Object

A **Button object** is a commonly used object in a graphical user interface. For example, you probably are familiar with the OK button that is used in many applications. Generally, when the program is executing, buttons are used to cause an event to occur. To place a Button object on the Windows Form object, you use the Toolbox. To create a Button object, you can complete the steps on the next page:

ONLINE REINFORCEMENT

To view a video of the process in the previous steps, visit scsite.com/vb2010/ch2 and then click Figure 2-45.

STEP 1   With the Toolbox displayed in the Visual Studio window, drag the Button .NET component in the Toolbox over the Windows Form object to the position where you want to place the button.

When you drag the button over the Windows Form object, the mouse pointer changes (Figure 2-47). The upper-left corner of the Button object will be placed where the upper-left corner of the rectangle is located.

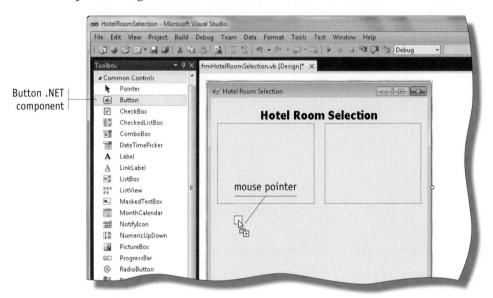

Button .NET
component

mouse pointer

FIGURE 2-47

STEP 2   When the mouse pointer is positioned properly, release the left mouse button.

A standard-sized Button object is added to the Windows Form object (Figure 2-48). The text on the button is the default, Button1. In addition, the button is selected as indicated by the heavier border and sizing handles.

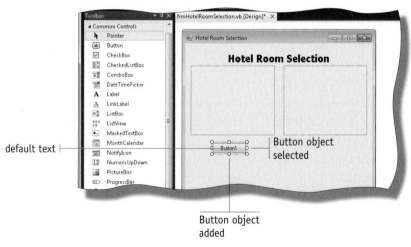

default text

Button object
selected

Button object
added

FIGURE 2-48

Name and Set Text for a Button Object

As with other objects added to the Windows Form object, the first step after adding the Button object is to name it. A Button object name should contain the prefix, btn. For example, the name for the button you just added could be, btnStandardRoom.

In most cases, you also will change the text that appears on the Button object. To change the text on the btnStandardRoom button, you can do the following:

STEP 1   With the Button object selected, scroll in the Properties dialog box until you find the Text property. Double-click the Text value in the right column, type `Standard Room` and then press the ENTER key.

The text for the Standard Room button is changed both on the button and in the Properties window (Figure 2-49). The button is not large enough to contain the words, Standard Room, so only the word, Standard, is displayed. In the next set of steps, you will learn how to enlarge the size of the Button object.

HEADS UP

In this chapter, you have named four different objects: a Windows Form object, a Label object, a PictureBox object, and a Button object. As you learned, each object name should have a prefix that identifies the type of object. In this chapter, the prefixes are:

Type of Object	Name Prefix
Windows Form object	frm
Label object	lbl
PictureBox object	pic
Button object	btn

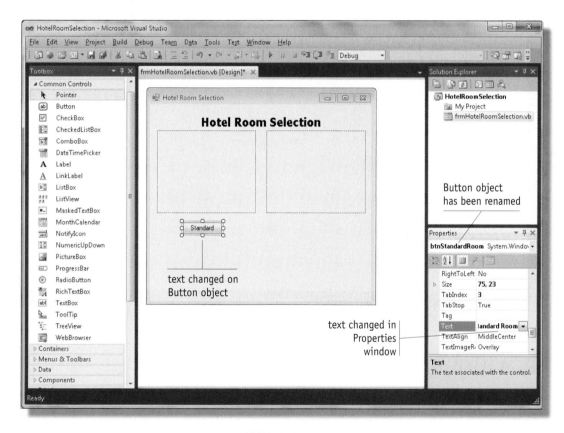

FIGURE 2-49

ONLINE REINFORCEMENT

To view a video of the process in the previous step, visit scsite.com/vb2010/ch2 and then click Figure 2-49.

Change Button Object Size

Sometimes, the button size may not be big enough to display the button text (see Figure 2-49 on the previous page). To change a Button object size to accommodate the text, you can perform the following steps:

STEP 1   Place the mouse pointer over the right edge of the Button object until the pointer changes to a double-headed arrow.

The mouse pointer changes to a double-headed arrow, which indicates you can drag the border of the button to increase or decrease its size (Figure 2-50).

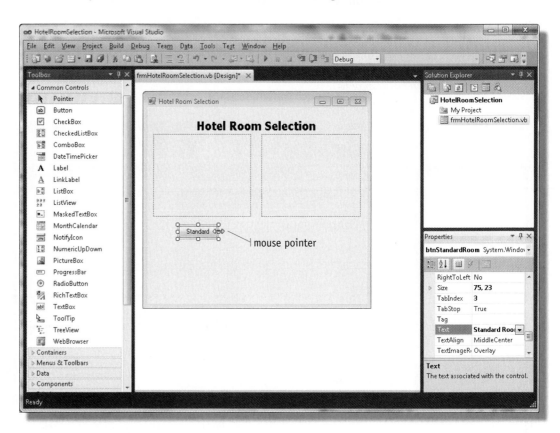

FIGURE 2-50

STEP 2 Drag the mouse pointer to the right until the Button object is just big enough to display the text, Standard Room, and then release the left mouse button.

As you drag the mouse pointer to the right, the button is made bigger (Figure 2-51). When the button is big enough to display the text, it is the right size.

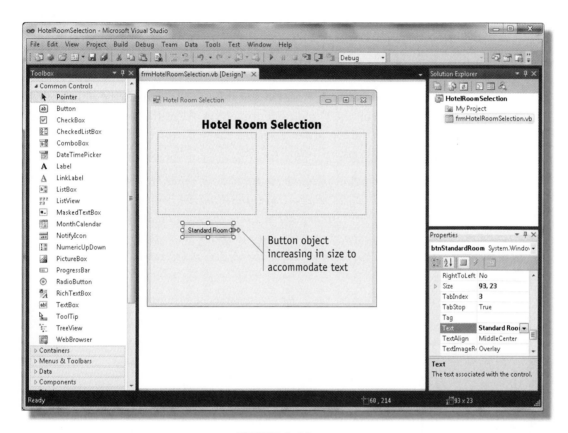

FIGURE 2-51

You can move a Button object by placing the mouse pointer on the button (the mouse pointer changes to a crosshair with four arrowheads) and then dragging the button to any location on the Windows Form object. You can move other objects on the Windows Form object using the same technique.

ONLINE REINFORCEMENT

To view a video of the process in the previous steps, visit scsite.com/vb2010/ch2 and then click Figure 2-50.

IN THE REAL WORLD

Some developers use the AutoSize property for a Button object to ensure the button always is large enough for text. By setting the AutoSize property for a Button object to True in the Properties window, the Button object will expand or contract when you change the text so the text fits precisely in the button.

Add and Align a Second Button

Often, a window requires more than one button. When a second button is added to the window, a normal requirement is that the buttons be aligned. As with PictureBox objects, you can align Button objects horizontally or vertically.

With the PictureBox objects, you saw that you can align objects after they have been placed on the Windows Form object. You also can align objects when you place them on the Windows Form object. To add a second button to the Windows Form object in Figure 2-51 and align it horizontally at the same time, you can complete the following steps:

STEP 1 Drag the Button .NET component from the Toolbox to the right of the Standard Room button on the Windows Form object. Align the top of the rectangle in the mouse pointer to the top of the Standard Room button until a blue line displays along the tops of the buttons.

*The blue line, called a **snap line**, indicates the top of the Standard Room button is aligned with the top of the Button object being added to the Windows Form object (Figure 2-52). You can drag the Button object left or right to obtain the desired spacing between the buttons. If the blue line disappears while you are dragging, move the mouse pointer up or down until the blue line reappears, signaling the objects are horizontally aligned.*

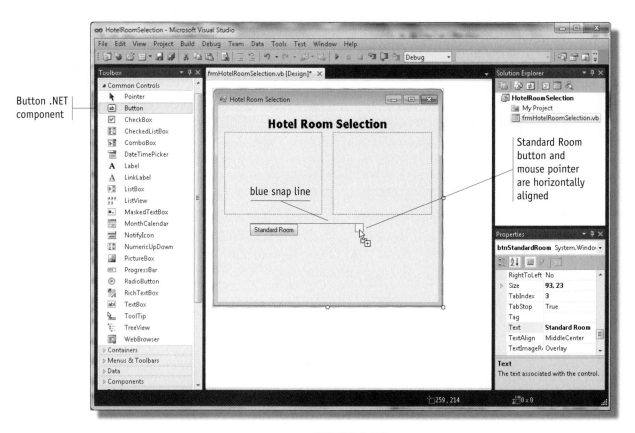

FIGURE 2-52

STEP 2 When the buttons are aligned and spaced as you like, release the left mouse button.

The Button1 object is aligned horizontally with the Standard Room button (Figure 2-53). Their tops are on the same line and, because they are the same vertical size, their bottoms are aligned as well.

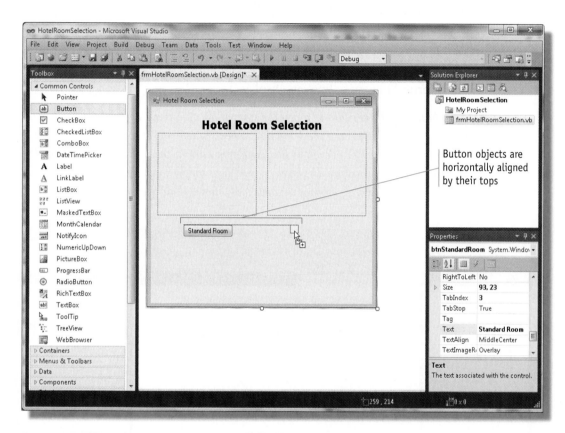

FIGURE 2-53

ONLINE REINFORCEMENT

To view a video of the process in the previous steps, visit scsite.com/vb2010/ch2 and then click Figure 2-52.

After adding the second Button object, you should name it, change the text as needed, and size the Button object if necessary. For the second Button object, assume you have named it btnDeluxeRoom, have changed the button text to Deluxe Room, and have made the two buttons the same size. You will recall that you can make the Deluxe Room button the same size as the Standard Room button by completing the following steps:

Step 1: Click the Standard Room button and then, while holding down the CTRL key, click the Deluxe Room button.

Step 2: Click Format on the menu bar, point to Make Same Size on the Format menu, and then click Both on the Make Same Size submenu.

Step 3: To unselect the Button objects, click anywhere on the Windows Form object except on another object.

Align Objects Vertically

The buttons in Figure 2-53 are aligned horizontally. They also can be aligned vertically. To illustrate this and to show how to align objects already on the Windows Form object using snap lines, assume that the Standard Room button and the Deluxe Room button should be vertically aligned on the left side of the Windows Form object with the Standard Room button above the Deluxe Room button. To vertically align the Button objects, you can complete the following steps:

STEP 1 If necessary, click anywhere in the Windows Form object to deselect any other objects. Then, slowly drag the Deluxe Room button below the Standard Room button until vertical blue snap lines are displayed.

*As you drag, **blue snap lines** indicate when the sides of the objects are aligned vertically. In Figure 2-54, since the buttons are the same size, when the left side of the Standard Room button is aligned with the left side of the Deluxe Room button, the right sides are aligned as well, so two blue vertical lines are displayed. If you drag the button a little further to the left or right, the buttons will not be aligned and the blue lines will disappear.*

FIGURE 2-54

STEP 2   When the blue lines appear, indicating the buttons are aligned vertically, drag the Deluxe Room button up or down to create the proper spacing between the buttons, and then release the left mouse button.

The vertical distance between the buttons is a judgment call, based on the needs of the application, the size of the Windows Form object, and the number of other elements within the window (Figure 2-55). As with many aspects of GUI design, the eye of the developer will be critical in determining the actual placement of objects in the window.

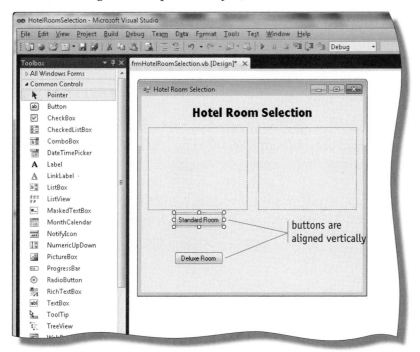

FIGURE 2-55

In the previous examples, you have seen the use of blue snap lines. As you drag objects, you also might see red snap lines flash on the screen. A **red snap line** indicates text within an object is aligned. For example, if you drag a button and the text in the button you are dragging aligns horizontally with the text in another button, a red snap line will be displayed. The use of red and blue snap lines allows you to align objects on the Windows Form object by dragging instead of selecting the objects and using the Format menu.

Visual Studio offers a variety of tools to create and align elements in the graphical user interface, and to make the user interface as effective and useful as possible.

Save a Visual Basic Project

As you are working on a Visual Basic project, a mandatory practice is to save your work on a regular basis. Some developers save every 10-15 minutes while others might wait for a natural break to save their work. Regardless, it is important to develop the habit of regularly saving your work.

To save the work you have completed, you can click the Save All button on the Standard toolbar. The first time you save a project, the Save Project dialog box shown in Figure 2-56 is displayed.

location for
saving project

FIGURE 2-56

Select the location where you want to store your program. You might use a USB drive, the hard drive on your computer, or a network drive. If you have any questions concerning where to store your program, check with your instructor or network administrator.

After you save the program the first time, each time you click the Save All button on the Standard toolbar, your program will be saved in the same location with the same name.

Close Visual Studio 2010

To close Visual Studio, you can click the Close button on the right of the Visual Studio window title bar. If, when you close Visual Studio, you have never saved your program, Visual Studio will display the Close Project dialog box (Figure 2-57).

FIGURE 2-57

You can choose to save your program or to discard your program. If you click the Save button, the Save Project dialog box will be displayed (Figure 2-56) and you can save your program. If you click the Discard button, your program will be discarded and not saved.

If, when you close Visual Studio, you have accomplished work since you last saved your project, Visual Studio will ask if you want to save the elements of the project that have changed since you last saved the project. In most cases, you should choose Yes.

Open a Visual Basic Project

After you save a project and close Visual Studio, you often will want to open the project and work on it again. To open a saved project, you can follow one of several methods:

Method 1: Double-click the solution file in the folder in which it is stored. This method will open the solution and allow you to continue your work.

Method 2: With Visual Studio open, click the Open File button on the Standard toolbar, locate the solution file, and open it in the same manner you use for most programs running under the Windows operating system.

Method 3: With Visual Studio open, click File on the menu bar and then point to Recent Projects and Solutions on the File menu. A list of the projects most recently worked on is displayed. Click the name of the project you want to open. This method might not work well if you are using a computer that is not your own because other persons' projects might be listed.

After using one of these methods, you can continue the work on your project.

> **WATCH OUT FOR**
>
> Sometimes when you open a Visual Basic project, the Form1.vb[Design] tabbed page is not displayed. (This page is renamed as frmHotelRoomSelection.vb in your project.) To display it, double-click Form1 or the new name in this project, frmHotelRoomSelection.vb, in the Solution Explorer window at the upper-right section of the Visual Studio window.

Program Development Life Cycle

Now that you have learned the Visual Studio and Visual Basic skills necessary to design a user interface, you are ready to learn about the program development life cycle. The **program development life cycle** is a set of phases and steps that are followed by developers to design, create, and maintain a computer program. The phases of the program development life cycle are:

1. **Gather and Analyze the Program Requirements** — The developer must obtain the information that identifies the program requirements and then document these requirements.
2. **Design the User Interface** — After the developer understands the program requirements, the next step is to design the user interface. The user interface provides the framework for the processing that will occur within the program.
3. **Design the Program Processing Objects** — A computer program consists of one or more processing objects that perform the tasks required within the program. The developer must determine what processing objects are required, and then determine the requirements of each object.
4. **Code the Program** — After the processing object has been designed, the object must be implemented in program code. **Program code** consists of the instructions written using a programming language such as Visual Basic 2010 that ultimately can be executed by a computer.
5. **Test the Program** — As the program is being coded, and after the coding is completed, the developer should test the program code to ensure it is executing properly. The testing process is ongoing, and includes a variety of stages.
6. **Document the Program/System** — As a program is being designed and coded, and after that process is completed, the developer should be documenting the program. **Documenting a program** means writing down in

a prescribed manner the instructions for using the program, the way in which a program performs its tasks, and other items that users, other developers, and management might require.

7. **Maintain the Program/System** — After a program is put into use, the program likely will have to be changed, or modified, some time in the future. For example, in the hotel room selection program, if a third type of room, such as a suite, is added to the rooms available in the hotel, the program must be changed to reflect the new room type. The process of changing and updating programs is called **program and system maintenance**.

The program development life cycle rarely is accomplished in a linear fashion, with one phase complete before the next phase starts. Rather, programs are developed iteratively, which means phases and steps within phases might have to be repeated a number of times before the program is completed. For example, the requirements for a program might be changed after the developer has begun coding the program. If this occurs, the developer must return to Phase 1 and gather and document the new requirements. Then, changes might have to be made to the user interface or other parts of the program to accommodate the updated requirements. This process of moving back and forth within the program development cycle is normal when developing a computer program.

The next sections in this chapter explain in detail Phase 1 and Phase 2 of the program development life cycle. The remaining phases are explained in Chapter 3.

Phase 1: Gather and Analyze the Program Requirements

An old programming adage states, "If you don't understand the problem to be solved, you will never develop a solution." While this seems self-evident, too often a program does not perform in the desired manner is because the designer did not understand the problem to be solved. Therefore, it is mandatory that, before beginning the user interface design, the developer understand the problem to be solved.

In many programming projects in industry, the developer is responsible for gathering the program requirements by interviewing users, reviewing current procedures, and completing other fact-gathering tasks. The emphasis in this book is on learning to program using the Visual Basic 2010 language, so the process of gathering program requirements is beyond the scope of the book. You will be given the program requirements for each program in this book.

When the requirements have been determined, they must be documented so the developers can proceed to design and implement the program. The exact form of the requirements documentation can vary significantly. The format and amount of documentation might be dictated by the application itself, or by the documentation standards of the organization for which the program is being developed. For Windows applications in this book, two types of requirements documentation will be provided for you. The first is the requirements document.

A **requirements document** identifies the purpose of the program being developed, the application title, the procedures to be followed when using the program, any equations and calculations required in the program, any conditions within the program that must be tested, notes and restrictions that must be followed by the program, and any other comments that would be helpful to understanding the problem.

Recall that the program to be developed in this chapter and in Chapter 3 is the Hotel Room Selection program (see Figure 2-1 on pages 30 and 31). The requirements document for the Hotel Room Selection program is shown in Figure 2-58.

The requirements document contains all the information that should be needed by a developer to design the program. In an event-driven program such as the Hotel Room Selection program, however, one additional document often is developed in

---

REQUIREMENTS DOCUMENT

Date submitted: January 23, 2013

Application title: Hotel Room Selection

Purpose: The hotel room selection program will allow a user to view different room types and make a room selection.

Program Procedures: From a window on the screen, the user should choose the room type and then make a room selection.

Algorithms, Processing, and Conditions:
1. The user must be able to view a standard room and a deluxe room until he or she makes a room selection.
2. When the user chooses a room type, a picture of that room type should appear in the window.
3. Only one picture should be displayed at a time, so if a user chooses a standard room, only the standard room picture should be displayed; if a user then chooses a deluxe room, the deluxe room picture should be displayed and the standard room picture should not be displayed.
4. When the user makes a room selection, a confirming message should be displayed. In addition, the user should be prevented from identifying a room type after the room selection is made.
5. After the user makes a room selection, the only allowable action is to exit the window.

Notes and Restrictions:
1. The user should not be able to make a room selection until he or she has chosen a room type.

Comments:
1. The pictures shown in the window should be selected from the pictures available on the Web.

FIGURE 2-58

order to clarify for the developer exactly what should occur in the program. The document is the Use Case Definition.

A **use case** is a sequence of actions a user will perform when using the program. The **Use Case Definition** specifies each of these sequences of actions by describing what the user will do and how the program will respond. The Use Case Definition for the Hotel Room Selection program is shown in Figure 2-59.

USE CASE DEFINITION

1. User clicks Standard Room or Deluxe Room button.
2. Program displays a picture of the room chosen by the user and enables the room selection button.
3. User clicks room buttons to view rooms if desired. Program displays the picture of the chosen room.
4. User clicks the Select Room button.
5. Program displays a room selection confirmation message, and disables both room buttons and the Select Room button. The Exit Window button becomes active.
6. User terminates the program by clicking the Exit Window button.

FIGURE 2-59

As you can see, the Use Case Definition specifies the actions performed by the user and the actions the program is to take in response.

The Use Case Definition is an important part of the requirements documentation for two reasons: 1) It defines for the developer exactly what is to occur as the user uses the program; 2) It allows the users to review the requirements documentation to ensure the specifications are correct before the developer actually begins designing the program.

When gathering and documenting the program requirements, it is critical that the users be involved. After all, the program is being developed for their use. When the users concur that the program requirements documentation is correct, the developer can move forward into the design phases for the program with the most confidence possible that the program will fulfill the needs of the users.

For the programs you will design in this book, the program requirements, including the requirements document and the Use Case Definition, will be provided to you. You should be aware, however, that in many cases in industry, an experienced developer must gather the requirements as well as implement them in a program.

Phase 2: Design the User Interface

Virtually all programs developed for a graphical user interface are driven by the user's actions when using the interface. It is these actions that dictate the processing the program should execute. Therefore, by designing the user interface, the developer will obtain a foundation for designing the rest of the program. In addition, by designing the user interface early in the design process, the developer can interact with users and ensure that the interface will fulfill the user requirements.

Expert program developers recognize the importance of the graphical user interface. These developers spend 25% to 40% of the program design time on the user interface, which sometimes is called the **presentation layer** of the program, because it is so critical to the program's success.

In the past, developers would draw the user interface on paper and present the drawings to users for their approval. When using Visual Studio 2010, however, with the rapid application development tools you have learned, the developer should use Visual Studio to create the user interface. The interface is created with no functionality; that is, none of the buttons or other GUI elements will cause processing to occur. Often, these interface designs are called **mock-ups** because they are provided for approval of the design only. When the users or others approve the interface design, the developer can design the program elements required to implement the functionality of the program.

An additional benefit when using Visual Studio to design the user interface is that when you have completed the design, you can use it in the actual program and you do not have to recreate it using other software.

Principles of User Interface Design

Because the presentation layer of the program is so important, a number of principles, or guidelines, have been developed over the years for user interface design. While the intent of this book is not to create expert user interface design specialists, nonetheless you should understand some of the principles so you can develop programs that are useful and usable. The following are some **design principles** you should incorporate into your user interface designs:

1. The most important principle to remember is that the user's ability to use the program effectively depends to a large extent on the design of the interface. If the GUI is easy to use and follow, the user will have a productive and enjoyable experience. If, on the other hand, the user must struggle to figure out how to enter data or which button to click, the user interface design is defeating the purpose of the program.
2. If the user interface is not easy to use, the user will not be satisfied with the application regardless of how well it does its work.
3. The user interface includes the windows, graphics, and text shown on the screen, as well as the methods used to interact with your program and cause operations to occur. Three primary means of interacting in a user interface are the keyboard, a pointing device such as a mouse, and voice input. The correct use of these tools significantly increases the probability of success for a user interface.
4. Use of the interface should feel natural and normal. This principle means the developer must be aware of who the user is and the manner in which the user is accustomed to working. For example, the interface for a banking program where a teller is entering account information will be different from that of a graphic arts program that allows manipulation of graphics and photographs. Each must reflect the needs of the user.

5. Visual Studio contains a wide variety of objects for use in the GUI, many of which can be used for similar purposes. A good user interface provides the most appropriate object for each requirement. You will learn about all these objects and their correct use throughout this text.

6. Once an object is used for a particular purpose in the user interface, such as a button being used to cause a particular action, then that object should be used for the same purpose throughout the program interface.

7. The objects in the interface must be arranged in the sequence in which they are used so the user can move from item to item on the screen in a logical, straightforward manner. Following this principle creates a clean and easy to use interface. It once again requires the developer to understand the needs of the user. When this principle is not followed, a confusing interface can result.

8. The interface should be kept as simple as possible, while containing all the functionality required for the program. Generally, the simpler the interface, the more effective it will be.

9. When implemented, the user interface should be intuitive, which means the user should be able to use it with little or no instruction. In fact, the user should feel that no other interface could have been designed because the one they are using is the most "natural."

By following these principles, you will create user interfaces that assist the user. The success of your program can depend on the user interface you design.

Sample Program

As you learned earlier, the Hotel Room Selection program is the sample program for this chapter and for Chapter 3 (see Figure 2-1 on page pages 30 and 31). The requirements document for this program is shown in Figure 2-58 on page 77 and the Use Case Definition is in Figure 2-59 on page 78. With these documents in hand, the first phase of the program development cycle is complete.

Sample Program — Phase 2: User Interface Design

When beginning the design of the user interface, the primary source of reference is the requirements document and the Use Case Definition for the program. Using these documents, the developer must analyze the program requirements and determine the elements required in the user interface.

On a line-for-line basis, the analysis of the requirements document in Figure 2-58 could proceed as follows:

1. The application will be presented in a window on the screen, so a Windows Forms Application using a Windows Form object is the appropriate means for creating the program.

2. The user will choose either a standard room or a deluxe room and then will make a room selection. In addition, when the room is chosen, a picture of the room should be displayed. While Visual Studio provides a variety of user interface tools for a user to make selections, a commonly used tool and one that is easily understood by users is the Button object. That is, when a user clicks a button, the user has made a choice and the program responds appropriately. In this application, a good design decision is to use buttons for the user to make a choice of rooms and make a room selection. When the user clicks the Standard Room button, a picture of the standard room will be displayed. When the user clicks the Deluxe Room button, a picture of the deluxe room will be displayed. When the user clicks the Select Room button, a room selection is made.

3. Two different pictures must be displayed in the user interface — a standard room picture and a deluxe room picture. While two different pictures can be displayed in a single PictureBox object, depending on the choice of the user, a simpler and more easily understood user interface can be developed if a PictureBox object and a button work together; that is, when the Standard Room button is clicked, the standard room picture is displayed in the standard room PictureBox object; and when the Deluxe Room button is clicked, the deluxe room picture is displayed in the deluxe room PictureBox object. In this way, the user can associate a button with a picture box location and the user interface is intuitive and easy to use.

4. When the user makes a room selection by clicking the Select Room button, a message must be displayed confirming the room selection. Therefore, a Label object must be included for the confirmation message.

5. After the user makes a room selection, the only action then available to the user is to exit the window, so an Exit Window button is required.

6. In addition to the exact requirements in the program requirements document, standard procedure usually dictates that a heading should appear in the program window. Also, it is common practice to include simple instructions in the window for the user so no confusion can result from using the interface. The heading and instructions can be included as Label objects.

7. As a result of this analysis, the user interface should include the following items: a Windows Form object that will contain all the other objects; two PictureBox objects to contain the pictures of the standard room and the deluxe room; four Button objects (Standard Room button, Deluxe Room button, Select Room button, and Exit Window button); and three Label objects (Heading, Instructions, and Room Selection Confirmation).

After the developer has determined the elements required for the user interface, Visual Studio 2010 can be used to create a mock-up of the user interface. The exact placement of objects in the window is a creative process, guided by the principles of user interface design you have learned. Usually, no "right answer" exists because each developer will see the solution to the problem a little differently, but you must adhere to good user interface design principles. Figure 2-60 shows the mock-up that was created for the Hotel Room Selection program.

FIGURE 2-60

Guided Program Development

This guided program development takes you step-by-step through the process of creating the sample program in this chapter. To create the mock-up shown in Figure 2-60, complete the steps on the following pages:

NOTE TO THE LEARNER

In the following activity, you should complete the tasks within the specified steps. Each of the tasks is accompanied by a Hint Screen. The purpose of the Hint Screen is to indicate where in the Visual Studio window you should perform the activity, and to serve as a reminder of the method that you should use. If you need further help completing the step, refer to the figure number identified by the term, ref:, in the step.

Guided Program Development

1

● **Open Visual Studio 2010**
Open Visual Studio using the
Start button on the Windows
taskbar and the All Programs
submenu *(ref: Figure 2-2)*. If
necessary, maximize the Visual
Studio window. If necessary,
close the Start page.

HINT

● **Create a new Visual Basic Windows Application**
Create a new Visual Basic Windows Forms Application
project by clicking the New Project button, selecting
Visual Basic in the left pane, selecting Windows
Forms Application in the right pane, naming the
project, and then clicking the OK button in the New
Project dialog box *(ref: Figure 2-3)*.

HINT

● **Keep the Toolbox Visible** If necessary, click
the Auto Hide button to keep the Toolbox visible
(ref: Figure 2-10).

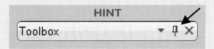

HINT

RESULT OF STEP I

*The Visual Studio
application opens
and a new project is
displayed in the
window (Figure
2-61). The Toolbox
remains visible
regardless of the
location of the
mouse pointer.*

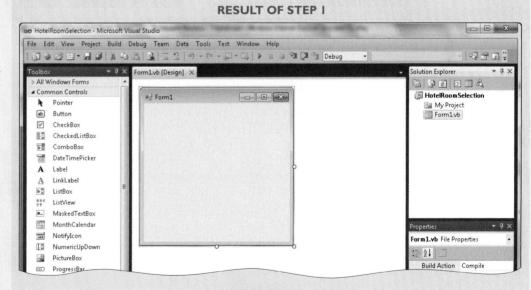

FIGURE 2-61

(continues)

2

● **Name the Windows Form Object** In the Solutions Explorer window, right-click Form1.vb. On the shortcut menu, click Rename. Name the form frmHotelRoomSelection *(ref: Figure 2-14)*.

● **Change the Windows Form Object Text Property** With the Windows Form object selected, double-click the text value in the Text property of the Properties window for the Windows Form object, and then change the Windows Form object title bar text to the value, Hotel Room Selection *(ref: Figure 2-16)*.

The text in the title bar of the Windows Form object has been changed to Hotel Room Selection (Figure 2-62). In addition, the name of the object has been changed to frmHotelRoom-Selection.

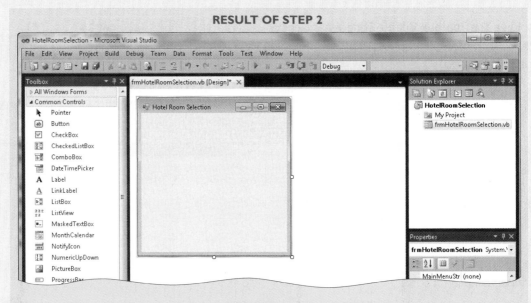

FIGURE 2-62

3

● **Resize the Windows Form Object** Resize the Windows
Form object to the approximate size shown in Figure 2-60
(430 × 395) by dragging the sizing handle in the lower-right
corner of the Windows Form object *(ref: Figure 2-18)*.

4

● **Add a Label Object** Add a Label object by dragging the
Label .NET component from the Toolbox to the Windows Form
object. Place the label near the center and top of the
Windows Form object *(ref: Figure 2-19)*.

● **Name the Label Object** Change the name of the Label object to lblHeading by using the (Name) property in the
Properties window for the Label object *(ref: Figure 2-21)*.

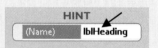

● **Change the Label Object Text Property** Double-click the
text value in the Text property in the Properties window for
the Label object, and then change the Text property
of the lblHeading Label object to Hotel Room Selection *(ref:
Figure 2-23)*.

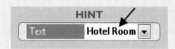

● **Open the Font Dialog Box** Click the Font property in the
Properties window for the Label object and then click the ellipsis button (...) for the Font property *(ref: Figure 2-27)*.

● **Change the Font for the Label Object** In the Font list of
the Font dialog box, change the font in the lblHeading Label
object to Tahoma *(ref: Figure 2-29)*.

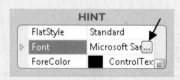

● **Change the Font Style for the Label Object** Using the Font
style list in the Font dialog box, change the Font style in the
lblHeading Label object to Bold *(ref: Figure 2-29)*.

(continues)

● **Change the Size for the Label Object** Using the Size list in the Font
dialog box, change the font size in the lblHeading Label object to
16 point *(ref: Figure 2-29)*.

● **Center the Heading Horizontally** If necessary,
select the lblHeading Label object. Then, using the
Center in Form command on the Format menu,
click the Horizontally command on the Center in
Form submenu to center the lblHeading Label
object horizontally on the Windows Form object
(ref: Figure 2-31).

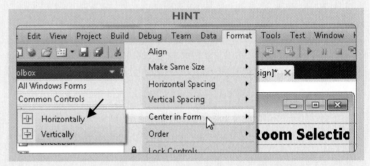

*The Heading Label object text has been changed and the Label object is centered horizontally on the Windows Form object
(Figure 2-63). The vertical placement of the label, that is, the distance from the top of the window frame, is dependent on
the eye of the developer, the size of the Windows Form object, and the other objects that are part of the graphical user interface. While you may have placed the label in your window a little higher or a little lower, your window should closely
resemble the one in Figure 2-63.*

RESULT OF STEPS 3 AND 4

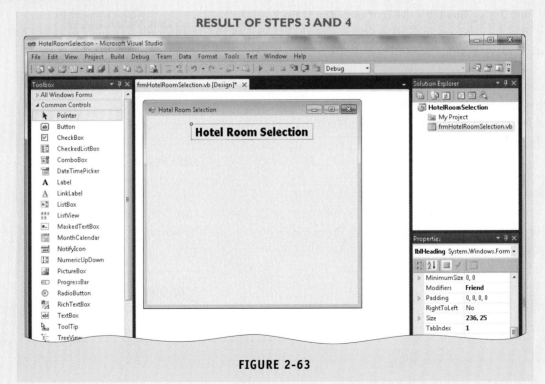

FIGURE 2-63

● **Add a PictureBox Object** Add a PictureBox object to the Windows Form object by dragging a PictureBox .NET component from the Toolbox to the Windows Form object. Place the PictureBox object below and to the left of the heading label in a location similar to that shown in Figure 2-64 *(ref: Figure 2-36)*.

HINT

● **Name the PictureBox Object** Using the (Name) property in the PictureBox Properties Window, name the PictureBox object, picStandardRoom.

● **Resize the PictureBox Object** Resize the PictureBox object to the approximate size of the PictureBox object in Figure 2-64 (185 × 150) by dragging the sizing handle in the lower-right corner of the PictureBox object *(ref: Figure 2-38)*.

HINT

A properly sized PictureBox object is displayed in the Windows Form object (Figure 2-64). This PictureBox object will be used to display a picture of a standard room when the program is completed in Chapter 3.

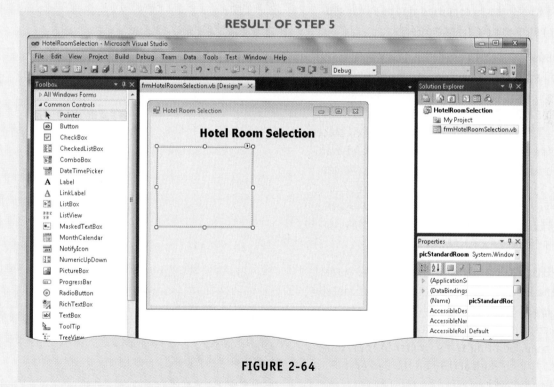

RESULT OF STEP 5

FIGURE 2-64

(continues)

6

● **Add a PictureBox Object** Add a second PictureBox object to the Windows Form object by dragging a PictureBox .NET component from the Toolbox to the Windows Form object. Place it to the right of the PictureBox object already in the Windows Form object *(ref: Figure 2-39)*.

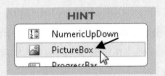

● **Name the PictureBox Object** Using the (Name) property in the PictureBox Properties window, name the PictureBox object picDeluxeRoom.

● **Size the PictureBox Object** Make the second PictureBox object on the right of the Windows Form object the same size as the PictureBox object on the left of the Windows Form object by using the Both command on the Make Same Size submenu of the Format menu *(ref: Figure 2-41)*.

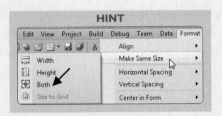

● **Align the PictureBox Objects Horizontally** Align the two PictureBox objects so their bottoms are horizontally aligned by using the Bottoms command on the Align submenu of the Format menu *(ref: Figure 2-43)*.

● **Set the Distance Between the PictureBox Objects** If necessary, adjust the distance between the two PictureBox objects so it is approximately the same as the distance in Figure 2-65. To do so, click the Windows Form object to unselect the two PictureBox objects. Then, place the mouse pointer in the right PictureBox object and drag the object left or right to set the correct distance. As you drag, blue snap lines should appear to indicate the PictureBox objects still are horizontally aligned. When the PictureBox objects are the correct distance apart, release the left mouse button.

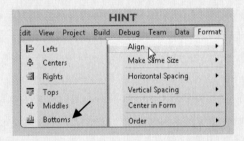

● **Center the PictureBox Objects in the Windows Form Object** Center the PictureBox objects as a unit horizontally within the Windows Form object by selecting both PictureBox objects, displaying the Center in Form command on the Format menu, pointing to the Center in Form command, and then clicking Horizontally on the Center in Form submenu *(ref: Figure 2-45)*.

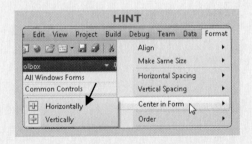

The PictureBox objects are sized and located properly within the Windows Form object (Figure 2-65).

RESULT OF STEP 6

FIGURE 2-65

7

● **Add Three Button Objects to the Windows Form Object** Add three Button objects to the Windows Form object by dragging three Button .NET components onto the Windows Form object. They should be horizontally aligned below the PictureBox objects at about the same locations as shown in Figure 2-60 on page 82. Use blue snap lines to horizontally align the buttons on the Windows Form object as you drag them onto the form (ref: Figure 2-47, Figure 2-52).

HINT

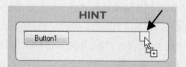

(continues)

● **Name the Three Button Objects** By using the (Name) property in the Properties window, name the leftmost Button object, btnStandardRoom; the center Button object, btnSelectRoom; and the rightmost Button object, btnDeluxeRoom.

● **Change the Text Property for Three Button Objects** By using the Text property in the Properties window, change the text for each of the Button objects to the text shown in Figure 2-66 on the next page *(ref: Figure 2-49)*.

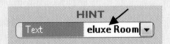

HINT

● **Change the Button Object Size** Change the size of the Standard Room button to accommodate the text, Standard Room *(ref: Figure 2-50)*.

HINT

● **Resize the Button Objects** Using the same technique you used for sizing the PictureBox objects, make all three Button objects the same size as the Standard Room Button object.

● **Align the btnStandardRoom Button Object** Center the Standard Room Button object under the standard room PictureBox object by: (a) selecting the standard room PictureBox first and then selecting the Standard Room Button object through the use of the CTRL key and clicking *(ref: Figure 2-40)*; (b) With the standard room PictureBox object as the controlling object, use the Centers command on the Align submenu of the Format menu to align the PictureBox object and the Standard Room Button object *(ref: Figure 2-43)*.

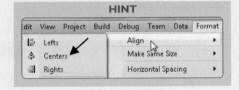

HINT

● **Align the btnDeluxeRoom Button Object** Using the same technique, center the Deluxe Room Button object beneath the deluxe room PictureBox object.

● **Center the btnSelectRoom Button Object** Center the Select Room Button object horizontally within the Windows Form object by selecting the Select Room Button object and then using the Horizontally command on the Center in Form submenu of the Format menu *(ref: Figure 2-31)*.

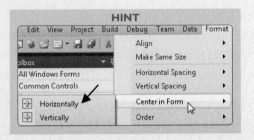

HINT

The Button objects are sized and placed properly within the Windows Form object (Figure 2-66). All three buttons are the same size. The Standard Room and Deluxe Room buttons are centered under their respective PictureBox objects, while the Select Room button is centered in the Windows Form object.

FIGURE 2-66

8

● **Add a Label Object** Add the instructions Label object to the Windows Form object by dragging a Label .NET object from the Toolbox to the Windows Form object. Place it below the Button objects at the approximate location shown in Figure 2-60 on page 82 *(ref: Figure 2-19).*

● **Name a Label Object** Using the techniques you have learned, give the Label object the name, lblInstructions.

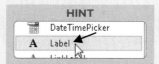

(continues)

● **Change the Label Object Text Property** Using the techniques you have learned, change the text in the lblInstructions Label object to, Choose a room type and then click the Select Room button.

● **Change the Label Object Font** Using the techniques you have learned, change the font for the lblInstructions Label object to Tahoma, change the Font style to Regular, and change the Size to 10 point.

● **Center the Label Object** Using the techniques you have learned, center the lblInstructions Label object horizontally within the Windows Form object.

● **Add a Label Object** Using the techniques you have learned, add the final message Label object whose text should read, You have completed your room selection, to the Windows Form object. Place the Label object in the location shown in Figure 2-67. Give it the name, lblConfirmationMessage. Change the font to Tahoma, the Font style to Regular, and the Size to 10 point. Center the Label object within the Windows Form object.

The two Label objects contain the correct text and are centered horizontally in the Windows Form object (Figure 2-67).

FIGURE 2-67

9

Add a Button Object Add the Exit Window Button object by dragging a Button .NET component onto the Windows Form object. Place it in the approximate location shown in Figure 2-68. Then, using techniques you have learned, give the name, btnExitWindow, to the Button object; change its text to Exit Window; make the Exit Window Button object the same size as the other Button objects in the window; and center the Exit Window Button object horizontally in the window.

The user interface mock-up now is complete (Figure 2-68).

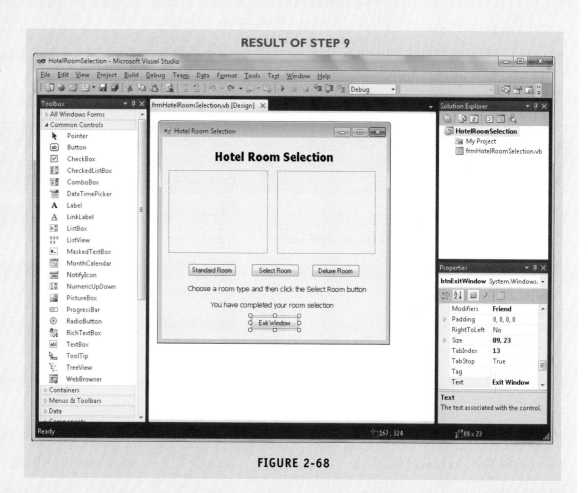

FIGURE 2-68

After completing the user interface mock-up, the designers would distribute the design to the users and others for their approval. In many cases, the developers must implement requested changes. They then will resubmit the design for approval.

Summary

You have completed the steps to create the graphical user interface mock-up for the Hotel Room Selection program. As you can see, many of the steps required are somewhat repetitive; that is, the same technique is used repeatedly to accomplish similar tasks. When you master these techniques, together with the principles of user interface design, you will be able to design user interfaces for a variety of different programs.

The items listed in the following table include all the new Visual Studio and Visual Basic skills you have learned in this chapter.

Visual Basic Skills		
Skill	**Figure Number**	**Web Address for Video**
Open Visual Studio 2010	Figure 2-2	scsite.com/vb2010/ch2/figure2-2
Create a New Visual Basic 2010 Windows Application	Figure 2-4	scsite.com/vb2010/ch2/figure2-4
Display the Toolbox	Figure 2-9	scsite.com/vb2010/ch2/figure2-9
Permanently Display the Toolbox	Figure 2-10	scsite.com/vb2010/ch2/figure2-10
Name an Object	Figure 2-12	scsite.com/vb2010/ch2/figure2-12
Set Title Bar Text in Windows Form Object	Figure 2-15	scsite.com/vb2010/ch2/figure2-15
Resize a Form	Figure 2-17	scsite.com/vb2010/ch2/figure2-17
Add a Label Object	Figure 2-19	scsite.com/vb2010/ch2/figure2-19
Name a Label Object	Figure 2-21	scsite.com/vb2010/ch2/figure2-21
Change the Text in a Label Object	Figure 2-23	scsite.com/vb2010/ch2/figure2-23
Enter Multiple Lines for a Label Object	Figure 2-26	scsite.com/vb2010/ch2/figure2-26
Change Label Font, Font Style, and Font Size	Figure 2-27	scsite.com/vb2010/ch2/figure2-27
Center a Label Object in the Windows Form Object	Figure 2-31	scsite.com/vb2010/ch2/figure2-31
Delete GUI Objects	Figure 2-33	scsite.com/vb2010/ch2/figure2-33
Use the Undo Button on the Standard Toolbar	Figure 2-35	scsite.com/vb2010/ch2/figure2-35
Add a PictureBox Object	Figure 2-36	scsite.com/vb2010/ch2/figure2-36
Resize a PictureBox Object	Figure 2-38	scsite.com/vb2010/ch2/figure2-38

Visual Basic Skills *continued*

Skill	Figure Number	Web Address for Video
Add a Second PictureBox Object	Figure 2-39	scsite.com/vb2010/ch2/figure2-39
Make Objects the Same Size	Figure 2-40	scsite.com/vb2010/ch2/figure2-40
Align PictureBox Objects	Figure 2-43	scsite.com/vb2010/ch2/figure2-43
Center Multiple Objects Horizontally	Figure 2-45	scsite.com/vb2010/ch2/figure2-45
Add a Button Object	Figure 2-47	scsite.com/vb2010/ch2/figure2-47
Name a Button Object	Page 67	
Change the Button Object Text	Figure 2-49	scsite.com/vb2010/ch2/figure2-49
Change Button Object Size	Figure 2-50	scsite.com/vb2010/ch2/figure2-50
Add a Button with Alignment (Use Snap Lines)	Figure 2-52	scsite.com/vb2010/ch2/figure2-52
Align Objects Vertically	Figure 2-54	scsite.com/vb2010/ch2/figure2-54
Save and Close a Visual Basic Project	Figure 2-56, 2-57	
Open a Visual Basic project	Page 75	

FIGURE 2-69

Learn It Online

Start your browser and visit scsite.com/vb2010/ch2. Follow the instructions in the exercises below.

1. **Chapter Reinforcement TF, MC, SA** Click one of the Chapter Reinforcement links for Multiple Choice, True/False, or Short Answer below the Learn It Online heading. Answer each question and submit to your instructor.

2. **Practice Test** Click the Practice Test link below the Learn It Online heading. Answer each question, enter your first and last name at the bottom of the page, and then click the Grade Test button. When the graded practice test is displayed on your screen, submit the graded practice test to your instructor. Continue to take the practice test until you are satisfied with your score.

3. **Crossword Puzzle Challenge** Click the Crossword Puzzle Challenge link below the Learn It Online heading. Read the instructions, and then click the Continue button. Work the crossword puzzle. When you are finished, click the Submit button. When the crossword puzzle is redisplayed, submit it to your instructor.

Knowledge Check

1–5. Label the following parts of the window:

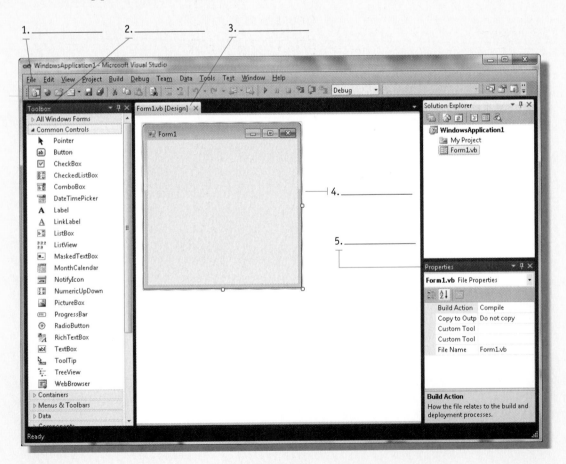

FIGURE 2-70

Knowledge Check *continued*

6. What does RAD stand for?

7. What is the purpose of the Auto Hide button on the Toolbox title bar?

8. What is the difference between red and blue snap lines?

9. Which Windows Form object property was changed to display the words "Welcome Screen" on the title bar in Figure 2-71?

FIGURE 2-71

10. A Button, a Label, and a PictureBox are all _____.

11. How do you select three Button objects on the Windows Form object at the same time for formatting purposes?

12. What is the purpose of a mock-up?

13. What are the first two phases of the program development life cycle?

14. Write the Label object name, Title, together with the correct prefix.

15. Write the Button object name, Submit, together with the correct prefix.

16. Write the PictureBox object name, Computer, together with the correct prefix.

17. Which property of the Label object do you use to change the name of the label from Label1 to a new name?

18. What is the name of the button you can click to sort the property names in the Properties window from A to Z?

19. How do you save the project you have created for the user interface mock-up?

20. Name the four objects you learned in Chapter 2 together with the purpose of each object.

Debugging Exercises

1. List the steps required to change the poorly aligned buttons on the left to the properly aligned buttons on the right.

BEFORE

FIGURE 2-72a

AFTER

FIGURE 2-72b

(continues)

Debugging Exercises *continued*

2. Change the order of the following Use Case Definition steps to correspond to the following problem definition: A college provides every incoming freshman with either a laptop or desktop PC. The student should select the type of computer she or he wants. A program opens a window that displays each computer type when the student clicks the corresponding button, one picture at a time. When a student makes a decision about the type of computer, the student should click the Select PC button. After the student selects the type of computer, the student should exit the application.

USE CASE DEFINITION

1. User clicks the Select PC button.
2. User clicks the Laptop or Desktop button.
3. User terminates the program by clicking the Exit Window button.
4. Program displays a PC confirmation message and disables both computer type buttons. The Exit Window button becomes active.
5. Program displays a picture of the type of PC clicked by the user and will enable the Select PC button.
6. Program displays a picture of the type of PC clicked by the user.

Program Analysis

1. After you have placed objects on the Windows Form object (Figure 2-73), list the steps you would follow to change the font for the Online Auction label to Tahoma font, bold, 18 point.

2. List the steps you would perform to center horizontally the On Line Auction label.

3. List the steps you would perform to center horizontally the PictureBox object on the Windows Form object in Figure 2-73.

4. List the steps you would perform to change the font for the Click to Bid label in Figure 2-73 to Tahoma, 12 point; and then center the label horizontally.

FIGURE 2-73

5. List the steps you would perform to align the two Button objects horizontally by the tops of the buttons on the Windows Form object in Figure 2-73.

6. List the steps you would perform to center both the Bid Now button and the Cancel button horizontally on the Windows Form object in Figure 2-73.

7. In the real world, why is it important to get a user interface mock-up approved before proceeding with the rest of the project?

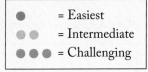

Case Programming Assignments

Complete one or more of the following case programming assignments. Submit the program and materials you create to your instructor. The level of difficulty is indicated for each case programming assignment.

● = Easiest
●● = Intermediate
●●● = Challenging

1 ●

EUROPEAN HOSTEL SELECTION

Create a Windows form mock-up for the following requirements document and Use Case Definition. The Windows Form object and the other objects in the user interface are shown in Figure 2-76.

REQUIREMENTS DOCUMENT

Date submitted: January 17, 2013

Application title: Vacation Hostel Location Selection

Purpose: The hostel selection application will allow a user to select the location in London or Dublin.

Program Procedures: From a window on the screen, the user should identify a hostel location (London or Dublin) and then indicate the location of the hostel.

Algorithms, Processing and Conditions:
1. The user must be able to identify the London or Dublin hostel, back and forth until the selection is made.
2. When the user identifies the hostel location, a picture of that hostel should appear in the window.
3. Only one picture should be displayed at a time. If a user identifies the London hostel, only the London hostel picture should be displayed; if a user identifies the Dublin hostel, only the Dublin hostel picture should be displayed.
4. When the user makes a hostel selection, a message stating that the selection of a hostel location has been made should be displayed. In addition, the user should be stopped from identifying a hostel location after the hostel selection has been made.
5. After the user makes a hostel selection, the only allowable action is to exit the window.

Notes and Restrictions
1. A user cannot make a hostel selection until he or she has identified a hostel location.

Comments:
1. The pictures shown in the window can be found on scsite.com/vb2010/ch3/images. The names of the pictures are LondonHostel and DublinHostel. Images will be added in Chapter 3.

FIGURE 2-74

(continues)

European Hostel Selection (continued)

USE CASE DEFINITION

1. User clicks London Hostel button or Dublin Hostel button.
2. Program displays a picture of the hostel identified by the user and enables the location selection button.
3. User clicks hostel buttons to view hostel locations if desired. Program displays the picture of the identified hostel.
4. User clicks the Select Location button.
5. Program displays a hostel selection confirmation message, and disables both hostel buttons and the Select Location button. The Exit Window button becomes active.
6. User terminates the program by clicking the Exit Window button.

FIGURE 2-75

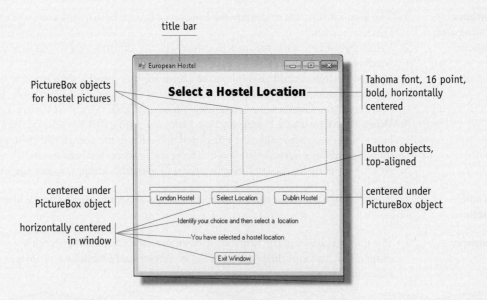

FIGURE 2-76

2 ● BANKING

Create a Windows form mock-up for the following requirements document and Use Case Definition. The Windows Form object and the other objects in the user interface are shown in Figure 2-79.

REQUIREMENTS DOCUMENT

Date submitted:	January 14, 2013
Application title:	Bank Welcome Screen with Banking Hours
Purpose:	This application displays a welcome screen for the First Corner National Bank. The user can choose an option to view the hours of the bank.
Program Procedures:	From a window on the screen, the user makes a request to see the bank's open hours.

Algorithms, Processing and Conditions:

1. The user first views a welcome screen that displays the bank's name (First Corner National Bank), bank picture, and a phrase that states the bank is FDIC insured.
2. When the user opts to view the bank hours, the following hours are displayed:

Monday – Thursday	9:00am – 5:00pm
Friday	9:00am – 8:00pm
Saturday	9:00am – 1:00 pm

3. After the user views the hours, the only allowable action is to exit the window.

Notes and Restrictions: n/a

Comments:

1. The picture shown in the window can be found on scsite.com/vb2010/ch3/images. The name of the picture is BankBuilding. Images will be added in Chapter 3.

FIGURE 2-77

(continues)

Case Programming Assignments

Banking *(continued)*

USE CASE DEFINITION

1. The window opens, displaying the title of the bank, the bank's picture, and a message that the bank is FDIC insured. All buttons are enabled.
2. User clicks the View Banking Hours button.
3. Program displays the banking hours above the buttons. The View Banking Hours button is disabled.
4. User clicks the Exit Window button to terminate the application.

FIGURE 2-78

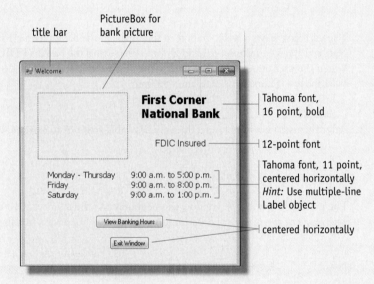

FIGURE 2-79

3

VISUAL BASIC 2010 TERMS

Create a Windows form mock-up for the following requirements document and Use Case Definition. The Windows Form object and the other objects in the user interface are shown in Figure 2-82.

REQUIREMENTS DOCUMENT

Date submitted: August 16, 2013

Application title: Visual Basic 2010 Terms

Purpose: This application displays the definitions of common Visual Basic terms. When the user chooses to view a definition, the term's definition is displayed.

Program Procedures: From a window on the screen, the user makes a request to see one of three VB definitions.

Algorithms, Processing, and Conditions:

1. The user first views a screen that displays three VB terms.
2. An image of a computer is displayed at the top of the window throughout the running of the application.
3. The user can select any of the three terms displayed on the buttons, and the definition appears after each selection is made.
4. The user can click any of the term buttons and the definition will appear. Any previous definitions will disappear.
5. An exit button is available at all times, allowing the user to end the application.

Notes and Restrictions:

1. Only one definition should be displayed at a time, so if a user selects a second term, the second definition only should be displayed.

Comments:

1. The computer picture shown in the window can be found on scsite.com/vb2010/ch3/images. The name of the picture is Computer. Images will be added in Chapter 3.

FIGURE 2-80

(continues)

Visual Basic 2010 Terms *(continued)*

USE CASE DEFINITION

1. The window opens and displays a computer image, the title (Visual Basic 2010 Terms), three buttons labeled with VB terms, and an Exit Window button. All buttons are enabled.
2. User clicks each of the term buttons to review the definitions.
3. Program displays the definitions to the right of the buttons.
4. Only one definition shows at a time.
5. User clicks the Exit Window button to terminate the application.

FIGURE 2-81

FIGURE 2-82

4 •• ONLINE STORE SPECIALS

Create a Use Case Definition document and design a Windows form mock-up based on the requirements document in Figure 2-83.

REQUIREMENTS DOCUMENT

Date submitted: January 6, 2014

Application title: Online Store Specials

Purpose: The online store specials program will display the daily, weekly, and holiday specials of the online store. The user can select the desired product and then add the product to the shopping cart.

Program Procedures: From a window on the screen, the user should select the daily special, the weekly special, or the holiday special. When a special is selected, the program should display a picture of the special product, the regular price of the product, and the special price of the product. The user should be able to select any special. Then, the user can add the product to the shopping cart.

Algorithms, Processing, and Conditions:
1. The user must select a special in order to display the special's product picture, regular price, and sales price.
2. The user cannot add a product to the shopping cart until a special is selected.
3. When a special is selected, only that special's picture and prices should be displayed in the window. No other special should be displayed.
4. After the user selects a special and adds it to the shopping cart, the only allowable user action is to exit the window.
5. A user should be able to exit the window at any time.

Notes and Restrictions: n/a

Comments:
1. The specials are: Daily Special: Cell Phone: Regular Price: $99.95; Special Price: $84.50
   Weekly Special: iPod: Regular Price: $39.95; Special Price: $29.95
   Holiday Special: Digital Camera: Regular Price: $259.95; Special Price: $203.19
2. The pictures shown in the window can be found on scsite.com/vb2010/ch3/images. The names of the pictures are CellPhone, iPod, and DigitalCamera.

FIGURE 2-83

5 ●●

RAFFLE PRIZE SELECTION

Create a Use Case Definition document and design a Windows form mock-up based on the requirements document in Figure 2-84.

REQUIREMENTS DOCUMENT

Date submitted: March 21, 2013

Application title: Raffle Prize Selection

Purpose: Your school has started selling raffle tickets for a scholarship fund that provides the winner a choice of raffle gifts. The winner can choose one of three prizes. So they can choose, the program must display each of the prizes upon request of the raffle winner. The winner then can make the choice of the prize he or she would like to receive.

Program Procedures: From a window on the screen, the user selects one of three raffle prizes. A picture of the prize is displayed in the window. The user then can choose the prize he or she wants to receive.

Algorithms, Processing, and Conditions:
1. The user selects a prize. Then, a picture of the prize is displayed in the window.
2. The user can select any of the three prizes. Only the picture for the selected prize should be displayed.
3. The user can select prizes back and forth to see the pictures for the prizes.
4. After the user finds a prize he or she wants, the user chooses that prize for delivery.
5. After the user chooses a prize, a message stating that a raffle prize has been chosen should be displayed.
6. After the user chooses a prize, the only allowable action is to exit the window.

Notes and Restrictions:
1. The user should not be able to choose a prize until they have viewed the picture of at least one raffle prize.

Comments:
1. The raffle prizes available are a gas grill, a flat-screen television, and a laptop.
2. The pictures shown in the window can be found on scsite.com/vb2010/ch3/ images. The names of the pictures are Grill, TV, and Laptop.

FIGURE 2-84

Case Programming Assignments

6 ●●●
SONG VOTING

Create a Use Case Definition document and design a Windows form mock-up based on the requirements document in Figure 2-85.

REQUIREMENTS DOCUMENT

Date submitted: February 22, 2013

Application title: Song Voting

Purpose: In your mall, a music store named "Millennium Music" wants a program that shows the #1 song in each of three music genres, and allows the user to vote for his or her overall favorite. The user should be able to select one of three music genres and then be able to vote for that song/genre as the user's overall favorite.

Program Procedures: From a window on the screen, the user selects one of three music genres. The name of the #1 song in the selected genre is displayed together with a picture of the artist or band for the song. Then, the user can vote for that song/genre as his or her overall favorite.

Algorithms, Processing, and Conditions:
1. The user selects a music genre. Then, the #1 song title in the genre and picture of the artist or band is displayed in the window.
2. The user can select any of the three music genres. Only the name of the song and the picture for the selected genre should be displayed.
3. The user can select music genres back and forth to see the #1 song for each genre and the associated artist or band.
4. After the user selects a genre, the user should be able to vote for that genre/song as the favorite. The user cannot vote until the user has selected a genre.
5. After the user votes, a message stating that voting has occurred should be displayed.
6. After the user votes, the only allowable action is to exit the window.

Notes and Restrictions:
1. The user should not be able to vote until he or she has selected a music genre.

Comments:
1. You (the developer) should select the three music genres and the #1 song for each of the genres.
2. The pictures of the artist or the band will depend on your selection of both the music genres and the #1 song in each of the genres. You should download a picture of the artist or band from the World Wide Web. You can search anywhere on the Web for the pictures. You will find that www.google.com/images is a good source.

FIGURE 2-85

Case Programming Assignments

7 ●●● ENGLISH-TO-SPANISH TRANSLATOR

Create a requirements document and a Use Case Definition document, and design a Windows form mock-up, based on the following case project:

The Bonita Travel Agency would like to create an English-to-Spanish translator of the most commonly used Spanish words for those booking a Spanish-speaking destination. Develop a Windows application for the Bonita Travel Spanish Translator. The English phrase should be displayed in a window. When the user selects an English phrase, the corresponding Spanish translation is displayed. Only one Spanish translation should be displayed at any given time. The user should be able to exit the window at any time.

English	Spanish Translation
Good morning	Buenos días
Thank you	Gracias
Goodbye	Adiós
Money	Dinero

FIGURE 2-86

Case Programming Assignments

8 ●●● TRAVEL SPECIALS

Create a requirements document and a Use Case Definition document, and design a Windows form mock-up, based on the following case project:

Your local travel agent would like a computer application to advertise the travel specials of the week from your city. This week's flight specials are:

Destination	Price
Orlando	$199 round trip
Las Vegas	$219 round trip
New Orleans	$320 round trip
Aruba	$519 round trip
Hawaii	$728 round trip

Write an application that will allow the user to select any of the five vacation destinations. When the user selects a vacation destination, the corresponding flight price and a picture of the destination should be displayed. Clear each prior price and picture when the user selects a different vacation destination. In addition to a picture of the destination, include a Web page address that features the location selected. After the user has selected a destination, the user should be able to book the flight and then exit the window.

FIGURE 2-87

Case Programming Assignments

9 ●●● FOOTBALL TICKETS

Create a requirements document and a Use Case Definition document, and design a Windows form mock-up, based on the following case project:

Your favorite university football team has asked you to develop a Windows application that allows the user to see the four types of seat ticket types offered, one at a time. Then, the user should be able to reserve a single game ticket for the seat type. The four types of stadium seating and their base prices are as follows:

Name of Service	Minimum Price
Upper Endzone Seating	$75.00
Lower Endzone Seating	$100.00
Sideline seating	$150.00
Club Seats	$500.00

For each type of seating, your program should display the base price and a picture depicting an example of the seating type. Clear each seating price and picture when the user selects a different seating type. After the user has selected a ticket, the user should be able to purchase the ticket and then exit the window.

FIGURE 2-88

CHAPTER 3

Program Design and Coding

OBJECTIVES

You will have mastered the material in this chapter when you can:

- Change the BackColor property of an object

- Add images to a PictureBox object

- Locate and save an image from the World Wide Web

- Import an image into the Program Resources folder

- Size an image

- Set the Visible property in the Properties window

- Set the Enabled property in the Properties window

- Run a Visual Basic 2010 program

- Enter Visual Basic 2010 code

- Understand Visual Basic 2010 code statement formats

- Use IntelliSense to enter Visual Basic 2010 code statements

- Using code, set the Visible property of an object

- Using code, set the Enabled property of an object

- Enter comments in Visual Basic 2010 code

- Correct errors in Visual Basic 2010 code

- Write code to use the Close() procedure

- Print code

- Prepare an Event Planning Document

Introduction

In Chapter 2 you completed the design of the graphical user interface (GUI) mock-up. While users and others can approve the mock-up as being functional, the developer normally must make a variety of changes to the GUI to prepare it for the actual production version of the program. Among these changes are:

1. Adding color to the interface to make it more visually appealing.
2. Acquiring and including images that are required for the program.
3. Setting interface object properties in accordance with the needs of the program.

Once these tasks have been completed, Phase 2 of the program development life cycle (PDLC) has been completed.

The next two phases of the PDLC are:

Phase 3: Design the program processing objects
Phase 4: Code the program

This chapter will provide the skills and knowledge necessary first to complete phase 2 of the PDLC and then complete phases 3 and 4.

Sample Program

You will recall that the sample program for Chapter 2 and this chapter is the Hotel Room Selection program. Windows for the program are shown in Figure 3-1.

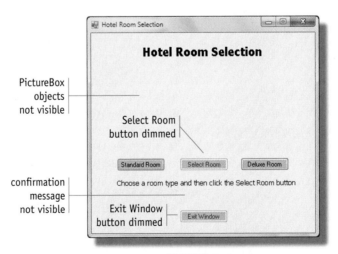

FIGURE 3-1a

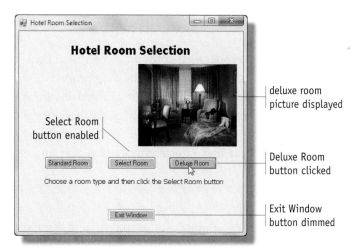

deluxe room
picture displayed

Select Room
button enabled

Deluxe Room
button clicked

Exit Window
button dimmed

FIGURE 3-1b

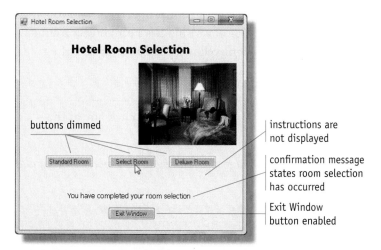

buttons dimmed

instructions are
not displayed

confirmation message
states room selection
has occurred

Exit Window
button enabled

FIGURE 3-1c

In the opening window (Figure 3-1a), you can see that no images appear in the
PictureBox objects that are included in the window, and that the Select Room button
and the Exit Window button are dimmed, which means they are disabled when the
program begins. In Figure 3-1b, the user clicked the Deluxe Room button, so the picture is displayed. In addition, the Select Room button is enabled. The Exit Window
button still is dimmed. In Figure 3-1c, the user has selected a room, so the room
selection confirmation message is displayed; the Standard Room, Select Room, and
Deluxe Room buttons are dimmed; and the Exit Window button is enabled. Each of
these changes occurs through the use of code you enter into the program, as you will
discover later in this chapter.

Fine-Tune the User Interface

You have learned about some properties of Visual Basic objects in Chapter 2, including the Name property and the Text property. As you probably noted in the Properties window in Chapter 2, more properties are available for each of the objects in a graphical user interface. In many cases, these properties are used to fine-tune the user interface to make it more usable. In the sample program, the BackColor property is used to make the user interface more attractive and effective.

BackColor Property

The **BackColor** of an object is the color that is displayed in its background. For example, in Figure 3-1 the BackColor of the Windows Form object is a light yellow, while the BackColor of the Button objects is an orange shade. You can select the BackColor of an object through the use of the **BackColor property** in the Properties window. For example, to change the BackColor of a Windows Form object from its default color of Control (gray) to Cornsilk (light yellow), you can complete the following steps:

STEP 1 Click the Windows Form object to select it. (Do not click any of the objects on the Windows Form object.)

The Windows Form object is selected, as indicated by the thick border and the sizing handles (Figure 3-2).

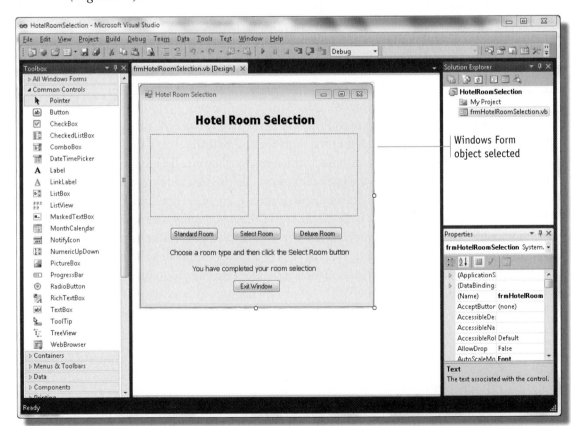

FIGURE 3-2

STEP 2   If necessary, scroll in the Properties window until the BackColor property is displayed, and then click the right column of the BackColor property.

The BackColor property is selected, and the BackColor arrow is displayed (Figure 3-3).

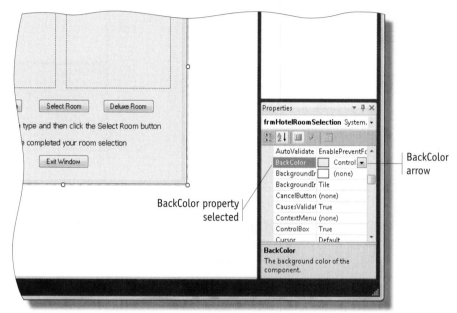

BackColor arrow

BackColor property selected

FIGURE 3-3

STEP 3   Click the BackColor arrow. Then, if necessary, click the Web tab to display the Web tabbed page.

The color window within the Properties window opens (Figure 3-4). The Web tabbed page contains more than 100 named colors you can select to display as the BackColor for the selected object, which in this case is the Windows Form object.

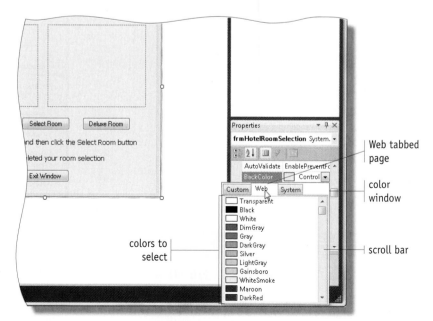

Web tabbed page

color window

colors to select

scroll bar

FIGURE 3-4

STEP 4   Scroll until the Cornsilk color is displayed in the list of colors.

The name and a sample of the Cornsilk color are displayed (Figure 3-5).

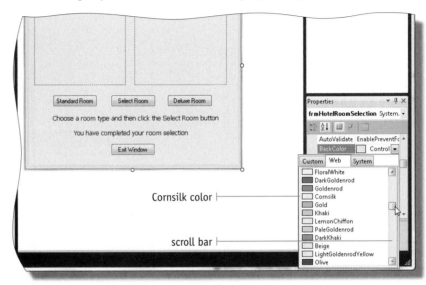

Cornsilk color

scroll bar

FIGURE 3-5

STEP 5   Click Cornsilk on the color list.

The background color in the Windows Form object is changed to Cornsilk (Figure 3-6).

BackColor changed to Cornsilk

Cornsilk selected

FIGURE 3-6

You can use the same technique to change the BackColor on any object that contains the BackColor property, including Button and Label objects.

Adding Images to a PictureBox Object

PictureBox objects are used to display a graphic image. In the sample program, a picture of both a standard room and a deluxe room are displayed. You must specify the image that will be displayed in a particular PictureBox object. Before specifying the image, however, you must locate the image and then place it in the Resources folder that is linked to the application. The steps for displaying an image in a PictureBox object are:

1. Locate the image to be displayed in the PictureBox object. You might locate this image on the Web, in which case you must then store the image in a folder on your computer; or it might already be stored on your computer or a local network.
2. Import the image into the **Resources folder**. This step makes the image available for display within the PictureBox object. Multiple images can be placed in the Resources folder.
3. Specify the image to be displayed within the PictureBox object.

Each of these steps will be shown on the following pages.

Locate and Save an Image from the World Wide Web

Images are available from a multitude of sources, ranging from your own digital camera to millions of publicly available images on the Web. If you work for a company, the company might have photos and graphic images that can be used in company applications.

For purposes of the images used in this book, you can use the scsite.com/vb2010 Web site to retrieve an image. For example, to retrieve the standard room image from this site, you could complete the steps beginning on page 118:

HEADS UP

While many Web sites offer images you can select, three sites are particularly useful. These sites are: bing.com/images, www.google.com/images, and www.webshots.com. When you visit sites, not all images are available for free download. In some cases, the images are copyrighted and you must acquire rights to use the image. In addition, some sites require a fee to be paid before the image can be used. Therefore, you should download only those images for which you have paid, or acquired the rights to use or those images that are free of copyright and can be used by anyone.

STEP 1 Open your Internet browser (in this example, Internet Explorer is used. Steps for other browsers might vary slightly). Then, enter `scsite.com/vb2010/ch3/images` in the Address box and press the ENTER key.

The browser window is open and the scsite.com/vb2010/ch3/images Web page is displayed (Figure 3-7). The names and thumbnails of the images used in this chapter are displayed on the Web page.

StandardRoom image

DeluxeRoom image

FIGURE 3-7

STEP 2 Locate the StandardRoom.jpg image and then right-click the image.

The shortcut menu is displayed (Figure 3-8).

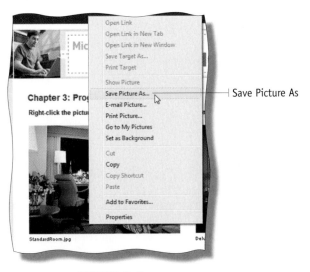

Save Picture As

FIGURE 3-8

STEP 3 Click Save Picture As on the shortcut menu.

The Save Picture dialog box opens (Figure 3-9). You must identify the drive and folder in which you want to store the image. Each of these items will be unique for your computer and drives. In all sample programs in this book, images are stored on a USB drive that is designated as drive E. You also must enter a file name under which the image will be stored.

Save Picture
dialog box

FIGURE 3-9

STEP 4 Identify the drive and folder where the image will be stored. Enter the image file name, `StandardRoom`, in the File name text box.

The information required to store the image is entered in the Save Picture dialog box (Figure 3-10). You must remember where you save the images because later you must locate them when you import them into the Resources folder for use within the program. Image file names should not contain spaces.

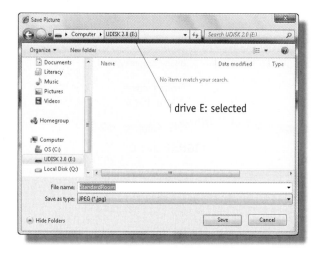

FIGURE 3-10

STEP 5 Click the Save button in the Save Picture dialog box to save the image in the selected location.

ONLINE REINFORCEMENT

To view a video of the process in the previous steps, visit scsite.com/vb2010/ch3 and then select Figure 3-7.

Import the Image into the Program Resources Folder

After you have saved an image on a storage device available to your computer, you should import the image into the Resources folder of the program so the image is available for use by the program. To import the Standard Room image into the Resources folder, you can complete the following steps:

STEP 1   With Visual Studio 2010 and the Hotel Room Selection Visual Basic program open, select the picStandardRoom PictureBox object by clicking it. Scroll in the PictureBox Properties window until the Image property is visible. Click the Image property name in the left list in the Properties window.

*With the PictureBox object selected, the Properties window displays all the properties of the object (Figure 3-11). The **Image property** specifies the image that should be displayed in the selected PictureBox object. The Image property is selected in the Properties window. The Image property Ellipsis button is displayed in the right column of the Image property.*

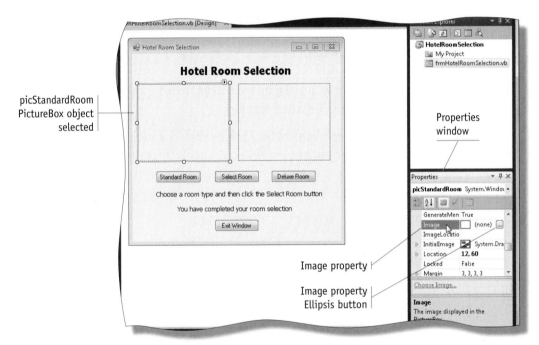

FIGURE 3-11

STEP 2   Click the Ellipsis button in the right column of the Image property.

*The **Select Resource dialog box** opens (Figure 3-12), and displays the resources that have been imported for the program. In Figure 3-12, no resources have been imported.*

Select Resource
dialog box

no resources
imported

Import button

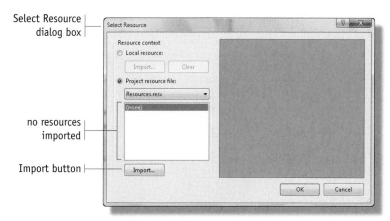

FIGURE 3-12

STEP 3   Click the Import button in the Select Resource dialog box. Then, using the features of the Open dialog box, locate the file you want to import into the program. In this case, the file is the StandardRoom.jpg file that is stored on drive E, which is a USB drive.

The Open dialog box opens when you click the Import button (Figure 3-13). The location of the StandardRoom.jpg file is on drive E.

Open dialog
box

drive E: selected

StandardRoom
image file selected

Open button

FIGURE 3-13

STEP 4   Click the Open button in the Open dialog box.

The Select Resource dialog box is displayed again, but now the StandardRoom image is identi-fied in the Project resource file list (Figure 3-14). The image appears in the preview window. This means the image has been made a part of the resources for the program. It no longer is nec-essary to locate the image on the USB drive in order to include the image in a PictureBox object.

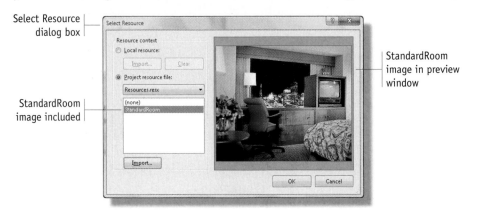

Select Resource dialog box

StandardRoom image included

StandardRoom image in preview window

FIGURE 3-14

STEP 5   With the StandardRoom file name selected in the Project resource file list, click the OK button in the Select Resource dialog box.

The StandardRoom image becomes the image displayed in the picStandardRoom PictureBox object (Figure 3-15). In addition, the Resources folder is added to the Solution Explorer window, indicating the Resources folder now is part of the program.

StandardRoom image in picStandardRoom PictureBox object

Resources folder

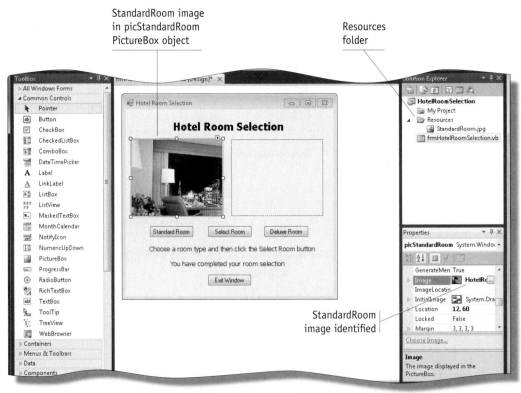

StandardRoom image identified

FIGURE 3-15

Size an Image

In most cases, when you import an image into a program, the image will not fit in the PictureBox object perfectly. This occurs for two reasons: the image is a different size from the PictureBox object, and/or the image has a dimension different than the PictureBox object. In both cases, the developer must adjust the size of the image to fit in the PictureBox object, or adjust the size of the PictureBox object to accommodate the image.

In Figure 3-15, you can see that the image is larger than the PictureBox object (compare the image in Figure 3-14 to the image in Figure 3-15). Because the PictureBox object must remain its current size, the image must be adjusted using the **SizeMode property**. To adjust an image size to fit in a PictureBox object, you can complete the following steps:

STEP 1   With the PictureBox object containing the StandardRoom image selected, scroll in the picStandardRoom Properties window until you see the SizeMode property. Click the SizeMode property name in the left column and then click the SizeMode arrow in the right column of the SizeMode property.

The SizeMode property list is displayed (Figure 3-16). The list contains five choices you can use to change either the size of the image or the size of the PictureBox object. Normal is selected because it is the default value.

picStandardRoom
PictureBox object
selected

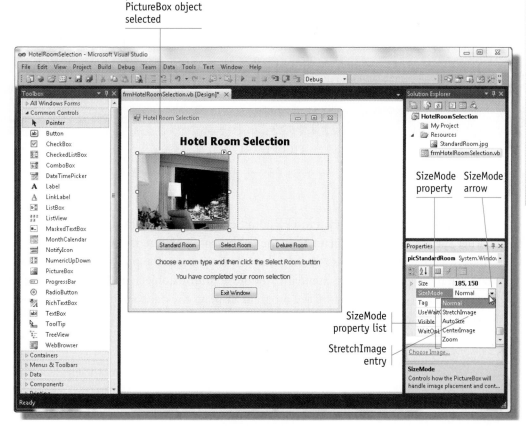

SizeMode
property list

StretchImage
entry

FIGURE 3-16

HEADS UP

StretchImage is not the only choice on the SizeMode list in the Properties window for PictureBox objects (see Figure 3-16). The other choices and their actions are: a) **Normal:** No changes are made to the image size or the size of the PictureBox object. Visual Studio places the image in the PictureBox object with the upper-left corner of the image and the upper-left corner of the PictureBox object aligned; b) **AutoSize:** Visual Studio increases or decreases the size of the PictureBox object to accommodate the size of the image. The entire image is visible and fits precisely in the PictureBox object; c) **CenterImage:** No changes are made to the image size or the size of the PictureBox object. Visual Studio places the image in the PictureBox object with the center of the image aligned with the center of the PictureBox object; d) **Zoom:** The image size is either reduced or enlarged so it fits in the PictureBox object. The fit can be left and right or up and down, depending on the dimensions of the image and the PictureBox object. If the image and Picture-Box object are not exactly proportional to another, the image will not fill out the entire PictureBox object.

STEP 2 Click StretchImage in the SizeMode list.

*The SizeMode list is closed and the image is resized to fit within the picStandardRoom Pic-tureBox object (Figure 3-17). When you use the **StretchImage option**, some distortion of the image might occur in order to make the image fit within the PictureBox object. This is why it is important to select an image that has the same approximate dimensions (or at least the same aspect ratio) as the PictureBox object in which the image will be placed.*

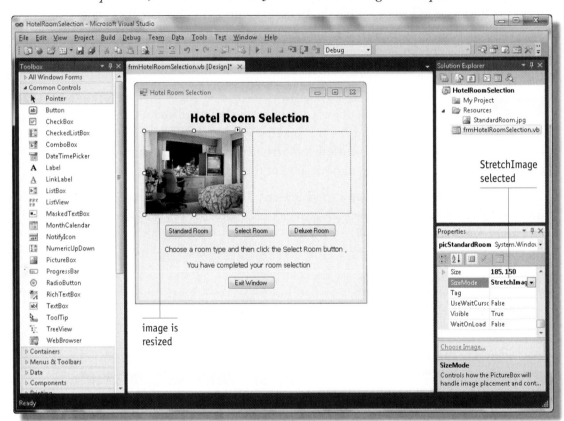

FIGURE 3-17

Visible Property

As you have learned, when the Hotel Room Selection program begins execution, neither the standard room picture nor the deluxe room picture is displayed in the window. When the user clicks the Standard Room button, the program displays the standard room picture in the Standard Room PictureBox object; and when the user clicks the Deluxe Room button, the program displays the deluxe room picture in the Deluxe Room PictureBox object.

The property that controls whether an object is displayed on the Windows Form object is the **Visible property**. By default, the Visible property is set to True so that any object you place on the Windows Form object will be displayed when the program runs. To cause the object not to display, you must set the Visible property to False. To set the Visible property for the picStandardRoom PictureBox object to False, you can complete the following steps:

STEP 1   If necessary, select the picStandardRoom PictureBox object. Scroll in the Properties window until the Visible property is displayed. Click the Visible property name in the left column, and then click the Visible arrow in the right column of the Visible property.

When you click the Visible arrow, the list displays the words True and False (Figure 3-18). To make the object visible when the program starts running, select True. To make the object not visible when the program starts running, select False.

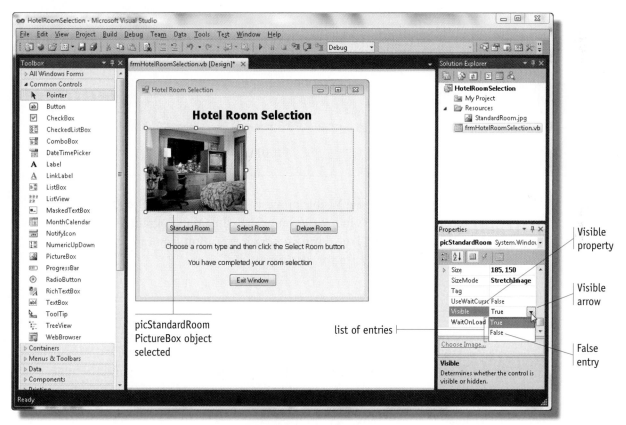

FIGURE 3-18

STEP 2　Click False on the Visible property list.

The Visible property is set to False (Figure 3-19). When the program begins running, the picStandardRoom object will not be displayed on the Windows Form object. Note that the image and object are displayed on the frmHotelRoomSelection.vb [Design] tabbed page regardless of the Visible property setting.

image is visible in Design mode

FIGURE 3-19

ONLINE REINFORCEMENT

To view a video of the process in the previous steps, visit scsite.com/vb2010/ch3 and then select Figure 3-18.

Once you have set the Visible property for an object to False, the only way to display the object on the Windows Form object while the program is running is to set the Visible property to True during program execution. You can do this by writing code, as you will see later in this chapter.

Enabled Property

In an event-driven program, objects such as Button objects can be used to cause events to occur. For example, in the sample program, when you click the Standard Room button, a picture of a standard room is displayed in the PictureBox object. In addition, the Select Room Button object becomes **enabled**, which means it can be clicked to cause an event to occur. When the program begins execution, however, the Select Room button is **disabled**, which means nothing will happen when you click the button. A disabled button is displayed as a dimmed button (see Figure 3-1a) on page 112).

The **Enabled property** controls when a Button object is enabled, which means clicking the button can cause an event to occur, and when a Button object is not enabled, which means clicking the button causes no action to occur. The default for the Enabled property is True, which means the associated Button object is enabled. To set the Enabled property to False for the Select Room button, you can complete the steps on the next page:

STEP 1   Select the btnSelectRoom object. Scroll in the Properties window until the Enabled property is displayed. Click the Enabled property name in the left column, and then click the Enabled arrow in the right column of the Enabled property.

The list displayed when you click the Enabled arrow contains the words, True and False (Figure 3-20). To make the object enabled when the program starts running, select True. To make the object not enabled when the program starts running, select False.

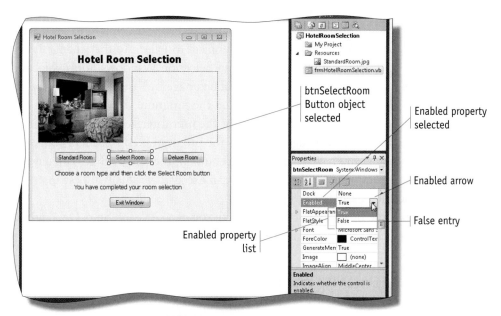

FIGURE 3-20

STEP 2   Click False on the Enabled property list.

The Enabled property is set to False (Figure 3-21). When the program begins running, the btnSelectRoom Button object will not be enabled on the Windows Form object.

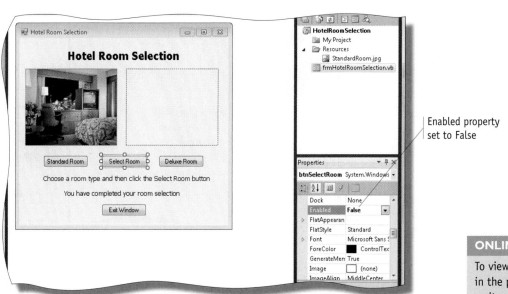

FIGURE 3-21

Once you have set the Enabled property to False, the only way to cause a Button object to be enabled on the Windows Form object while the program is running is to set the Enabled property to True. You can do this by writing code, as you will see later in this chapter.

Running a Program

When you set some object properties, the effect of the property change might not be evident until you run the program. For example, you have set the Visible property for the picStandardRoom PictureBox object to False, and you have set the Enabled property for the btnSelectRoom Button object to False. Neither change is evident, however, when you view the Hotel Room Selection Windows Form object on the frmHotelRoomSelection.vb [Design] tabbed page in Visual Studio. These settings will take place only when you actually run the program.

To ensure the settings are correct for the user interface, you must run the program. **Running the program** means the program is compiled, or translated, from the instructions you have written or generated in the Visual Basic language into a form of instructions that the computer can execute eventually. These instructions are saved and then executed as a program.

To run the program you have created, you can click the Start Debugging button on the Standard toolbar, as shown in the following steps:

STEP 1   Point to the Start Debugging button on the Standard toolbar.

The pointer points to the Start Debugging button (Figure 3-22).

Start Debugging
button

FIGURE 3-22

STEP 2 Click the Start Debugging button on the Standard toolbar.

The program is compiled and saved, and then is run on the computer. When the program runs, the Hotel Room Selection window is displayed on the screen (Figure 3-23). Notice that the Standard Room image is not displayed in the window because the Visible property for the picStandardRoom PictureBox object was set to False (see Figure 3-19 on page 126). Notice also that the Select Room button is dimmed, which indicates its Enabled property is set to False.

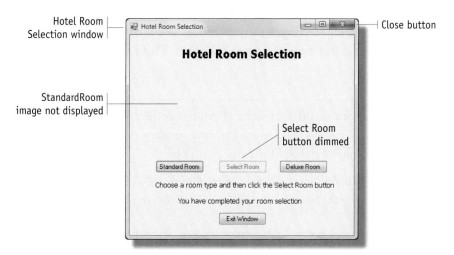

Hotel Room Selection window

Close button

StandardRoom image not displayed

Select Room button dimmed

FIGURE 3-23

Once you have started running the program, it will continue to run until you close it. To close a program, click the Close button on the right of the window title bar (see Figure 3-23).

Once you have set all the properties for the objects in the user interface, the design of the user interface is complete. You now are ready to move to the next phase of the program development life cycle — designing the program processing objects.

Visual Basic Program Coding

Prior to beginning the design of the program processing objects, the developer must understand certain program coding principles and techniques so he or she can apply this knowledge to the program design. **Program code** is the set of instructions written by the developer that direct the program to carry out the processing required in the program. The following sections explain the Visual Basic 2010 code required for the Hotel Room Selection program.

Entering Visual Basic Code for Event Handling

As you have learned, most program processing in an event-driven program occurs when the user triggers an event. For example, when a user clicks a button on the graphical user interface, this activity can trigger an event and the program performs the required processing. The developer writes program code to carry out the processing. This code is placed in a section of the program called an **event handler** — so-called because it "handles" the event that the user action triggers by executing code that performs the required processing.

To write the code for an event handler, the developer first must identify the GUI object that will be used to trigger the event. For example, in the sample program, you have learned that when the Standard Room button is clicked, the standard room picture should appear in the picStandardRoom PictureBox object. To write the code that will display the standard room picture, the developer must inform Visual Studio that the Standard Room button is the object for which the code is to be written, and that an event handler must be created for the click event. This can be done using the following steps:

STEP 1   With Visual Studio 2010 and the Hotel Room Selection program open and the frmHotelRoomSelection.vb [Design] tabbed window visible, point to the Standard Room Button object in the Windows Form object.

The pointer points to the Standard Room Button object (Figure 3-24). The four-headed arrow pointer indicates you can drag the Button object to another location in the window if desired.

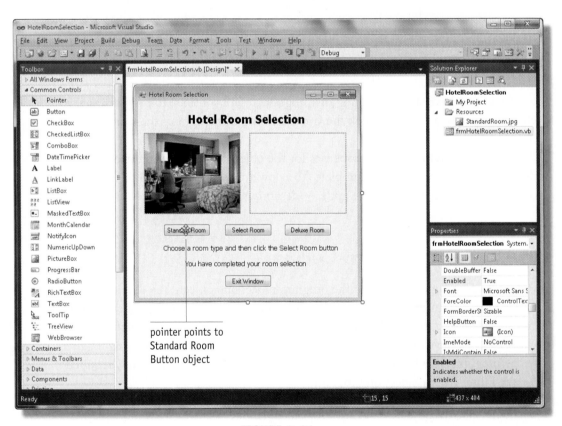

FIGURE 3-24

STEP 2 Double-click the Standard Room Button object.

The code window is displayed on the frmHotelRoomSelection.vb* tabbed page (Figure 3-25). The code in the window is generated by Visual Studio. This code identifies an event handler, which is the code that executes when an event is triggered. In this case, when the Standard Room button is clicked, the code in this event handler will be executed by the program. The list box at the upper-left of the tabbed page identifies the object for which the event hander will execute — in this case, the btnStandardRoom object. The list box at the upper-right of the tabbed page identifies the event that must occur in order to execute the code in the event handler. The event identified in Figure 3-25 is Click. So, when the user clicks the Standard Room button, the program will execute the code between the Private Sub statement and the End Sub statement. In Figure 3-25, no code other than the event handler identification code generated by Visual Studio has been entered. The insertion point is located where the developer should begin entering the code that executes when the user clicks the btnStandardRoom Button object.

frmHotelRoomSelection.vb* tabbed page   object for which event handler will execute

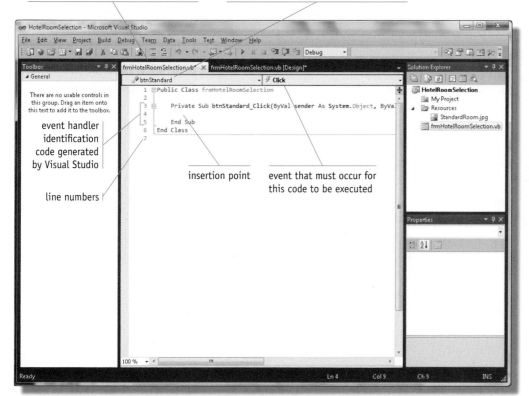

event handler identification code generated by Visual Studio

line numbers

insertion point   event that must occur for this code to be executed

FIGURE 3-25

HEADS UP

In the left column of the coding window in Figure 3-25, line numbers appear. These line numbers help identify each line of code in the coding window. They do not appear by default, however, so you must instruct Visual Studio to display the line numbers. If line numbers do not appear in the coding window on a computer you are using, you can display them by completing the following steps: 1) Click Tools on the menu bar; 2) Click Options on the Tools menu; 3) If necessary, click the triangle next to Text Editor in the Options dialog box; 4) If necessary, click the triangle next to Basic in the list below Text Editor; 5) Click Editor in the list below Basic; 6) Place a check mark in the Line numbers check box; 7) Click the OK button in the Options dialog box.

ONLINE REINFORCEMENT

To view a video of the process in the previous steps, visit scsite.com/vb2010/ch3 and then select Figure 3-24.

Visual Basic 2010 Coding Statements

A Visual Basic 2010 coding statement contains instruction(s) that the computer eventually executes. Visual Basic has a set of rules, or **syntax**, that specifies how each statement must be written.

In the Hotel Room Selection program, you will recall that when the user clicks the Standard Room Button while the program is running, the standard room image should be displayed in the picStandardRoom PictureBox object. Figure 3-26 shows a Visual Basic coding statement that sets the Visible property for the picStandardRoom PictureBox object to True so the image is displayed in the picture box after the statement is executed.

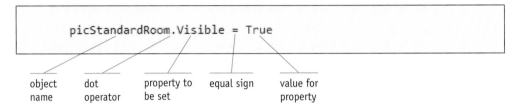

FIGURE 3-26

The first part of the statement, picStandardRoom, identifies the object containing the property to set. The name of the object is followed by the dot operator (period) with no intervening spaces. The dot operator separates the name of the object from the next entry in the statement and is required.

Following the dot operator is the name of the property to set. In Figure 3-26, the name of the property is Visible. You will recall that the Visible property determines whether an image is displayed in the PictureBox object when the program is running. In Figure 3-19 on page 126, the Visible property for the picStandardRoom PictureBox object was set to False so the image would not be displayed when the program was started. This statement sets the Visible property to True so the image will be displayed.

The property name is followed by a space and then an equal sign. The space is not required, but good coding practice dictates that elements within a statement should be separated by a space so the statement is easier to read. One or more spaces can be used, but most developers use only one space. The equal sign is required because it indicates that the value to be used for setting the property follows. A space follows the equal sign for ease of readability.

The word True follows the space. The value True in the Visible property indicates that the image in the PictureBox object should be displayed. When the program is running, as soon as the Visible property is set to True, the image appears in the picture box.

Each entry within the program statement must be correct or the program will not compile. This means the object name must be spelled properly, the dot operator must be placed in the correct location, the name of the property must be spelled properly, the equal sign must be present, and a valid entry for the property must follow the equal sign. For the Visible property, the only valid entries are True and False, so the word True or the word False must follow the equal sign.

General Format of a Visual Basic Statement

The general format of the Visual Basic statement shown in Figure 3-26 appears in Figure 3-27.

General Format: Property Value Assignment Statement
`objectname.property = propertyvalue`

EXAMPLE	RESULT
picStandardRoom.Visible = True	Picture is visible
btnSelectRoom.Enabled = False	Button is dimmed

FIGURE 3-27

In the general format, the object name always is the first item in the Visual Basic statement. The object name is the name you specified in the (Name) property in the Properties window. In Figure 3-26, the object name is picStandardRoom because that is the name given to the standard room PictureBox object.

The dot operator (period) is required. It follows the object name with no space between them. Immediately following the dot operator is the name of the property that will be set by the statement. The property name must be spelled correctly and must be a valid property for the object named in the statement. Valid properties that can be specified in the statement are identified in the Properties window associated with the object.

The equal sign must follow zero or more spaces in the statement. Visual Basic statements do not require spaces, nor is there is a limit on how many spaces can be contained between elements in the statement. The equal sign identifies the statement as an **assignment statement**, which means the value on the right side of the equal sign is assigned to the element on the left side of the equal sign. When setting properties, it means the value on the right side of the equal sign is assigned to the property identified on the left side of the equal sign.

The property value specified in the assignment statement must be a valid value for the property identified on the left side of the equal sign. You can see the valid values for a given property by looking in the Properties window for the object whose property you are setting.

After you have entered the property value, the Visual Basic statement is complete. Because correct programming protocol states that only one statement should appear on a line, the next step is to press the ENTER key to move the insertion point to the next line in the coding window.

The general statement format shown in Figure 3-27 is used for all statements in which the code sets the value of an object property.

IntelliSense

In Figure 3-25 on page 131, the insertion point is located in the coding window. To enter the statement in Figure 3-26 into the actual program in the coding window, you can type the entire statement. Visual Studio, however, provides help when entering a statement so that you will be less prone to make an error when entering the statement. This help is called IntelliSense.

IntelliSense displays all allowable entries you can make in a Visual Basic statement each time a dot (period), equal sign, or other special character required for the statement is typed. When you type the prefix pic as shown in Figure 3-28, an IntelliSense window opens with all the objects that begin with that prefix. Instead of possibly misspelling the object name, you can select it from the IntelliSense list. Therefore, when using IntelliSense, the complete Visual Basic statement would be as shown in Figure 3-28:

```
picStandardRoom.Visible = True
```

FIGURE 3-28

When you type the first few letters of the object name, IntelliSense displays a list of all the entries, including all the objects, that can be specified in the statement.

Enter a Visual Basic Statement

To enter the Visual Basic statement in Figure 3-28 using IntelliSense, you can complete the following steps:

STEP 1   With the code editing window open and the insertion point positioned as shown in Figure 3-25 on page 131, type `pic`.

The characters pic are displayed in the code window (Figure 3-29). IntelliSense displays a list of all the entries that can follow the prefix in the statement. Sometimes the entry selected in the list is the correct entry for the statement you are entering, but often it is not the correct entry. Therefore, you must identify the correct statement in the list before entering it.

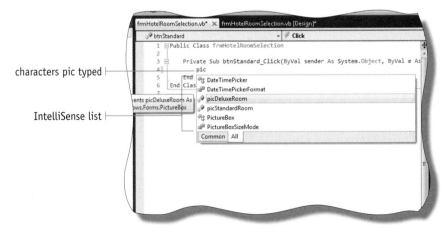

FIGURE 3-29

STEP 2 To identify the correct entry, type the next letter of the entry until the entry is selected. In this case, type s on your keyboard.

When you type characters, IntelliSense highlights in the list an entry that begins with the letters you type (Figure 3-30). When you enter pics, IntelliSense highlights the only term in the list that begins with pics, which is picStandardRoom. This is the object name you want to enter into the Visual Basic statement.

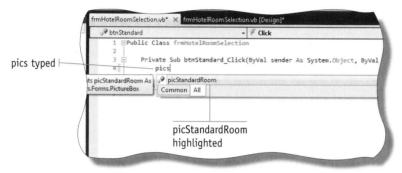

FIGURE 3-30

STEP 3 When IntelliSense highlights the correct object name, press the key on the keyboard corresponding to the entry that is to follow the object name. In this case, press the PERIOD key.

IntelliSense automatically enters the entire object name into the Visual Basic statement and the period (the character you typed) following the object name (Figure 3-31). In addition, because IntelliSense realizes that the dot you entered means more information is required in the statement, a list of the allowable entries following the dot is displayed.

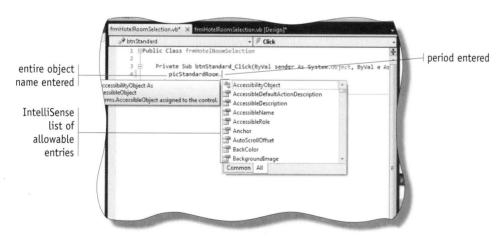

FIGURE 3-31

STEP 4 As with the object name in Step 2, the next step is to enter one or more characters until IntelliSense highlights the desired property in the list. Type the letter v on your keyboard.

IntelliSense highlights the properties in the list that begins with the letter v (Visible), or that contains the letter v such as in ProductVersion (Figure 3-32). Because the Visible property is highlighted, no further action is required to select the Visible property.

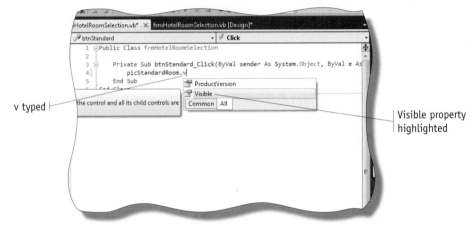

v typed

Visible property highlighted

FIGURE 3-32

STEP 5 Press the key for the character that is to follow the property name. In this case, press the SPACEBAR on the keyboard.

IntelliSense enters the highlighted property name (Visible) followed by the character you typed (space) (Figure 3-33). The space indicates to Visual Basic that the object name and property name entry is complete. Notice also that the IntelliSense tip specifies what the statement will be able to do. In Figure 3-33, it states that the statement "gets or sets a value indicating whether the control is displayed." This means the Visible property indicates whether the picStandardRoom PictureBox object is displayed.

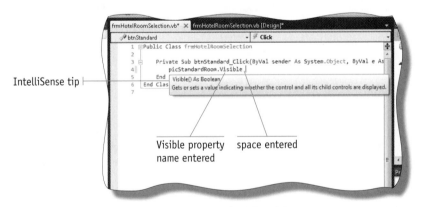

IntelliSense tip

Visible property name entered

space entered

FIGURE 3-33

STEP 6 Press the EQUAL SIGN key on the keyboard and then press the SPACEBAR. On the IntelliSense list, click the Common tab to display the most common results.

The equal sign and a space are displayed and then IntelliSense displays a list containing the entries you can make (Figure 3-34). For the Visible property, the only possible entries following the equal sign are False (which indicates the PictureBox object should not be visible) and True (which indicates the PictureBox object should be visible).

FIGURE 3-34

STEP 7 Type t on the keyboard.

IntelliSense highlights the True entry (Figure 3-35).

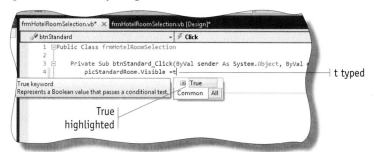

FIGURE 3-35

STEP 8 Press the key for the character that is to follow the True entry. In this case, press the ENTER key.

Because you pressed the ENTER key, IntelliSense enters True into the statement and then Visual Studio moves the indented insertion point to the next line (Figure 3-36). The Visual Basic statement now is completely entered.

FIGURE 3-36

Visual Studio and IntelliSense automatically create the indentations in the program statements in Figure 3-36 because the indentations make the statements easier to read and understand. As programs become more complex, proper indentation of program statements can be an important factor in developing error-free programs.

The following steps summarize the procedure for using IntelliSense to enter a Visual Basic statement that sets a property:

1. Type the first letter(s) of the name of the object whose property will be set until the object name is selected in the IntelliSense list.
2. Press the PERIOD key.
3. Type the first letter(s) of the name of the property to be set until the name is highlighted in the IntelliSense list.
4. Press the SPACEBAR to complete the first portion of the statement.
5. Press the EQUAL SIGN key.
6. Press the SPACEBAR.
7. Press the first letter(s) of the entry you want to select in the list until the entry is highlighted; or if IntelliSense does not display a list, type the value for the property.
8. Press the ENTER key.

Using IntelliSense to enter a Visual Basic statement provides two significant advantages: 1) It is faster to enter a statement using IntelliSense than it is to enter a statement by typing it; 2) Using IntelliSense reduces the number of errors committed when entering a statement to almost zero. By using only the entries contained on the IntelliSense lists, the developer seldom will make a mistake by entering an invalid entry. In addition, because the entry is chosen from a list, it is not possible for the entry to be misspelled or mistyped.

Entering a programming statement is a fundamental skill of a Visual Basic programmer. You should understand thoroughly how to enter a programming statement using IntelliSense.

Set Visible Property to False

In Figure 3-36 on page 137, the programming statement set the Visible property for the picStandardRoom PictureBox object to True, which will cause the image in the picture box to be displayed when the statement is executed. The statement will be executed when the user clicks the Standard Room button because the statement is within the btnStandardRoom_Click event handler.

Another setting that must take place when the user clicks the Standard Room button is to set the Visible property for the picDeluxeRoom PictureBox to False so the deluxe room picture is not displayed when the standard room picture is displayed. To set the Visible property for the picDeluxeRoom PictureBox object to False, you could complete the steps on the following pages:

STEP 1   With the insertion point on the second line of the code editing window for the Click event of the Standard Room button, type pic on your keyboard.

The letters you typed are displayed in the code editing window and the IntelliSense list shows the valid entries you can choose (Figure 3-37). The entry picStandardRoom is highlighted because it is the last entry that was selected from this list.

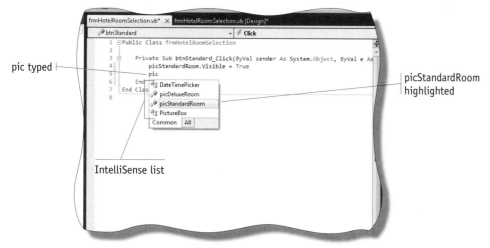

FIGURE 3-37

STEP 2   Type d to highlight the picDeluxeRoom entry in the IntelliSense list.

IntelliSense highlights picDeluxeRoom in the list because this is the only entry that starts with the characters, picd (Figure 3-38).

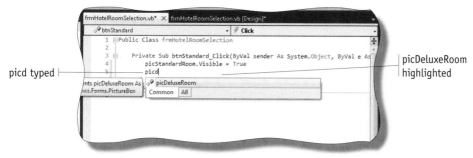

FIGURE 3-38

STEP 3 Press the key on the keyboard for the character that is to follow the object name. In this case, press the PERIOD key.

The picDeluxeRoom entry is placed in the statement followed by the dot operator (period) you typed (Figure 3-39). In addition, IntelliSense displays the list of allowable entries.

Visible is highlighted in the list because it was the entry selected the last time the list was used. If Visible was not highlighted, you could type the letter v to highlight Visible in the list.

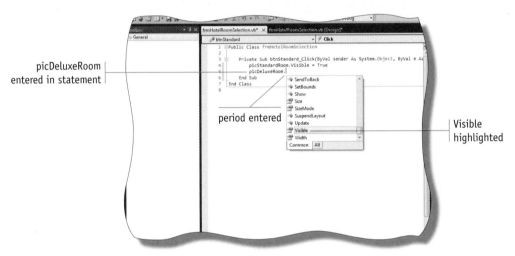

picDeluxeRoom entered in statement

period entered

Visible highlighted

FIGURE 3-39

STEP 4 Press the SPACEBAR, press the EQUAL SIGN key, and then press the SPACEBAR.

IntelliSense places the Visible entry in the statement (Figure 3-40). Next, the space you typed appears, followed by the equal sign and the space you typed. When you typed the equal sign, IntelliSense displayed the list of allowable entries following the equal sign.

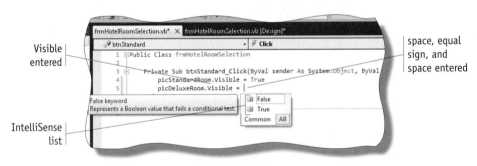

Visible entered

space, equal sign, and space entered

IntelliSense list

FIGURE 3-40

STEP 5 Type f and then press the ENTER key.

*When you type the letter f, IntelliSense highlights False in the list. When you press the
ENTER key, IntelliSense inserts False (Figure 3-41).*

indented
insertion point

False inserted

FIGURE 3-41

ONLINE REINFORCEMENT

To view a video of the process
in the previous steps, visit
scsite.com/vb2010/ch3 and
then select Figure 3-37.

Once again, using IntelliSense to enter a Visual Basic programming statement results in a correct statement in minimum time with reduced chance of error.

Enabled Property

You learned earlier that if the Enabled property for a Button object is True, the
click event code for the button will be executed when the user clicks the button. If
the Enabled property for a Button object is False, the event code for the button will
not be executed. In Figure 3-21 on page 127, the Enabled property for the Select
Room button was set to False so that the button is not active when the program
begins execution. When a picture button such as the Standard Room button is
clicked, however, the Enabled property must be set to True so the Select button is
active. To set the Enabled property to True, a coding statement to set the Enabled
property for the btnSelectRoom Button object is required. To enter the coding
statement into the btnStandardRoom_Click event handler, you can complete the
following steps:

STEP 1 Type btn to display the IntelliSense list (Figure 3-42).

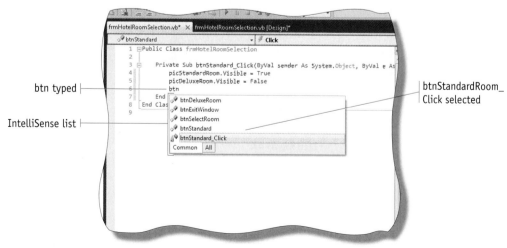

btn typed

IntelliSense list

btnStandardRoom_
Click selected

FIGURE 3-42

STEP 2 Type se (or more characters if necessary) until IntelliSense highlights the btnSelectRoom entry in the list.

IntelliSense highlights btnSelectRoom, the only entry that starts with the characters, btnse (Figure 3-43). Sometimes, the correct entry will be highlighted before you type all the distinguishing characters. If so, you need not type any more characters.

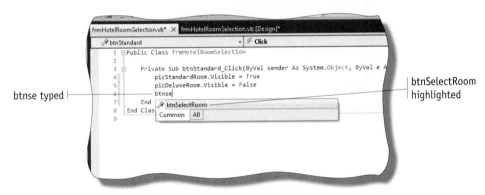

btnse typed

btnSelectRoom highlighted

FIGURE 3-43

STEP 3 Type a period, type e, press the SPACEBAR, press the EQUAL SIGN key, press the SPACEBAR again, and then type t to select True in the IntelliSense list.

IntelliSense places the highlighted entry (btnSelectRoom) into the statement and displays a list of the next allowable entries. When you typed e, Enabled was selected in the list. Pressing the SPACEBAR caused IntelliSense to place the entry, Enabled, and then the space into the statement. When you typed the equal sign and space, IntelliSense inserted the equal sign and space, and displayed the list of entries that can follow the equal sign (Figure 3-44). When you typed the letter t, IntelliSense highlighted True in the list.

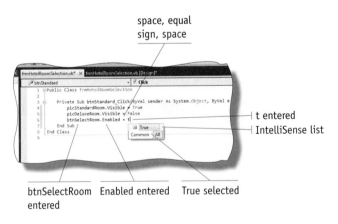

space, equal sign, space

t entered

IntelliSense list

btnSelectRoom entered

Enabled entered

True selected

FIGURE 3-44

STEP 4 Press the ENTER key to enter the completed statement and place the insertion point on the next line.

IntelliSense enters the entry, True, into the statement (Figure 3-45). Pressing the ENTER key completes the statement and moves the indented insertion point to the next line.

indented
insertion
point

True entered

FIGURE 3-45

ONLINE REINFORCEMENT

To view a video of the process in the previous steps, visit scsite.com/vb2010/ch3 and then select Figure 3-42.

Learning the process of entering program statements through the use of IntelliSense is fundamental to writing programs using the Visual Basic 2010 language.

Comments in Program Statements

A well-written Visual Basic 2010 program normally contains **comment statements** within the code itself to document what the code is doing. An example of comment statements in code is shown in Figure 3-46.

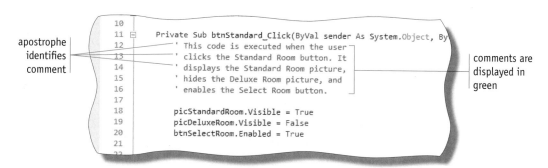

apostrophe
identifies
comment

comments are
displayed in
green

FIGURE 3-46

A comment is preceded by an apostrophe. Whenever the Visual Basic compiler encounters an apostrophe in the code, it ignores the remaining characters on the line. To the compiler, it's as if the comments do not exist.

The comments in the code, which are displayed in green text, describe the processing that will occur in the code that follows. Because comments are ignored by the Visual Basic compiler, no programming language syntax must be followed within the comments. Any letters or characters are allowed within comments. The general reason for comments is to aid the code reader in understanding the purpose of the code and how it accomplishes its tasks.

To enter comments, type an apostrophe in the code. All characters following the apostrophe on that line of code are considered a comment. To enter the comment code shown in Figure 3-46, you could complete the following steps:

STEP 1   To insert a blank line following the event code generated by Visual Studio that begins with the word Private, click anywhere in that line and then press the END key on your keyboard.

Visual Studio positions the insertion point at the end of the line that you clicked (Figure 3–47).

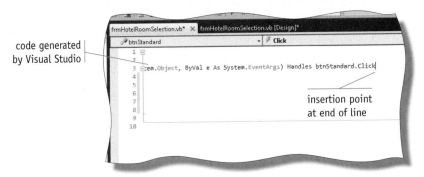

FIGURE 3-47

STEP 2   Press the ENTER key.

Visual Studio inserts a blank line in the code and then moves the insertion point to the blank line (Figure 3–48). The comments can be inserted on the blank line.

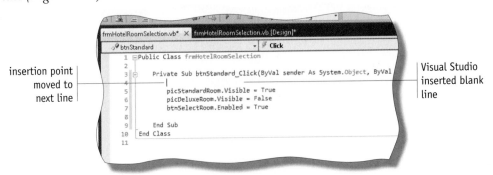

FIGURE 3-48

STEP 3 Type the first line of the comments, beginning with an apostrophe, as shown in Figure 3-46 on page 143, and then press the ENTER key.

The apostrophe as the first character typed identifies the rest of the line as a comment (Figure 3-49). The comment line is displayed in green text. When you press the ENTER key, Visual Studio creates a new blank line and places the indented insertion point on that line.

FIGURE 3-49

ONLINE REINFORCEMENT

To view a video of the process in the previous steps, visit scsite.com/vb2010/ch3 and then select Figure 3-47.

You can continue to enter lines of comments by typing an apostrophe and the comment, and then pressing the ENTER key until all comments are completed.

Same Line Comments

Because the Visual Basic compiler treats all characters following an apostrophe as comments, it is possible to place a comment on the same line as executable code. In Figure 3-50, a comment is shown on the same line as the statement that sets the btnSelectRoom Enabled property to True.

```
frmHotelRoomSelection.vb*  ×  frmHotelRoomSelection.vb [Design]*
[General]                          ▼  [Declarations]
1  ⊟Public Class frmHotelRoomSelection
2
3  ⊟    Private Sub btnStandard_Click(ByVal sender As System.Object, ByVa
4          ' This code is executed when the user
5          ' clicks the Standard Room button. It
6          ' displays the Standard Room picture,
7          ' hides the Deluxe Room picture, and
8          ' enables the Select Room button.
9
10         picStandardRoom.Visible = True
11         picDeluxeRoom.Visible = False
12         btnSelectRoom.Enabled = True 'Enable button
13
14     End Sub
15  End Class
16
17
```

apostrophe identifies comment

FIGURE 3-50

In Figure 3-50, the apostrophe specifies that all characters remaining on the line are to be treated as comments. Therefore, the text, Enable button, is displayed in green and is treated as a comment. To enter a comment on any line, enter an apostrophe and then type the comment. Remember that all characters following an apostrophe on a line of code are treated as comments.

Introductory Comments

Every program should begin with comments that state the name of the program, the developer's name, the date, and the purpose of the program. These comments should precede any other statements in the program (Figure 3-51).

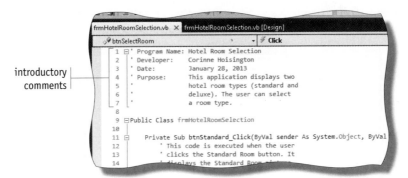

FIGURE 3-51

Notice that the introductory comments precede all code in the program — even the code generated by Visual Studio. To enter introductory comments, you can complete the following steps:

STEP 1 Click to the left of the word Public on line 1 in the program to place the insertion point on that line.

The insertion point is positioned at the beginning of line 1 in the code (Figure 3-52).

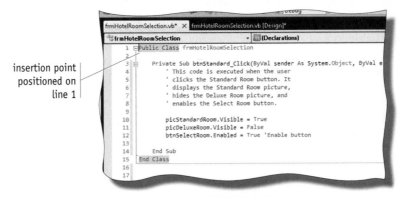

FIGURE 3-52

STEP 2 Press the ENTER key one time, and then press the UP ARROW key one time.

When you press the ENTER key, Visual Studio inserts a blank line on line 1 of the code and moves the line that begins with the words, Public Class, down to line 2 (Figure 3-53). Visual Studio also moves the insertion point to line 2 when you press the ENTER key. When you press the UP ARROW key, the insertion point moves to the first line, which is blank.

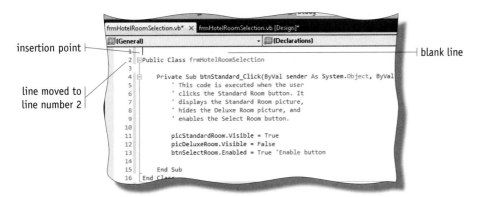

FIGURE 3-53

STEP 3 Type an apostrophe, a space, the text, `Program Name:` and then press the TAB key one time.

The apostrophe identifies all characters and words that follow as comments, so the characters are displayed in green (Figure 3-54). The first line of introductory comments normally specifies the name of the program. Pressing the TAB key moves the insertion point to the right.

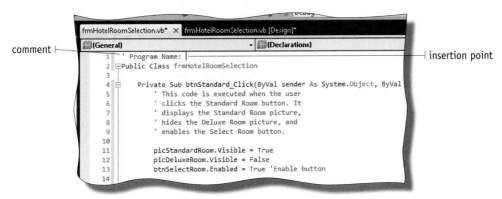

FIGURE 3-54

STEP 4 Type Hotel Room Selection as the name of the program. Then, press the ENTER key.

The program name appears in the first line of comments and the insertion point is moved to line 2 (Figure 3-55).

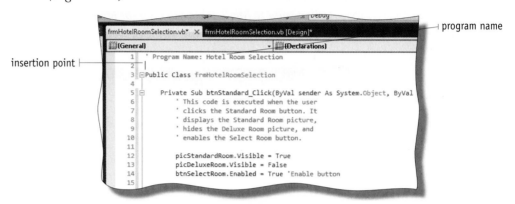

FIGURE 3-55

ONLINE REINFORCEMENT

To view a video of the process in the previous steps, visit scsite.com/vb2010/ch3 and then select Figure 3-52.

You can enter the remaining comments using the same techniques. Press the TAB key one or more times to align vertically the paragraphs on the right so they appear as shown in Figure 3-51 on page 146.

Correcting Errors in Code

Using IntelliSense to assist you when entering code reduces the likelihood of coding errors considerably. Nevertheless, because you could create one or more errors when entering code, you should understand what to do when a coding error occurs.

One possible error you could commit would be to forget an apostrophe in a comment statement. In Figure 3-56, a comment was entered without a leading apostrophe.

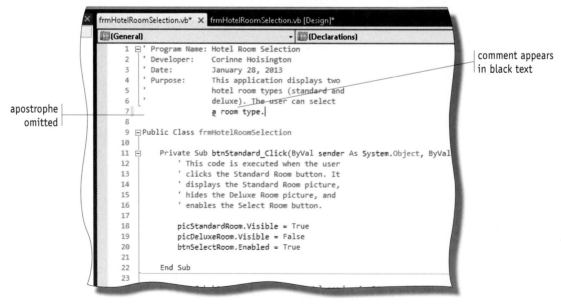

FIGURE 3-56

In Figure 3-56, the comment words are displayed in black text, which is a clue that this is an error because comment characters normally are displayed in green text. Nonetheless, Visual Studio gives no other indication that an error has occurred.

From this point where the error occurred, the developer might take any course of action. For example, she might immediately run the program. Or, she might click anywhere in the window to move the insertion point, or press the ENTER key to insert a blank line. If the program in Figure 3-56 is executed immediately by clicking the Start Debugging button on the Standard toolbar, the window shown in Figure 3-57 will be displayed.

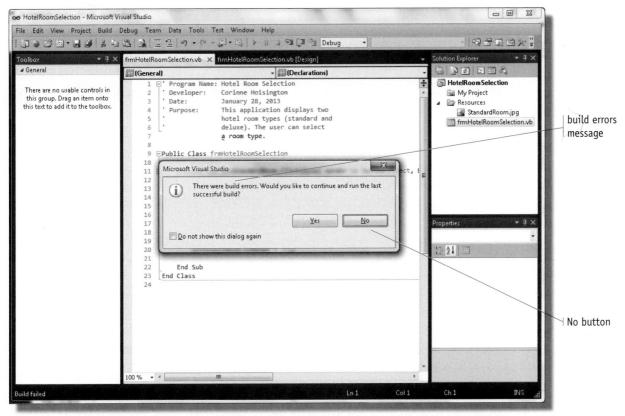

FIGURE 3-57

The **build errors message** means the Visual Basic compiler detected a coding error in the program. An absolute requirement when programming Visual Basic programs is that when you see the build errors message, you *always click the No button*. Under no circumstances should you click the Yes button in the dialog box. When you click the No button, you can perform the steps on the next page to make corrections in your program:

STEP 1 Click the No button in the Microsoft Visual Studio dialog box that informs you of a build error (see Figure 3-57).

*When you click the No button, Visual Studio displays the program code and the Error List window (Figure 3-58). The **Error List window** identifies the number of errors that occurred and displays a description of the error detected. The description, Declaration expected, in Figure 3-58 means Visual Studio expected to find a different type of statement than it found. In addition, the window contains the file in which the error occurred (frmHotelRoomSelection.vb), the line number of the statement in error (7), and the vertical column within the statement where the error was detected (17). In the code editing window, the location of the error is noted by a blue squiggly line.*

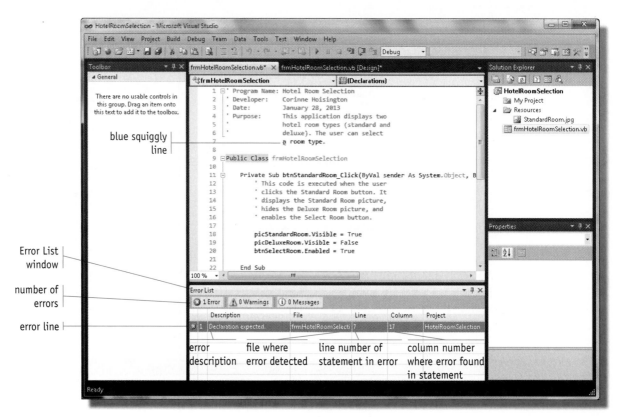

FIGURE 3-58

STEP 2 Double-click anywhere on the error line.

Visual Studio highlights the error in blue so the developer, if desired, can type and replace the highlighted text with the correct code (Figure 3-59). With the error highlighted, the developer must examine the statement to determine the error. By looking at line 7, column 17, where the letter a is highlighted, it is clear that a line intended to be a comment was not treated as a comment by Visual Studio. Further examination reveals the required apostrophe is missing.

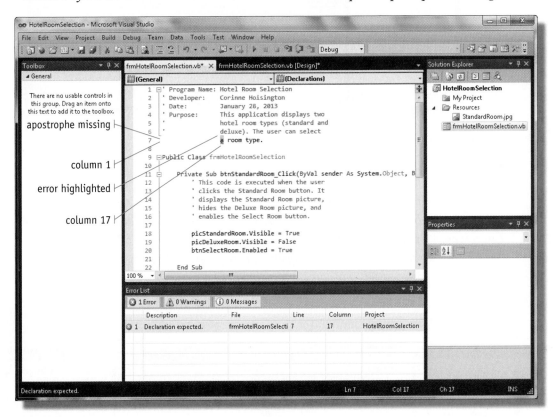

FIGURE 3-59

STEP 3 Click in the leftmost column on line 7 to place the insertion point at that location.

The insertion point is located in the leftmost column on line 7 of the program (Figure 3-60).

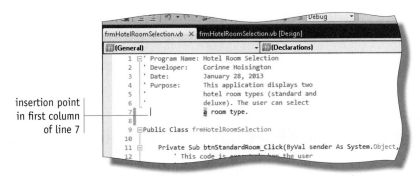

FIGURE 3-60

STEP 4 Type an apostrophe.

The apostrophe is located in the first column on line 7 of the program (Figure 3-61).

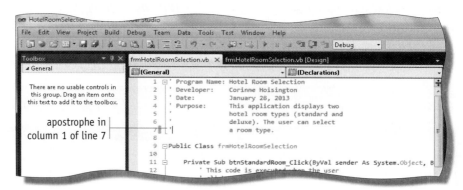

FIGURE 3-61

STEP 5 Click anywhere in the code editing window.

When you click anywhere in the window, the insertion point moves to that location (Figure 3-62). If the statement has been corrected, the error line is removed from the Error List window, and the number of errors is reduced by one. In Figure 3-62, the number of errors is zero because only one error was found in the program. It is possible to have multiple errors detected when the program is compiled.

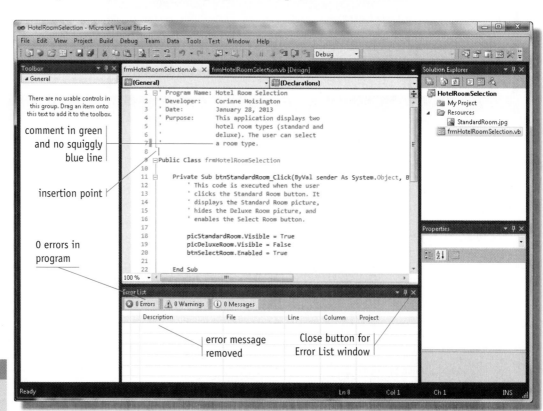

ONLINE REINFORCEMENT

To view a video of the process in the previous steps, visit scsite.com/vb2010/ch3 and then select Figure 3-58.

FIGURE 3-62

You can close the Error List window by clicking the Close button for the window (see Figure 3-62).

In Figure 3-57 on page 149, it was assumed the developer, after making the error, immediately ran the program. If, before running the program, the developer moved the insertion point to any other part of the program, or clicked any other element in the window, then Visual Studio would provide a visual cue that an error was made by displaying a blue squiggly line under the error. The line shown in Figure 3-58 is the type of line that Visual Studio would display. If you see a blue squiggly line in your code, it means you have made an error entering the code. You do not have to run the program to find coding errors. If a blue squiggly line appears in your code, an error has been made and you must correct it.

Additional Click Events

In the sample program in this chapter, multiple buttons can trigger events. For example, when the user clicks the Exit Window button, the program window should close and the program should terminate. To indicate that clicking the Exit Window button will trigger an event, and to prepare to write the code for the event, complete the same steps for the Exit Window button that you learned for the Standard Room button, as shown in the following figure:

STEP 1   On the frmHotelRoomSelection.vb [Design] tabbed page, double-click the Exit Window Button object.

Visual Studio opens the code editing window and displays the frmHotelRoomSelection.vb tabbed page (Figure 3-63). Visual Studio also inserts the event handler code for the click event on the btnExitWindow object. Two horizontal lines separate the event handler code for the btnExitWindow object from code for other event handlers that might be in the program. The developer must write the code that will be executed when the click event occurs. The insertion point is located in the proper place to begin writing code.

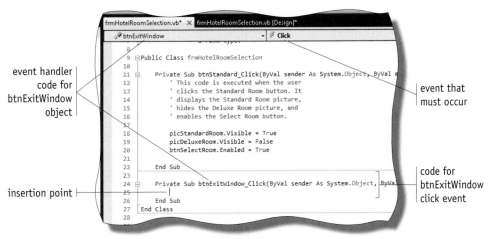

FIGURE 3-63

ONLINE REINFORCEMENT

To view a video of the process in the previous steps, visit scsite.com/vb2010/ch3 and then select Figure 3-63.

Entering Code

As you have seen, you can enter code in the code window using the IntelliSense tools you have learned. The first code written for an event, however, should be comment code that indicates what the event is and what processing will occur. The comment code for the Exit Window event handler is shown in Figure 3-64.

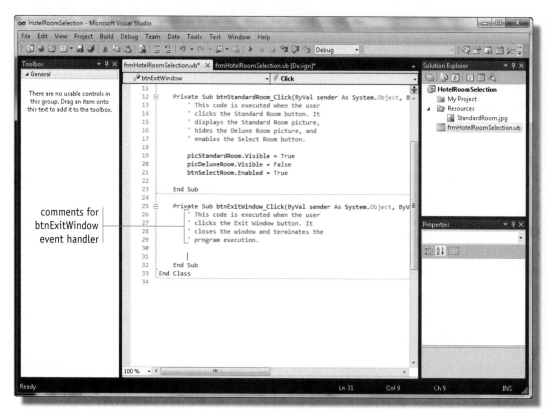

FIGURE 3-64

Close Procedure

The Visual Basic statement to close the window and terminate the program calls a procedure that performs the actual processing. A **procedure** is a set of prewritten code that can be called by a statement in the Visual Basic program. When the procedure is called, it performs its processing. The procedure used to close a window and terminate a program is the Close procedure.

You can use the statement in Figure 3-65 to call the Close procedure:

FIGURE 3-65

The word Close specifies the name of the procedure to be called. The left and right parentheses immediately following the name of the procedure identifies the Visual Basic statement as a **procedure call statement**.

When the statement in Figure 3-65 is executed, the Close procedure will be called and control will be given to the prewritten programming statements in the Close procedure. These statements will close the window and terminate the application.

To enter the Close statement into the program, you can type `clo` and then select Close in the IntelliSense list, as shown in the following steps.

STEP 1   With the insertion point positioned as shown in Figure 3-64 on page 154, type `clo` to highlight Close in the IntelliSense list.

When you type the letters clo IntelliSense highlights the word Close in the IntelliSense list (Figure 3-66).

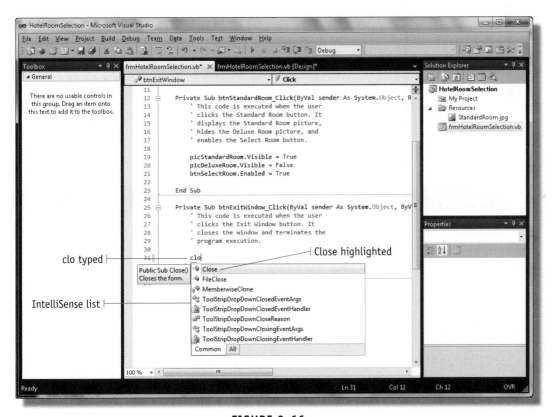

FIGURE 3-66

STEP 2   Press the ENTER key.

IntelliSense enters Close in the statement and, because it knows Close is a procedure call, automatically appends the open and closed parentheses to the statement (Figure 3-67). Then, Visual Studio returns the insertion point to the next line.

Close entered

open and closed
parentheses added
automatically

FIGURE 3-67

ONLINE REINFORCEMENT

To view a video of the process in the previous steps, visit scsite.com/vb2010/ch3 and then select Figure 3-66.

IN THE REAL WORLD

Developers can write their own procedures to perform required processing and then store the procedures in a library so they and other programmers can use the procedures. You will learn more about using procedures throughout this book.

Prewritten procedures available to Visual Basic developers through Visual Studio are an important element when using rapid application development because the developer is not required to write the procedure code. The developer merely writes a single statement to call the procedure. You will use many procedures in this book for a variety of reasons.

Printing Code

In some instances, you will find the need to print the code in the program. Sometimes as you review the code, you might find it easier to read and understand the code on a printed page rather than on your computer screen. In other cases, you might want to share the code with another developer and the printed page often is a better tool for this than a monitor screen. To print the code in a program, you can complete the following steps:

1. Click File on the menu bar to display the File menu.
2. Click Print on the File menu to display the Print dialog box.

3. Ensure that a check mark appears in the Include line numbers check box if you want line numbers on your printout. Most developers prefer line numbers on printouts.
4. Make any other selections you find necessary in the Print dialog box.
5. Click the OK button in the Print dialog box to print the code.

If you have a color printer, the code will be printed with correct color. Otherwise, shades of gray will represent the colors shown in the code editing window. If a line of code extends beyond one printed line, an arrow will appear at the end of the first printed line to indicate it continues to the next printed line.

Coding Summary

Writing code is the essence of programming in Visual Basic 2010. Much of the emphasis in this book will be on writing the code required to implement applications of all kinds.

Once you understand coding and the statements shown in this chapter, you are ready to continue the process of designing and implementing the Hotel Room Selection program.

Phase 3 — Design the Program Processing Objects

The next phase in the program development life cycle requires determining the processing objects for the program and creating the event planning document. In the Hotel Room Selection program and in programs of similar complexity, the designer need not be concerned about determining the processing objects. The only processing object required for the program is the Windows Form object. In later, more complex programs, this task will become important.

So, for the Hotel Room Selection program, the next task is to design the event planning document.

Event Planning Document

As you have learned, programs written using a graphical user interface normally are event-driven programs. An **event** means the user has initiated an action that causes the program to perform the type of processing called for by the user's action. Once the mock-up for the user interface has been created, the developer must document the events that can occur based on the user interface.

The **event planning document** consists of a table that specifies an object in the user interface that will cause an event, the action taken by the user to trigger the event, and the event processing that must occur. The event planning document for the Hotel Room Selection program is shown in Figure 3-68 on the next page.

HEADS UP

Visual Studio 2010 does not provide a tool to print the user interface designed on the frmHotelRoomSelection.vb [Design] tabbed page. You can implement a workaround to print the user interface using the following steps: 1) Open Microsoft Word; 2) Make Visual Studio 2010 the active program window; 3) With the user interface displayed on the frmHotelRoomSelection.vb [Design] tabbed page, hold down the ALT key and then press the PRINT SCREEN key; 4) Make Microsoft Word the active window; 5) Click the Paste button on the Word Standard Toolbar. The screen shot created in Step 3 will be pasted into the Word document; 6) Print the Word document.

EVENT PLANNING DOCUMENT

Program Name: Hotel Room Selection	Developer: Corinne Hoisington	Object: frmHotelRoomSelection	Date: January 28, 2013
OBJECT	**EVENT TRIGGER**	**EVENT PROCESSING**	
btnStandardRoom	Click	Display the standard room picture Hide the deluxe room picture Enable the Select Room button	
btnSelectRoom	Click	Disable the Standard Room button Disable the Select Room button Disable the Deluxe Room button Hide the Instructions label Display the Confirmation Message label Enable the Exit Window button	
btnDeluxeRoom	Click	Display the deluxe room picture Hide the standard room picture Enable the Select Room button	
btnExitWindow	Click	Close the window and terminate the program	

FIGURE 3-68

The leftmost column on the event planning document identifies the object in the graphical user interface that can be used to trigger an event. In the Hotel Room Selection program, the four Button objects each can be used to trigger an event, so each of the Button objects must be included in the event planning document. Notice each of the Button objects is identified by its name. Using this technique ensures that the documentation is precise, and provides little room for error when the developer creates the code to implement these events.

The middle column identifies the event trigger, which is the action a user takes to cause the event to occur. In all four event cases in Figure 3-68, clicking the button triggers the event. As you will learn in this book, a variety of acts by a user can trigger an event. For example, a user might point to an object, right-click the object, or double-click the object. Each of these event triggers could trigger a different event.

The rightmost column on the event planning document specifies the event processing that the program must accomplish when the event occurs. This list of tasks for each event is a critical element in the program design. It must be precise and accurate. No processing step that must occur should be left out of the event processing column. The tasks should be in the same sequence as they will be accomplished in the program.

For example, the first task for the btnStandardRoom_Click event is to display the standard room picture. This is the primary task for the Standard Room button. In addition, however, several other tasks must be completed. When the program begins, the deluxe room picture is not visible, but if the user clicks the Deluxe Room button, then the picture will be visible. When the user clicks the Standard Room button, however, the deluxe room picture should not be visible. Therefore, each time the user clicks the Standard Room button, the processing must hide the deluxe room picture.

You also will recall that when program execution begins, the Select Room button is dimmed (disabled) and, after the user clicks a room button, it should be enabled. Therefore, each time the user clicks the Standard Room button, the Select Room button must be enabled because it might be the first time the user clicked the Standard Room button.

As you review the event planning document in Figure 3-68 on page 158, be sure you understand the processing that must occur for each event.

You should note that the event processing tasks in the right column identify *what* processing must be done when the event occurs. The manner in which these tasks will be accomplished is not identified specifically, although the information in the event planning document must be precise enough that the developer easily can write the code to implement the tasks specified.

Phase 4 — Code the Program

After the events and tasks within the events have been identified, the developer is ready to code the program. As you have learned in this chapter, coding the program means entering Visual Basic statements to accomplish the tasks specified on the event planning document. As the developer enters the code, she also will implement the logic to carry out the required processing.

Guided Program Development

To fine-tune the user interface in the Hotel Room Selection program and enter the code required to process each event in the program, complete the following steps to create the program shown in Figure 3-1 on pages 112 and 113.

NOTE TO THE LEARNER

In the following activity, you should complete the tasks within the specified steps. Each of the tasks is accompanied by a Hint Screen. The purpose of the Hint Screen is to indicate where in the Visual Studio window you should perform the activity; it also serves as a reminder of the method that you should use to create the user interface or enter code. If you need further help completing the step, refer to the figure number identified by the term, ref:, in the step.

Guided Program Development

1

- **Open the Mock-Up File** Open Visual Studio and then open the mock-up file for the user interface you created in Chapter 2. (If you did not create a mock-up file in Chapter 2, consult with your instructor to obtain the file).

HINT

- **Show the Windows Form Object BackColor Property** To finish the user interface, the back color of the Windows Form object must be specified. Select the frmHotelRoomSelection Windows Form object. In the Properties window, scroll until the BackColor property is visible, click the BackColor property name in the left column, and then click the BackColor arrow in the right column. If necessary, click the Web tab *(ref: Figure 3-3)*.

HINT

- **Choose the Windows Form Object BackColor** Scroll in the Web tabbed page until Cornsilk is visible and then click Cornsilk in the list *(ref: Figure 3-5)*.

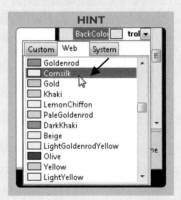
HINT

- **Select the Buttons** Next, you must spec-ify the BackColor for the Button objects. Select the four buttons in the window using techniques you have learned previously.

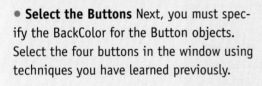

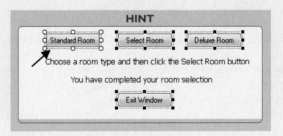
HINT

● **Choose the BackColor for the Buttons**
Scroll in the Properties window until the
BackColor property is visible. Click the
BackColor property name in the left column,
click the BackColor arrow in the right
column, if necessary click the Web tab, scroll
until the LightSalmon color is visible, and
then click LightSalmon in the Web list. Click
anywhere in the window to deselect the
buttons *(ref: Figure 3-4)*.

*The BackColor
for the Windows
Form object is
changed to
Cornsilk and the
BackColor for
the buttons in
the window is
changed to
LightSalmon
(Figure 3-69).*

FIGURE 3-69

(continues)

2

● **Download the StandardRoom Image** To display
the pictures in the PictureBox object, you must
download the pictures from the Web and store them
on your computer. Download the StandardRoom
image from scsite.com/vb2010/ch3/images. Save
the StandardRoom image on a USB drive or other
storage media you have available on your computer
(ref: Figure 3-7).

● **Download the DeluxeRoom Image** Download the
DeluxeRoom image from scsite.com/vb2010/
ch3/images. Save the DeluxeRoom image on a USB
drive or other storage media you have available on
your computer *(ref: Figure 3-7)*.

3

● **Display the Select Resource Dialog Box** After
acquiring the pictures, you must import them into
the Resources folder and specify the PictureBox
object where they will be displayed. Select the pic-
StandardRoom PictureBox object. In the Properties
window, click Image and then click
the Ellipsis button in the right column *(ref:
Figure 3-11)*.

● **Import the StandardRoom Image** In the Select
Resource dialog box, click the Import button,
import the StandardRoom image from where you
saved it in Step 2, and then click the OK button
(ref: Figure 3-14).

● **Import the DeluxeRoom Image** Using the Properties window and the same techniques, specify the DeluxeRoom image as the image for the picDeluxeRoom PictureBox object.

● **Set the SizeMode Property for the StandardRoom Image to StretchImage** When you import a picture, normally you must resize either the picture or the PictureBox object so the picture is displayed properly. To resize the StandardRoom image, select the picStandardRoom PictureBox object. In the Properties window for the picStandardRoom PictureBox object, click the SizeMode property name, click the SizeMode arrow, and then set the property to StretchImage *(ref: Figure 3-16)*.

● **Set the SizeMode Property for the DeluxeRoom Image to StretchImage** Using the same technique, set the SizeMode property for the picDeluxeRoom PictureBox object to StretchImage.

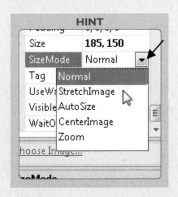

(continues)

The images are displayed in the correct PictureBox objects (Figure 3-70).

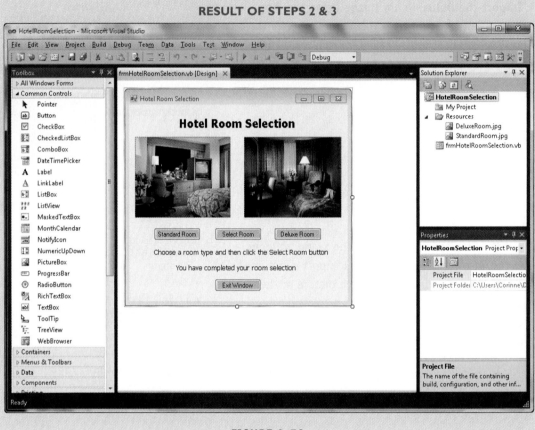

RESULT OF STEPS 2 & 3

FIGURE 3-70

4

● **Set the Visible Property for the StandardRoom Image to False** When program execution begins, the pictures are not displayed in the window, so their Visible property must be set to False. In the Properties window for the picStandardRoom PictureBox object, click the Visible property name in the left column, click the Visible arrow for the Visible property, and then set the Visible property for the picStandardRoom Picture-Box object to False *(ref: Figure 3-18)*.

HINT

- **Set the Visible Property for the DeluxeRoom Image to False** Using the same technique, in the Properties window set the Visible property for the picDeluxeRoom PictureBox object to False *(ref: Figure 3-18)*.

HINT

- **Set the Visible Property for the Confirmation Message to False** The confirmation message is not displayed when program execution begins. Therefore, using the same technique, in the Properties window set the Visible property for the lblConfirmationMessage Label object to False *(ref: Figure 3-18)*.

HINT

- **Run the Program** After you have made changes to a program, you should run it to ensure your changes work properly. Run the program to ensure the changes you have made are correct *(ref: Figure 3-22)*.

HINT

In Figure 3-71, the room pictures are not displayed. In addition, the confirmation message is not displayed.

RESULT OF STEP 4

FIGURE 3-71

(continues)

5

● **Set the Select Room Button Enabled Property to False** Initially, the Select Room button and the Exit Window button must be dimmed. In the Properties window for the btnSelectRoom object, click the Enabled property name, click the Enabled arrow, and then set the Enabled property for the btnSelectRoom Button object to False *(ref: Figure 3-20)*.

HINT

● **Set the Exit Window Button Enabled Property to False** Using the same technique, set the Enabled property for the btnExitWindow Button object to False *(ref: Figure 3-20)*.

HINT

● **Run the Program** Once again, after you make changes always ensure the changes are correct. Run the program.

Both the Select Room button and the Exit Window button are dimmed, indicating the Enabled property for both buttons is False (Figure 3-72).

RESULT OF STEP 5

FIGURE 3-72

6

● **Open the Code Editing Window for the btnStandardRoom Event Handler** The user interface now is complete, so you should begin writing the code for the program. To write code, you must open the code editing window. Double-click the Standard Room button to open the code editing window for the btnStandardRoom_Click event *(ref: Figure 3-24)*.

HINT

● **Position the Insertion Point** When you begin writing the code for a program, the first step is to write the introductory comments. Click in the leftmost position of the first coding line (Public Class) *(ref: Figure 3-52).*

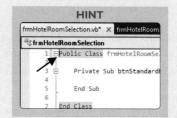

● **Create a Blank Line and Position the Insertion Point** Press the ENTER key and then press the UP ARROW key *(ref: Figure 3-53).*

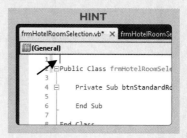

● **Enter the First Line of the Introductory Comments** The introductory comments provide the code reader with important information regarding the program. The first line normally specifies the name of the program. Type an apostrophe, press the SPACEBAR one time, type `Program Name:` on your keyboard, press the TAB key one time, type `Hotel Room Selection` and then press the ENTER key *(ref: Figure 3-54).*

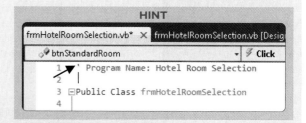

● **Enter the Developer Identification Comment Line** Type an apostrophe, press the SPACEBAR one time, type `Developer:` on your keyboard, press the TAB key one time, type your name and then press the ENTER key.

● **Enter the Date Comment Line** Type an apostrophe, press the SPACEBAR one time, type `Date:` on your keyboard, press the TAB key three times, enter the current date, and then press the ENTER key.

● **Enter the First Program Purpose Comment Line** Type an apostrophe, press the SPACEBAR one time, type `Purpose:` on your keyboard, press the TAB key two times, enter the first line of your own comments about the program, and then press the ENTER key.

● **Enter the Remaining Program Purpose Comment Lines** Insert additional lines of comments concerning the purpose of the program as you see fit.

(continues)

Guided Program Development *continued*

The comments appear at the top of the program (Figure 3-73).

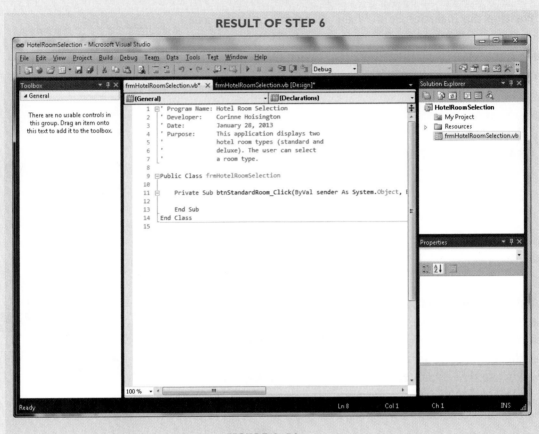

RESULT OF STEP 6

FIGURE 3-73

7

● **Position the Insertion Point Inside the Click Event Handler** With the insertion point located on the line above the line of code that begins with Public Class (see Figure 3-73), press the DOWN ARROW key four times and then press the TAB key two times to position the insertion point *(ref: Figure 3-48)*.

HINT

```
 9  ⊟Public Class frmHotelRoomSelection
10
11  ⊟    Private Sub btnStandardRoom_Click(ByVal sender As System.Obj
12       |
13  →    End Sub
14
```

● **Enter the First Line of the Event Handler Comments** Each event handler should begin with comments describing what the event handler accomplishes. Type an apostrophe, press the SPACEBAR one time, and then enter the first line of comments for the btnStandardRoom_Click event handler. Press the ENTER key *(ref: Figure 3-49)*.

HINT

```
10
11  ⊟    Private Sub btnStandardRoom_Click(ByVal sender As System.Object,
12  →        ' This code is executed when the user
13
14       End Sub
15
16   End Class
```

● **Enter the Remaining Event Handler Comments** Enter the remaining comments for the btnStandardRoom_Click event handler.

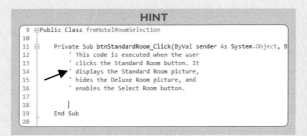

● **Make the StandardRoom PictureBox Object Visible** The first executable line of code in the Standard Room Button object click event handler must make the StandardRoom PictureBox object visible. Using IntelliSense, enter the Visual Basic code statement to set the Visible property for the picStandardRoom PictureBox object to True *(ref: Figure 3-29)*.

● **Make the DeluxeRoom Picture Box Object Not Visible** As documented in the event planning document, the next task is to make the Deluxe Room picture not visible in the window. Using IntelliSense, enter the Visual Basic code statement to set the Visible property for the picDeluxeRoom PictureBox object to False *(ref: Figure 3-37)*.

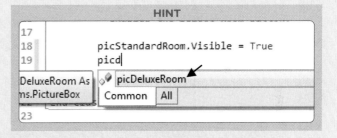

● **Enable the Select Room Button Object** The last task for the Standard Room button click event is to enable the Select Room button. Using IntelliSense, enter the Visual Basic code statement to set the Enabled property for the btnSelectRoom Button object to True *(ref: Figure 3-44)*.

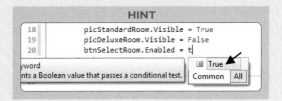

The lines of code are entered in the Standard Room Button object click event handler (Figure 3-74).

(continues)

Guided Program Development *continued*

The code will set the Visible property for the picStandardRoom PictureBox object to True, set the Visible property for the picDeluxeRoom PictureBox object to False, and set the Enabled property for the btnSelectRoom Button object to True.

RESULT OF STEP 7

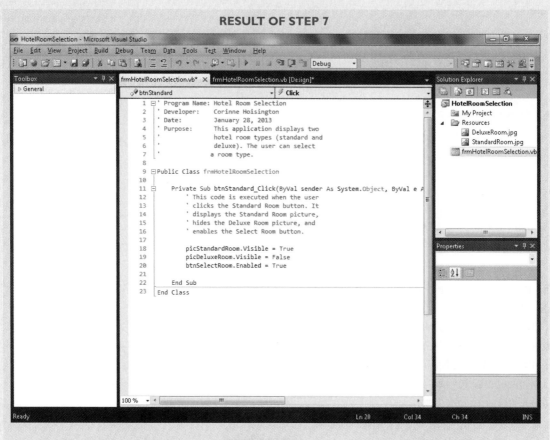

FIGURE 3-74

8

● **Run the Program** When the code for an event handler is complete, good practice dictates that you should run the program to ensure the event handler code works properly. Run the program. Click the Standard Room button.

When you click the Standard Room button, the Standard Room picture is displayed, the Deluxe Room picture is not displayed, and the Select Room button is enabled (Figure 3-75). These are the correct results. Note that if you click any of the other buttons in the window nothing happens. This is because you have not yet written the event handler code for these objects.

RESULT OF STEP 8

FIGURE 3-75

9

● **Display the Design Window** When the code for an event handler is completed, the next task is to write the code for another event handler. To do so, you must indicate the object for which the code will be written. You can do this on the Design tabbed page. Click the frmHotelRoomSelection.vb [Design] tab to return to the Design tabbed page.

HINT

● **Open the Code Editing Window for the btnSelectRoom Event Handler** You must open the code editing window for the btnSelectRoom Button object to enter code for the event handler. Double-click the Select Room button to open the code editing window for the btnSelectRoom_Click event *(ref: Figure 3-24)*.

HINT

● **Enter Event Handler Comments** When beginning the code for an event handler, the first step is to enter the event handler comments. Enter the comments that describe the processing in the btnSelectRoom_Click event handler.

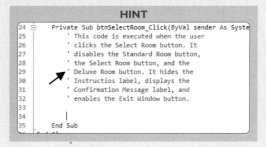

HINT

(continues)

● **Disable the btnStandardRoom Button Object** Referencing the event planning document (Figure 3-68 on page 158) the first task is to disable the Standard Room button. Using IntelliSense, enter the Visual Basic code statement to set the Enabled property for the btnStandardRoom Button object to False *(ref: Figure 3-42)*.

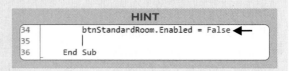

● **Disable the btnSelectRoom Button Object** The next task is to disable the Select Room button. Using IntelliSense, enter the Visual Basic code statement to set the Enabled property for the btnSelectRoom Button object to False *(ref: Figure 3-42)*.

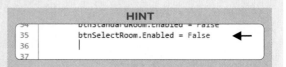

● **Disable the btnDeluxeRoom Button Object** Using IntelliSense, enter the Visual Basic code statement to set the Enabled property for the btnDeluxeRoom Button object to False *(ref: Figure 3-42)*.

● **Hide the Instructions Label Object** When the Select Room button is clicked, the instructions should not be displayed. Using IntelliSense, enter the Visual Basic code statement to set the Visible property for the lblInstructions Label object to False *(ref: Figure 3-29)*.

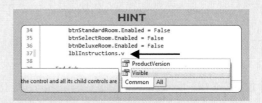

● **Display the Confirmation Message** The confirmation message must be displayed when the user clicks the Select Room button. Using IntelliSense, enter the Visual Basic code statement to set the Visible property for the lblConfirmationMessage Label object to True *(ref: Figure 3-29)*.

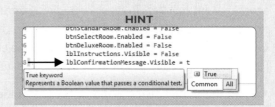

● **Enable the Exit Window Button** After the user clicks the Select Room button, the only allowable action is to click the Exit Window button and close the application. Therefore, the Exit Window button must be enabled. Using IntelliSense, enter the Visual Basic code statement to set the Enabled property for the btnExitWindow Button object to True *(ref: Figure 3-42)*.

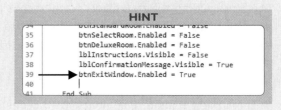

- **Run the Program** Run the program to ensure that it works correctly. Click the Standard Room button and then click the Select Room button.

After clicking the two buttons, the standard room picture is displayed; the Standard Room, Select Room, and Deluxe Room buttons are disabled; the Instructions label is not displayed; the Confirmation Message label is displayed; and the Exit Window button is enabled (Figure 3-76).

RESULT OF STEP 9

FIGURE 3-76

10

- **Display the Design Window** The next task is to write the code for the btnDeluxeRoom event handler. To return to the Design tabbed page so you can select the Deluxe Room button, click the frmHotelRoomSelection.vb [Design] tab.

- **Open the Code Editing Window for the btnDeluxeRoom Event Handler** Double-click the Deluxe Room button to open the code editing window for the btnDeluxeRoom_Click event *(ref: Figure 3-24)*.

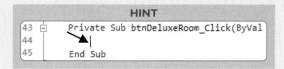

- **Enter the Event Handler Comments** Using the techniques you have learned, enter the comments that describe the processing in the btnDeluxeRoom_Click event handler.

- **Make the DeluxeRoom PictureBox Object Visible** By referencing the event planning document, you can see the first task is to make the Deluxe Room picture visible. Using IntelliSense, enter the Visual Basic code statement to set the Visible property for the picDeluxeRoom PictureBox object to True *(ref: Figure 3-29)*.

(continues)

Guided Program Development *continued*

● **Make the Standard Room Picture Not Visible** Using
IntelliSense, enter the Visual Basic code statement to set
the Visible property for the picStandardRoom PictureBox
object to False *(ref: Figure 3-29)*.

● **Enable the Select Room Button** Using IntelliSense,
enter the Visual Basic code statement to set the Enabled
property for the btnSelectRoom Button object to True
(ref: Figure 3-42).

● **Run the Program** Run the program and then click the
Deluxe Room button to ensure your code works correctly.

*The completed
code for the Select
Room button event
handler and the
Deluxe Room
button event
handler is shown
in Figure 3-77.*

FIGURE 3-77

When you click the Deluxe Room button, the Deluxe Room picture is displayed, the Standard Room picture is not displayed, and the Select Room button is enabled (Figure 3-78). The program is working properly.

**RESULT OF STEP 10
(PROGRAM EXECUTION)**

FIGURE 3-78

11

● **Display the Design Window** Click the frmHotelRoom-Selection.vb [Design] tab to return to the Design tabbed page.

● **Open the Code Editing Window for the btnExitWindow Event Handler** Double-click the Exit Window button to open the code editing window for the btnExitWindow_Click event *(ref: Figure 3-24)*.

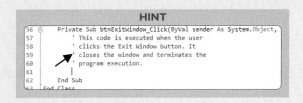

● **Enter the Event Handler Comments** Using the techniques you have learned, enter the comments that describe the processing in the btnExitWindow_Click event handler.

● **Enter the Close() Procedure Call** Using IntelliSense, enter the Visual Basic code statement to close the window and terminate the program *(ref: Figure 3-66)*.

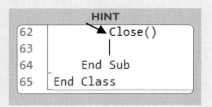

(continues)

*The Close()
procedure call
statement
is entered
(Figure 3-79).
When the proce-
dure call is
executed, the
application will
be closed.*

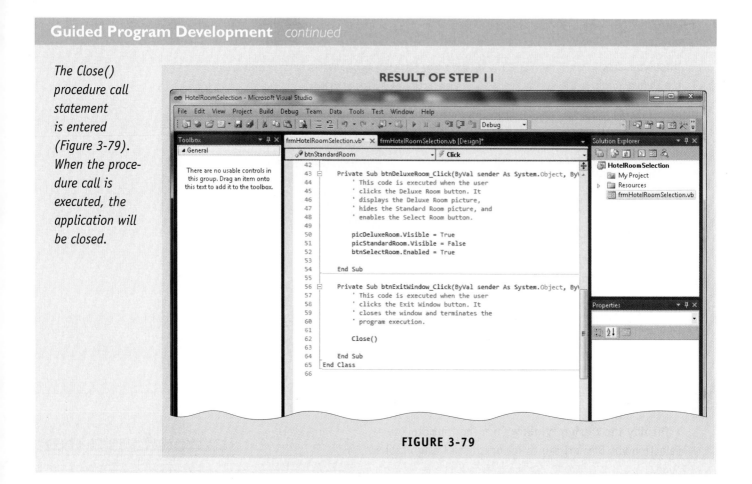

RESULT OF STEP 11

FIGURE 3-79

12

● **Run the Program** Run the program to ensure that it works correctly: 1. Click the Standard Room button; 2. Click the Deluxe Room button; 3. Click the Standard Room button; 4. Click the Select Room button; 5. Click the Exit Window button.

Code Listing

The complete code for the sample program is shown in Figure 3-80.

```vbnet
 1 ☐' Program Name: Hotel Room Selection
 2  ' Developer:      Corinne Hoisington
 3  ' Date:           January 28, 2013
 4  ' Purpose:        This application displays two
 5  '                 hotel room types (standard and
 6  '                 deluxe). The user can select
 7  '                 a room type.
 8
 9 ☐Public Class frmHotelRoomSelection
10
11 ☐    Private Sub btnStandardRoom_Click(ByVal sender As System.Object, ByVal e As System.EventArgs) Handles btnStandardRoom.Click
12          ' This code is executed when the user
13          ' clicks the Standard Room button. It
14          ' displays the Standard Room picture,
15          ' hides the Deluxe Room picture, and
16          ' enables the Select Room button.
17
18          picStandardRoom.Visible = True
19          picDeluxeRoom.Visible = False
20          btnSelectRoom.Enabled = True
21
22      End Sub
23
24 ☐    Private Sub btnSelectRoom_Click(ByVal sender As System.Object, ByVal e As System.EventArgs) Handles btnSelectRoom.Click
25          ' This code is executed when the user
26          ' clicks the Select Room button. It
27          ' disables the Standard Room button,
28          ' the Select Room button, and the
29          ' Deluxe Room button. It hides the
30          ' Instructios label, displays the
31          ' Confirmation Message label, and
32          ' enables the Exit Window button.
33
34          btnStandardRoom.Enabled = False
35          btnSelectRoom.Enabled = False
36          btnDeluxeRoom.Enabled = False
37          lblInstructions.Visible = False
38          lblConfirmationMessage.Visible = True
39          btnExitWindow.Enabled = True
40
41      End Sub
42
43 ☐    Private Sub btnDeluxeRoom_Click(ByVal sender As System.Object, ByVal e As System.EventArgs) Handles btnDeluxeRoom.Click
44          ' This code is executed when the user
45          ' clicks the Deluxe Room button. It
46          ' displays the Deluxe Room picture,
47          ' hides the Standard Room picture, and
48          ' enables the Select Room button.
49
50          picDeluxeRoom.Visible = True
51          picStandardRoom.Visible = False
52          btnSelectRoom.Enabled = True
53
54      End Sub
55
56 ☐    Private Sub btnExitWindow_Click(ByVal sender As System.Object, ByVal e As System.EventArgs) Handles btnExitWindow.Click
57          ' This code is executed when the user
58          ' clicks the Exit Window button. It
59          ' closes the window and terminates the
60          ' program execution.
61
62          Close()
63
64      End Sub
65 End Class
```

FIGURE 3-80

Summary

In this chapter you have learned to fine-tune a graphical user interface to maximize its usefulness and to enter code for object event handlers.

The items listed in the table in Figure 3-81 include all the new Visual Studio and Visual Basic skills you have learned in this chapter.

Visual Basic Skills		
Skill	Figure Number	Web Address for Video
Set the BackColor property	Figure 3-2	scsite.com/vb2010/ch3/figure3-2
Locate and Save an Image from the World Wide Web	Figure 3-7	scsite.com/vb2010/ch3/figure3-7
Import an Image into the Program Resources Folder	Figure 3-11	scsite.com/vb2010/ch3/figure3-11
Size an Image	Figure 3-16	scsite.com/vb2010/ch3/figure3-16
Set the Visible Property in the Properties Window	Figure 3-18	scsite.com/vb2010/ch3/figure3-18
Set the Enabled Property in the Properties Window	Figure 3-20	scsite.com/vb2010/ch3/figure3-20
Run a Visual Basic 2010 Program	Figure 3-22	scsite.com/vb2010/ch3/figure3-22
Enter Visual Basic 2010 Code for Event Handling	Figure 3-24	scsite.com/vb2010/ch3/figure3-24
Enter a Visual Basic 2010 Statement using IntelliSense	Figure 3-29	scsite.com/vb2010/ch3/figure3-29
Enter a Visual Basic 2010 Statement to Set the Visible Property to True	Figure 3-29	scsite.com/vb2010/ch3/figure3-29
Enter a Visual Basic 2010 Statement to Set the Visible Property to False	Figure 3-37	scsite.com/vb2010/ch3/figure3-37
Enter a Visual Basic 2010 Statement to Set the Enabled Property to True	Figure 3-42	scsite.com/vb2010/ch3/figure3-42
Enter Comments in Visual Basic 2010 Code	Figure 3-47	scsite.com/vb2010/ch3/figure3-47
Enter Introductory Comments in Visual Basic 2010 Code	Figure 3-52	scsite.com/vb2010/ch3/figure3-52
Correct Errors in a Visual Basic 2010 Program	Figure 3-58	scsite.com/vb2010/ch3/figure3-58
Enter a Close() Statement into Visual Basic 2010 Code	Figure 3-66	scsite.com/vb2010/ch3/figure3-66
Print Code	Pages 156–157	

FIGURE 3-81

Learn It Online

Start your browser and visit scsite.com/vb2010/ch3. Follow the instructions in the exercises below.

1. **Chapter Reinforcement TF, MC, SA** Click one of the Chapter Reinforcement links for Multiple Choice, True/False, or Short Answer below the Learn It Online heading. Answer each question and submit to your instructor.

2. **Practice Test** Click the Practice Test link. Answer each question, enter your first and last name at the bottom of the page, and then click the Grade Test button. When the graded practice test is displayed on your screen, submit the graded practice test to your instructor. Continue to take the practice test until you are satisfied with your score.

3. **Crossword Puzzle Challenge** Click the Crossword Puzzle Challenge link below the Learn It Online heading. Read the instructions, and then click the Continue button. Work the crossword puzzle. When you are finished, click the Submit button. When the crossword puzzle is redisplayed, submit it to your instructor.

Knowledge Check

1. Which property controls the background color of the Form object?

2. Which property controls the background color of a Button object?

3. Which color palette is guaranteed to be displayed properly on every computer?

4. What is the use of the Image property for a PictureBox object?

5. To display an image in a PictureBox object in your application, you first must store the image in which folder within the application?

6. When you click the Ellipsis button for the Image property of a PictureBox object (Figure 3-82), what action does Visual Studio 2010 take?

FIGURE 3-82

7. What is the default setting of the PictureBox object SizeMode property?

8. Which option in the SizeMode property should be selected to make the image fit within the PictureBox object?

9. Which property has been set to False if a Button object in a window is dimmed when program execution begins?

(continues)

10. Which property has been set to False if a PictureBox object is not displayed when you run the application?

11. What two options can you select for the Visible property in the Properties window?

12. Write a line of code that would set the Visible property for a PictureBox object named picHomeTown to False.

13. Write a line of code that would set the Enabled property for a Button object named btnStart to True.

14. Write a line of code that would set the Visible property for a Label object named lblDisplayTuition to True.

15. Write a comment line of code that states, "The following code displays the image".

16. What color text is used to display comments in the code editing window of Visual Basic 2010?

17. Write a line of code that will close an application window and terminate the application.

18. What does a blue squiggly line mean in the code editing window?

19. Why is it best that you use IntelliSense when you enter code in the code editing window? List two reasons.

20. Which symbol is associated with the assignment statement?

Debugging Exercises

1. Fix the following line of code to set the Visible property for the picCompanyLogo PictureBox object to True.

```
picCompanyLogo.Visible.True
```

2. Fix the following line of code to disable the btnExitProgram Button object.

```
btnExitProgram.Enabled = No
```

3. Fix the following line of code to set the Visible property for the lblDirections Label object to False.

```
lblDirections.Visible = ' False
```

4. Fix the following comment line of code.

```
The ' following line of code makes the college logo visible
```

5. Fix the following line of code.

```
Close
```

6. Examine the code window and the Error List window in Figure 3-83. Then, write a line of code to replace the line of code in error.

FIGURE 3-83

Program Analysis

1. For a bakery application shown in Figure 3-84, write the Visual Basic 2010 coding statement to view the cake picture when the user clicks the btnView button, assuming the Visible property for the picCake PictureBox object had been set to False in the Properties window.

FIGURE 3-84

2. Which property in the Properties window controls whether the btnPlaceOrder button is dimmed when the program begins execution? Which option for the property would you select to cause the button to be dimmed when the program begins execution?

3. When you import the picture of the cake into the Resources folder and select the image for use in the pic-Cake PictureBox object, which SizeMode property option would you select to view the complete picture?

4. Write the Visual Basic 2010 coding statement for the btnView click event that would cause the btnPlaceOrder button to be active (not dimmed).

5. To make the window background color White as shown in Figure 3-84, what property should you modify?

6. What property is used to cause the text, Birthday Cake Order Form, to be displayed in the window title bar?

7. What procedure should be used to close the window and terminate the application when the user clicks the Place Order button?

Case Programming Assignments

Complete one or more of the following case programming assignments. Submit the program and materials you create to your instructor. The level of difficulty is indicated for each case programming assignment.

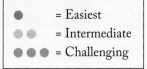

● = Easiest
●● = Intermediate
●●● = Challenging

1 ●

EUROPEAN HOSTEL SELECTION

Based on the Windows form mock-up you created in Chapter 2, complete the Hostel Location Selection program by changing the window background color, downloading and adding the images, and writing the code that will execute according to the program requirements. Before writing the code, create an event planning document for each event in the program. The completed Windows Form object and the other objects in the user interface are shown in Figure 3-87a, Figure 3-87b, and Figure 3-87c.

REQUIREMENTS DOCUMENT

Date submitted: January 17, 2013

Application title: Vacation Hostel Location Selection

Purpose: The hostel selection application will allow a user to select the location in London or Dublin.

Program Procedures: From a window on the screen, the user should identify a hostel location (London or Dublin) and then indicate the location of the hostel.

Algorithms, Processing and Conditions:
1. The user must be able to identify the London or Dublin hostel, back and forth until the selection is made.
2. When the user identifies the hostel location, a picture of that hostel should appear in the window.
3. Only one picture should be displayed at a time. If a user identifies the London hostel, only the London hostel picture should be displayed; if a user identifies the Dublin hostel, only the Dublin hostel picture should be displayed.
4. When the user makes a hostel selection, a message stating that the selection of a hostel location has been made should be displayed. In addition, the user should be stopped from identifying a hostel location after the hostel selection has been made.
5. After the user makes a hostel selection, the only allowable action is to exit the window.

Notes and Restrictions:
1. A user cannot make a hostel selection until he or she has identified a hostel location.

Comments:
1. The pictures shown in the window can be found on scsite.com/vb2010/ch3/ images. The names of the pictures are LondonHostel and DublinHostel.

FIGURE 3-85

(continues)

European Hostel Selection (continued)

USE CASE DEFINITION

1. User clicks London hostel button or Dublin hostel button.
2. Program displays a picture of the hostel identified by the user and enables the hostel selection button.
3. User clicks hostel buttons to view hostel locations if desired. Program displays the picture of the identified hostel.
4. User clicks the Select Location button.
5. Program displays a hostel selection confirmation message, and disables both hostel buttons and the Select Location button. The Exit Window button becomes active.
6. User terminates the program by clicking the Exit Window button.

FIGURE 3-86

In Figure 3-87a, no button has been clicked. In Figure 3-87b, the user has clicked the Dublin Hostel button. In Figure 3-87c, the user has clicked the Select Location button.

background color is Beige

picture boxes not visible

button background color is Moccasin

buttons dimmed

selected message not visible

FIGURE 3-87a

Dublin hostel image is displayed

Select Location button is active

Dublin Hostel button clicked

FIGURE 3-87b

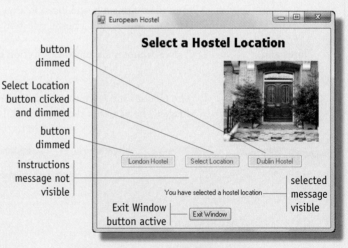

button dimmed

Select Location button clicked and dimmed

button dimmed

instructions message not visible

Exit Window button active

selected message visible

FIGURE 3-87c

2

BANKING

Based on the Windows form mock-up you created in Chapter 2, complete the Banking program by changing the window background color, downloading and adding the image, and writing the code that will execute according to the program requirements. Before writing the code, create an event planning document for each event in the program. The completed Windows Form object and the other objects in the user interface are shown in Figure 3-90a and Figure 3-90b.

REQUIREMENTS DOCUMENT

Date submitted: January 14, 2013

Application title: Bank Welcome Screen with Banking Hours

Purpose: This application displays a welcome screen for the First Corner National Bank. The user can choose an option to view the hours of the bank.

Program Procedures: From a window on the screen, the user makes a request to see the bank's open hours.

Algorithms, Processing, and Conditions:

1. The user first views a welcome screen that displays the bank's name (First Corner National Bank), bank picture, and a phrase that states the bank is FDIC insured.
2. When the user opts to view the bank hours, the following hours are displayed:

Monday–Thursday	9:00AM – 5:00PM
Friday	9:00AM – 8:00PM
Saturday	9:00AM – 1:00PM

3. After the user views the hours, the only allowable action is to exit the window.

Notes and Restrictions: n/a

Comments:

1. The picture shown in the window can be found on scsite.com/vb2010/ch3/images. The name of the picture is BankBuilding.

FIGURE 3-88

(continues)

Case Programming Assignments

Banking (continued)

USE CASE DEFINITION

1. The window opens, displaying the title of the bank, the bank's picture, and a message that the bank is FDIC insured. The View Banking Hours button and the Exit Window button are enabled.
2. User clicks View Banking Hours button.
3. Program displays the banking hours above the buttons. The View Banking Hours button is disabled.
4. User clicks the Exit Window button to terminate the application.

FIGURE 3-89

In Figure 3-90a, no button has been clicked. In Figure 3-90b, the user has clicked the View Banking Hours button.

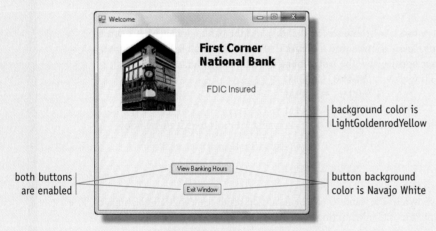

FIGURE 3-90a

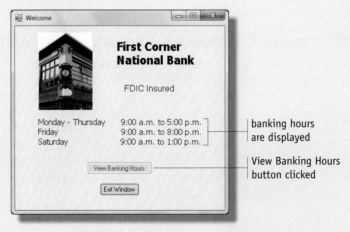

FIGURE 3-90b

3

VISUAL BASIC 2010 TERMS

Based on the Windows form mock-up you created in Chapter 2, complete the Visual Basic 2010 Terms program by changing the window background color, downloading and adding the image, and writing the code that will execute according to the program requirements. Before writing the code, create an event planning document for each event in the program. The completed Windows Form object and the other objects in the user interface are shown in Figure 3-93a and Figure 3-93b.

REQUIREMENTS DOCUMENT

Date submitted: August 16, 2013

Application title: Visual Basic 2010 Terms

Purpose: This application displays the definitions of common Visual Basic terms. When the user chooses to view the definition, the term's definition is displayed.

Program Procedures: From a window on the screen, the user makes a request to see one of three VB definitions.

Algorithms, Processing, and Conditions:
1. The user first views a screen that displays three VB terms.
2. An image of a computer is displayed at the top of the window throughout the running of the application.
3. The user can select any of the three terms displayed on the buttons, and the definition appears after each selection is made.
4. The user can click any of the terminology buttons and the definition will appear. Any previous definitions will disappear.
5. An exit button is available at all times allowing the user to end the application.

Notes and Restrictions:
1. Only one definition should be displayed at a time, so if a user selects a second term, the second definition only should be displayed.

Comments:
1. The computer picture shown in the window can be found on scsite.com/vb2010/ch3/images. The name of the picture is Computer.

FIGURE 3-91

(continues)

Visual Basic 2010 Terms (continued)

USE CASE DEFINITION

1. The window opens and displays a computer image, the title (Visual Basic 2010 Terms), three buttons labeled with VB terms, and an Exit Window button. The Exit Window button is enabled.
2. User clicks each of the terminology buttons to review the definitions.
3. Program displays the definitions to the right of the buttons.
4. Only one definition shows at a time.
5. User clicks the Exit Window button to terminate the application.

FIGURE 3-92

In Figure 3-93a, no button has been clicked. In Figure 3-93b, the user has clicked the Developer button.

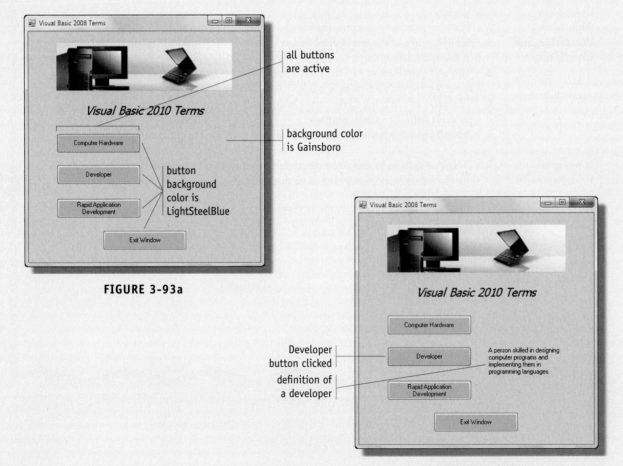

FIGURE 3-93a

FIGURE 3-93b

4 ●●
ONLINE STORE SPECIALS

Based on the Windows form mock-up you created in Chapter 2, complete the Online Store Specials program by finishing the user interface, downloading and adding the images, and writing the code that will execute according to the program requirements. Before writing the code, create an event planning document for each event in the program.

REQUIREMENTS DOCUMENT

Date submitted: January 6, 2014

Application title: Online Store Specials

Purpose: The online store specials program will display the daily, weekly, and holiday specials of the online store. The user can select the desired product and then add the product to the shopping cart.

Program Procedures: From a window on the screen, the user should select the daily special, the weekly special, or the holiday special. When a special is selected, the program should display a picture of the special product, the regular price of the product, and the special price of the product. The user should be able to select any special. Then, the user can add the product to the shopping cart.

Algorithms, Processing, and Conditions:
1. The user must select a special in order to display the special's product picture, regular price, and sales price.
2. The user cannot add a product to the shopping cart until a special is selected.
3. When a special is selected, only that special's picture and prices should be displayed in the window. No other special should be displayed.
4. After the user selects a special and adds it to the shopping cart, the only allowable user action is to exit the window.
5. A user should be able to exit the window at any time.

Notes and Restrictions: n/a

Comments:
1. The specials are: Daily Special: Cell Phone: Regular Price: $99.95; Special Price: $84.50
    Weekly Special: iPod Shuffle: Regular Price: $39.95: Special Price: $29.95
    Holiday Special: Digital Camera: Regular Price: $259.95; Special Price: $203.19
2. The pictures shown in the window can be found on scsite.com/vb2010/images. The names of the pictures are CellPhone, iPod, and DigitalCamera.

FIGURE 3-94

5

RAFFLE PRIZE SELECTION

Based on the Windows form mock-up you created in Chapter 2, complete the Raffle Prize Selection program by finishing the user interface, downloading and adding the images, and writing the code that will execute according to the program requirements. Before writing the code, create an event planning document for each event in the program.

REQUIREMENTS DOCUMENT

Date submitted: March 21, 2013

Application title: Raffle Prize Selection

Purpose: Your school has started selling raffle tickets for a scholarship fund that provides the winner a choice of raffle gifts. The winner can choose one of three prizes. So they can choose, the program must display each of the prizes upon request of the raffle winner. The winner then can make the choice of the prize he or she would like to receive.

Program Procedures: From a window on the screen, the user selects one of three raffle prizes. A picture of the prize is displayed in the window. The user then can choose the prize he or she wants to receive.

Algorithms, Processing, and Conditions:
1. The user selects a prize. Then, a picture of the prize is displayed in the window.
2. The user can select any of the three prizes. Only the picture for the selected prize should be displayed.
3. The user can select prizes back and forth to see the pictures for the prizes.
4. After the user finds a prize he or she wants, the user chooses that prize for delivery.
5. After the user chooses a prize, a message stating that a raffle prize has been chosen should be displayed.
6. After the user chooses a prize, the only allowable action is to exit the window.

Notes and Restrictions:
1. The user should not be able to choose a prize until they have viewed the picture of at least one raffle prize.

Comments:
1. The raffle prizes available are a gas grill, a flat-screen television, and a laptop.
2. The pictures shown in the window can be found on scsite.com/vb2010/ch3/ images. The names of the pictures are Grill, TV, and Laptop.

FIGURE 3-95

6 ●● SONG VOTING

Based on the Windows form mock-up you created in Chapter 2, complete the Song Voting program by finishing the user interface, downloading and adding the images, and writing the code that will execute according to the program requirements. Before writing the code, create an event planning document for each event in the program.

REQUIREMENTS DOCUMENT

Date submitted: February 22, 2013

Application title: Song Voting

Purpose: In your mall, a music store named "Millennium Music" wants a program that shows the #1 song in each of three music genres and allows the user to vote for his or her overall favorite. The user should be able to select one of three genres and then be able to vote for that song/genre as the user's overall favorite.

Program Procedures: From a window on the screen, the user selects one of three music genres. The name of the #1 song in the selected genre is displayed together with a picture of the artist or band for the song. Then, the user can vote for that song/genre as their overall favorite.

Algorithms, Processing, and Conditions:
1. The user selects a music genre. Then, the #1 song title in the genre and picture of the artist or band is displayed in the window.
2. The user can select any of the three music genres. Only the name of the song and the picture for the selected genre should be displayed.
3. The user can select music genres back and forth to see the #1 song for each genre and the associated artist or band.
4. After the user selects a genre, the user should be able to vote for that genre/song as the favorite. The user cannot vote until the user has selected a genre.
5. After the user votes, a message stating that voting has occurred should be displayed.
6. After the user votes, the only allowable action is to exit the window.

Notes and Restrictions:
1. The user should not be able to vote until he or she has selected a music genre.

Comments:
1. You (the developer) should select the three music genres and the #1 song for each of the genres.
2. The pictures of the artist or the band will depend on your selection of both the music genres and the #1 song in each of the genres. You should download a picture of the artist or band from the World Wide Web. You can search anywhere on the Web for the pictures. You will find that www.google.com/images is a good source.

FIGURE 3-96

Case Programming Assignments

7 ●●● ENGLISH-TO-SPANISH TRANSLATOR

Based on the problem definition (Figure 3-97) and the Windows form mock-up you created in Chapter 2, complete the English-to-Spanish translator program by finishing the user interface, downloading and adding any required images, and writing the code that will execute according to the program requirements. Before writing the code, create an event planning document for each event in the program.

The Bonita Travel Agency would like to create an English-to-Spanish translator of the most commonly used Spanish words for those booking a trip to a Spanish-speaking destination. Develop a Windows application for the Bonita Travel Spanish Translator. The English phrase should be displayed in the window. When the user selects an English phrase, the corresponding Spanish translation is displayed. Only one Spanish translation should be displayed at any given time. The user should be able to exit the window at any time.

English	Spanish Translation
Good morning	Buenos días
Thank you	Gracias
Goodbye	Adiós
Money	Dinero

FIGURE 3-97

Case Programming Assignments

8 ●●●
TRAVEL SPECIALS

Based on the problem definition (Figure 3-98) and the Windows form mock-up you created in Chapter 2, complete the Travel Specials program by finishing the user interface, downloading and adding any required images, and writing the code that will execute according to the program requirements. Before writing the code, create an event planning document for each event in the program.

Your local travel agent would like a computer application to advertise the travel specials of the week from your city. This week's flight specials are:

Destination	Price
Orlando	$199 round trip
Las Vegas	$219 round trip
New Orleans	$320 round trip
Aruba	$520 round trip
Hawaii	$728 round trip

Write an application that will allow the user to select any of the five vacation destinations. When the user selects a vacation destination, the corresponding price and a picture of the destination should be displayed. Clear each prior price and picture when the user selects a different vacation destination. In addition to a picture of the destination, include a Web page address that features the selected location. After the user has selected a destination, the user should be able to book the vacation and then exit the window.

FIGURE 3-98

Case Programming Assignments

9 ●●● FOOTBALL TICKETS

Based on the problem definition (Figure 3-99) and the Windows form mock-up you created in Chapter 2, complete the Football Tickets program by finishing the user interface, downloading and adding any required images, and writing the code that will execute according to the program requirements. Before writing the code, create an event planning document for each event in the program.

Your favorite university football team has asked you to develop a Windows application that allows the user to see the four types of seat ticket types offered, one at a time. Then, the user should be able to reserve a single game ticket for the seat type. The four types of stadium seating and their base prices are as follows:

Name of Service	Minimum Price
Upper Endzone Seating	$75.00
Lower Endzone Seating	$100.00
Sideline seating	$150.00
Club Seats	$500.00

For each type of seating, your program should display the base price and a picture depicting an example of the seating type. Clear each seating price and picture when the user selects a different seating type. After the user has selected a ticket, the user should be able to purchase the ticket and then exit the window.

FIGURE 3-99

CHAPTER 4

Variables and Arithmetic Operations

OBJECTIVES

You will have mastered the material in this chapter when you can:

- Create, modify, and program a TextBox object

- Use code to place data in the Text property of a Label object

- Use the AcceptButton and CancelButton properties

- Understand and declare String and Numeric variables

- Use assignments statements to place data in variables

- Use literals and constants in coding statements

- Understand scope rules for variables

- Convert string and numeric data

- Understand and use arithmetic operators and arithmetic operations

- Format and display numeric data as a string

- Create a form load event

- Create a concatenated string

- Debug a program

Introduction

In the Hotel Room Selection program developed in Chapter 2 and Chapter 3, when the user clicked buttons in the user interface, events were triggered; but the user did not enter data. In many applications, users must enter data and then the program uses the data in its processing.

When processing data entered by a user, a common requirement is to perform arithmetic operations on the data in order to generate useful output information. Arithmetic operations include adding, subtracting, multiplying, and dividing numeric data.

To illustrate the use of user data input and arithmetic operations, the application in this chapter allows the user to enter the number of songs to be downloaded from the World Wide Web. The application then calculates the total cost of the downloads. The user interface for the program is shown in Figure 4-1.

FIGURE 4-1

In Figure 4-1, the user entered 5 as the number of songs to download. When the user clicked the Calculate Cost button, the program multiplied 5 times the cost per song (99 cents) and then displayed the result as the total cost of downloads. When the user clicks the Clear button, the values for the number of song downloads and the total cost of downloads are cleared so the next user can enter a value. Clicking the Exit button closes the window and terminates the program.

To create this application, the developer must understand how to perform the following processes, among others:

1. Define a text box for data entry.
2. Define a label to hold the results of arithmetic operations.
3. Convert data in a text box to data that can be used for arithmetic operations.
4. Perform arithmetic operations on data a user enters.

The following pages describe the tools and techniques required to create the program shown in Figure 4-1.

User Interface

As you have learned in Chapter 2 and Chapter 3, after the program requirements document for an application has been completed, the first step is to define the graphical user interface. In this chapter, three new elements are introduced:

1. TextBox objects
2. Labels intended for variable text property values
3. Accept buttons

Each of these elements is described in the following sections:

TextBox Objects

A **TextBox object** allows users to enter data into a program. In Figure 4-2, the user can enter a value into the text box.

FIGURE 4-2

In Figure 4-2, the TextBox object is placed on the Windows Form object. A TextBox object automatically allows the user to enter data into the text box. To place a TextBox object on the Windows Form object, you can complete the steps on the following pages. (Note: The examples in this chapter illustrate new objects in the user interface. Portions of the user interface have already been completed. You should not expect to "click along" with these examples unless you create these elements or unless you follow the steps using an unformatted user interface.)

STEP 1   With Visual Studio open and the frmDigitalDownloads.vb [Design] tabbed page visible, point to the TextBox .NET component in the Toolbox.

The TextBox .NET component is highlighted in the Toolbox (Figure 4–3).

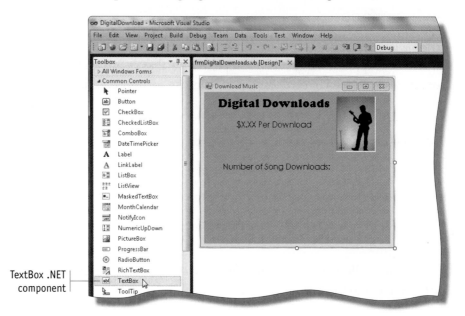

FIGURE 4-3

STEP 2   Drag the TextBox .NET component onto the Windows Form object at the desired location.

While you drag, the mouse pointer changes to indicate a TextBox object will be placed on the Windows Form object (Figure 4–4). Snap lines indicate where the TextBox object aligns with other objects on the Windows Form object. In Figure 4–4, the top of the TextBox object aligns with the top of the Label object. When adding a TextBox object to the Windows Form object, top alignment often provides a good beginning position.

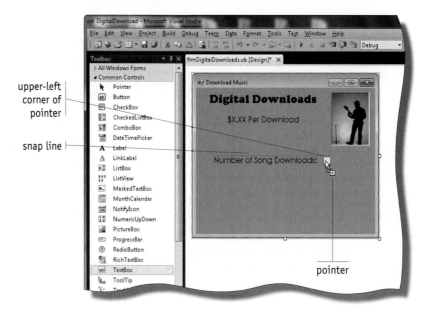

FIGURE 4-4

STEP 3   When the upper-left corner of the pointer is located where you want the TextBox object's upper-left corner, release the left mouse button.

Visual Studio places the TextBox object at the location identified by the mouse pointer (Figure 4-5). The default size of the TextBox object is 100 pixels wide by 20 pixels high. Notice that by default the TextBox object contains no text. You can change that by entering text in the Text property of the TextBox object.

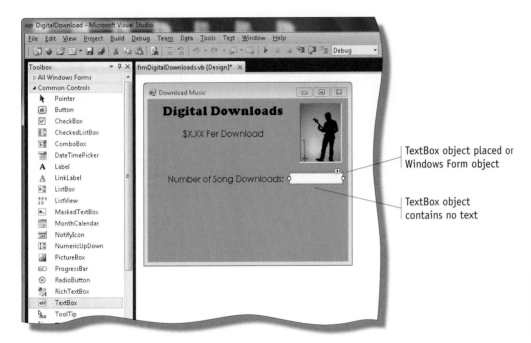

TextBox object placed or Windows Form object

TextBox object contains no text

FIGURE 4-5

ONLINE REINFORCEMENT

To view a video of the process in the previous steps, visit scsite.com/vb2010/ch4 and then select Figure 4-3.

As you have learned, whenever you place an object on the Windows Form object, you must name the object. When naming a TextBox object, the prefix should be txt. Therefore, the name of the TextBox object in Figure 4-5 could be txtNumberOfDownloads.

Sizing and Positioning a TextBox Object

To properly place a TextBox object on the Windows Form object, you need to know the minimum and maximum size of the text box. The minimum size of the text box normally is determined by the maximum number of characters the user will enter into the text box. For example, if in the sample program the maximum number of downloads the user should order is 999, the minimum size of the text box must be large enough to display three numbers. Although it can be larger, it should not be smaller.

The maximum size of the text box often is determined by the design of the user interface; that is, the size should look and feel good in the user interface. To determine the minimum size of the text box, you can use the technique on the following pages:

STEP 1 Select the TextBox object. Select the (Name) property and name the TextBox object txtNumberOfDownloads. Scroll in the Properties window until the Text property is visible and then click the right column for the Text property.

The TextBox object is selected, as shown by the thick border and sizing handles (Figure 4-6). The Textbox object is named txtNumberOfDownloads. The Text property for the TextBox object is highlighted and the insertion point indicates you can enter text for the Text property.

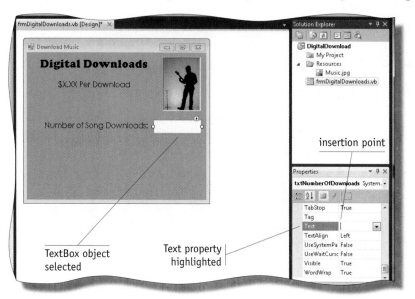

FIGURE 4-6

STEP 2 Type the maximum number of characters the user normally will enter into the text box and then press the ENTER key. When entering numbers, the digit 8 often is entered because it is wider than other digits. In this example, the value 888 is entered because three digits is the maximum number of digits the user normally will enter.

When the value is entered in the Text property of the TextBox object, the value is displayed in the TextBox object (Figure 4-7).

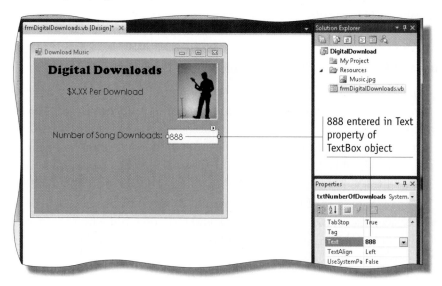

FIGURE 4-7

STEP 3 Using the Font property in the Properties window, change the Font property to the correct font and font size. For this application, change the font to Century Gothic and change the font size to 12. Then, drag the right edge of the TextBox object to resize the TextBox object so it is slightly wider than the 888 entry.

As you drag, the size of the TextBox object changes (Figure 4-8). When you release the left mouse button, the text box will be resized. When the font size is changed, the horizontal alignment of the text will change.

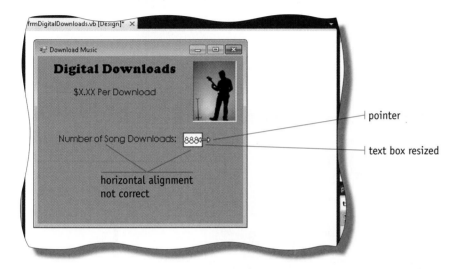

FIGURE 4-8

STEP 4 To horizontally align the text in the label and the text in the text box, drag the text box up until a red snap line indicates the bottoms of the text are aligned (Figure 4-9). Then, release the left mouse button.

When you drag the TextBox object, the red snap line indicates when the bottoms of the text are aligned (Figure 4-9). When you release the left mouse button, the TextBox object will be placed so the bottoms of the text are aligned.

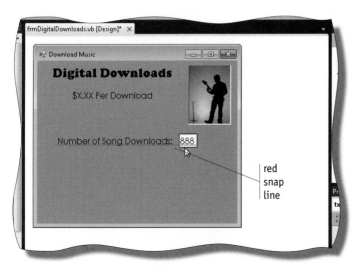

FIGURE 4-9

ONLINE REINFORCEMENT

To view a video of the process in the previous steps, visit scsite.com/vb2010/ch4 and then select Figure 4-6.

Aligning Text in a TextBox Object

In Figure 4-9, the numbers are left-aligned in the text box. Often, the user interface will be more useful if the value the user enters is centered in the text box. To align the text in a TextBox object, you can use the following method:

STEP 1   Select the TextBox object. In the Properties window, scroll until the TextAlign property is visible, click the TextAlign property in the left column, and then click the list arrow in the right column of the TextAlign property.

The TextAlign property list contains the values Left, Right, and Center (Figure 4-10).

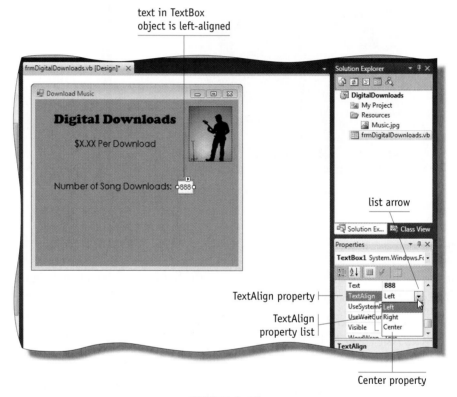

FIGURE 4-10

STEP 2 Click Center in the TextAlign property list.

The text in the TextBox object is centered (Figure 4-11). When a user enters data into the text box, the text also will be centered.

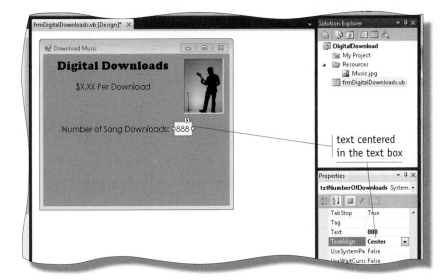

FIGURE 4-11

STEP 3 Because the TextBox object is sized properly, remove the digits in the TextBox object. Select the characters 888 in the Text property, press the DELETE key on your keyboard, and then press the ENTER key.

The TextBox object contains no text and is ready for use in the user interface (Figure 4-12).

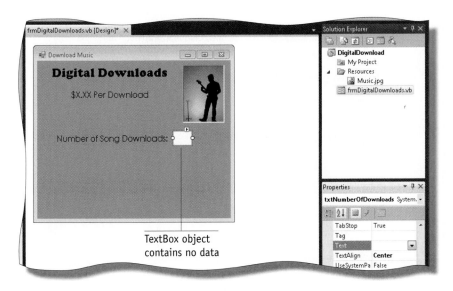

FIGURE 4-12

ONLINE REINFORCEMENT

To view a video of the process in the previous steps, visit scsite.com/vb2010/ch4 and then select Figure 4-10.

Entering Data in a TextBox Object

When the program is executed, the user can enter data in the text box. Users can enter both numbers and characters. In a text box, the user can enter many characters even though the program expects to find only a few. If the user enters more characters than can be displayed in the text box, the characters already entered scroll to the left and no longer are visible. A text box does not contain a scroll bar, so if a user enters more characters than can be visible in the text box, the user must move the insertion point left or right with the arrow keys on the keyboard to view the data in the text box. In most situations, a user should not enter more characters than are expected, and the text box should be designed to display all the characters that are expected.

In a default text box, only a single line of text can be entered regardless of the number of characters entered. A special option for a text box can be selected to allow the user to enter multiple lines of text. Additionally, the MaskedTextBox object can be used to control the format of the data a user enters. These types of text boxes are explained in the following sections.

Creating a MultiLine Text Box

A MultiLine text box allows the user to enter multiple lines in the text box. The TextBox object must be resized vertically to display the multiple lines. To create a TextBox object that can accept multiple lines, you can complete the following step:

STEP 1   Select the TextBox object, click the Action tag, and point to the MultiLine check box.

The TextBox Tasks list is displayed with the MultiLine check box (Figure 4-13). When you click the MultiLine check box, the TextBox object will be able to accept multiple lines.

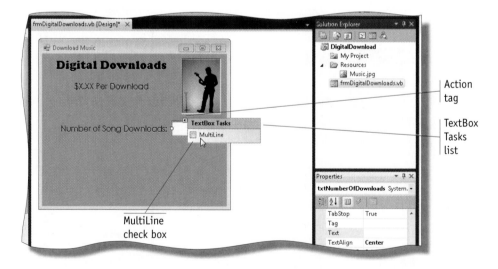

FIGURE 4-13

STEP 2 Click the MultiLine check box.

The text box is enabled to accept multiple lines.

ONLINE REINFORCEMENT

To view a video of the process in the previous steps, visit scsite.com/vb2010/ch4 and then select Figure 4-13.

In addition to enabling multiple lines, you should increase the vertical size of the TextBox object so the multiple lines will be visible when the user enters them.

Creating a MaskedTextBox Object

The MaskedTextBox object allows you to specify the data format of the value typed into the text box. Using the MaskedTextBox object removes confusion concerning what format should be used for the data the user enters. The term, mask, refers to a predefined layout for the data a user must enter. Figure 4-14 shows three examples of the use of the MaskedTextBox for the Short date input mask, the Phone number input mask, and the Social Security number input mask.

Prior to Data Entry

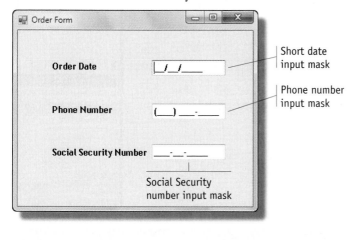

After Data Entry

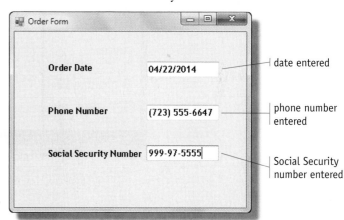

FIGURE 4-14

In Figure 4-14, before the user enters data the mask demonstrates to the user the format of the data to be entered. To enter data, the user merely selects the text box and then types data into the text box. The user need not enter any punctuation or any spacing. Therefore, to enter the date in the Order Date text box, the user typed 04222012, with no spaces, punctuation, or other keystrokes. Similarly, for the phone number, the user typed 7235556647, again with no spaces or other keystrokes. For the Social Security number, the user typed 999975555.

ONLINE REINFORCEMENT

To view a video of the process in the previous figure, visit scsite.com/vb2010/ch4 and then select Figure 4-14.

To place a MaskedTextBox object on the Windows Form object, you can complete the following steps:

STEP 1   Drag a MaskedTextBox .NET component from the Toolbox to the Windows Form object. Then, click the Action tag on the TextBox object and point to the Set Mask command.

The MaskedTextBox object is placed on the Windows Form object (Figure 4-15). When the Action button is clicked, the MaskedTextBoxTasks list is displayed. The Set Mask command is the only command in the list.

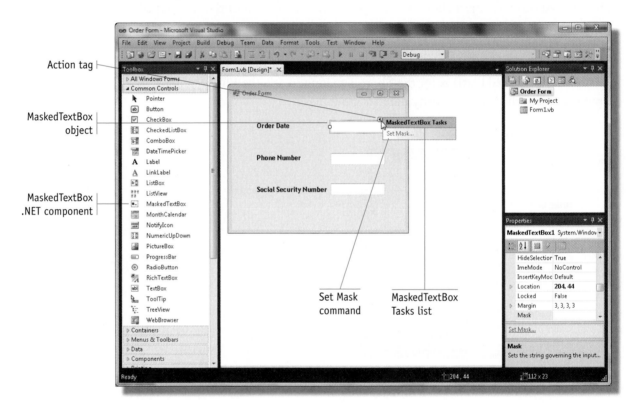

FIGURE 4-15

STEP 2   Click Set Mask on the MaskedTextBox Tasks list and then click the Short
date mask description in the Input Mask dialog box.

*Visual Studio displays the Input Mask dialog box (Figure 4–16). The Mask Description
column contains all the masks that can be used for the MaskedTextBox object. The Short
date mask description is highlighted. In the Preview box, you can type data to see how the
mask will perform when it is used in the MaskedTextBox object. The Use Validating Type
check box is selected so the object will verify the user entered valid numeric data.*

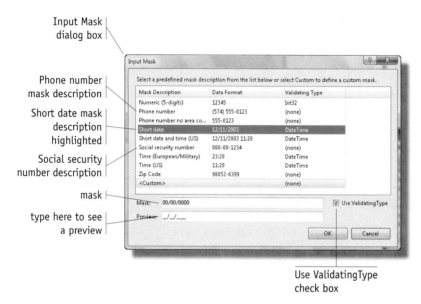

Input Mask
dialog box

Phone number
mask description

Short date mask
description
highlighted

Social security
number description

mask

type here to see
a preview

Use ValidatingType
check box

FIGURE 4-16

STEP 3 Click the OK button in the Input Mask dialog box and then click any-where in the Windows Form object.

The mask is placed in the MaskedTextBox object (Figure 4-17).

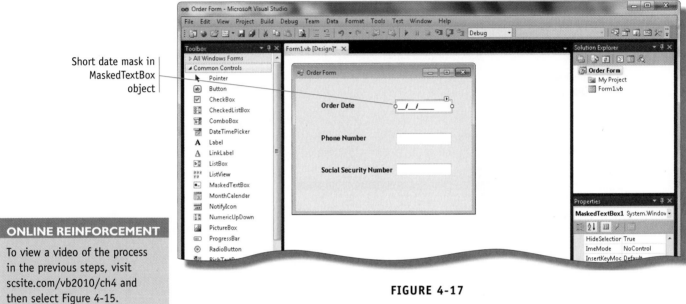

FIGURE 4-17

You can use the same technique to place the Phone number and Social Security number in the MaskedTextBox.

Label Objects

In the sample program, a Label object is used to display the total cost of down-loads (see Figure 4-1 on page 196). The developer must accomplish two tasks to prepare the label for this purpose: a) Place the label on the Windows Form object at the correct location; b) Ensure that when the Label object contains its maximum value, its location on the Windows Form object will work within the user interface design.

To accomplish these two tasks, you can complete the steps on the following page:

STEP 1 Drag a Label object onto the Windows Form object to the correct location. Name the label lblTotalCostOfDownloads. Change the label to the appropriate font size (Century Gothic, 12 point). In the Text property for the Label object, enter the maximum number of characters ($888.88) that will appear in the label during execution of the program.

The properly sized characters appear in the label (Figure 4-18). The label is aligned vertically, but should be moved up to align horizontally with the Total Cost of Downloads label.

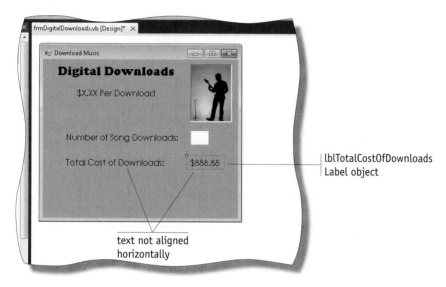

lblTotalCostOfDownloads
Label object

text not aligned
horizontally

FIGURE 4-18

STEP 2 Drag the Label object up until the red snap line appears (Figure 4-19). Then release the left mouse button.

The label is aligned (Figure 4-19).

red snap line

FIGURE 4-19

When program execution begins (see Figure 4-1 on page 196), the label that will contain the total cost of downloads should be blank. In Figure 4-19, however, it contains the value in the Text property of the Label object ($888.88). If the Text property in a Label object is set to no content, the Label object will not be displayed in the Windows Form object during design time, which makes the Label object difficult to work with in Design mode. Therefore, most designers place a value in the Text property of the Label object and leave it there during user interface design. Then, when program execution begins, the Label Text property will be set to blank. You will learn to do this later in this chapter.

Accept Button in Form Properties

Computer users often press the ENTER key to enter data into a text box and cause processing to occur. For example, in the sample program for this chapter, instead of typing the number of downloads and clicking the Calculate Cost button, users might prefer to have the option of typing the number of downloads and pressing the ENTER key.

You can assign a button in the user interface to be an Accept button, which means the program will carry out the event handler processing associated with the button if the user clicks the button or if the user presses the ENTER key. To assign the Calculate Cost button as the Accept button, you can complete the following steps:

STEP 1   Click a blank area in the Windows Form object to select it. Scroll in the Properties window until the AcceptButton property is visible. Click the AcceptButton property name in the left column and then click the AcceptButton property list arrow in the right column.

The AcceptButton property list displays the names of the Button objects on the selected Windows Form object (Figure 4-20). Any of these buttons can be chosen as the Accept button.

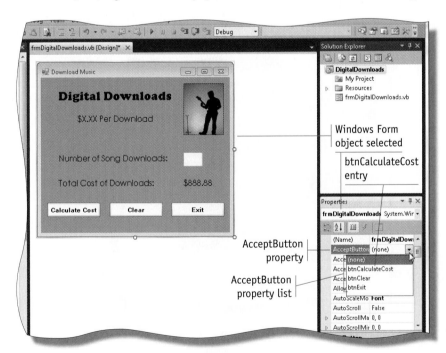

FIGURE 4-20

STEP 2   Click btnCalculateCost in the AcceptButton property list.

The btnCalculateCost Button object is designated as the Accept button. When the program is running, the user can press the ENTER key after entering data and the event handler processing for the Calculate Cost button will be executed.

ONLINE REINFORCEMENT

To view a video of the process in the previous steps, visit scsite.com/vb2010/ch4 and then select Figure 4-20.

Cancel Button in Form Properties

In the same manner as the Accept button, you can designate a Cancel button for the Windows Form object. When the user presses the ESC key, the event handler processing for the button identified as the Cancel button will be executed. In the sample program, the Cancel button will be used to clear the text box and the total cost of downloads, and place the insertion point in the text box. Thus, it performs the same activity as if the user clicks the Clear button. To specify the Cancel button for the sample program, you complete the following steps.

Step 1: Click a blank area in the Windows Form object to select it.
Step 2: Click the CancelButton property name in the left column in the Properties window for the Windows Form object, and then click the CancelButton list arrow.
Step 3: Click the button name (btnClear) in the CancelButton property list.

When the program is executed, the user can press the ESC key to perform the same processing as when the Clear button is clicked.

Visual Studio Preparation for Code Entry

When designing and creating the user interface, the Toolbox in Visual Studio 2010 provides the objects that you can place in the interface. When writing the code in the code editing window, however, the Toolbox is of little use. Therefore, many developers close the Toolbox when writing code in order to increase the space used for coding. To close the Toolbox, you can complete the step on the following page:

STEP 1   With the Toolbox visible (see Figure 4-21), click the Toolbox Close button. The Toolbox closes and the work area expands in size. To reshow the Toolbox after it has been closed, click the Toolbox button on the Standard toolbar.

Figure 4-21 illustrates the screen before the Toolbox is closed. The Toolbox Close button is visible. When the Toolbox is closed, clicking the Toolbox button on the Standard toolbar will open the Toolbox.

Toolbox button

Toolbox Close button

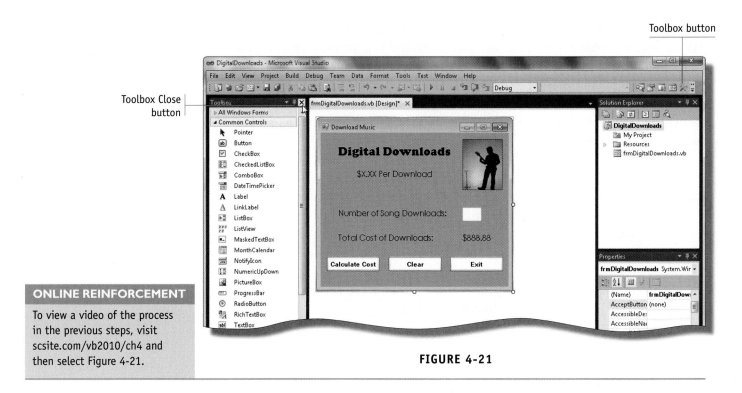

ONLINE REINFORCEMENT

To view a video of the process in the previous steps, visit scsite.com/vb2010/ch4 and then select Figure 4-21.

FIGURE 4-21

In the following sections, the Toolbox has been closed in the windows that show code.

Introduction to Data Entry and Data Types

As you have seen, the user can enter data into the program through the use of the TextBox object. When the user enters the data, the data becomes the value stored in the Text property of the object. For example, if the user enters the value 15 as the number of downloads, the Text property for the txtNumberOfDownloads TextBox object will contain the value 15.

String Data Type

Whenever data is stored in RAM, it is stored as a particular data type. Each data type allows data to be used in a specific manner. For example, to add two values together, the values must be stored in one of the numeric data types. The data type for the value the user enters in a TextBox object and that is stored in the Text property of the TextBox object is string. A **String** data type allows every character available on the computer to be stored in it.

When the user enters data into a TextBox object, often it is good programming style to copy the value entered from the Text property of the TextBox object to a String variable. A **variable** is a named location in RAM where data is stored. A **String variable** is a named location in RAM that can store a string value. Thus, a person's name, a dollar amount, a telephone number, or the number of song downloads can be stored in a String variable.

A variable is defined in the coding of the program. The statement in Figure 4-22 defines a string.

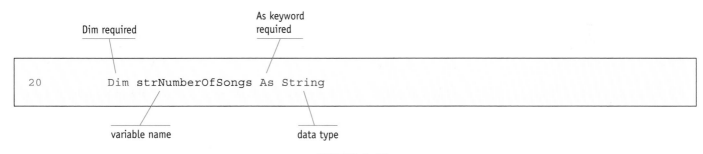

FIGURE 4-22

To begin the statement, the keyword Dim is required. This keyword stands for variable dimension. It indicates to the Visual Basic compiler that the entries that follow it are defining a variable.

The next entry is the variable name. Every variable must have a name so it can be referenced in other statements within the program. By convention, every String variable name begins with the letters, str, followed by a descriptive name. The name in Figure 4-22 (strNumberOfSongs) indicates the variable is a String variable that will contain the number of songs entered by the user.

The keyword As must follow the name of the variable as shown in Figure 4-22. If it is not included, a compilation error will occur. Following the word As is the declaration for the data type of variable being defined. In Figure 4-22, the data type is specified as String.

As a result of the statement in Figure 4-22, when the program is compiled, the Visual Basic compiler will allocate an area in RAM that is reserved to contain the value in the string.

VARIABLE NAME RULES

Variable names used in Visual Basic must follow a few simple rules: 1) The name must begin with a letter or an underline symbol (_); 2) The name can contain letters, numbers, and the underline symbol. It cannot contain spaces or other special characters; 3) No Visual Basic reserved words (words that appear in blue in the code editing window) can be used for variable names.

The general format to define any variable is shown in Figure 4-23.

General Format: Define a Variable

`Dim VariableName As DataType`

EXAMPLE	RESULT
Dim strNumberOfSongs As String	String variable
Dim intNumberOfSongs As Integer	Integer variable
Dim decFinalCosts As Decimal	Decimal variable

FIGURE 4-23

The Integer and Decimal variables defined as examples in Figure 4-23 are numeric variables. You will learn about numeric variables shortly.

Assignment Statements

When a variable is defined as shown in Figure 4-22, the variable does not contain any data. One method to place data in the variable is to use an **assignment statement**. The assignment statement shown in Figure 4-24 will copy the data from the Text property of the txtNumberOfDownloads TextBox object into the strNumberOfSongs String variable.

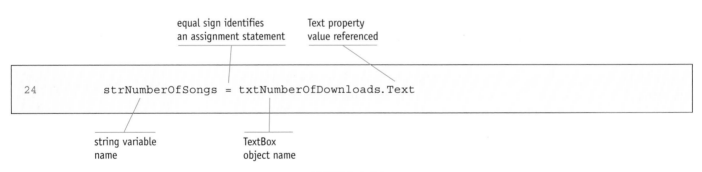

FIGURE 4-24

The variable name on the left of the assignment statement (strNumberOfSongs) identifies the variable to which a value will be copied. The equal sign indicates to the Visual Basic compiler that the statement is an assignment statement. It is required.

The value on the right of the equal sign is the value that will be copied to the variable on the left of the equal sign. In Figure 4-24, the value in the Text property of the txtNumberOfDownloads TextBox object will be copied to the strNumberOfSongs variable.

To enter the definition of the strNumberOfSongs variable and then enter the assignment statement in Figure 4-24 using IntelliSense, you can complete the following steps:

STEP 1   With Visual Studio displaying the code editing window and the insertion point located in the desired column, type `Dim` followed by a space. Then, type the name of the String variable you want to define, `strNumberOfSongs` on your keyboard.

The Dim keyword and the string name you typed are displayed in the code window (Figure 4-25). Notice the word, Dim, is blue to indicate it is a keyword.

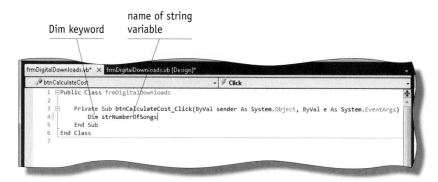

FIGURE 4-25

STEP 2   Press the SPACEBAR, type the word `As` and then press the SPACEBAR again.

The letters you typed are entered and when you typed the space following the word As, IntelliSense displayed a list (Figure 4-26). The IntelliSense list contains all the allowable entries that can follow the As keyword. To define a String variable, the entry should be String.

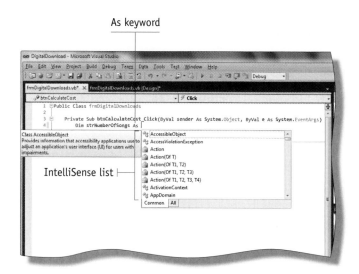

FIGURE 4-26

STEP 3 Because the entry should be String, type `str` on your keyboard.

IntelliSense highlights String in the IntelliSense list (Figure 4-27).

str typed ⊢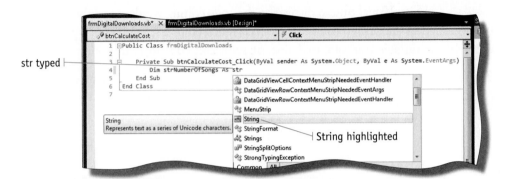

FIGURE 4-27

STEP 4 Press the ENTER key.

The Dim statement is entered (Figure 4-28). The green squiggly underline indicates the variable is not referenced within the program. Visual Studio will remove the line when the variable is used in an assignment statement or other statement.

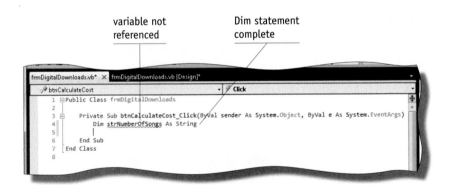

FIGURE 4-28

STEP 5   To begin the assignment statement, type `strn`. IntelliSense displays
the only variable name that starts with the letters strn, the String variable
strNumberOfDownloads.

*IntelliSense displays a list of the entries that can be made in the statement (Figure 4-29).
Whenever you want to reference a variable name in a statement, you can begin to type the
first few letters of the variable name to have IntelliSense display a list of the allowable
entries. The variable name strNumberOfSongs is highlighted because you typed strn.*

IntelliSense
list   strn typed

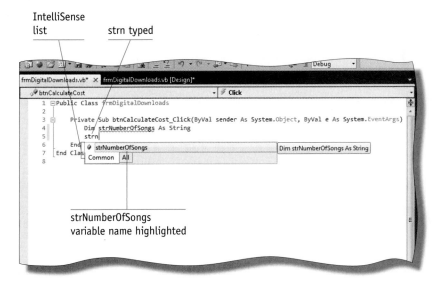

strNumberOfSongs
variable name highlighted

FIGURE 4-29

STEP 6   Press the SPACEBAR, press the EQUAL SIGN key, and then press the SPACEBAR.

*IntelliSense enters the highlighted variable name, the spaces, and the equal sign you typed
(Figure 4-30). The spaces are not required in Visual Basic but should be included in the
statement for ease of reading. An IntelliSense listing automatically appears displaying the
possible valid entries.*

IntelliSense entered   equal sign and
the variable name   spaces

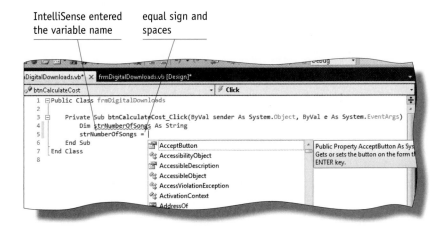

FIGURE 4-30

STEP 7 Type txt to display the IntelliSense list of the Form objects, and then type n to identify the txtNumberOfDownloads TextBox object in the IntelliSense list.

The IntelliSense list contains the valid entries for the statement; in this case only one object has the prefix of txt. The TextBox object txtNumberOfDownloads is highlighted in the list (Figure 4-31).

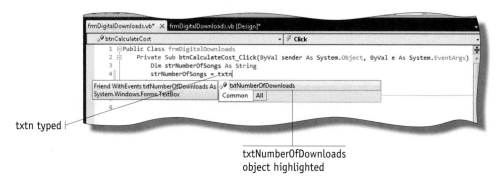

txtn typed

txtNumberOfDownloads
object highlighted

FIGURE 4-31

STEP 8 Press the PERIOD key and then, if necessary, type te to highlight the Text entry in the IntelliSense list.

After the dot operator (period) and the strNumberOfSongs object name are entered, Visual Studio displays the IntelliSense list (Figure 4-32). When you typed te, the Text entry was highlighted in the IntelliSense list.

dot operator   te typed

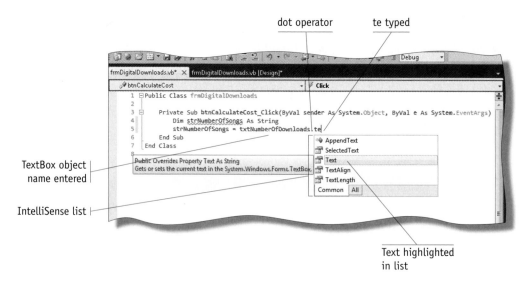

TextBox object
name entered

IntelliSense list

Text highlighted
in list

FIGURE 4-32

STEP 9   Press the ENTER key.

The assignment statement is entered (Figure 4-33). When the statement is executed, the value in the Text property of the txtNumberOfDownloads TextBox object will be copied to the location in memory identified by the strNumberOfSongs variable name. Notice also that the green squiggly lines in the Dim statement are removed because the variable now is referenced in a statement.

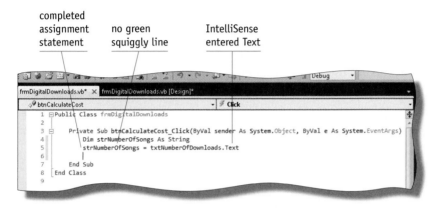

FIGURE 4-33

ONLINE REINFORCEMENT

To view a video of the process in the previous steps, visit scsite.com/vb2010/ch4 and then select Figure 4-25.

You can use the method shown in the previous steps to declare a variable name and include it in assignment statements for all the variables you might define within a program. IntelliSense works the same with each variable name, regardless of the variable type.

Numeric Data Types

As you will recall, the String data type can contain any character that can be entered or stored on a computer. String data types, however, cannot be used in arithmetic operations. A **numeric data type** must be used in arithmetic operations. So, in order to multiply two values, the values must be stored in one of the numeric data types.

Visual Basic allows a variety of numeric data types, depending on the need of the application. Each numeric data type requires a different amount of RAM in which the numeric value is stored, can contain a different type of numeric data, and can contain a different maximum range of values. The table in Figure 4-34 illustrates three widely used numeric data types. The data types are explained in the following sections.

HEADS UP

The rule for using IntelliSense to enter object names and variable names into a Visual Basic statement is: 1) To enter the name of an object that has been defined in the user interface, type the prefix; 2) To enter a variable name you have declared in the program, type the first few letters of the variable name to display an IntelliSense listing of possible names. In each case, IntelliSense will display a list of the allowable entries.

Data Type	Sample Value	Memory Allocation	Range of Values
Integer	48	4 bytes	$-2{,}147{,}483{,}648$ to $+2{,}147{,}483{,}647$
Decimal	3.14519	16 bytes	Decimal values that may have up to 28 significant digits
Double	5.3452307 or 673.6529	8 bytes	$-1.79769313486232\mathrm{e}308$ to $+1.79769313486232\mathrm{e}308$

FIGURE 4-34

Integer Data Type

An **Integer data type** holds a nondecimal whole number in Visual Basic. As you can see from Figure 4-34, an Integer data type can store a value greater or less than 2 billion. Examples of an integer would be the number of songs to download, the number of credit hours you are taking in a semester, and the number of points your favorite football team scored. Notice that each of these examples is a whole number.

Normally, an Integer data type is stored in an Integer variable. An **Integer variable** identifies a location in RAM where an integer value is stored. To define an Integer variable and place a value in the variable through the use of an assignment statement, you can use the Dim statement and the assignment statement, as shown in Figure 4-35.

```
6          Dim intNumberOfSongs As Integer
7          intNumberOfSongs = 34
```

FIGURE 4-35

The Dim statement in Figure 4-35 is the similar to the Dim statement used to define the String variable (Figure 4-28 on page 216) except that the variable name begins with the prefix int; and the word Integer follows the word As. Four bytes of RAM will be reserved for any value that is stored in the intNumberOfSongs Integer variable as a result of the Dim statement in Figure 4-35.

The definition in Figure 4-35 will not place a value in the intNumberOfSongs variable. To place a value in the variable, you can use an assignment statement. The variable into which the value is to be placed (intNumberOfSongs) is entered on the left side of the equal sign, and the value to be placed in the variable (34) is entered on the right side of the equal sign. When the statement is executed, the value 34 will be copied to the RAM location identified by the variable name intNumberOfSongs.

You also can place an initial value in the variable. For example, to define an Integer variable to hold the number of credit hours you are taking, and to place the value 12 in that variable, you could write the Dim statement in Figure 4-36.

value placed in
intCreditHours
Integer variable

```
9          Dim intCreditHours As Integer = 12
```

FIGURE 4-36

The statement in Figure 4-36 defines the Integer variable named intCreditHours. The equal sign following the word Integer indicates to the Visual Basic compiler that the value to its right should be placed in the variable. As a result, the value 12 will be placed in the intCreditHours Integer variable when the program is compiled.

Decimal Data Type

A **Decimal data type** can represent accurately large or very precise decimal numbers. It is ideal for use in the accounting and scientific fields to ensure numbers keep their precision and are not subject to rounding errors. The Decimal data type can be accurate to 28 significant digits. (Significant digits are those that contribute to the precision of a number.) Often, Decimal data types are used to store dollar amounts. For example, to define the cost of downloads Decimal variable for the sample program in this chapter, the statement in Figure 4-37 can be used.

```
22          Dim decTotalCostOfDownloads As Decimal
```

FIGURE 4-37

The Dim statement is used to define the Decimal variable. The dec prefix is used for all Decimal variable names. When the compiler processes the statement in Figure 4-37, 16 bytes of RAM will be reserved for a value to be placed in the decTotalCostOfDownloads variable. Initially, no value will be present in the variable unless you specify a value, as shown in Figure 4-36. You can use an assignment statement to place data into the decTotalCostOfDownloads variable.

Double Data Type

A **Double data type** can represent huge positive and very small negative numbers that can include values to the right of the decimal point. Sometimes, a Double data type is said to represent floating-point numbers, which means the decimal point can be anywhere within the number. The Dim statement in Figure 4-38 declares a Double variable that could be used in a tax application.

```
13          Dim dblTaxRate As Double
14          dblTaxRate = 0.07875
```

FIGURE 4-38

In Figure 4-38, the dblTaxRate Double variable is declared and then the assignment statement places the value 0.07875 in the memory location identified by the variable name. Note that a Double variable begins with the dbl prefix.

Other Data Types

Visual Basic supports a number of other data types that are used for more specialized situations. The two most widely used other types are the Char data type and the Boolean data type. These data types are summarized in the table in Figure 4-39.

Data Type	Sample Value	Memory Allocation	Range of Values
Char	A single character such as ? or M	2 bytes	Any single character
Boolean	True or False	2 bytes	True or False

FIGURE 4-39

Char Data Type

The **Char data type** represents a single keystroke such as a letter of the alphabet, punctuation, or a symbol. The prefix for a Char variable name is chr. When you assign a value to a Char variable, you must place quotation marks around the value. This is shown in Figure 4-40, where the value A is assigned to the chrTopGrade Char variable.

```
16        Dim chrTopGrade As Char
17        chrTopGrade = "A"
```

FIGURE 4-40

The value A in the assignment statement has quotation marks around it. In addition, Visual Studio displays the letter and the quotation marks in red text, indicating they are not Visual Basic keywords nor are they variable or object names. In fact, the value is called a literal. You will learn more about literals in a few pages.

Visual Studio allows 65,534 different characters in a program. These characters consist of numbers, letters, and punctuation symbols. In addition, a wide variety of technical characters, mathematical symbols, and worldwide textual characters are available, allowing developers to work in almost every known language, such as the Korean shown in Figure 4-41. These characters are represented by a coding system called Unicode. To learn more about Unicode, visit www.unicode.org.

유니코드에 대해 ?

어떤 플랫폼,
어떤 프로그램,
어떤 언어에도 상관없이
유니코드는 모든 문자에 대해 고유 번호를 제공합니다.

FIGURE 4-41

Even though you can assign a number to a Char variable, a Char variable cannot be used in arithmetic operations. A number to be used in an arithmetic operation must be assigned to a numeric variable.

Boolean Data Type

A Boolean data variable, whose name begins with the bln prefix, can contain a value that Visual Basic interprets as either True or False. If a variable in your program is intended to represent whether a condition is true or a condition is not true, then the variable should be a Boolean variable. In Figure 4-42, a Boolean variable called blnFullTimeStudent is declared and then the assignment statement sets the Boolean variable to True.

```
19        Dim blnFullTimeStudent As Boolean
20        blnFullTimeStudent = True
```

FIGURE 4-42

In Figure 4-42, the Dim statement is used to declare the blnFullTimeStudent Boolean variable. The assignment sets the Boolean variable to True. This variable can be checked in the program to determine if it is true or false, and appropriate processing can occur based on the finding.

Miscellaneous Data Types

Visual Basic also has a number of other data types that are used less often than the ones you have seen. These data types are summarized in the table in Figure 4-43.

Data Type	Sample Value	Memory Allocation	Range of Values
Byte	A whole number such as 7	1 bytes	0 to 255
Date	April 22, 2014	8 bytes	Dates and times
Long	A whole number such as 342,534,538	8 bytes	−9,223,372,036,854,775,808 through +9,223,372,036,854,775,807
Object	Holds a reference	4 bytes	A memory address
Short	A whole number such as 16,546	2 bytes	−32,786 through 32,767
Single	A number such as 312,672.3274	4 bytes	−3.4028235E+38 through 1.401298E−45 for negative values; and from 1.401298E−45 through 3.4028235E+38 for positive values

FIGURE 4-43

As a review, the prefixes for each of the data type variable names are shown in Figure 4-44.

Data Type	Prefix
String	str
Integer	int
Decimal	dec
Double	dbl
Char	chr
Boolean	bln
Byte	byt
Date	dtm
Long	lng
Short	shr
Single	sng

FIGURE 4-44

Literals

When you include a value in an assignment statement, such as in Figure 4-38 on page 221 and Figure 4-40 on page 222, this value is called a **literal** because the value being used in the assignment statement is literally the value that is required. It is not a variable. The Visual Basic compiler determines the data type of the value you have used for a literal based on the value itself. For example, if you type "Chicago," the compiler treats the literal as a String data type, while if you type 49.327, the compiler treats the literal as a Double data type. The table in Figure 4-45 displays the default literal types as determined by the Visual Basic compiler.

Standard Literal Form	Default Data Type	Example
Numeric, no fractional part	Integer	104
Numeric, no fractional part, too large for Integer data type	Long	3987925494
Numeric, fractional part	Double	0.99 8.625
Enclosed within double quotes	String	"Brittany"
Enclosed within number signs	Date	#3/17/1990 3:30 PM#

FIGURE 4-45

Forced Literal Types

Sometimes you might want a literal to be a different data type than the Visual Basic default. For example, you may want to assign the number 0.99 to a Decimal data variable to take advantage of the precision characteristics of the Decimal data type. As you can see in Figure 4-45, Visual Basic will, by default, consider the value 0.99 to be a Double data type. To define the literal as a Decimal literal, you must use special literal-type characters to force the literal to assume a data type other than the one Visual Basic uses as the default. You do this by placing the literal-type character at the end of the literal value. The table in Figure 4-46 shows the available literal-type characters, together with examples of their usage.

Literal-Type Character	Data Type	Example
S	Short	Dim shoAge As Short shoAge = 40S
I	Integer	Dim intHeight as Integer intHeight = 76I
D	Decimal	Dim decPricePerSong As Decimal decPricePerSong = 0.99D
R	Double	Dim dblWeight As Double dblWeight = 8491R
C	Char	Dim chrNumberOfDays As Char chrNumberOfDays = "7"C

FIGURE 4-46

In the first example, the value 40 will be processed by Visual Basic as a Short data type literal even though the value would by default be considered a Integer value. In the second example, the literal-type character confirms the value should be treated as an Integer data type. In the third example, the value 0.99 will be processed as a Decimal data type even though it would by default be considered a Double data type. In the fourth example, the value 8491 would, by default, be considered an Integer data value but because the R literal-type character is used, Visual Basic will treat it as a Double data type. In example 5, the value 7 will be treated as a Char data type.

Constants

Recall that a variable identifies a location in memory where a value can be stored. By its nature, the value in a variable can be changed by statements within the program. For example, in the sample program in this chapter, if one user requested 5 downloads and another user requested 12 downloads, the value in the strNumberOfSongs variable would be changed based on the needs of the user. In some instances, however, you might not want the value to be changed. For example, the price per download in the sample program is $0.99 per song. This value will not change, regardless of how many songs the user wants to download.

When a value in a program will remain the same throughout the execution of the program, a special variable called a constant should be used. A **constant** variable will contain one permanent value throughout the execution of the program. It cannot be changed by any statement within the program. To define a constant variable, you can use the code in Figure 4-47.

```
12      Const cdecPricePerDownload As Decimal = 0.99D
```

FIGURE 4-47

The following rules apply to a constant:

1. The declaration of a constant variable begins with the letters Const, not the letters Dim.
2. You must assign the value to be contained in the constant on the same line as the definition of the constant. In Figure 4-47, the value 0.99D is assigned to the constant variable on the same line as the Const definition of the constant.
3. You cannot attempt to change the value in the constant variable anywhere in the program. If you attempt this, you will produce a compiler error.
4. The letter c often is placed before the prefix of the constant variable name to identify throughout the program that it is a constant variable and cannot be changed.
5. Other than the letter c constant variable names are formed using the same rules and techniques as nonconstant names.

Using a named constant variable instead of a literal provides several significant advantages and should be done whenever a constant value is required in a program. These advantages include:

1. The program becomes easier to read because the value is identified through the use of the name. For example, instead of using the value 0.99D in a literal, it is used in a constant called cdecPricePerDownload. This variable name describes the use of the value 0.99D and makes the program easier to read.
2. If the constant is used in more than one place in the program and it must be changed in the code, it is much easier and more reliable to change the value one time in the constant as opposed to changing every occurrence of the value in a literal.

Referencing a Variable

You learned earlier that when a variable is declared, it will be underlined with a green squiggly line until it is referenced in a statement. This feature of Visual Basic is intended to ensure that you do not declare a variable and then forget to use it. It also helps ensure you do not waste memory by declaring an unnecessary variable.

It is mandatory when using a variable in a program that the variable is defined prior to using the variable name in a statement. For example, the code in the statements in Figure 4-48 *will cause an error* because the variable is used in an assignment statement before it is declared.

```
25          strNumberOfSongs = txtNumberOfDownloads.Text
26          Dim strNumberOfSongs As String
```

FIGURE 4-48

In the code in Figure 4-48, the variable strNumberOfSongs is referenced in an assignment statement (line 25) before it is defined (line 26). This creates a compile error as indicated by the blue squiggly line beneath the variable name strNumberOfSongs on line 25. If you attempt to compile the statements on lines 25 and 26, you will receive a build error. Always define a variable before it is used in a statement.

Scope of Variables

When you declare a variable in Visual Basic, you not only declare the data type of the variable, you also, implicitly, define the scope of the variable. The **scope of a variable** specifies where within the program the variable can be referenced in a Visual Basic statement. In larger programs, with multiple classes and multiple forms, scope becomes critical, but it is important that you understand the concept at this point.

You declare a variable in a region within a program. For example, in the sample program in this chapter, you can declare a variable in the click event handler for the Calculate Cost button. You could declare another variable in the click event handler for the Clear button. Scope determines where each of these variables can be referenced and used in the Visual Basic program. **The rule is: A variable can be referenced only within the region of the program where it is defined.** A region in the programs you have seen thus far in the book is the code between the Sub statement and the End Sub statement in the event handlers. The code between the Sub statement and the End Sub statement is a **procedure**.

Therefore, if you declare a variable within the click event handler for the Calculate Cost button, that variable cannot be referenced in the click event handler for the Clear button, and vice versa. A variable that can only be referenced within the region of the program where it is defined is called a **local variable**. This means the value in a variable defined in one region of the program cannot be changed by a statement in another region of the program.

In addition, when a variable is defined in a procedure and the procedure ends, the values in the local variables defined in the procedure are destroyed. Thus, local variables have a certain **lifetime** in the program. They are only "alive" from the time the procedure begins executing until the procedure ends. If the procedure is executed again, whatever value the variable once contained no longer is present. One execution of the procedure is a variable's lifetime. Therefore, if a user clicks the Calculate Cost button, the values in the variables are valid until the click event execution is completed. When the user clicks the Calculate Cost button again, all values from the first click are gone.

It is possible in a Visual Basic program to define variables that can be used in multiple regions of a program. These variables are called **global variables**. In most programs, local variables should be used because they minimize the errors than can be generated when using global variables.

Understanding the scope of a variable is important when developing a program. You will learn more about the scope of variables later in this chapter and throughout this book.

Converting Variable Data

Variables used in arithmetic statements in a Visual Basic program must be numeric variables. String variables cannot be used in arithmetic statements. If you attempt to do so, you will create a compilation error.

A user often enters data in a text box. Data in the Text property of a TextBox object is treated as String data. Because String data cannot be used in an arithmetic statement, the String data entered by a user must be converted to numeric data before it can be used in an arithmetic statement.

For example, in the sample program in this chapter, before the number of songs to download a user enters can be used in an arithmetic statement to determine the total cost of the downloads, that value must be converted to an Integer data type.

Visual Basic includes several procedures that allow you to convert one data type to another data type. You will recall that a **procedure** is a prewritten set of code that can be called by a statement in the Visual Basic program. When the procedure is called, it performs a particular task. In this case, the task is to convert the String value the user entered into an Integer data type that can be used in an arithmetic operation. A procedure to convert a String data type to an Integer data type is named ToInt32. The number 32 in the procedure name identifies that the representation of the integer will require 32 bits or 4 bytes, which is the memory required for the Integer data type. The procedure is found in the Convert class, which is available in a Visual Studio 2010 class library.

Using a Procedure

When you require the use of a procedure to accomplish a task in your program, you need to understand what the procedure does and how to code the procedure call in a program statement. A procedure can operate in one of two ways: it can perform its task and return a value, or it can perform its task and not return a value. You will recall in the Chapter 3 program that the Close() procedure closed the window and terminated the program. This is an example of a procedure that performs its task but does not return a value. A procedure of this type is called a **Sub procedure**.

In the Song Download program in this chapter, the requirement is to convert the number of songs String value the user enters into an Integer data type. Then, it can be used in an arithmetic operation. Therefore the procedure must return a value (the Integer value for the number of songs). A procedure that returns a value is called a **Function procedure**, or a **function**.

In addition, a procedure might require data to be passed to it when it is called in order to carry out its processing. In the sample program in this chapter, the Function procedure to convert a String variable to an Integer variable must be able to access the String variable in order to convert it. Therefore, in the statement that calls the Function procedure, the variable name for the String variable to be converted must be passed to the procedure. A value is passed to a procedure through the use of an argument.

An **argument** identifies a value required by a procedure. It is passed to the procedure by including its name within parentheses following the name of the procedure in the calling statement. For example, to pass the value stored in the strNumberOfSongs variable to the ToInt32 procedure, the statement in Figure 4-49 could be used.

FIGURE 4-49

The name of the procedure is ToInt32. The argument is strNumberOfSongs, which is the String variable that contains the value to be converted to an Integer data type by the ToInt32 procedure. Notice that the argument is enclosed within parentheses.

Every procedure is a part of a class in Visual Basic. You will recall from Chapter 1 that a **class** is a named grouping of program code. When the calling statement must call a procedure, it first must identify the class that contains the procedure. Thus, in Figure 4-49 the calling statement is incomplete because the class name is not included in the statement. The class containing the ToInt32 procedure is the Convert class. To complete the procedure call statement, the class must be added, as shown in Figure 4-50.

FIGURE 4-50

In Figure 4-50, the class name Convert begins the procedure call. A dot operator separates the class name from the procedure name (ToInt32). The argument (strNumberOfSongs) within the parentheses completes the procedure call.

When a Function procedure returns a value, such as the ToInt32 procedure that returns an integer value, in effect the returned value replaces the procedure call in the assignment statement containing the Function procedure call. So, in Figure 4-51, you can see that when the processing within the Function procedure is completed, the integer value is substituted for the procedure call in the assignment statement.

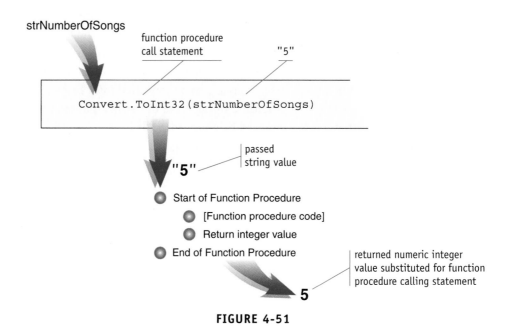

FIGURE 4-51

The complete assignment statement to convert the String data type in the strNumberOfSongs variable to an Integer data type and place it in the intNumberOfSongs variable is shown in Figure 4-52.

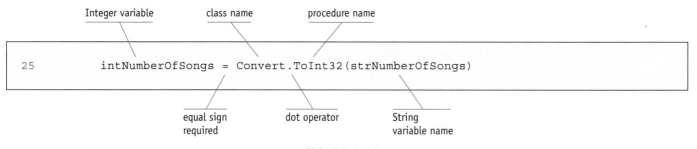

FIGURE 4-52

The intNumberOfSongs variable name on the left of the equal sign identifies the Integer variable where the converted value will be copied. The equal sign in the assignment statement is required. As a result of the assignment statement in Figure 4-52, the ToInt32 Function procedure found in the Convert class will convert the value in the strNumberOfSongs String variable to an integer value. The assignment statement will place that integer value in the intNumberOfSongs variable.

The use of Function procedures, and arguments with the procedure calls, is common when programming in Visual Basic. You will encounter many examples of Function procedure calls throughout this book.

Option Strict On

In the previous section, you saw an example of explicitly changing a value from one data type to another. Visual Basic will, by default, automatically convert data types if the data type on the right side of the equal sign in an assignment statement is different from the data type on the left side of the equal sign. Quite often, however, the automatic conversion can introduce errors and produce an incorrect converted value. Therefore, allowing automatic conversion normally is not good programming style.

To prevent automatic conversion of values, the developer must insert the Option Strict On statement in the program prior to any event handler code in the program. In Figure 4-53, the Option Strict On statement is shown just following the introductory comments in the sample program for this chapter.

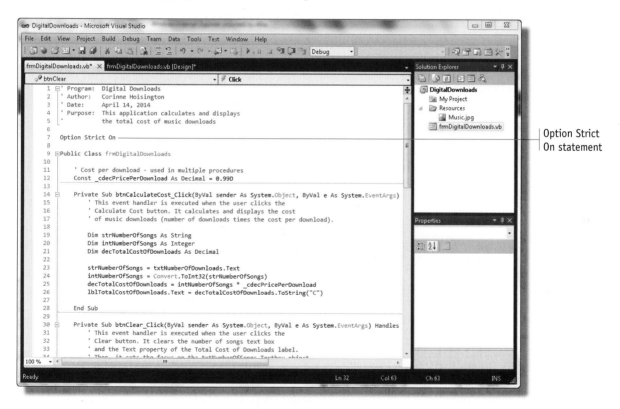

FIGURE 4-53

The Option Strict On statement explicitly disallows any default data type conversions in which data loss would occur and any conversion between numeric types and strings. Therefore, you must write explicit conversion statements in order to convert from one data type to another. This approach minimizes potential errors that can occur from data conversion.

Arithmetic Operations

The ability to perform arithmetic operations on numeric data is fundamental to computer programs. Many programs require arithmetic operations to add, subtract, multiply, and divide numeric data. For example, in the Digital Downloads program in this chapter, the price per song downloaded must be multiplied by the number of songs to be downloaded in order to calculate the total cost of downloads. The formula is shown in Figure 4-54.

Total Cost of Downloads = Number of Song Downloads times Price per Download

FIGURE 4-54

An assignment statement is used in Visual Basic 2010 to perform the arithmetic operation shown in Figure 4-54. The statements used in the sample program and a depiction of the operation are shown in Figure 4-55.

```
20          Dim strNumberOfSongs As String
21          Dim intNumberOfSongs As Integer
22          Dim decTotalCostOfDownloads As Decimal
23          Const cdecPricePerDownload As Decimal = 0.99D
24
25          strNumberOfSongs = txtNumberOfDownloads.Text
26          intNumberOfSongs = Convert.ToInt32(strNumberOfSongs)
27          decTotalCostOfDownloads = intNumberOfSongs * cdecPricePerDownload
```

decTotalCostOfDownloads = intNumberOfSongs * cdecPricePerDownload

FIGURE 4-55

In the code in Figure 4-55, the variable strNumberOfSongs is assigned the value the user entered by the assignment statement on line 25 (see Figure 4-24 for a detailed explanation of this statement). The statement on line 26 converts the value in the strNumberOfSongs variable to an integer and copies it to the intNumberOfSongs variable (see Figure 4-52 for an explanation of this statement).

The statement on line 27 multiplies the integer value in the intNumberOfSongs variable times the constant value in the cdecPricePerDownload variable, and then copies the result to the decTotalCostOfDownloads variable. For example, if the user enters the value 5 as the number of downloads, as depicted in the diagram, the value 5 is multiplied by the value .99 (the value in the cdecPricePerDownload variable), and the result (4.95) is copied to the decTotalCostOfDownloads variable.

Arithmetic Operators

An important element on the right side of the equal sign in the assignment statement on line 27 is the multiply **arithmetic operator**, which is an asterisk (*). Whenever the compiler encounters the multiply arithmetic operator, the value on the left of the operator is multiplied by the value on the right of the operator and these values are replaced in the assignment statement by the product of the two numbers. Thus, in Figure 4-55 the arithmetic expression intNumberOfSongs * cdecPricePerDownload is replaced by the value 4.95. Then, the assignment statement places the value 4.95 in the decTotalCostOfDownloads variable.

The multiply arithmetic operator is only one of the arithmetic operators available in Visual Basic 2010. The table in Figure 4-56 lists the Visual Basic 2010 arithmetic operators, their use, and an example of an arithmetic expression showing their use.

Arithmetic Operator	Use	Assignment Statement Showing Their Use
+	Addition	decTotal = decPrice + decTax
−	Subtraction	decCost = decRegularPrice − decDiscount
*	Multiplication	decTax = decItemPrice * decTaxRate
/	Division	decClassAverage = decTotalScores / intNumberOfStudents
^	Exponentiation	intSquareArea = intSquareSide ^ 2
\	Integer Division	intResult = 13 \ 5
Mod	Modulus Arithmetic (remainder)	intRemainder = 13 Mod 5

FIGURE 4-56

The arithmetic operators shown in Figure 4-56 are explained in the following paragraphs.

Addition

The **addition arithmetic operator** (+) causes the numeric values immediately to the left and immediately to the right of the operator to be added together and to replace the arithmetic expression in the assignment statement. For example, in Figure 4-57, the value in the decPrice variable is added to the value in the decTax variable.

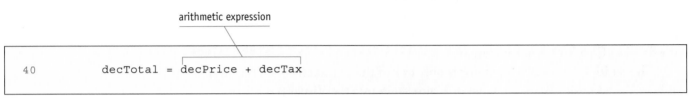

```
40            decTotal = decPrice + decTax
```

FIGURE 4-57

In Figure 4-57, the arithmetic expression (decPrice + decTax) is evaluated by adding the value in the decPrice variable to the value in the decTax variable. Then, the assignment statement copies the sum to the decTotal variable in RAM.

An arithmetic expression that uses the addition operator can contain more than two numeric values to be added. For example, in Figure 4-58, three variables are used in the arithmetic expression.

```
47        decTotalPay = decRegularPay + decOvertimePay + decBonusPay
```

FIGURE 4-58

In Figure 4-58, the value in decRegularPay is added to the value in decOvertimePay. The result then is added to decBonusPay. That sum is copied to the decTotalPay variable. Visual Basic imposes no limit on the number of variables that can be used in an arithmetic expression.

In addition to variables, arithmetic expressions can contain literals. The assignment statement in Figure 4-59 uses a literal.

```
53        decTicketCost = decInternetTicketCost + 10.25
```

FIGURE 4-59

In Figure 4-59, the value 10.25 is added to the value in the decInternetTicketCost variable and that sum is placed in the decTicketCost variable. Generally, literals should not be used in arithmetic expressions unless it is known that the value will not change. For example, if the extra cost for the ticket could change in the future, good program design would dictate that the value be placed in a variable (perhaps even a constant).

Subtraction

In order to subtract one value from another in an assignment statement, the **subtraction arithmetic operator** ($-$) is used, as shown in Figure 4-60.

```
59          decNetProfit = decRevenue - decCosts
```

FIGURE 4-60

In Figure 4-60, the value in the decCosts variable is subtracted from the value in the decRevenue variable. The result then is copied into the decNetProfit variable. If the value in decCosts is greater than the value in decRevenue, the value placed in the decNetProfit variable will be negative.

Using Arithmetic Results

After an arithmetic operation has been performed using an assignment statement, the values used in the arithmetic operation together with the answer obtained can be used in subsequent arithmetic operations or for other purposes within the program. For example, the result of one operation can be used in a subsequent calculation (Figure 4-61).

```
67          decComputerCost = decMonitorCost + decSystemUnitCost
68          decNetComputerCost = decComputerCost - decSystemDiscount
```

FIGURE 4-61

In Figure 4-61, the statement on line 67 determines the computer cost by adding the cost of the monitor and the cost of the system unit. The statement on line 68 calculates the net computer cost by subtracting the system discount from the computer cost that is calculated on line 67. Whenever a value is stored in a variable, it can be used in other statements within the program.

Multiplication

Multiplication is accomplished through the use of an assignment statement and the multiplication operator (*), as shown in Figure 4-62.

```
74        intLandPlotArea = intLandPlotLength * intLandPlotWidth
```

FIGURE 4-62

In Figure 4-62, the value in the intLandPlotLength variable is multiplied by the value in the intLandPlotWidth variable. The product of the multiplication is placed in the intLandPlotArea variable.

When multiplication takes place, the signs of the numbers are considered. If two positive numbers are multiplied, the answer is positive. If two negative numbers are multiplied, the answer is positive. If one positive number and one negative number are multiplied, the answer is negative.

When two numbers are multiplied, you must be aware of the size of the result. The largest number of digits that can appear in the product of two numbers is the sum of the number of digits in each of the values being multiplied. If the product is greater than the value that can be stored in the variable on the left of the assignment statement, an overflow error can occur and the program will be terminated.

Division

Visual Basic 2010 provides three arithmetic operators for division and related calculations. These operators are the slash (/), the backslash (\), and the entry MOD.

You use the slash for normal division. For example, in Figure 4-63, the value in the decTestScores variable is divided by 3 in order to obtain the average test score.

```
79        decAverageTestScore = decTestScores / 3
```

FIGURE 4-63

WATCH OUT FOR

Be sure that the divisor (the number on the right of the division operator) is not zero. If you attempt to divide by zero, your program will be terminated with an error.

You use the backslash (\) for integer division. With integer division, the quotient returned from the division operation is an integer. If the division operation produces a quotient with a remainder, the remainder is dropped, or truncated. The examples in Figure 4-64 illustrate the use of the integer division arithmetic operator.

Division Operation	Result
12\5	2
25\4	6
30\7	4

FIGURE 4-64

Notice in each example in Figure 4-64 that the result is a whole number with the remainder truncated.

The MOD operator divides the number on the left of the operator by the number on the right of the operator and returns an integer value that is the remainder of division operation. Integer division and the MOD operator often are used together, as shown in Figure 4-65.

```
86          intHours = intTotalNumberOfMinutes \ 60
87          intMinutes = intTotalNumberOfMinutes Mod 60
```

FIGURE 4-65

In Figure 4-65, the operation on line 86 will return only the integer value of the division. For example, if the intTotalNumberOfMinutes variable contains 150, a result of 2 (2 = 150\60) will be placed in the intHours variable. The operation on line 87 will place the remainder in the intMinutes variable. The remainder in the example is 30 (150 divided by 60 is 2, with a remainder of 30).

Exponentiation

Exponentiation means raising a number to a power. Exponentiation is accomplished by using the exponentiation arithmetic operator (^), as shown in Figure 4-66.

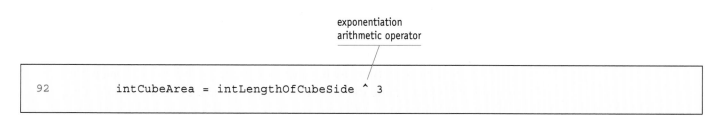

exponentiation
arithmetic operator

```
92          intCubeArea = intLengthOfCubeSide ^ 3
```

FIGURE 4-66

In Figure 4-66, the arithmetic expression is the same as intLengthOfCubeSide * intLengthOfCubeSide * intLengthOfCubeSide. So the value is cubed and copied to the intCubeArea variable.

The exponent used in the exponentiation operation can be a fraction. If the exponent is a fraction, the root is taken (Figure 4-67).

```
94          intLengthOfCubeSide = intCubeArea ^ (1 / 3)
```

FIGURE 4-67

In Figure 4-67, the cube root of the value in the intCubeArea variable is calculated and the result is copied to the intLengthOfCubeSide variable. Thus, if the area of the cube is 64, the value calculated for the length of the cube side would be 4 (4 * 4 * 4 = 64). The fractional exponent can never be negative, and it must be placed within parentheses.

Multiple Operations

A single assignment statement can contain multiple arithmetic operations. In Figure 4-68, the addition and subtraction operators are used to calculate the new balance in a savings account by adding the deposits to the old balance and subtracting withdrawals.

```
101         decNewBalance = decOldBalance + decDeposits - decWithdrawals
```

FIGURE 4-68

When the assignment statement in Figure 4-68 is executed, the value in the decOldBalance variable is added to the value in the decDeposits variable. Then, the value in the decWithdrawals variable is subtracted from that sum and the result is copied to the decNewBalance variable.

Notice in Figure 4-68 that the calculations proceed from the left to the right through the arithmetic expression.

Hierarchy of Operations

When multiple operations are included in a single assignment statement, the sequence of performing the calculations is determined by the following rules:

1. Exponentiation (^) is performed first.
2. Multiplication (*) and division (/) are performed next.
3. Integer division (\) is next.
4. MOD then occurs.
5. Addition (+) and subtraction (−) are performed last.
6. Within each of these five steps, calculations are performed left to right.

As a result of this predetermined sequence, an arithmetic expression such as decBonus + decHours * decHourlyRate would result in the product of decHours * decHourlyRate being added to decBonus.

An arithmetic expression such as decGrade1 + decGrade2 / 2 would result in the value in the decGrade2 variable being divided by 2, and then the quotient being added to the value in decGrade1 because division is performed before addition. It is likely that this is not the intended calculation to be performed. Instead, the intent was to add the value in decGrade1 to the value in decGrade2 and then divide the sum by 2. To force certain operations to be performed before others, you can use parentheses. Any arithmetic expression within parentheses is evaluated before expressions outside the parentheses, as shown in Figure 4-69.

```
108          decAverageGrade = (decGrade1 + decGrade2) / 2
```

FIGURE 4-69

In Figure 4-69, because it is inside the parentheses, the addition operation will be completed before the division operation. Therefore, the result of the arithmetic expression is that the value in decGrade1 is added to the value in decGrade2. That sum then is divided by the value 2 and the quotient is copied to the decAverageGrade variable.

It is advisable to use parentheses around multiple arithmetic operations in an arithmetic expression even if the predetermined sequence of operations will produce the correct answer because then the sequence of operations is explicitly clear.

Displaying Numeric Output Data

As you have learned, the result of an arithmetic expression is a numeric value that normally is stored in a numeric variable. In most cases, to display the numeric data as information in a graphical user interface, the numeric data must be placed in the Text property of a Label object or a TextBox object. The Text property of these objects, however, requires that this data be a String data type. Therefore, to display a numeric value in a label or a text box, the numeric data must be converted to a String data type.

Each of the numeric data types provides a function called the ToString function that converts data from the numeric data type to the String data type. The general format of the function call for a Decimal numeric variable is shown in Figure 4-70.

> **General Format: ToString Function**
>
> ```
> decimalvariable.ToString()
> ```

FIGURE 4-70

The statement shown in Figure 4-70 consists of the name of the decimal variable containing data to be converted, the dot operator (.), and the name of the function (ToString). Notice that the function name is followed immediately by closed parentheses, which indicates to the Visual Basic compiler that ToString is a procedure name. When the function call is executed, the value returned by the ToString function replaces the call.

The function call normally is contained within an assignment statement to assign the returned string value to the Text property of a Label or TextBox object. The example in Figure 4-71 shows the assignment statement to convert the numeric value in the decTemperature variable to a String value that then is placed in the Text property of the lblTemperature Label object.

name of decimal variable

ToString
function call

```
118        lblTemperature.Text = decTemperature.ToString()
```

FIGURE 4-71

In Figure 4-71, the name of the decimal variable (decTemperature) is followed by the dot operator and then the name of the function (ToString) with the required parentheses. When the statement on line 118 is executed, the ToString function is called. It converts the numeric value in the decTemperature variable to a String data type and returns the String data. The assignment statement then copies the returned String data to the Text property of the Temperature Label object.

Format Specifications for the ToString Function

In the example in Figure 4-71, the conversion from numeric value to String value is a straight conversion, which means the value is returned but it is not formatted in any manner. For example, if the numeric value in the Decimal variable was 47.235, then this same value was returned as a String value.

The ToString function, however, can convert numeric data to String data using a specified format. For example, the value 2317.49 could be returned as $2,317.49. Notice that the returned value is in the form of dollars and cents, or currency. To identify the format for the numeric data to be returned by the ToString function, the **format specifier** must be included as an argument in the parentheses following the ToString function name. The table in Figure 4-72 identifies the commonly used format specifiers (assume the value in the numeric field is 8976.43561).

Format Specifier	Format	Description	Output from the Function
General(G)	ToString("G")	Displays the numbers as is	8976.43561
Currency(C)	ToString("C")	Displays the number with a dollar sign, a thousands separator (comma), two digits to the right of the decimal and negative numbers in parentheses	$8,976.44
Fixed(F)	ToString("F")	Displays the number with 2 digits to the right of the decimal and a minus sign for negative numbers	8976.44
Number(N)	ToString("N")	Displays a number with a thousands separator, 2 digits to the right of the decimal and a minus sign for negative numbers	8,976.44
Percent(P)	ToString("P")	Displays the number multiplied by 100 with a % sign, a thousands separator, 2 digits to the right of the decimal and a minus sign for negative numbers	897,643.56%
Scientific(E)	ToString("E")	Displays the number in E-notation and a minus sign for negative numbers	8.976436E+03

FIGURE 4-72

In Figure 4-72, each format specifier is used as an argument within parentheses. The argument must be included in the quotation marks (" ") on each side of the format specifier, as shown. The letter for the format specifier can either be uppercase or lowercase.

Precision Specifier

Each format specifier has a default number of digits to the right of the decimal point that will be returned. You can use a precision specifier, however, to override the default number of positions to the right of the decimal point. The **precision specifier** is a number that is included within the quotation marks in the function call to identify the number of positions to the right of the decimal point that should be returned. The examples in Figure 4-73 illustrate the use of the precision specifier (assume the value in the decNumericValue variable is 8976.43561):

Statement	Copied to Text Property of lblOutput Label Object
lblOutput = decNumericValue.ToString("C2")	$8,976.44
lblOutput = decNumericValue.ToString("C3")	$8,976.436
lblOutput = decNumericValue.ToString("F1")	8976.4
lblOutput = decNumericValue.ToString("N4")	8,976.4356
lblOutput = decNumericValue.ToString("P0")	897,644%

FIGURE 4-73

As you can see, the precision specifier identifies the number of digits to the right of the decimal point that should be displayed in the string returned from the ToString function. Notice that if the precision specifier is 0, no digits to the right of the decimal point are returned.

As with all conversions, when the number of positions to the right of the decimal point in the returned string is less than the number of digits to the right of the decimal point in the numeric value being converted, the returned value is rounded to the specified number of decimal places.

Clearing the Form — Clear Procedure and Focus Procedure

You will recall from the explanation of the Digital Downloads program in this chapter that when the user clicks the Clear button (see Figure 4-1 on page 196), the event handler for the Clear button must clear the results from window, allowing the user to enter the next value for the number of downloads. To perform this task, the Clear button event handler must complete the following tasks: 1) Clear the Text property of the TextBox object; 2) Clear the Text property of the Label object that displays the total cost of the downloads; 3) Set the focus on the TextBox object, which means place the insertion point in the text box. You will learn to accomplish these tasks in the following sections.

Clear Procedure

The Clear procedure clears any data currently placed in the Text property of a TextBox object. The general format of the Clear procedure is shown in Figure 4-74.

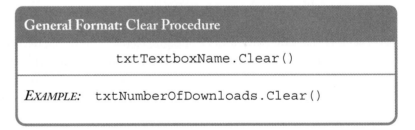

General Format: Clear Procedure

```
txtTextboxName.Clear()
```

EXAMPLE: `txtNumberOfDownloads.Clear()`

FIGURE 4-74

When the Clear procedure is executed, the Text property is cleared of any data. As with every procedure call, the name of the procedure must be followed by parentheses.

Clear the Text Property of a Label

The Clear procedure cannot be used with a Label object. Instead, to clear the Text property of a Label object, you must write an assignment statement that assigns a null length string to the Text property of a Label object. A null length string is a string with no length, which means no characters. A null length string is represented by two quotation marks with no character between them (" "). To assign a null length string to the Text property, you can use the statement shown in Figure 4-75.

```
39          lblTotalCostOfDownloads.Text = ""
```

FIGURE 4-75

In Figure 4-75, the null length string represented by the two quotation marks with no character between them is assigned to the Text property of the lblTotalCostOfDownloads Label object. As a result of the assignment statement, the Text property of the Label object is cleared.

Set the Focus

When the focus is on a TextBox object, the insertion point is located in the text box (Figure 4-76).

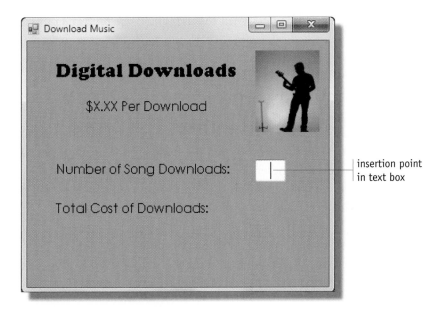

insertion point in text box

FIGURE 4-76

When the user clicks a button or any other item in the graphical user interface, the focus shifts to that item. Therefore, to place the focus on a text box, the user can click the text box. To place the focus on a text box without requiring to user to click it first, and thus making it easier for the user to enter data in the text box, the Focus procedure is used (Figure 4-77).

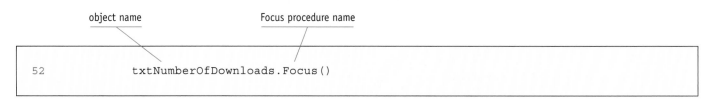

object name   Focus procedure name

```
52               txtNumberOfDownloads.Focus()
```

FIGURE 4-77

As with most procedure calls, the name of the object is stated first in the statement, followed immediately by the dot operator (period). The name of the procedure (Focus) follows the dot operator. When the statement on line 52 is executed, the focus is placed on the txtNumberOfDownloads TextBox object, which means the insertion point is placed in the text box.

Form Load Event

In the program in Chapter 3 and in the program in this chapter, you have seen that an event can occur when the user clicks a button. The code in the event handler for the button click is executed when the user clicks the button. For example, in the Digital Downloads program in this chapter, when the user clicks the Calculate Cost button, the event handler code multiplies the number of songs times the price per song and displays the result (see Figure 4-1 on page 196).

Clicking a button is not the only action that can trigger an event. For example, a form load event occurs each time a program is started and the Windows Form object is loaded into computer memory. For the program in this chapter, a form load event occurs when the program starts and the Digital Downloads form is loaded. In some programs, an event handler is not written for this particular event and no processing occurs. In the Digital Downloads program, however, a form loading event handler is required. This event handler completes the following tasks:

1. Display the cost per download heading.
2. Clear the placeholder from the lblTotalCostOfDownloads Text property.
3. Set the focus on the txtNumberOfDownloads text box.

Concatenation

In the Digital Downloads program, the lblCostHeading Label object displays the cost per download (see Figure 4-1). In the user interface design, the lblCostHeading Label contains words for the placement of the label, but does not contain the actual cost per download (Figure 4-78).

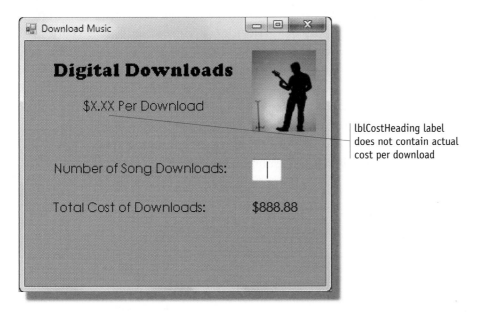

lblCostHeading label does not contain actual cost per download

FIGURE 4-78

In Figure 4-78, the label contains placeholder information for the actual cost per download. The reason the actual cost is not placed in the label at design time is twofold: 1) In the original implementation of the program, the cost per download is 99 cents. In the future, however, the cost might change. Generally, data that might change should be placed in the Text property of a Label object during execution time, not at design time. Therefore, the cost should be placed in the label when the form opens (in the form load event handler); 2) The cost per download is used in two places in the program — in the label and when the actual calculation to determine total cost is performed (see Figure 4-55 on page 232). When a value is to be used more than one time, it should be declared one time in a variable and then used wherever necessary. If the value must be changed in the future, it must be changed only one time. For example, if the cost per download changed to 85 cents, the cost can be changed in the cost per download variable and it then will be correct for all uses of the variable. To illustrate, the variable for the cost per download is shown in Figure 4-79.

```
12      Const cdecPricePerDownload As Decimal = 0.99D
```

FIGURE 4-79

As you can see, the price per download is declared as a constant that cannot be changed during program execution. If the price changes in the future, the developer can make one change to this declaration and all elements of the program that use the value will be correct.

To create the actual heading for the Digital Downloads program, the value in the variable declared in Figure 4-79 must be combined with the words Per Download and that result must be placed in the Text property of the lblCostHeading Label object. The process of joining two different values into a single string is called **concatenation**. Whenever you use concatenation, the values being concatenated must be String data types. You will note in Figure 4-79 that the cdecPricePerDownload variable is a Decimal data type. Therefore, it must be changed to a String data type before being joined with the words in the heading.

The statement in Figure 4-80 converts the Decimal data type to a String data type, concatenates (or joins) the two strings together, and then places that result in the Text property of the lblCostHeading Label object.

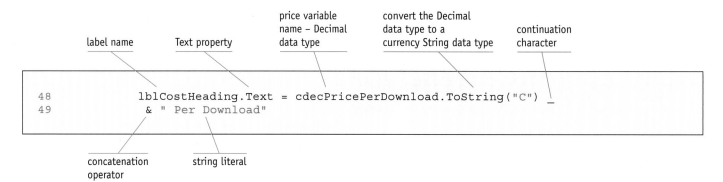

FIGURE 4-80

In Figure 4-80, the string generated on the right of the equal sign will be placed in the Text property of the lblCostHeading Label object. The first entry on the right of the equal sign is the price variable name (see Figure 4-79). Following the dot operator is the ToString procedure name, followed by the currency argument within parentheses. You will recall from earlier in this chapter that the ToString procedure converts a numeric value to a String data type. When the currency argument ("C") is used, the String value returned is in a currency format (see Figure 4-72 on page 241 for a detailed explanation).

Following the conversion statement is the **concatenation operator (&)**. Whenever the Visual Basic compiler encounters the concatenation operator, the string on the left of the operator is joined with the string data on the right of the operator to create a single concatenated string. The resulting concatenated string then is placed in the Text property of the lblCostHeading Label object.

The process that occurs on the right of the equal sign is illustrated in Figure 4-81.

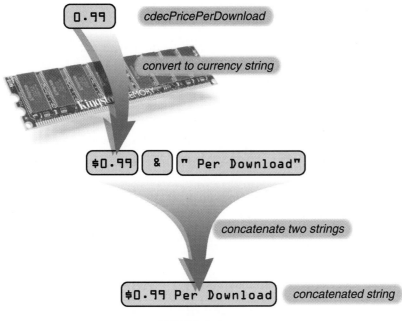

FIGURE 4-81

In Figure 4-81 you can see that to obtain the concatenated string, the Decimal value in the cdecPricePerDownload decimal variable is converted to a currency String data type. Then, that value is concatenated with the string literal to create the concatenated string. In the assignment statement in Figure 4-80, the concatenated string is assigned to the Text property of the lblCostHeading Label object.

Class Scope

You will recall from earlier in this chapter that when you declare a variable you also define the scope of the variable. The scope of a variable identifies where within the program the variable can be referenced. For example, if a variable is declared within an event handler procedure, the variable can be referenced only within that procedure.

Sometimes, a variable must be referenced in multiple event handlers. In the Digital Downloads program, the value in the cdecPricePerDownload variable is referenced in the Calculate button event handler when the total cost is calculated (see Figure 4-55 on page 232). The value also is referenced in the form load event when the heading is displayed (see Figure 4-80 on page 246). Because the variable is referenced in two different event handling procedures, it must be defined at the class level instead of the procedure (event handler) level. This means that the variable must be declared in the code prior to the first procedure, or event handler, in the program.

As you can see in Figure 4-82, the declaration of the cdecPricePerDownload variable follows the class definition statement but appears before the first event handler procedure.

beginning of program

class definition statement

```
' Program:   Digital Downloads
' Author:    Corinne Hoisington
' Date:      April 14, 2014
' Purpose:   This application calculates and displays
'            the total cost of music downloads

Option Strict On

Public Class frmDigitalDownloads

    ' Cost per download - used in multiple procedures
    Const _cdecPricePerDownload As Decimal = 0.99D

    Private Sub btnCalculateCost_Click(ByVal sender As System.Object, ByVal e As System
    .EventArgs) Handles btnCalculateCost.Click
        ' This event handler is executed when the user clicks the
        ' Calculate Cost button. It calculates and displays the cost
        ' of music downloads (number of downloads times the cost per download).
```

first event handler

declaration of Price Per Download variable

FIGURE 4-82

IN THE REAL WORLD

When a variable is declared for use throughout a class, the naming convention specifies that the name should begin with an underscore character (_). So, whenever you see a variable name that begins with the underscore character, you know that variable has class scope.

As a result of the code in Figure 4-82, the scope of the _cdecPricePerDownload variable will be all procedures within the class; that is, code within any event handler procedure within the class can reference the variable. Because the variable is declared as a constant, the value in the variable cannot be changed by code within the class; however, the value in the class can be referenced to calculate the total cost and to create the cost heading.

Debugging Your Program

When your program processes numeric data entered by a user, you should be aware of several errors that can occur when users enter data that the program does not expect. The three errors that occur most often are: 1) Format Exception; 2) Overflow Exception; 3) Divide By Zero Exception.

A **Format Exception** occurs when the user enters data that a statement within the program cannot process properly. In the Digital Downloads program, you will recall that the user is supposed to enter a numeric value for the number of song downloads desired. When the user clicks the Calculate Cost button, the program converts the value entered to an integer and then uses the numeric value in the calculation (see Figure 4-52 on page 230). If the user enters a nonnumeric value, such as abc shown in Figure 4-83a, the conversion process cannot take place because the argument passed to the Convert class is not a numeric value. When this occurs, a Format Exception error is recognized and the error box shown in Figure 4-83b is displayed.

FIGURE 4-83a

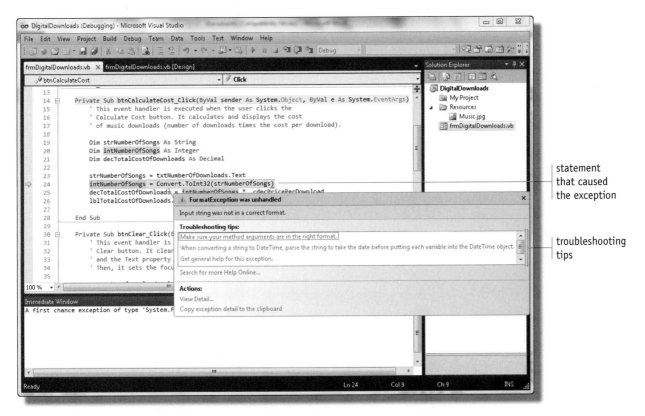

FIGURE 4-83b

In Figure 4-83a, the user entered the value abc and then clicked the Calculate Cost button. When control was passed to the ToInt32 procedure to convert the value from the String value entered in the text box to an Integer, the Format Exception was triggered because the value in the strNumberOfSongs was not numeric. When an exception occurs, the execution of the program is terminated. With Visual Studio running, click the Stop Debugging button on the Standard toolbar.

An **Overflow Exception** occurs when the user enters a value greater than the maximum value that can be processed by the statement. For example, in the Digital Downloads program, if the user enters a value in the text box that is greater than the value that can be converted by the ToInt32 procedure, an Overflow Exception occurs.

An Overflow Exception also can occur when a calculation creates a value larger than one that can be processed by a procedure. For example, if two large but valid numbers are multiplied, the product of the multiplication might be larger than can be processed.

The third type of common error is the **Divide By Zero Exception**. It is not possible to divide by zero, so if your program contains a division operation and the divisor is equal to zero, the Divide By Zero Exception will occur.

Whenever an exception occurs, a window similar to that shown in Figure 4-83b will be displayed.

To avoid exceptions, which should always be your goal, you can use certain techniques for editing the data and ensuring that the user has entered valid data that will not cause an exception. You will learn in Chapter 5 and Chapter 6 how to write code that checks user input to ensure exceptions do not occur because of the data users enter.

Program Design

As you have learned, the requirements document identifies the purpose of the program being developed, the application title, the procedures to be followed when using the program, any equations and calculations required in the program, any conditions within the program that must be tested, notes and restrictions that must be followed by the program, and any other comments that would be helpful to understanding the problem. The requirements document for the Digital Downloads application is shown in Figure 4-84.

REQUIREMENTS DOCUMENT

Date submitted: April 14, 2014

Application title: Digital Downloads

Purpose: The Digital Downloads program allows the user to enter the number of songs to be downloaded. The program calculates the total cost of the downloads based on a price of $0.99 per song.

Program Procedures: In a Windows application, the user enters the number of songs she wants to download. The program calculates the total cost of downloads. The user can clear the values on the screen and enter a new value for the number of downloads.

Algorithms, Processing, and Conditions:

1. The user must be able to enter the number of songs to be downloaded.
2. The user can initiate the calculation and display the total cost of the downloads.
3. The application computes the total cost of downloads by multiplying the number of downloads times the cost per download ($0.99).
4. The total cost of downloads is displayed as a currency value.
5. The user should be able to clear the value entered for the number of downloads and the total cost of downloads.
6. The user should be provided with a button to exit the program.

Notes and Restrictions: n/a

Comments:

1. A graphic should depict a musical image named Music. The graphic is available at scsite.com/vb2010/ch4/images.

FIGURE 4-84

The use case definition identifies the steps the user will take when using the program. The use case definition for the Digital Downloads program is shown in Figure 4-85.

USE CASE DEFINITION

1. The Windows application opens with a text box where the user can enter the number of song downloads. The user interface includes the text box, an area to display the total cost of downloads, a Calculate Cost button, a Clear button, and an Exit button.
2. The user enters the number of songs downloads.
3. The user clicks the Calculate Cost button.
4. The program displays the total cost of the song downloads.
5. The user clicks the Clear button to clear the Number of Song Downloads text box and erase the total cost of downloads amount.
6. The user repeats steps 2-5 if desired.
7. The user clicks the Exit button to terminate the application.

FIGURE 4-85

Event Planning Document

You will recall that the event planning document consists of a table that specifies an object in the user interface that will cause an event, the action taken by the user to trigger the event, and the event processing that must occur. The event planning document for the Digital Downloads program is shown in Figure 4-86.

EVENT PLANNING DOCUMENT

Program Name: Digital Downloads	Developer: Corinne Hoisington	Object: frmDigitalDownloads	Date: April 14, 2014
OBJECT	**EVENT TRIGGER**	**EVENT PROCESSING**	
btnCalculate	Click	Assign data entered in text box to a String variable Convert data entered to numeric integer Calculate total cost of downloads (number of downloads * price per download) Display total cost of downloads	
btnClear	Click	Clear number of song downloads text box Clear total cost of downloads label text Set focus on number of song downloads text box	
btnExit	Click	Close the window and terminate the program	
frmDigitalDownloads	Load	Display heading with price per download Clear the placement digits for total cost of downloads Label object Set focus on number of song downloads text box	

FIGURE 4-86

Code the Program

After identifying the events and tasks within the events, you are ready to code the program. As you have learned, coding the program means entering Visual Basic statements to accomplish the tasks specified on the event planning document. As you enter the code, you also will implement the logic to carry out the required processing.

Guided Program Development

To design the user interface for the Digital Downloads program and enter the code required to process each event in the program, complete the following steps:

NOTE TO THE LEARNER

As you will recall, in the following activity, you should complete the tasks within the specified steps. Each of the tasks is accompanied by a Hint Screen. The purpose of the Hint Screen is to indicate where in the Visual Studio window you should perform the activity; it also serves as a reminder of the method that you should use to create the user interface or enter code. If you need further help completing the step, refer to the figure number identified by the term ref: in the step.

Guided Program Development *continued*

Phase 1: Create User Interface Mockup

1

- **Create a Windows Application** Open Visual Studio using the Start button on the Windows taskbar and the All Programs submenu. Close the Start page by clicking the Start Page Close button. To create a Windows application, click the New Project button on the Standard toolbar; if necessary, click Visual Basic in the Installed Templates pane; click Windows Forms Application in the center pane; double-click the term WindowsApplication1 in the Name text box and then type `DigitalDownload`. Click the OK button in the New Project dialog box.

- **Display the Toolbox** Ensure the Toolbox is displayed in the Visual Studio window. If it is not, click the Toolbox button on the Standard toolbar. If necessary, click the plus sign next to the Common Controls category name in the Toolbox to display the tools *(ref: Figure 4-21)*.

- **Name the Windows Form Object** In the Solution Explorer window, right-click the Form1.vb form file and select Rename. Type frmDigitalDownloads.vb and press the ENTER key.

- **Change the Title on the Title Bar** To change the title on the Windows Form object, click the form, scroll in the Properties window until the Text property is displayed, double-click in the right column of the Text property, type `Download Music`, and then press the ENTER key.

● **Resize the Windows Form Object** Drag the lower-right corner of the Windows Form object to resize it to approximately the size shown in Figure 4-87 on page 257. To match Figure 4-87 exactly, make the form size (397,338).

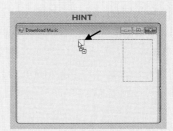

● **Add a PictureBox Object** Add a PictureBox object to the Windows Form object by dragging the PictureBox .NET component onto the Windows Form object. Place it in the upper-right corner of the Windows Form object.

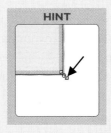

● **Name the PictureBox Object** With the PictureBox object selected, scroll in the Properties window until the (Name) property is visible. Double-click in the right column of the (Name) property, type `picDownloadHeading`, and then press the ENTER key.

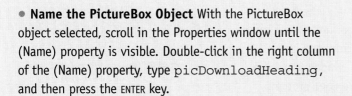

● **Resize the PictureBox Object** To resize the picDownloadHeading PictureBox object, if necessary select the PictureBox object. Click to the right of the Size property and change it to 81,110.

● **Add a Heading Label** To insert the Digital Downloads heading label, drag the Label .NET component from the Toolbox to the Windows Form object. Top-align the Label object and the PictureBox object through the use of blue snap lines. Position the PictureBox object and the Label object as shown in Figure 4-87.

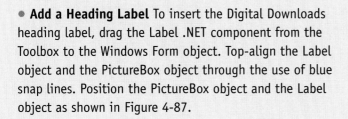
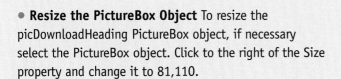

(continues)

● **Name the Label Object** Give the name lblDigitalDownloads to the Label object by scrolling to the (Name) property in the Properties window, double-clicking in the right column of the (Name) property, typing lblDigitalDownloads and then pressing the ENTER key.

● **Change the Text of the Label Object** To change the text displayed in the Label object, scroll until the Text property is visible, double-click in the right column of the Text property, type Digital Downloads and then press the ENTER key.

● **Change the Heading Font, Font Style, and Size** To make the heading stand out on the Windows form, its font should be larger and more prominent. To change the font to Cooper, its style to Black, and its Size to 18, with the Label object selected, scroll in the Properties window until the Font property is visible. Click in the right column of the Font property, and then click the Ellipsis button that is displayed in the right column. In the Font dialog box that appears, scroll if necessary and then click Cooper (or a similar font) in the Font list, click Black in the Font style list, and click 18 in the Size list. Then click the OK button in the Font dialog box.

● **Horizontally Center the PictureBox Object and the Label Object** The PictureBox object and the Label object should be centered horizontally as a group. To complete this task, click the Windows Form object to unselect any object, click the PictureBox object to select it, hold down the CTRL key and then click the Label object. Click Format on the menu bar, point to Center in Form on the Format menu, and then click Horizontally on the Center in Form submenu.

The PictureBox object and the Label object are placed on the re-sized Windows Form object (Figure 4-87). The font and font size for the Label object are appropriate for a heading in the window.

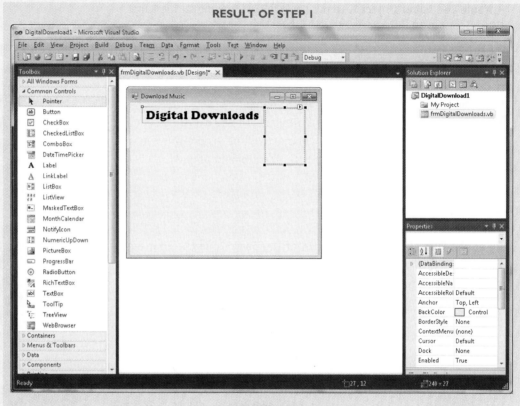

FIGURE 4-87

2

● **Add a Second Heading Label** To add the second heading label required for the Window, drag a Label .NET component from the Toolbox to the Windows Form object. Place the second Label object below the Digital Downloads Label object.

(continues)

● **Name the Label Object** Give the name lblCostHeading to the Label object you just placed on the Windows Form object.

● **Change the Text in the Label Object** Change the text in the lblCostHeading object to $X.XX Per Download. This text is a placeholder in the Label object so that the Label object will be visible when it is not selected, and so the Label object can be properly aligned.

● **Set the Font, Font style, and Size of the Font** Using the Font property and Ellipsis button in the Properties window to display the Font dialog box, change the font to Century Gothic, the Font style to Regular, and the Size to 12.

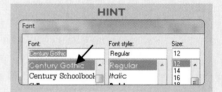

● **Center-Align the Two Label Objects** The lblCostHeading Label object should be centered under the lblDigitalDownloads Label object. To accomplish this, click the Windows Form object to unselect any other objects, select the lblDigitalDownloads Label object, hold down the CTRL key, and click the lblCostHeading Label object. Click Format on the menu bar, point to Align on the Format menu, and then click Centers on the Align submenu.

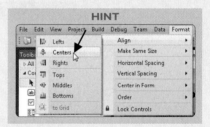

The PictureBox object and the Label objects are properly aligned in the Windows Form object (Figure 4-88).

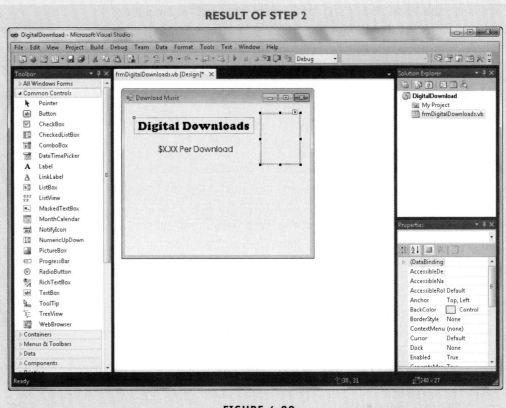

RESULT OF STEP 2

FIGURE 4-88

3

● **Add a Label for Number of Song Downloads** Add the Label object for the number of song downloads label by dragging it from the Toolbox. Place it below the lblDigitalDownloads object, and align the Label object using the blue snap lines.

HINT

HEADS UP

As you work through the development of your program, remember to save the program frequently. To save the program, you can click the Save All button on the Standard toolbar.

(continues)

● **Change the Name, Enter Text, and Change the Font for Number of Song Downloads Label** Using techniques you have learned previously, change the name of the Label object to lblNumberOfDownloads. In the Text property, enter Number of Song Downloads:. Using the Font property in the Properties dialog box, change the font to Century Gothic, Regular style, 12 point Size.

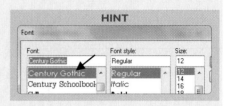

● **Add a TextBox Object for the Number of Song Downloads** Drag and drop a TextBox object onto the Windows Form object. Use the blue snap lines to align the top of the TextBox object with the top of the Number of Song Downloads Label object and align with the left edge of the picDownloadHeading Picture object. Name the TextBox object txtNumberOfDownloads *(ref: Figure 4-3)*.

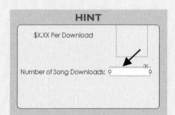

● **Enter Data into Text Property** As you learned in this chapter, even though the TextBox object will not contain text when the program begins execution, it still is necessary to enter text in the Text property of the TextBox object to size it properly. To enter text into the TextBox, select the TextBox object. Then, in the Properties window, change the Text property to 888 *(ref: Figure 4-6)*.

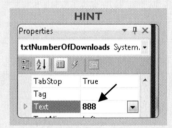

● **Change the Font and Size of the TextBox Object** Using the Properties dialog box, change the font for the TextBox object to Century Gothic, Regular style, 12 point Size. Drag the right border of the TextBox object so the numbers fit properly in the text box *(ref: Figure 4-8)*.

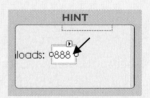

● **Align the Resized TextBox Object** To realign the resized TextBox object, drag it up until the red snap line indicates the text in the TextBox object is bottom-aligned with the label *(ref: Figure 4-9)*.

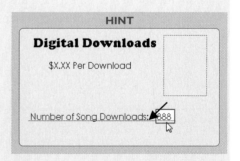

● **Center-Align Text in the TextBox Object** To center-align the text in the TextBox object, select the TextBox object, scroll in the Properties window until the TextAlign property is visible, click the list arrow in the right column of the TextAlign property, and then click Center on the TextAlign property list *(ref: Figure 4-10)*.

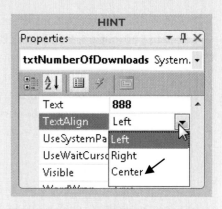

● **Remove Text from TextBox Object** Because the TextBox object is sized properly, remove the digits from the TextBox object by selecting the digits in the Text property of the object and pressing the DELETE key *(ref: Figure 4-12)*.

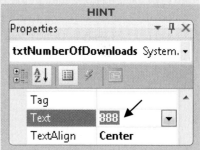

● **Add the Total Cost of Downloads Label Objects** The total cost of the downloads that is calculated by the program must be displayed as the Text property in a Label object. In addition, another label actually identifies the total cost. Drag two labels onto the Windows Form object and place them on the same horizontal line (use blue snap lines). Vertically align the left side of the left label with the label above it. Vertically align the left side of the right label with the text box above it. Name the Label object on the left lblTotalCostLabel. Name the label on the right lblTotalCostOfDownloads *(ref: Figure 4-18)*.

● **Enter Text for the Labels and Change the Font** Select the lblTotalCostLabel Label object and then double-click in the right column of the Text property for the label. Type the text Total Cost of Downloads: and then press the ENTER key. Select the lblTotalCostOfDownloads Label object and then double-click in the right column of the Text property for the label. Enter the value $888.88 because this represents the largest expected value for the label. With the right label selected, hold down the CTRL key and then click the left label. With both labels selected, change the font to Century Gothic, Regular style, 12 point Size.

(continues)

●　**Add Buttons** Three buttons are required for the user interface: the Calculate Cost button, the Clear button, and the Exit button. Drag three buttons onto the Windows Form object below the labels. Use blue snap lines to horizontally align the tops of the buttons. Using the (Name) property for each button, name the first button btnCalculateCost, name the second button btnClear, and name the third button btnExit.

●　**Change the Button Text and Change the Font Style** Using the Text property for each button, change the text for the btnCalculateCost Button object to Calculate Cost. Change the text for the btnClear button to Clear. Change the text for the btnExit button to Exit. Select all three buttons (click the Calculate Cost button, hold down the CTRL key, and then click the other two buttons), click the Font property, click the Ellipsis button in the right column of the Font property, and in the Font dialog box, change the Font style to Bold.

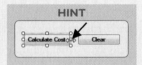

HINT

●　**Change Button Size** The btnCalculateCost button does not display the entire Text property, so it must be enlarged. Drag the right border of the btnCalculateCost button until the entire Text property is visible.

HINT

●　**Change the Size of the Other Buttons** Click the btnCalculateCost button first, and then hold down the CTRL key and click the other two buttons to select all three buttons. Make these buttons the same size by clicking Format on the menu bar, pointing to Make Same Size on the Format menu, and clicking Both on the Make Same Size submenu.

HINT

●　**Space and Center the Buttons** With all three buttons selected, display the Format menu, point to Horizontal Spacing on the Format menu, and then click Make Equal on the Horizontal Spacing submenu. Display the Format menu, point to Center in Form on the Format menu, and then click Horizontally on the Center in Form submenu to center all three buttons horizontally in the Windows Form object.

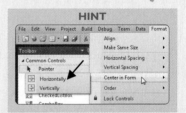

HINT

The mockup for the user interface is complete (Figure 4-89).

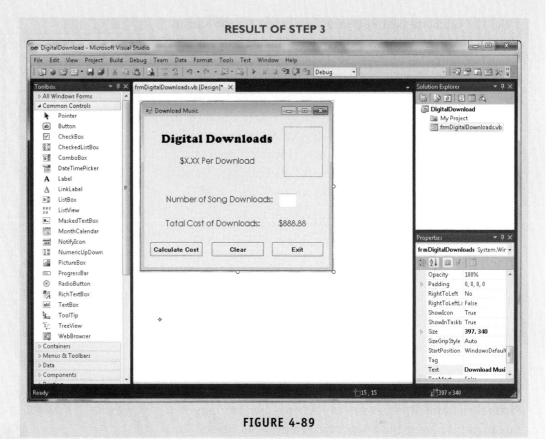

RESULT OF STEP 3

FIGURE 4-89

Phase 2: Fine-Tune the User Interface

4

HINT

● **Set the BackColor Property for the Windows Form Object** The user interface must be finished by setting the colors, adding images, and preparing the user interface for program execution. To set the BackColor property for the user interface to DarkSeaGreen, select the Windows Form object. In the Properties window, click the BackColor property; click the BackColor arrow in the right column of the BackColor property; if necessary, click the Web tab; scroll as required; and then click DarkSeaGreen in the BackColor list.

● **Set the BackColor for the Button Objects** To set the BackColor for the button objects to White, select all three buttons. Click the BackColor property in the Properties window; click the BackColor arrow in the right column of the BackColor property; if necessary, click the Web tab; scroll as required; and then click White in the BackColor list.

(continues)

● **Set the Calculate Cost Button Object as the Accept Button**
When the user enters the number of song downloads, she should
able to calculate the total cost of downloads by clicking the
Calculate Cost button or by pressing the ENTER key on the
keyboard. To assign the Calculate Cost button as the Accept
button, select the Windows Form object by clicking anywhere in
the window except on another object; scroll in the Properties
window until the AcceptButton property is visible; click the
AcceptButton property; click the AcceptButton property arrow;
and then click btnCalculateCost in the list *(ref: Figure 4-20)*.

● **Set the Clear Button Object as the Cancel Button** When the
user presses the ESC key on the keyboard, the same action as
clicking the Clear button should occur. To set the Clear button
as the Cancel button, click the Windows Form object, click
the CancelButton property in the Properties window, click the
CancelButton arrow, and then click btnClear in the list
(ref: Page 211).

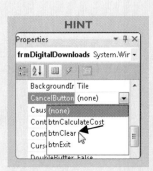

● **Insert the Music Image into the picDownloadHeading
PictureBox Object** The last step to ready the user interface for
execution is to insert the image into the PictureBox object. To
do so, if necessary download and save the Music image from
scsite.com/vb2010/ch4/images. Then, with the picture box
selected, click the ellipsis button of the Image property in the
Properties window, click the Import button in the Select
Resource dialog box, locate the image, and then import the
image into the Resource folder. Click the OK button in the
Select Resource dialog box.

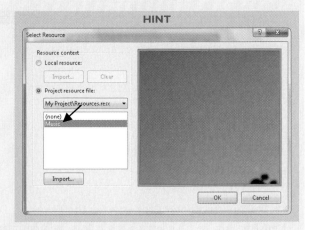

● **Resize the Image** To resize the Music image, with the
picDownloadHeading PictureBox object selected, in the Properties
window click the SizeMode property in the left column, click the
SizeMode arrow in the right column, and then click StretchImage
in the list.

The user interface is complete (Figure 4-90).

RESULT OF STEP 4

FIGURE 4-90

Phase 3: Code the Application

5

● **Code the Comments** Double-click the btnCalculateCost Button object on the frmDigitalDownloads Windows Form object to open the code editing window and create the btnCalculateCost_Click Event Handler. Click the Close button on the Toolbox title bar to close the Toolbox. Click in front of the first words, Public Class frmDigitalDownloads, and press the ENTER key to create a blank line. Press the UP ARROW key on your keyboard. Insert the first four standard comments. Insert the Option Strict On command at the beginning of the code to turn on strict type checking *(ref: Figure 4-53).*

HINT

(continues)

● **Enter the _cdecPricePerDownload Class Variable**
The next step is to enter the class variable that is
referenced in more than one event handler within
this program. This variable, which contains the price
per download, is referenced for calculating the total
cost and also for the heading. To enter this variable,
press the DOWN ARROW key on your keyboard until the
insertion point is on the blank line following the
Public Class command (line 9). Press the ENTER key to
add a blank line, then type the comment that identifies the variable. Press the ENTER key and then write
the declaration for the _cdecPricePerDownload variable. The constant decimal variable should contain
the value 0.99. The underline character (_) in the
variable name indicates the variable is a class variable that is referenced in multiple procedures within
the class *(ref: Figure 4-47)*.

● **Comment the btnCalculateCost_Click Event
Handler** Following the Private statement for the
btnCalculateCost_Click event handler, enter a
comment to describe the purpose of the
btnCalculateCost_Click event.

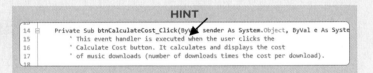

● **Declare and Initialize the Variables** This event
handler requires three variables: 1) strNumberOfSongs:
Holds the number of song downloads entered by
the user. 2) intNumberOfSongs: Holds the integer
value for the number of song downloads entered
by the user; 3) decTotalCostOfDownloads: Holds the
calculated total cost of downloads. Declare these
three variables *(ref: Figure 4-22, Figure 4-35,
Figure 4-37)*.

```
19        Dim strNumberOfSongs As String
20        Dim intNumberOfSongs As Integer
21        Dim decTotalCostOfDownloads As Decimal
```

● **Write the Statements to Place the Number of Downloads in a Variable and Convert the Value to an Integer** The first steps in the event handler are to move the number of songs value from the Text property of the txtNumberOfDownloads TextBox object to a string variable and then convert that value to an integer value. Using IntelliSense, write the code to complete these steps *(ref: Figure 4-29, Figure 4-52).*

```
HINT
22
23        strNumberOfSongs = txtNumberOfDownloads.Text
24        intNumberOfSongs = Convert.ToInt32(strNumberOfSongs)
```

● **Calculate Total Cost of Downloads** To calculate the total cost of downloads and place the result in the decTotalCostOfDownloads variable, the number of songs is multiplied by the price per download. Using IntelliSense, write the statement to perform this calculation *(ref: Figure 4-55).*

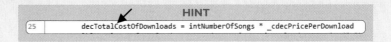

```
HINT
25        decTotalCostOfDownloads = intNumberOfSongs * _cdecPricePerDownload
```

● **Convert the Decimal Total Cost of Downloads to a String Currency Value and Place It in the Text Property of the lblTotalCostOfDownloads Label Object** Once the total cost of downloads has been calculated, it must be converted from a Decimal value to a currency String value so it can be displayed as the value in the Text property of a Label object. Write the statement to perform this conversion and place the converted value in the Text property of the lblTotalCostOfDownloads Label object *(ref: Figure 4-72).*

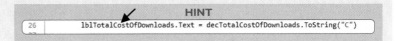

```
HINT
26        lblTotalCostOfDownloads.Text = decTotalCostOfDownloads.ToString("C")
```

(continues)

The coding for the btnCalculateCost_Click event handler is complete (Figure 4-91).

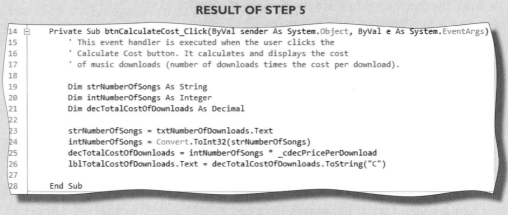

RESULT OF STEP 5

```
14 ⊟      Private Sub btnCalculateCost_Click(ByVal sender As System.Object, ByVal e As System.EventArgs)
15            ' This event handler is executed when the user clicks the
16            ' Calculate Cost button. It calculates and displays the cost
17            ' of music downloads (number of downloads times the cost per download).
18
19            Dim strNumberOfSongs As String
20            Dim intNumberOfSongs As Integer
21            Dim decTotalCostOfDownloads As Decimal
22
23            strNumberOfSongs = txtNumberOfDownloads.Text
24            intNumberOfSongs = Convert.ToInt32(strNumberOfSongs)
25            decTotalCostOfDownloads = intNumberOfSongs * _cdecPricePerDownload
26            lblTotalCostOfDownloads.Text = decTotalCostOfDownloads.ToString("C")
27
28        End Sub
```

FIGURE 4-91

6

● **Run the Application** After you have entered code, you should run the application to ensure it is working properly. Run the Digital Downloads application by clicking the Start Debugging button on the Standard toolbar. Enter 10 for the number of song downloads and then click the Calculate Cost button. The Total Cost of Downloads should be $9.90. Enter 15 for the number of song downloads and then press the ENTER key on the keyboard.

When the number of downloads is 10 songs, the total cost of downloads is $9.90 (Figure 4-92).

RESULT OF STEP 6

FIGURE 4-92

● **Write the Code for the Clear Button Event
Handler** Click the frmDigitalDownloads.vb [Design]
tab in the coding window to return to the design
window. Double-click the Clear button to create the
event handler for the Clear button. The Clear button event handler must accomplish the following
tasks: Clear the txtNumberOfDownloads text
box; clear the value in the Text property of the
lblTotalCostOfDownloads Label object; set the focus
to the txtNumberOfDownloads text box. Write the
comments for the event handler and then, using
IntelliSense, write the code for the event handler
(ref: Figure 4-74, Figure 4-75, Figure 4-77).

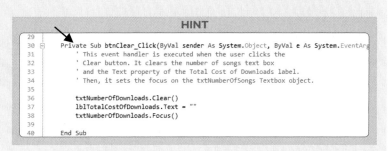

```
HINT
29
30 ⊟     Private Sub btnClear_Click(ByVal sender As System.Object, ByVal e As System.EventArg
31              ' This event handler is executed when the user clicks the
32              ' Clear button. It clears the number of songs text box
33              ' and the Text property of the Total Cost of Downloads label.
34              ' Then, it sets the focus on the txtNumberOfSongs Textbox object.
35
36              txtNumberOfDownloads.Clear()
37              lblTotalCostOfDownloads.Text = ""
38              txtNumberOfDownloads.Focus()
39
40          End Sub
```

● **Write the Code for the Form Load Event
Handler** Click the frmDigitalDownloads.vb [Design]
tab in the coding window to return to the design
window. Double-click the Windows Form object to
create the event handler for the Form Load event.
The Form Load event handler must accomplish the
following tasks: Using concatenation, create
and display the Price per Download heading
in the Text property of the lblCostHeading
Label object; clear the Text property of the
lblTotalCostOfDownloads Label object; set the
focus in the txtNumberOfDownloads TextBox
object. Write the comments for the event handler
and then, using IntelliSense, write the code for
the event handler *(ref: Figure 4-75, Figure 4-77,
Figure 4-80).*

```
HINT
41
42 ⊟     Private Sub frmDigitalDownloads_Load(ByVal sender As System.Object, ByVal e As Syst
43              ' This event handler is executed when the form is loaded.
44              ' It displays the cost heading, clears the Text property of the
45              ' Total Cost of Downloads label, and sets the focus on
46              ' the txtNumberOfSongs Textbox object.
47
48              lblCostHeading.Text = _cdecPricePerDownload.ToString("C") & " Per Download"
49              lblTotalCostOfDownloads.Text = ""
50              txtNumberOfDownloads.Focus()
51
52          End Sub
```

● **Write the Code for the Exit Button Event
Handler** Click the frmDigitalDownloads.vb [Design]
tab in the coding window to return to the design
window. Double-click the Exit button to create the
event handler for the Exit button. The Exit button
event handler must close the window and terminate the application. Write the comments and
code for this event handler.

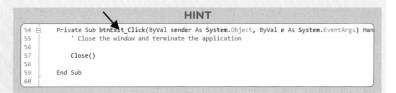

```
HINT
54 ⊟     Private Sub btnExit_Click(ByVal sender As System.Object, ByVal e As System.EventArgs) Han
55              ' Close the window and terminate the application
56
57              Close()
58
59          End Sub
60
```

(continues)

The coding is complete for the Clear button event handler, the Form load event handler, and the Exit button event handler (Figure 4-93).

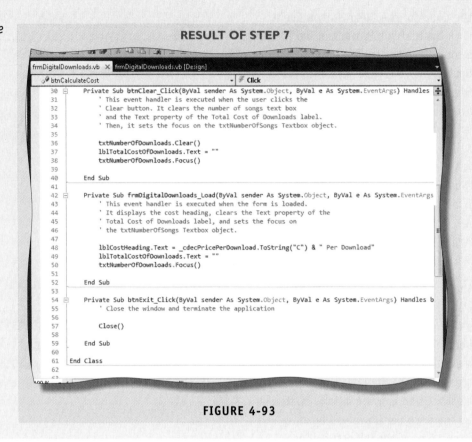

RESULT OF STEP 7

```vb
      Private Sub btnClear_Click(ByVal sender As System.Object, ByVal e As System.EventArgs) Handles
30
31         ' This event handler is executed when the user clicks the
32         ' Clear button. It clears the number of songs text box
33         ' and the Text property of the Total Cost of Downloads label.
34         ' Then, it sets the focus on the txtNumberOfSongs Textbox object.
35
36         txtNumberOfDownloads.Clear()
37         lblTotalCostOfDownloads.Text = ""
38         txtNumberOfDownloads.Focus()
39
40      End Sub
41
42      Private Sub frmDigitalDownloads_Load(ByVal sender As System.Object, ByVal e As System.EventArgs
43         ' This event handler is executed when the form is loaded.
44         ' It displays the cost heading, clears the Text property of the
45         ' Total Cost of Downloads label, and sets the focus on
46         ' the txtNumberOfSongs Textbox object.
47
48         lblCostHeading.Text = _cdecPricePerDownload.ToString("C") & " Per Download"
49         lblTotalCostOfDownloads.Text = ""
50         txtNumberOfDownloads.Focus()
51
52      End Sub
53
54      Private Sub btnExit_Click(ByVal sender As System.Object, ByVal e As System.EventArgs) Handles b
55         ' Close the window and terminate the application
56
57         Close()
58
59      End Sub
60
61   End Class
62
```

FIGURE 4-93

8

• **Test the Program** After finishing the coding, you should test the program to ensure it works properly. Run the Digital Downloads application by clicking the Start Debugging button on the Standard toolbar. Enter 20 for the number of song downloads and then click the Calculate Cost button. The Total Cost of Downloads should be $19.80. Click the Clear button to clear the text box and the label containing the total cost of downloads. Enter 5 for the number of song downloads and then press the ENTER key on the keyboard. The Total Cost of Downloads should be $4.95. Press the ESC key to clear the text box and the label containing the total cost of downloads. Enter other values to completely test the program.

The program runs properly (Figure 4-94).

RESULT OF STEP 8

FIGURE 4-94

Code Listing

The complete code for the sample program is shown in Figure 4-95.

```vb
 1  ' Program:  Digital Downloads
 2  ' Author:   Corinne Hoisington
 3  ' Date:     April 14, 2014
 4  ' Purpose:  This application calculates and displays
 5  '           the total cost of music downloads
 6
 7  Option Strict On
 8
 9  Public Class frmDigitalDownloads
10
11      ' Cost per download - used in multiple procedures
12      Const _cdecPricePerDownload As Decimal = 0.99D
13
14      Private Sub btnCalculateCost_Click(ByVal sender As System.Object, ByVal e As System.EventArgs) Handles btnCalculateCost.Click
15          ' This event handler is executed when the user clicks the
16          ' Calculate Cost button. It calculates and displays the cost
17          ' of music downloads (number of downloads times the cost per download).
18
19          Dim strNumberOfSongs As String
20          Dim intNumberOfSongs As Integer
21          Dim decTotalCostOfDownloads As Decimal
22
23          strNumberOfSongs = txtNumberOfDownloads.Text
24          intNumberOfSongs = Convert.ToInt32(strNumberOfSongs)
25          decTotalCostOfDownloads = intNumberOfSongs * _cdecPricePerDownload
26          lblTotalCostOfDownloads.Text = decTotalCostOfDownloads.ToString("C")
27
28      End Sub
29
30      Private Sub btnClear_Click(ByVal sender As System.Object, ByVal e As System.EventArgs) Handles btnClear.Click
31          ' This event handler is executed when the user clicks the
32          ' Clear button. It clears the number of songs text box
33          ' and the Text property of the Total Cost of Downloads label.
34          ' Then, it sets the focus on the txtNumberOfSongs Textbox object.
35
36          txtNumberOfDownloads.Clear()
37          lblTotalCostOfDownloads.Text = ""
38          txtNumberOfDownloads.Focus()
39
40      End Sub
41
42      Private Sub frmDigitalDownloads_Load(ByVal sender As System.Object, ByVal e As System.EventArgs) Handles MyBase.Load
43          ' This event handler is executed when the form is loaded.
44          ' It displays the cost heading, clears the Text property of the
45          ' Total Cost of Downloads label, and sets the focus on
46          ' the txtNumberOfSongs Textbox object.
47
48          lblCostHeading.Text = _cdecPricePerDownload.ToString("C") & " Per Download"
49          lblTotalCostOfDownloads.Text = ""
50          txtNumberOfDownloads.Focus()
51
```

FIGURE 4-95 (continues)

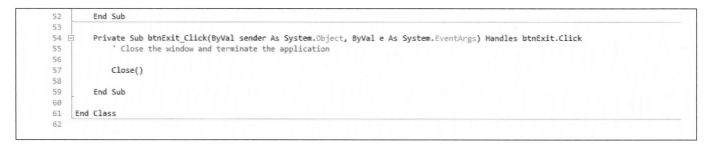

```
52        End Sub
53
54 ⊟      Private Sub btnExit_Click(ByVal sender As System.Object, ByVal e As System.EventArgs) Handles btnExit.Click
55            ' Close the window and terminate the application
56
57            Close()
58
59        End Sub
60
61   End Class
62
```

FIGURE 4-95 (continued)

Summary

In this chapter you have learned to declare variables and write arithmetic operations. The items listed in the table in Figure 4-96 include all the new Visual Studio and Visual Basic skills you have learned in this chapter.

Visual Basic Skills		
Skill	**Figure Number**	**Web Address For Video**
Place a TextBox object on the Windows Form object	Figure 4-3	scsite.com/vb2010/ch4/figure4-3
Size and position a TextBox object	Figure 4-6	scsite.com/vb2010/ch4/figure4-6
Align text in a TextBox object	Figure 4-10	scsite.com/vb2010/ch4/figure4-10
Create a MultiLine TextBox object	Figure 4-13	scsite.com/vb2010/ch4/figure4-13
Place a masked TextBox object on the Windows Form object	Figure 4-15	scsite.com/vb2010/ch4/figure4-15
Place and size a Label object on the Windows Form object	Figure 4-18	scsite.com/vb2010/ch4/figure4-18
Assign a Button object as the Accept button	Figure 4-20	scsite.com/vb2010/ch4/figure4-20
Assign a Button object as the Cancel button	Page 211	
Close the Toolbox	Figure 4-21	scsite.com/vb2010/ch4/figure4-21
Define a String variable	Figure 4-22	
Write an assignment statement	Figure 4-24	
Use IntelliSense to enter a variable and an assignment statement	Figure 4-25	scsite.com/vb2010/ch4/figure4-25
Declare an Integer data type	Figure 4-35	
Declare a Decimal data type	Figure 4-37	

Visual Basic Skills (continued)

Skill	Figure Number	Web Address For Video
Declare a Char data type	Figure 4-40	
Declare a Boolean data type	Figure 4-42	
Declare a constant variable	Figure 4-47	
Use an argument in a procedure call statement	Figure 4-49	
Write a procedure call statement for the ToInt32 procedure in the Convert class	Figure 4-52	
Enter the Option Strict On statement	Figure 4-53	
Perform arithmetic operations using arithmetic operators	Figure 4-56	
Display numeric output data	Figure 4-72	
Write a procedure call for the Clear procedure	Figure 4-74	
Write a procedure call for the Focus procedure	Figure 4-76	
Write a String concatenation statement	Figure 4-80	
Write a variable with class scope	Figure 4-82	
Understand a Format Exception	Figure 4-83	

FIGURE 4-96

Learn It Online

Start your browser and visit scsite.com/vb2010/ch4. Follow the instructions in the exercises below.

1. **Chapter Reinforcement TF, MC, SA** Click one of the Chapter Reinforcement links for Multiple Choice, True/False, or Short Answer below the Learn It Online heading. Answer each question and submit to your instructor.

2. **Practice Test** Click the Practice Test link below the Learn It Online heading. Answer each question, enter your first and last name at the bottom of the page, and then click the Grade Test button. When the graded practice test is displayed on your screen, submit the graded practice test to your instructor. Continue to take the practice test until you are satisfied with your score.

3. **Crossword Puzzle Challenge** Click the Crossword Puzzle Challenge link below the Learn It Online heading. Read the instructions, and then click the Continue button. Work the crossword puzzle. When you are finished, click the Submit button. When the crossword puzzle is redisplayed, submit it to your instructor.

Knowledge Check

1. Name three numeric data types that can contain a decimal point.

2. Write a Dim statement for each of the following variables using the variable type and variable name that would be best for each value.

   a. The population of the state of Alaska

   b. Your weekly pay

   c. The smallest data type you can use for your age

   d. A constant for the first initial of your first name

   e. The minimum wage

   f. The name of the city in which you live

   g. The answer to a true/false question

3. Determine if each of the following variable names is valid or invalid. Please state the error in the invalid variable names.

   a. _intRadian

   b. PercentOfSales#

   c. first_Input_Value

   d. R743-L56

   e. 3CPO

   f. Close

   g. Name Of Client

4. List the steps specifying how you would perfectly align a group of TextBox objects along their left edges.

5. Which data type would be best for currency amounts?

6. Explain the precedence for the order of operations.

7. What is the solution to each of the following arithmetic expressions?

   a. $3 + 4 * 2 + 6$

   b. $16 / 2 * 4 - 3$

   c. $40 - 6 \wedge 2 / 3$

   d. 68 Mod 9

   e. $9 \setminus 4 + 3$

   f. $2 \wedge 3 + (8 - 5)$

   g. $(15 \text{ Mod } 2) - 1 + 4 * (16 \setminus 5)$

8. What is the difference between a method and a procedure?

9. What is the difference between a variable and a literal?

10. Correct the following statements:

    a. `Dim itAge As Integr`

    b. `Dim dblDiscountRate As Dbl`

    c. `Constant cstrCollege As String = "CVCC"`

    d. `Dim strLastName As String`

       `strLastName = 'McNamara'`

    e. `1.5 * decHourlyPay = decOverTimePayRate`

11. Write a statement that sets the focus on the txtLastName TextBox object.

12. Write a statement that removes the contents of the txtAge TextBox object.

13. Write a statement that blanks the Text property of the lblEligibilityAge Label object.

14. Write a statement to convert the value in the String variable strWaistSize to an integer value and place the integer value in a variable named intWaistSize.

15. Write a statement to convert the value in the String variable strHourlyPay to a Decimal value and place the Decimal value in a variable named decWage.

16. Write a statement that closes the form that currently is open.

17. Write a statement that declares a constant named decInsuranceDeductible as a Decimal data type and set its value to 379.25.

18. Which Windows Form property allows the user to press the ENTER key while the form is active and activate a button's event handler?

(continues)

19. What is a local variable? How does its scope differ from that of a global variable?

20. When the following statements are executed, what would be displayed in the lblHourlyWage Label object?

```
decHourlyWage = 12.637
lblHourlyWage.Text = decHourlyWage.ToString("C")
```

Debugging Exercises

1. Fix the following code:

```
Option Strict On
Dim intDistance As Integer

intDistance = 17.5
```

2. Fix the following code:

```
Dim dblRegularPay As Double
Dim dblOvertimePay As Double

intRegularPay = 783.87
intOvertimePay = 105.92
lbl.TotalPay = (dblRegularPay + dblOvertimePay).ToString('C')
```

3. Analyze the following code and then correct it:

```
1  ⊟Public Class Form1
2  |
3  ⊟    Private Sub btnCalculate_Click(ByVal sender
4  |
5          Dim strLengthOfSide As String
6          Dim intArea As Integer
7
8          strLengthOfSide = txtLengthOfSide.text
9          intArea = strLengthOfSide ^ 2
10         lblArea.text = intArea.ToString("C")
11    End Sub
12
13  End Class
```

FIGURE 4-97

Program Analysis

1. What will occur when the user clicks the btnSlope Button?

```
Private Sub btnSlope_Click(ByVal sender As System.Object, ByVal e As
System.EventArgs) Handles btnSlope.Click
  Dim decRise As Decimal
  Dim decRun As Decimal
  Dim decSlope As Decimal

  decRise = 12.3D
  decRun = 2.1D
  decSlope = decRise / decRun
  lblSlope.Text = "The Line Slope is " & decSlope.ToString("F3")
End Sub
```

2. How would the number .0256 be displayed if the format specifier ("P") is used in a Convert.ToString statement?

3. How would the number 3746.35555 be displayed if the format specifier ("F3") is used in a Convert.ToString statement?

4. If you want the user to enter her telephone number with the area code, which .NET component would be best to use on the Windows Form object?

5. Using the Format Specification with the ToString procedure, write the statement that would display:

   a. The value in the decDvdCost variable with a dollar sign and two places to the right of the decimal place in a label named lblDvd.

   b. The value in the decWithholdingTaxRate variable with a percent sign and one place to the right of the decimal point in a label named lblWithholdingTaxRate.

   c. The value in the decOilRevenue variable with commas as needed, two places to the right of the decimal place, and no dollar sign in a label called lblOilRevenue.

6. Write a single line of code to declare a variable decWindSpeed as a Decimal data type and assign it the value 25.47. Use a forced literal to ensure the compiler views this number as a Decimal data type.

7. What would the values of the following variables be at the end of the code that follows:

   a. intParts

   b. intBoxes

   c. intLeftovers

   ```
   Dim intParts As Integer
   Dim intBoxes As Integer
   Dim intLeftovers As Integer

   intParts = 77
   intPartsPerBox = 9

   intBoxes = intParts \ intPartsPerBox
   intLeftovers = intParts Mod intBoxes
   ```

(continues)

8. Are the following statements written correctly? If not, how should they be written?

```
Dim dblPay as Double
lblPay.Text = dblPay.ToString("C2")
```

9. For a Button object named btnCalories, write the click event handler to implement the following requirements to calculate the number of calories burned in a run:

   a. Declare variables named strMilesRan, decCaloriesConsumed, and decMilesRan.

   b. Declare a constant named cdecCaloriesBurnedPerHour and assign it the value 700 (assume you burn 700 calories for every mile you run).

   c. Allow the user to enter the number of miles she ran today.

   d. Convert the number of miles to a Decimal data type.

   e. Calculate the number of calories the user burned during her run.

   f. Display the result rounded to zero decimal places in a label named lblCaloriesBurned.

10. What would the output be when the user clicks the btnDrivingAge Button?

```
Private Sub btnDrivingAge_Click(ByVal sender As System.Object, ByVal e As
System.EventArgs) Handles btnDrivingAge.Click
    Dim intPresentAge As Integer
    Const cintDrivingAge As Integer = 16
    Dim intYearsToDrive As Integer

    intPresentAge = 13
    intYearsToDrive = cintDrivingAge - intPresentAge
    lblYearsLeft.Text = intYearsToDrive.ToString() & " year(s) until you
can drive."
  End Sub
```

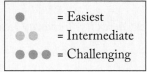

Complete one or more of the following case programming assignments. Submit the program and materials you create to your instructor. The level of difficulty is indicated for each case programming assignment.

● = Easiest
●● = Intermediate
●●● = Challenging

1 ●
NEW YORK CITY BROADWAY TICKETS

Design a Windows application and write the code that will execute according to the program requirements in Figure 4-98 and the Use Case definition in Figure 4-99. Before writing the code, create an event planning document for each event in the program. The completed program is shown in Figure 4-100.

REQUIREMENTS DOCUMENT

Date submitted: January 31, 2014

Application title: New York City Broadway Tickets

Purpose: The Broadway tickets selection program allows a user to purchase tickets to a theatre production.

Program Procedures: From a window on the screen, the user chooses the number of tickets for her favorite artist/group and the total cost amount for the tickets will be displayed.

Algorithms, Processing, and Conditions:
1. The user must be able to enter the number of Broadway tickets for their favorite theatre production.
2. A picture of a Broadway theatre sign will be displayed throughout the entire process.
3. After the user enters the number of tickets needed, the user clicks the Display Cost button.
4. The total cost of the tickets at $153.50 per ticket will be displayed in currency format (total cost = number of tickets * 153.50).

Notes and Restrictions:
1. The user can clear the number of tickets entered and the total cost of the tickets with a clear button and enter another number of tickets.
2. An exit button should close the application.
3. The cost per ticket can vary, so the program should allow a different price to be placed in any headings and be used in any calculations.

Comments:
1. The picture is named Broadway and is found at scsite.com/vb2010/ch4/images.

FIGURE 4-98

(continues)

Case Programming Assignments

New York City Broadway Tickets (continued)

USE CASE DEFINITION

1. The Windows Application opens.
2. The user enters the number of Broadway tickets.
3. The user clicks the Display Cost button.
4. The program displays the total cost of the concert tickets.
5. The user can click the Clear button and repeat steps 2–4.
6. The user terminates the program by clicking the Exit button.

FIGURE 4-99

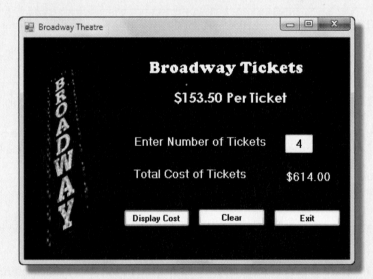

FIGURE 4-100

2

TAXI METER

Design a Windows application and write the code that will execute according to the program requirements in Figure 4-101 and the Use Case definition in Figure 4-102. Before writing the code, create an event planning document for each event in the program. The completed program is shown in Figure 4-103.

REQUIREMENTS DOCUMENT

Date submitted:	October 19, 2014
Application title:	Taxi Fare
Purpose:	The Taxi Fare Windows application computes the cost of a taxi fare.
Program Procedures:	From a window on the screen, the user enters the number of miles traveled in the taxi. The program calculates and displays the cost of the total fare.
Algorithms, Processing, and Conditions:	1. The user must be able to enter the number of miles traveled in a taxi cab.
	2. The title and a taxi logo (logo is named Taxi and is found at scsite.com/vb2010/ch4/images) will be displayed throughout the entire process.
	3. After entering the number of miles traveled, the user clicks the Display Fare button.
	4. The formula for calculating the fare is: Flat fee ($1.25) + (number of miles * $2.25 per mile).
	5. The program displays the fare in currency format.
Notes and Restrictions:	1. The user can clear the number of miles and make another entry.
	2. An exit button should close the application.
Comments:	n/a

FIGURE 4-101

(continues)

Taxi Meter (continued)

USE CASE DEFINITION

1. The Windows Application opens.
2. The user enters the number of miles traveled.
3. The user clicks the Display Fare button.
4. The program displays the total fare.
5. The user can click the Clear button and repeat steps 2-4.
6. The user terminates the program by clicking the Exit button.

FIGURE 4-102

FIGURE 4-103

3

WEEKLY PAY CALCULATOR

Design a Windows application and write the code that will execute according to the program requirements in Figure 4-104 and the Use Case definition in Figure 4-105. Before writing the code, create an event planning document for each event in the program. The completed program is shown in Figure 4-106.

REQUIREMENTS DOCUMENT

Date submitted:	May 11, 2014
Application title:	Weekly Pay Calculator
Purpose:	The Weekly Pay Calculator Windows application computes the weekly pay for an hourly employee.
Program Procedures:	From a window on the screen, a payroll clerk enters the total minutes an employee worked in a week and the hourly pay rate. The program displays the weekly pay for the employee.
Algorithms, Processing, and Conditions:	1. The payroll clerk must be able to enter the total minutes worked during the week and the hourly pay rate.
	2. The company name (Western Distribution) and the picture (Payroll found at scsite.com/vb2010/ch4/images) will be displayed throughout the entire process.
	3. After entering the total minutes worked and hourly pay rate, the payroll clerk clicks the weekly pay button.
	4. The weekly pay is displayed in currency format together with the number of hours and minutes worked.
Notes and Restrictions:	1. The user can clear the total minutes worked, the hourly pay rate, the hours and minutes worked, and the weekly pay by clicking a clear button. He then can enter another employee's data.
	2. An exit button should close the application.
	3. In this application, if hours worked is greater than 40, the hourly pay rate still applies.
Comments:	n/a

FIGURE 4-104

(continues)

Case Programming Assignments

Weekly Pay Calculator *(continued)*

USE CASE DEFINITION

1. The Windows Application opens.
2. The payroll clerk enters the total minutes worked by an employee and the employee's hourly pay rate.
3. The payroll clerk clicks the Weekly Pay button.
4. The program displays the hours worked, the minutes worked, and the employee's weekly pay.
5. The payroll clerk can click the Clear button and then repeat steps 2 through 4.
6. The user terminates the program by clicking the Exit button.

FIGURE 4-105

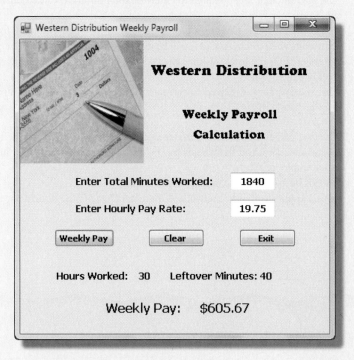

FIGURE 4-106

Case Programming Assignments

4 ●●
CASH REGISTER

Design a Windows application and write the code that will execute according to the program requirements in Figure 4-107. Before designing the user interface, create a Use Case definition. Before writing the code, create an event planning document for each event in the program.

REQUIREMENTS DOCUMENT

Date submitted: June 6, 2014

Application title: Cash Register

Purpose: The Cash Register Windows application will compute the tax and the final cost of a purchased item.

Program Procedures: From a window on the screen, the user enters the item name and amount of the item purchased. The program calculates the tax for the item and the final total, and then displays these values.

Algorithms, Processing, and Conditions:
1. The user must be able to enter the name of the item purchased and the cost of the item before tax.
2. The store name and store picture will be displayed throughout the entire process.
3. After the user enters the item name and the cost of the item, the user clicks the Display Cost button.
4. The program displays the item name with the cost, tax, and final total.
5. The cost, tax, and final total should appear in currency format.
6. The tax rate for all items is 7.75%.
7. The final total is calculated by adding the cost and the tax.

Notes and Restrictions:
1. The user can clear the item name, cost, tax, and final total with a clear button.
2. The user can click an exit button to close the application.

Comments:
1. The store picture shown in the window should be selected from the pictures available on the Web.

FIGURE 4-107

5 GRADE CALCULATOR

Design a Windows application and write the code that will execute according to the program requirements in Figure 4-108. Before designing the user interface, create a Use Case definition. Before writing the code, create an event planning document for each event in the program.

REQUIREMENTS DOCUMENT

Date submitted: January 4, 2014

Application title: Grade Calculator

Purpose: The Grade Calculator Windows application will compute and display the average of four numeric test grades.

Program Procedures: From a window on the screen, the user enters the Social Security number of a student and the four numeric scores from four tests taken by the student. The program determines the average of the four test scores and displays the result.

Algorithms, Processing, and Conditions:
1. The user must be able to enter the Social Security number of the student and the four test scores.
2. The Social Security number must be formatted properly with hyphens.
3. To determine the average test score, add the four entered test scores and divide by four.
4. The average score should be shown with one position to the right of the decimal point.

Notes and Restrictions:
1. The user can clear the Social Security number, test scores, and average score; and then enter new data.
2. The user can use an exit button to close the application.

Comments:
1. The designer should design the user interface, including all graphics and words used.

FIGURE 4-108

6 ●●
CONVERT CURRENCY

Design a Windows application and write the code that will execute according to the program requirements in Figure 4-109. Before designing the user interface, create a Use Case definition. Before writing the code, create an event planning document for each event in the program.

REQUIREMENTS DOCUMENT

Date submitted:	November 4, 2014
Application title:	Convert Currency
Purpose:	The Convert Currency Windows application will display the value of U.S. dollars in euros, English pounds, and Mexican pesos.
Program Procedures:	From a window on the screen, the user should enter the number of U.S. dollars to be converted. The program will display the equivalent value in euros, British pounds, and Mexican pesos.
Algorithms, Processing, and Conditions:	1. The user must be able to enter the number of U.S. dollars to be converted.
	2. After entering the number of U.S. dollars to be converted, the user clicks the Convert Currency button.
	3. The program converts the number of U.S. dollars entered into the equivalent number of euros, English pounds, and Mexican pesos. The program displays all three currencies together with the U.S. dollars.
	4. To find the conversion rates, the developer must consult the appropriate Web sites. A possible site is www.xe.com.
	5. Because the currency rates change dynamically, the user should enter both the date and the time that the conversion rates were applied. The date and time should be displayed in U.S. format.
	6. The user should be able to clear the date and time, the number of U.S. dollars entered, and the results of the calculations, and then enter new values.
Notes and Restrictions:	1. The user should be able to click an exit button to close the application.
Comments:	1. The designer must determine the design of the user interface, and the words and graphics used in the user interface.

FIGURE 4-109

Case Programming Assignments

7 ●●● SWIMMING POOL FILL

Create a requirements document and a Use Case Definition document, and then design a Windows application based on the following case project. Before writing the code, create an event planning document for each event in the program.

Because filling a swimming pool with water requires much more water than normal usage, your local city charges a special rate of $0.77 per cubic foot of water to fill a swimming pool. In addition, it charges a one-time fee of $100.00 for pool filling. The city water works department has requested that you write a Windows application that allows the user to enter a swimming pool's length, width, and average depth to find the volume of the pool in cubic feet (volume = length * width * depth); and then display the pool's volume and the final cost of filling the pool, including the one-time fee. Allow the user to enter values with decimal places and compute the volume to one decimal place past the decimal point. The user should be able to clear all entries and then reenter data. To close the program, the user should be able to click a button.

FIGURE 4-110

Case Programming Assignments

8 ●●● HOT TUB DIMENSIONS

Create a requirements document and a Use Case Definition document, and then design a Windows application based on the following case project. Before writing the code, create an event planning document for each event in the program.

You are interested in purchasing a hot tub. The hot tub listings on the Internet describe hot tubs that are all perfectly round in shape. Each ad states the diameter. Create a Windows application that computes the area and circumference of a hot tub by entering the diameter in feet and inches (example 7 feet and 4 inches). The area and circumference results should each go out two decimal places. You should be able to clear the entry, enter a new diameter, and exit the form.

FIGURE 4-111

Case Programming Assignments

9 ●●● HOURS AND YEARS SLEPT

Create a requirements document and a Use Case Definition document, and then design a Windows application based on the following case project. Before writing the code, create an event planning document for each event in the program.

The science museum has asked you to write a Windows application that children can use to find the total number of hours and years they have slept during their lifetime, assuming they sleep an average of 8 hours per night. The user should enter her first name, her birth date (ask for the month, day, and year separately in numeric form) and the current date (ask for the month, day, and year separately in numeric form). To calculate the number of hours slept, assume 360 days per year and 30 days per month. The program must display the user's name and the number of hours slept. Based on 360 days per year and 8 hours of sleep per day, the program also should show how many years, months, and days the user has slept in her lifetime. The user can click a Clear button to clear all entries and results. An Exit button must be available to close the application. Because children normally will use this program, the museum has asked you to develop a colorful and fun user interface.

FIGURE 4-112

CHAPTER 5

Decision Structures

OBJECTIVES

You will have mastered the material in this chapter when you can:

- Use the GroupBox object

- Place RadioButton objects in applications

- Display a message box

- Make decisions using If…Then statements

- Make decisions using If…Then… Else statements

- Make decisions using nested If statements

- Make decisions using logical operators

- Make decisions using Case statements

- Insert code snippets

- Test input to ensure a value is numeric

Introduction

Developers can code Visual Basic applications to make decisions based on the input of users or other conditions that occur. Decision-making is one of the fundamental activities of a computer program. In this chapter, you will learn to write decision-making statements in Visual Basic 2010.

Visual Basic allows you to test conditions and perform different operations depending on the results of that test. You can test for a condition being true or false and change the flow of what happens in a program based on the user's input.

Chapter Project

The sample program in this chapter is designed to be used by a carpenter or cabinet-maker to calculate an estimate for the wood needed for a job. The Wood Cabinet Estimate application is written for a cabinetmaker who wants a program on the job site that can provide a cost estimate for building wood cabinets.

The application requests that the user enter the number of linear feet of cabinetry required and the desired wood type. The Windows application then computes the cost of the cabinets based on the rate of $150.00 per linear foot for pine, $200.00 per linear foot for oak, and $350.00 per linear foot for cherry. Figure 5-1 shows the user interface for the application.

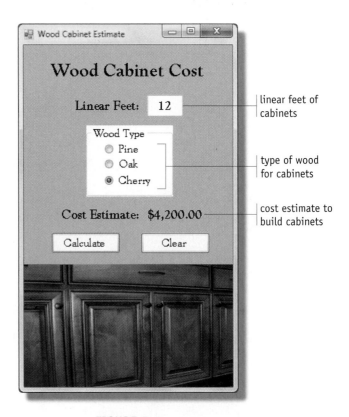

FIGURE 5-1

In Figure 5-1 on the previous page, the Wood Cabinet Estimate Windows application displays the title Wood Cabinet Estimate in the title bar. The linear footage the user enters in the TextBox object includes all cabinets for the job. The user chooses the wood type by selecting a RadioButton from the following list: Pine (the most common choice), Oak, or Cherry. After the user has entered the number of linear feet of cabinetry and selected a type of wood, the user clicks the Calculate button to obtain the cost estimate. The calculation is based on the linear feet multiplied by the cost of the selected wood. The cost estimate is displayed in currency format. In the example in Figure 5-1 on the previous page, the user entered 12 linear feet of cabinetry and selected cherry wood. After clicking the Calculate button, the application displayed a cost of \$4,200.00 (12 × \$350.00).

Clicking the Clear button will clear the linear footage, reset the RadioButton selection to Pine, which is the most common wood type, and clear the calculation result.

Checking the validity of data entered by the user is a requirement of this chapter project program. In Chapter 4, you learned that if you enter nonnumeric data and attempt to use it in a calculation, the program will be terminated. To check for invalid data, the Wood Cabinet Estimate program ensures that the user enters a numeric value greater than zero in the Linear Feet TextBox object. A warning dialog box appears if the user leaves the linear feet TextBox blank or does not enter a valid number. Figure 5-2 displays the Input Error warning dialog box, called a Message Box, which directs the user to enter the linear feet for the cabinets.

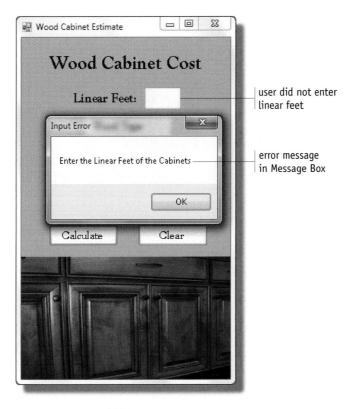

FIGURE 5-2

Checking input data for validity is an important task in Visual Basic programs. You will learn several data validation techniques in this chapter.

User Interface Design

The user interface for the Wood Cabinet Estimate Windows application includes three new objects: a GroupBox, RadioButtons, and Message Boxes. The Message Boxes appear when the user inputs a negative number or a nonnumeric value.

Using the GroupBox Object

The Wood Cabinet Estimate Form object requires a GroupBox object and RadioButton objects (Figure 5-3).

RadioButton objects

GroupBox object

FIGURE 5-3

A GroupBox object associates items as a group, allowing the user to select one item from the group. It also includes caption text. RadioButton objects allow the user to make choices. In Figure 5-3, the GroupBox object groups the radio buttons for selecting the wood type. When RadioButton objects are contained in a group box, the user can select only one of the radio buttons. For example, in Figure 5-3 the Cherry radio button is selected. If the user clicks the Oak radio button, it will be selected and the Cherry radio button automatically will be deselected.

The GroupBox object shown in Figure 5-3 on the previous page is displayed with the Text property of Wood Type as the caption text. The prefix for the GroupBox object (Name) property is grp. To place a GroupBox object on the Form object, you can complete the following steps:

STEP 1   Drag the GroupBox object in the Containers category of the Toolbox over the Form object to the approximate location where you want to place the GroupBox object.

The mouse pointer changes when you place it over the Form object (Figure 5-4). The GroupBox object will be placed on the form at the location of the outline in the pointer.

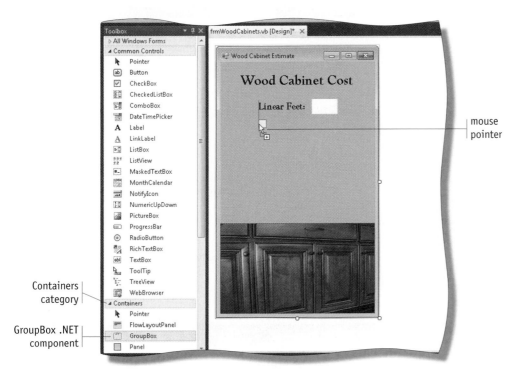

FIGURE 5-4

STEP 2 When the mouse pointer is in the correct location, release the mouse button. With the GroupBox object selected, scroll in the Properties window to the (Name) property. Double-click in the right column of the (Name) property and then enter the name grpWoodType. Double-click in the right column of the Text property to change the caption of the GroupBox object. Enter the text Wood Type.

The name you entered is displayed in the (Name) property in the Properties window, and the caption Wood Type is displayed in the caption (Figure 5-5).

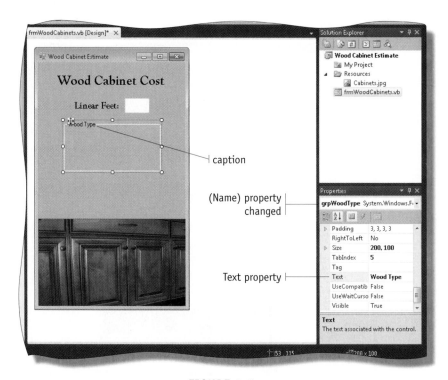

FIGURE 5-5

STEP 3   Click to the right of the Size property of the GroupBox object and enter
`125,100` as the size. Change the Font property to Goudy Old Style, Regular, Size
12. Change the BackColor property to White.

*The GroupBox object is sized on the form. If you want to move the panel to another location
on the form, place the mouse pointer over the drag box on the border of the GroupBox object
and then drag the GroupBox object to the desired location. The Font property is set to Goudy
Old Style, and BackColor is white (Figure 5-6).*

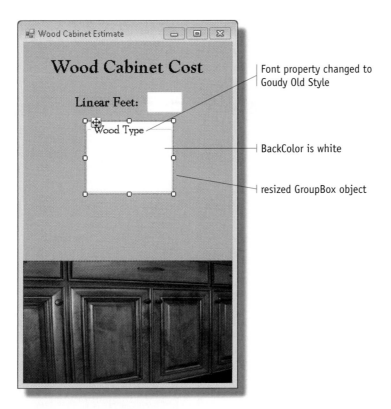

Font property changed to
Goudy Old Style

BackColor is white

resized GroupBox object

FIGURE 5-6

ONLINE REINFORCEMENT

To view a video of the process
in the previous steps, visit
scsite.com/vb2010/ch5 and
then select Figure 5-4.

Grouping all options in a GroupBox object gives the user a logical visual cue.
Also, when you move the GroupBox object, all its contained objects move as well.

Adding the RadioButton Objects

The GroupBox object in the Wood Cabinet Estimate application contains a set of RadioButton objects (see Figure 5-3 on page 294). The user may select only one type of wood: pine, oak, or cherry. To place RadioButton objects within the GroupBox object, you can complete the following steps:

STEP 1   Drag and drop one RadioButton object from the Toolbox into the GroupBox object on the Form object. Drag a second RadioButton object from the Toolbox into the GroupBox object, using blue snap lines to align and separate the RadioButton objects vertically.

The second RadioButton object is aligned vertically with a blue snap line, which separates it vertically from the first RadioButton object (Figure 5-7).

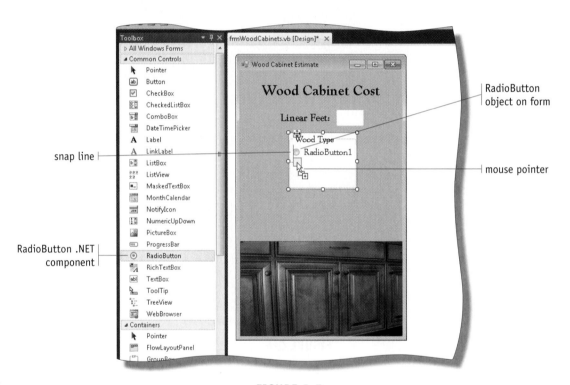

FIGURE 5-7

STEP 2 Release the mouse button to place the RadioButton object on the
Form object within the GroupBox object. Using the same technique, add a third
RadioButton object.

*Three RadioButton objects are placed on the form and aligned within the GroupBox object
(Figure 5-8).*

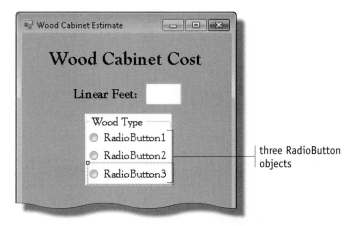

FIGURE 5-8

STEP 3 Name the RadioButton objects by selecting a RadioButton object, double-
clicking in the right column of the (Name) property in the Properties window, and
entering the name. The names for the radio buttons, from top to bottom, should be
radPine, radOak, and radCherry.

*The (Name) property is selected. The names radPine, radOak, and radCherry are entered
(Figure 5-9).*

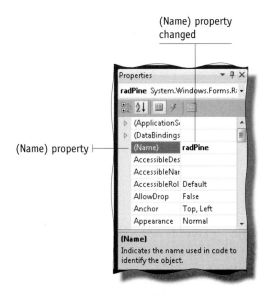

FIGURE 5-9

STEP 4 Change the Text property for each RadioButton by double-clicking in the right column of the Text property and typing `Pine` for the first RadioButton, `Oak` for the second RadioButton, and `Cherry` for the third RadioButton.

The Text property has been changed to the types of wood available: Pine, Oak, and Cherry (Figure 5-10).

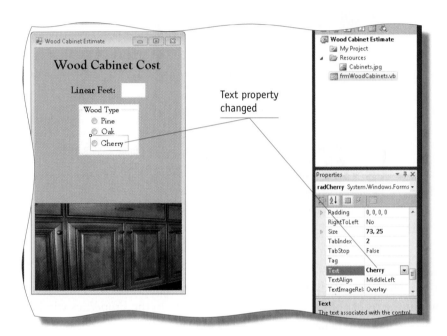

FIGURE 5-10

Using the Checked Property of RadioButton Objects

You will recall that the RadioButton objects in the Wood Cabinet Estimate application allow the user to select one wood type. When the user selects Cherry as the wood type, as shown in Figure 5-11 on the next page, the RadioButton is selected (the small circle in the radio button is shaded). When a RadioButton is selected, the Checked property of the Cherry RadioButton changes from False (unselected) to True (selected).

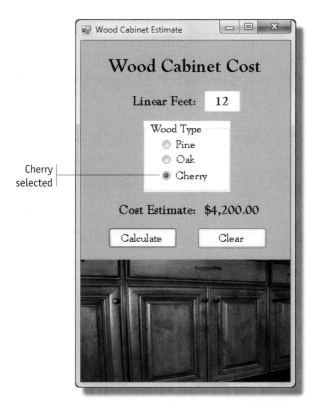

FIGURE 5-11

Often, during design time, you should set the Checked property to True for the most commonly selected RadioButton to save the user from having to select the most common choice. In the Wood Cabinet Estimate application, the cabinetmaker uses Pine most often. To cause the Pine RadioButton object named radPine to appear selected (shaded) when the program begins, you change the Checked property for the radPine RadioButton from False to True (Figure 5-12).

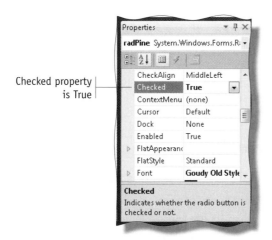

FIGURE 5-12

Windows Application Container Objects

The Panel object in a Windows application performs in the same manner as the GroupBox object. For Windows applications, Visual Basic provides four additional container objects: FlowLayoutPanel, SplitContainer, TabControl, and TableLayoutPanel. The GroupBox object is used most often; it provides several options not available with the Panel object. The table in Figure 5-13 shows the differences between the GroupBox and the Panel objects.

Option	GroupBox Object	Panel Object
Have a caption	Yes	No
Have scroll bars	Yes	No
Display a labeled border	Yes	No

FIGURE 5-13

Figure 5-14 shows the Windows application Toolbox, the Containers group of .NET components, and a GroupBox object and a Panel object in a Windows application. Notice in the Toolbox that the GroupBox and Panel objects are in a subcategory called Containers.

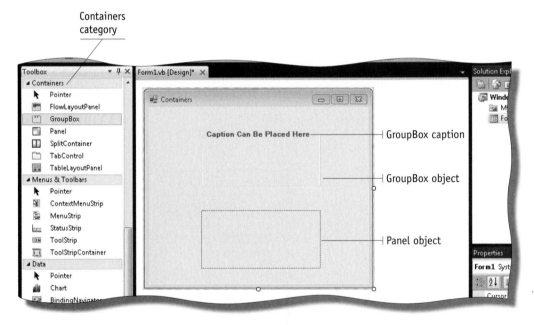

FIGURE 5-14

The GroupBox object in Figure 5-14 displays a border around the edges of the object, with a text area in the upper-left for a caption. The Panel object has a black dashed border that does not appear when the application is executed. GroupBox and Panel objects have the same purpose of grouping RadioButtons and other objects, but they differ in their appearance.

Related RadioButtons should be placed in a separate container object so that the user can select one radio button from each group. Always place the container object on the form first, and then drag the RadioButton objects into the container object.

The Course Sign-up example in Figure 5-15 displays a Windows application that allows the user to sign up for a Web Design course. Notice the two separate groups of RadioButton objects. In the Choose Course Level GroupBox object, the user should select a course level. In the Choose Semester GroupBox object, the user should identify the semester for the course. As you can see, the user selects one radio button from the left group and one radio button from the right group.

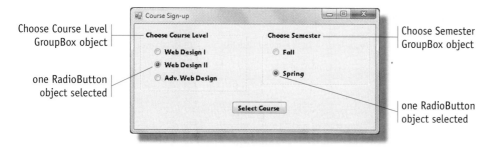

FIGURE 5-15

Displaying a Message Box

In the Wood Cabinet Estimate chapter project, a message box, also called a dialog box, opens if the user does not enter the length of the cabinets correctly. The dialog box displays an error message if the user omits the length or enters nonnumeric data (Figure 5-16).

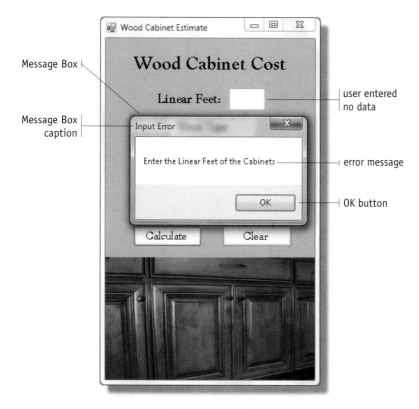

FIGURE 5-16

If the user enters a negative number for the length of the cabinets, a message box appears (Figure 5-17) stating that a positive number is necessary.

FIGURE 5-17

This message box reminds the user to enter the linear feet of the cabinets. A message box window must be closed before the application can continue. The user can continue the application by clicking the OK button in the message box.

In Visual Basic, the message to the user in a message box window is displayed using a procedure named Show that is found in the MessageBox class. The syntax for the statement to display a message in a message box is shown in Figure 5-18 on the next page.

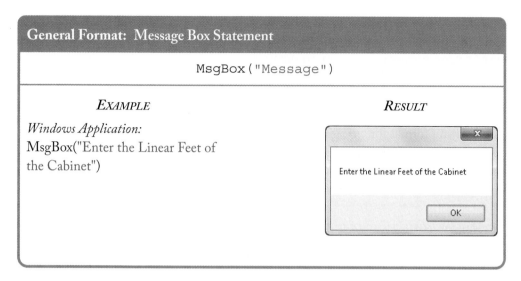

FIGURE 5-18

The string message shown in the parentheses will appear in the message box when the code is executed. The string message is considered an argument of the procedure. You will recall that an argument is a value that is passed to a procedure. The first argument for the MsgBox command contains the message to be printed in the message box window on top of the form during execution.

The example in Figure 5-19 illustrates the code that could be used in the Calculate button click event handler. This code could be executed if the user clicks the Calculate button without entering a numeric value in the Linear Feet text box (see Figure 5-17 on the previous page).

Displaying Message Box Captions

A message box can be displayed during execution with a variety of arguments. For example, a message box can display a message and a caption in the title bar (two arguments with two commas between the two arguments) using the syntax shown in Figure 5-19.

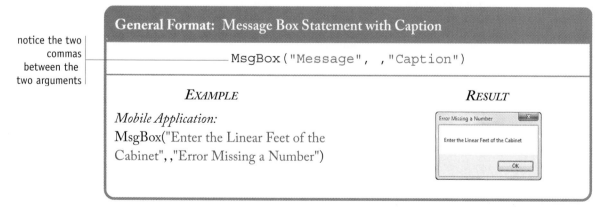

FIGURE 5-19

The title bar in the example in Figure 5-19 on the previous page displays a caption and the message box displays a message. In many applications, the caption is used to give further information to the user.

Message Box Buttons

The general format for changing the button command from OK to another button type is shown in Figure 5-20. The button entry can be a command or a value representing a command.

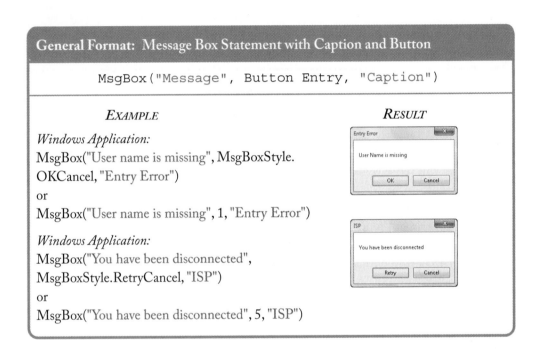

General Format: Message Box Statement with Caption and Button

```
MsgBox("Message", Button Entry, "Caption")
```

EXAMPLE

Windows Application:
MsgBox("User name is missing", MsgBoxStyle.
OKCancel, "Entry Error")
or
MsgBox("User name is missing", 1, "Entry Error")

Windows Application:
MsgBox("You have been disconnected",
MsgBoxStyle.RetryCancel, "ISP")
or
MsgBox("You have been disconnected", 5, "ISP")

RESULT

FIGURE 5-20

In the first example in Figure 5-20, the buttons specified are the OK button and the Cancel button. In the second example, the buttons shown are the Retry button and the Cancel button.

The table in Figure 5-21 shows all the possible entries that can be placed in the Button Entry portion of the argument passed to the Show procedure.

MsgBoxButtons Arguments	Value	Use
MsgBoxStyle.OKOnly	0	Displays an OK button — default setting
MsgBoxStyle.OKCancel	1	Displays an OK and Cancel button
MsgBoxStyle.AbortRetryIgnore	2	After a failing situation, the user can choose to Abort, Retry, or Ignore
MsgBoxStyle.YesNoCancel	3	Displays Yes, No, and Cancel buttons
MsgBoxStyle.YesNo	4	Displays Yes and No buttons
MsgBoxStyle.RetryCancel	5	After an error occurs, the user can choose to Retry or Cancel

FIGURE 5-21

Message Box Icons

In the button entry portion of the argument (the second argument), a message box icon can be added (Figure 5-22). The word "or" connects the button entry to the icon entry.

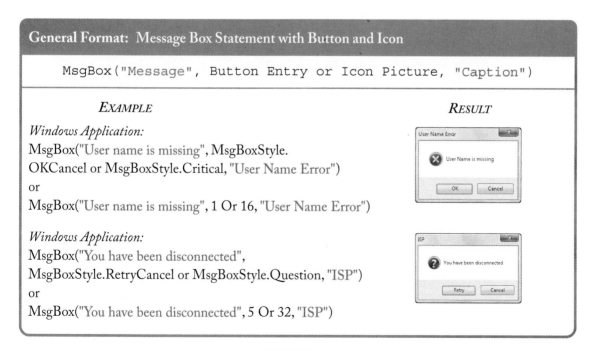

FIGURE 5-22

The picture icon represents the MsgBoxStyle that can be displayed as a graphic icon in the message box. Both examples in Figure 5-22 on the previous page show a graphic icon added to the message box.

The picture icon in the second argument can contain any of the entries shown in Figure 5-23.

MsgBoxStyle Icons	Value	Icon	Use
MsgBoxStyle.Critical	16		Alerts the user to an error
MsgBoxStyle.Question	32		Displays a question mark
MsgBoxStyle.Exclamation	48		Alerts the user to a possible problem
MsgBoxStyle.Information	64		Displays an information icon

FIGURE 5-23

In the general formats shown for a message box, you must follow the syntax of the statements exactly, which means the commas, quotation marks, and parentheses must be placed in the statement as shown in the general formats.

You can also add values to display both the buttons and a picture icon. In Figure 5-24, the value of the message button type AbortRetryIgnore is 2 and the value of the critical icon is 16. If you add 16 plus 2, the result is 18.

General Format: MsgBox("Message", Button Entry Value + Icon Picture Value, "Caption")

EXAMPLE

Windows Application:
MsgBox("Enter a Number Only", 18, "Illegal Operation")

RESULT

FIGURE 5-24

Message Box IntelliSense

When you enter the code for a message box, IntelliSense can assist you. To use IntelliSense to enter code for the message box shown in Figure 5-22 on the previous page that contains a message, caption, and button, you can complete the following steps:

STEP 1   In the code editing window, inside the event handler you are coding, type msg to display MsgBox in the IntelliSense list.

IntelliSense displays a list of the allowable entries (Figure 5-25). When you type msg *MsgBox is selected in the IntelliSense list.*

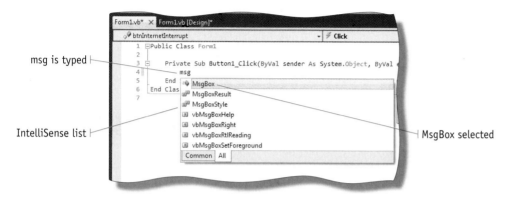

FIGURE 5-25

STEP 2   Press the Tab key to select MsgBox from the IntelliSense list. Type the following text: ("You have been disconnected from the Internet", m)

The first argument for the message box is entered (Figure 5-26). IntelliSense displays a list of the allowable entries for the second argument.

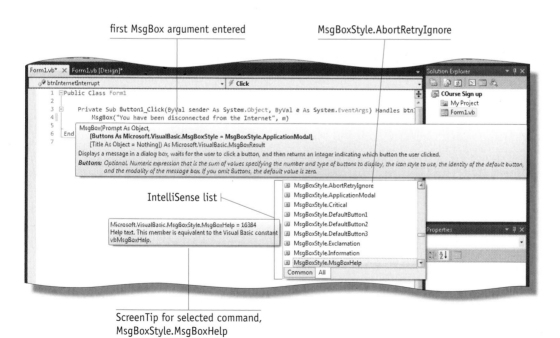

FIGURE 5-26

STEP 3   Select the MsgBoxStyle.AbortRetryIgnore argument by pressing the UP ARROW until the correct argument is highlighted. Type a comma. Then type `"ISP"` and a right parenthesis.

The MsgBoxStyle.AbortRetryIgnore argument is selected. After the comma is typed following the second argument, the caption "ISP" is typed with a right parenthesis (Figure 5-27).

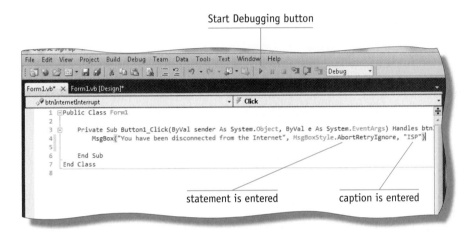

FIGURE 5-27

STEP 4   Click the Start Debugging button on the Standard toolbar.

The application runs, displaying the message box that shows the message, buttons, and caption (Figure 5-28).

FIGURE 5-28

ONLINE REINFORCEMENT

To view a video of the process in the previous steps, visit scsite.com/vb2010/ch5 and then select Figure 5-25.

String Concatenation

Recall that when the Wood Cabinet Estimate application runs, the user enters the linear footage of the wood cabinets. If the user enters a number that is not greater than zero, such as −6, a message box appears that states "You entered −6. Enter a Positive Number", as shown in Figure 5-29.

message box with error message

message created using concatenation

FIGURE 5-29

To create the message in the message box, you can use concatenation, which you learned about in Chapter 4. In Figure 5-29, the string message is constructed by joining a string ("You entered"), a variable named decFootage containing the linear footage entered (which must be converted to a string), and a string for the final part of the message (". Enter a Positive Number."). The code in Figure 5-30 creates the desired message box.

```
45        MsgBox("You entered " & decFeet.ToString() & ". Enter a Positive Number", , "Input Error")
```

FIGURE 5-30

You will recall that the operator to concatenate strings is the ampersand (&). When the statement is executed, the three string elements are joined together (concatenated) to form the one string that is displayed in the message box.

HEADS UP

In older versions of Visual Basic, the plus (+) sign was used to concatenate strings instead of the ampersand (&) symbol. The + sign still functions for concatenation, but it can be confusing because it looks like the plus sign used in addition. You should always use the ampersand.

Making Decisions with Conditional Statements

In the Wood Cabinet Estimate chapter project, which calculates the cost of wood cabinets, the application allows the user to select one of three different types of wood: pine, oak, or cherry. The price per square foot is based on the user's choice of wood. To select the wood type, the user must click one of three radio buttons titled Pine, Oak, and Cherry. Then, based on the choice, the application uses a different wood cost.

Visual Basic uses decision structures to deal with the different conditions that occur based on the values entered into an application. A **decision structure** is one of the three fundamental control structures used in computer programming. For example, if the user clicks the Pine radio button, the wood cost is set to $150.00 per linear foot. The statement that tests the radio button is called a **conditional statement**. The condition checked is whether the Pine radio button is selected. If so, the wood cost is set to $150.00.

When a condition is tested in a Visual Basic program, the condition either is true or false. For example, when checking to determine if the Pine radio button is selected, the condition can either be true (the Pine radio button is checked) or false (the Pine radio button is not checked). All conditional statements result in the tested condition either being true or false.

To implement a conditional statement and the statements that are executed when a condition is true and statements executed when a condition is false, Visual Basic uses the If statement and its variety of formats. You will learn about the If statement in the following sections.

Using an If . . . Then Statement

In the sample program, an If . . . Then statement is used to determine the cost of the wood. The simplest form of the If . . . Then statement is shown in Figure 5-31.

```
5        If condition Then
6            Statement(s) executed when condition is true
7        End If
8
```

FIGURE 5-31

In Figure 5-31, when the condition tested in the If statement on line 5 is true, the statement(s) between the If and the End If keywords will be executed. If the condition is not true, no statements between the If and End If keywords will be executed, and program execution will continue with the statement(s) that follows the End If statement.

Visual Basic automatically indents statements to be executed when a condition is true or not true to indicate the lines of code are within the conditional If...Then structure. This is why the statement on line 6 in Figure 5-31 on the previous page is indented. The End If keyword terminates the If...Then block of code. After executing the If...Then block, execution continues with any statements that follow the closing End If statement.

Relational Operators

In Figure 5-31 on the previous page, the condition portion of the If...Then statement means a condition is tested to determine if it is true or false. The conditions that can be tested are:

1. Is one value equal to another value?
2. Is one value not equal to another value?
3. Is one value greater than another value?
4. Is one value less than another value?
5. Is one value greater than or equal to another value?
6. Is one value less than or equal to another value?

To test these conditions, Visual Basic provides relational operators that are used within the conditional statement to express the relationship being tested. The table in Figure 5-32 shows these relational operators.

	Relational Operator	Meaning	Example	Resulting Condition
1	=	Equal to	8 = 8	True
2	<>	Not equal to	6 <> 6	False
3	>	Greater than	7 > 9	False
4	<	Less than	4 < 6	True
5	>=	Greater than or equal to	3 >= 3	True
6	<=	Less than or equal to	7 <= 5	False

FIGURE 5-32

A condition tested using a relational operator is evaluated as true or false. Example 1 tests whether 8 is equal to 8. Because it is, the resulting condition is true. Example 2 tests if 6 is not equal to 6. Because they are equal, the resulting condition is false. Similarly, Example 5 tests if 3 is greater than or equal to 3. Because they are equal, the resulting condition is true.

As an example of using a conditional operator, consider the following problem where an If statement is used to determine if someone is old enough to vote. If the

HEADS UP

If Visual Basic does not automatically indent the code in an If...Then statement, follow these steps:
1) Click Tools on the menu bar at the top of the screen and then click Options; 2) if necessary, click the triangle next to Text Editor in the left panel; 3) if necessary, click the triangle next to Basic in the left panel; 4) if necessary, click VB Specific in the left panel; 5) ensure the Pretty listing (reformatting) of code check box contains a check mark; 6) click the OK button in the Options dialog box.

value in the intAge variable is greater than or equal to 18, then the person is old enough to vote. If not, the person is not old enough to vote. The If . . . Then statement to test this condition is shown in Figure 5-33.

```
8        If intAge >= 18 Then
9            lblVotingEligibility.Text = "You are old enough to vote"
10       End If
```

FIGURE 5-33

In Figure 5-33, if the value in the intAge variable is greater than or equal to 18, the string value "You are old enough to vote" is assigned to the Text property of the lblVotingEligibility Label object. If not, then no processing occurs based on the conditional statement and any statement(s) following the End If keyword will be executed.

You can see in Figure 5-33 that several keywords are required in an If . . . Then statement. The word If must be the first item. Next, the condition(s) to be tested are stated, followed by the word Then. This keyword is required in an If statement.

The End If keyword follows the statements to be executed when the condition is true. This entry also is required. It signals to the Visual Basic compiler that statements following it are to be executed regardless of the result of the conditional statement; that is, the End If keyword is the last element within the If block and no subsequent statements depend on it for execution.

To enter the If . . . Then statement shown in Figure 5-33, you can complete the following steps:

STEP 1   With the insertion point in the correct location in the code, type if and then press the SPACEBAR.

The statement begins with the word if (Figure 5-34). The If command is displayed in blue because it is a Visual Basic keyword. You can type uppercase or lowercase letters.

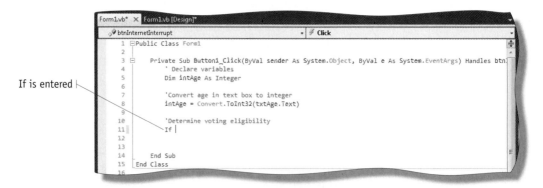

FIGURE 5-34

STEP 2   Type inta to select the variable named intAge in the IntelliSense list. Then, type >=18 as the condition to be tested. Press the ENTER key.

The If . . . Then statement is entered in the code editing window (Figure 5-35). When the
ENTER *key is pressed, Visual Basic adds the keyword Then to the end of the If statement line
of code and inserts spaces between the elements in the statement for ease of reading. In addition, Visual Basic inserts the End If keyword following a blank line. Notice the keywords
Then and End If are capitalized and displayed in blue.*

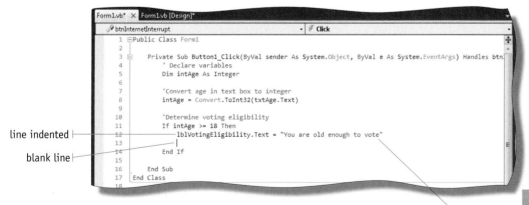

FIGURE 5-35

STEP 3   On the blank line (line 12 in Figure 5-35), enter the statement that should
be executed when the condition is true. To place the message, "You are old enough to
vote" in the Text property of the lblVotingEligibility Label object, insert the code
shown in Figure 5-33 on the previous page. Remember to use IntelliSense to
reference the lblVotingEligibility Label object.

*The resulting statement is entered between the If and End If keywords (Figure 5-36).
Notice that Visual Basic automatically indents the line for ease of reading. The blank line
allows you to enter more statements. If you have no further statements, you can press the*
DELETE *key to delete the blank line in the If . . . Then statement.*

FIGURE 5-36

Comparing Strings

You also can write an If … Then statement using the relational operators shown in Figure 5-32 on page 313 to compare string values. A string value comparison compares each character in two strings, starting with the first character in each string. For example, in the two strings in Figure 5-37, the comparison begins with the first character in each string, a. Because the characters are equal, the comparison continues with the second character in each string, b. Because these characters are equal, the comparison continues with the third characters in each string, c. Because all three characters are equal, the strings are considered equal and the resulting condition from the If statement is true.

```
13          Dim String1 As String = "abc"
14          Dim String2 As String = "abc"
15
16          If String1 = String2 Then
17              Me.lblStringTest.Text = "Equal"
18          End If
```

FIGURE 5-37

All characters found in strings, including letters, numbers, and special characters, are in a sequence from low to high based on the manner in which the characters are coded internally on the computer. When using Visual Studio 2010, characters are stored and sequenced in Unicode, which is a coding methodology that can accommodate more than 60,000 characters. Appendix A in this book shows the Unicode sequence for the standard keyboard characters. You will find that the numbers are considered less than uppercase letters, and uppercase letters are considered less than lowercase letters.

Using the If … Then statement, the following comparisons produce the following resulting conditions:

Example 1:
```
Dim String1 As String = "Powder"
Dim String2 As String = "Power"

If String1 < String2 Then
```

Resulting Condition: True because in the fourth character position, the letter d is less than the letter e.

Example 2:
```
Dim String1 As String = "6"
Dim String2 As String = "T"

If String1 < String2 Then
```

Resulting Condition: True because in a string comparison, a number is less than an uppercase letter.

Example 3:

```
Dim String1 As String = "12"
Dim String2 As String = "9"

If String1 < String2 Then
```

Resulting Condition: True because in a string comparison, the characters in the first position of the string are compared first. Because the value 1 in String1 is less than the value 9 in String2, the entire value in String1 is considered less than the value in String2.

Example 4:

```
Dim String1 As String = "anchor"
Dim String2 As String = "Anchorline"

If String1 > String2 Then
```

Resulting Condition: True because a lowercase letter (the a in the first position of String1) is considered greater than an uppercase letter (the A in the first position of String2).

Comparing Different Data Types

Every type of data available in Visual Basic can be compared. Different numeric types can be compared to each other using an If statement. A single string character can be compared to a Char data type. The following examples illustrate some of the allowable comparisons.

Example 1: Decimal compared to Double

```
If decQuarterlySales > dblSalesQuota Then
```

If decQuarterlySales = 110,324.54 and dblSalesQuota = 112,435.54, the condition is false.

Example 2: Decimal compared to Integer

```
If decTirePressureReading > intTirePressureMaximum Then
```

If decTirePressureReading = 30.21 and intTirePressureMaximum = 30, the condition is true.

Example 3: Double compared to Integer

```
If dblCurrentTemperature >= intHeatDanger Then
```

If dblCurrentTemperature = 94.543 and intHeatDanger = 98, the condition is false.

Example 4: String compared to Char

```
If strChemistryGrade < chrPassingGrade Then
```

If strChemistryGrade = "B" and chrPassingGrade = "C", the condition is true.

Visual Basic allows comparisons between most data types. If you are unsure whether a comparison can be made, write an If statement to ensure the comparison is working properly.

Using the If . . . Then . . . Else Statement

An If . . . Then statement executes a set of instructions if a condition is true. If the condition is false, the instructions between the If statement and the End If statement are not executed and program execution continues with the statement(s) following the End If statement.

In many applications, the logic requires one set of instructions to be executed if a condition is true, and another set of instructions to be executed if a condition is false. For example, a requirement in a program could specify that if a student's test score is 70 or greater, a message stating "You passed the examination" should be displayed, while if the test score is less than 70, a message stating "You failed the examination" should be displayed.

To execute one set of instructions if a condition is true, and another set of instructions if the condition is false, you can use the If . . . Then . . . Else statement. Figure 5-38 illustrates the syntax of the If . . . Then . . . Else statement.

```
16      If condition Then
17          Statement(s) executed if condition is true
18      Else
19          Statement(s) executed if condition is false
20      End If
```

FIGURE 5-38

In the code in Figure 5-38, if the condition tested by the If statement is true, the statement(s) between the Then keyword and the Else keyword will be executed. If the condition tested is false, the statement(s) between the Else keyword and the End If keyword will be executed.

The example in Figure 5-39 on the next page shows the use of the If . . . Then . . . Else statement to calculate student fees by testing the student status.

statement is executed if
student is a graduate

```
27          If strStudentStatus = "Graduate" Then
28              decStudentFees = decGraduateFee * intNumberOfUnits
29          Else
30              decStudentFees = decUndergraduateFee * intNumberOfUnits
31          End If
```

statement is executed if
student is not a graduate

FIGURE 5-39

If the student is a graduate student, the student fees are calculated by multiplying the graduate fee times the number of units. If the student is not a graduate student, fees are calculated by multiplying the undergraduate fee times the number of units. Notice that a student cannot be both an undergraduate student and a graduate student, so either the statement following the Then keyword will be executed or the statement following the Else keyword will be executed.

> **HEADS UP**
>
> A condition cannot be true and false at the same time, so statements for a true condition and statements for a false condition cannot both be executed based on a single comparison.

Comparing to an Arithmetic Expression

An If statement can compare an arithmetic expression to a constant or other data type. For example, in Figure 5-40, the withdrawals from a bank account are compared to the value obtained by adding the current balance to deposits and then subtracting account charges.

```
41          If decWithdrawals > decCurrentBalance + decDeposits - decAccountCharges Then
42              lblAccountStatus.Text = "Overdrawn"
43          Else
44              lblAccountStatus.Text = "Balance is Positive"
45          End If
```

FIGURE 5-40

In Figure 5-40, if the value in the decWithdrawals variable is greater than the current balance plus the deposits minus the account charges, the Text property of the lblAccountStatus Label object is set to Overdrawn. If the value in decWithdrawals is less than or equal to the value from the arithmetic expression, the message Balance is Positive is placed in the Text property of the lblAccountStatus Label object. Notice that the arithmetic expression is evaluated prior to the comparison. If the condition is true, the statement between the Then and Else keywords is executed. If the condition is false, the statement between the Else and End If keywords is executed.

Using the If . . . Then . . . Elseif Statement

Complex logic problems might require a more complex structure than the If . . . Then . . . Else logic structure. For example, consider the following logical problem that must be solved in a computer program:

An online store charges a shipping amount based on the dollar amount of the order being shipped. The rules are: 1) If the order amount is above $500, the shipping cost is $30; 2) If the order amount is more than $400 and not greater than $500, the shipping cost is $25; 3) If the order amount is more than $200 and not greater than $400, the shipping cost is $20; 4) If the order amount is equal to or less than $200, the shipping cost is $15.

When one of the conditions is found to be true, the rest of the conditions are not tested because the correct condition has been found. To solve this problem, you should think this way:

1. If the order amount is greater than $500.00, then the shipping cost is $30.00 and no more processing must be done to determine the shipping cost.
2. If, however, the order amount is not greater than $500.00, I must check further to see if it is greater than $400.00 (400.01 through 500.00). If so, the shipping cost is $25.00.
3. If the order amount is not greater than $400.00, the next step is to check if it is greater than $200.00. Notice that if it is greater than $200.00 but not greater than $400.00, it must be in the range $201.00 to $400.00. If this is true, the shipping cost is $20.00.
4. If none of the above is true, then the order amount must be less than or equal to $200. In this case, the shipping cost is $15.00.

As you can see, a simple If . . . Then . . . Else statement could not solve this logic problem because the If . . . Then . . . Else structure tests only a single condition and specifies the processing based on whether the condition is true or false. For a problem where multiple conditions must be tested, the If . . . Then . . . ElseIf statement might be appropriate. The general format of the If . . . Then . . . ElseIf statement is shown in Figure 5-41.

```
105        If decOrderAmount > 500D Then
106            Statement(s) executed if condition is true
107        ElseIf decOrderAmount > 400D Then
108            Statement(s) executed if condition is true
109        ElseIf decOrderAmount > 200D Then
110            Statement(s) executed if condition is true
111        ElseIf decOrderAmount > 0D Then
112            Statement(s) executed if condition is true
113        End If
```

FIGURE 5-41

Once a condition in the code in Figure 5-41 on the previous page is true, Visual Basic bypasses the rest of the ElseIf statements. For example, assume the order amount is $455. The first condition tests if the order amount is greater than 500. The first condition would test false because 455 is not greater than 500.

Next, the ElseIf entry will test if 455 is greater than 400. Because the value 455 is greater than 400, the condition is true and the statement(s) on line 108 will be executed. The remaining ElseIf statements will not be evaluated because the true condition has been found.

Separate If . . . Then statements are not used in the example in Figure 5-41 on the previous page because each condition would have to be tested even though a condition had already been found to be true. When using an If . . . Then . . . ElseIf statement, after the condition is found to be true, the remaining conditions are not tested, making the process faster and more efficient.

Trailing Else Statements

You may want to include a trailing Else statement at the end of an If . . . Then . . . ElseIf conditional statement to handle a condition that does not meet any of the conditions tested. In the example in Figure 5-42, the code is determining if the user is eligible for Social Security benefits. If the user's age is greater than or equal to 65, the user receives full benefits. If the user's age is between 0 and 65, the user is not eligible for benefits.

```
115          If intAge >= 65 Then
116              lblSocialSecurity.Text = "Full Benefits"
117          ElseIf intAge > 0 Then
118              lblSocialSecurity.Text = "Not Eligible for Benefits"
119          Else
120              lblSocialSecurity.Text = "Invalid Age"
121          End If
```

FIGURE 5-42

In Figure 5-42, the statement on line 120 that follows the trailing Else statement on line 119 is executed if the number in the intAge variable does not meet the conditions stated in the previous If statements. For example, if the intAge variable contains a negative value such as −12, the Text property of the lblSocialSecurity Label object will be set to "Invalid Age".

Nested If Statements

At times, more than one decision has to be made to determine what processing must occur. For example, if one condition is true, a second condition may need to be tested before the correct code is executed. To test a second condition only after determining that a first condition is true (or false), you must place an If statement within another If statement. When you place one If statement within another If statement, the inner If statement is said to be nested within the outer If Statement. The syntax of a nested If statement is shown in Figure 5-43.

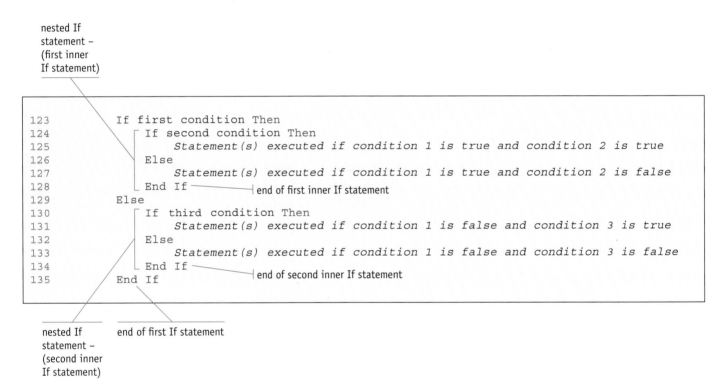

nested If
statement –
(first inner
If statement)

```
123        If first condition Then
124            If second condition Then
125                Statement(s) executed if condition 1 is true and condition 2 is true
126            Else
127                Statement(s) executed if condition 1 is true and condition 2 is false
128            End If              end of first inner If statement
129        Else
130            If third condition Then
131                Statement(s) executed if condition 1 is false and condition 3 is true
132            Else
133                Statement(s) executed if condition 1 is false and condition 3 is false
134            End If              end of second inner If statement
135        End If
```

nested If
statement –
(second inner
If statement)

end of first If statement

FIGURE 5-43

In Figure 5-43, if the first condition tested is true, the statements following the keyword Then are executed. The statement to be executed when the first condition is true is another If statement (line 124) that tests the second condition. This second If statement is said to be a nested If statement or an inner If statement. If the second condition is true, the statement(s) on line 125 following the keyword Then for the first inner If statement are executed. If the second condition is not true, the statement(s) on line 127 following the keyword Else for the first inner If statement are executed. The End If entry (line 128) follows the first inner If statement, indicating the end of the effect of the first inner If statement.

If the first condition is not true, then the statements following the keyword Else on line 129 for the first If statement are executed. The statement to be executed when the first condition is not true is an If statement that tests the third condition (line 130). If the third condition is true, the statement(s) on line 131 following the Then keyword of the second inner If statement are executed. Finally, if the second inner If statement that tests the third condition is false, the statement(s) on line 133 are executed for the case when condition 1 is false and condition 3 is false.

To illustrate a nested If statement, assume a college has the following admissions policy: If an applying student has a GPA greater than 3.5 and an SAT score greater than 1000, then that student is granted admission. If an applying student has a GPA greater than 3.5 but an SAT score of 1000 or lower, the student is advised to retake the SAT exam. If an applying student has a GPA of 3.5 or lower but an SAT score greater than 1200, the student is granted a probationary admission, which means a 2.5 GPA must be achieved in the first semester of college. If an applying student has a GPA lower than 3.5 and an SAT score of 1200 or lower, the student is denied admission. The nested If statement to process this admission policy is shown in Figure 5-44.

```
140        If decGPA > 3.5D Then
141            If intSatScore > 1000 Then
142                lblAdmissionStatus.Text = "You have earned admission"
143            Else
144                lblAdmissionStatus.Text = "Retake the SAT exam"
145            End If
146        Else
147            If intSatScore > 1200 Then
148                lblAdmissionStatus.Text = "You have earned probationary admission"
149            Else
150                lblAdmissionStatus.Text = "You have been denied admission"
151            End If
152        End If
```

FIGURE 5-44

Notice in Figure 5-44 that the test for greater than 1000 on the SAT (line 141) must take place only after the test for a GPA greater than 3.5 (line 140), because the test for greater than 1000 is required only after it has been determined that the GPA is greater than 3.5. Therefore, a nested If statement is required. In addition, the test for greater than 1200 (line 147) should occur only after it has been determined that the GPA is less than 3.5. As you can see, you should use a nested If statement when a condition must be tested only after another condition has been tested.

Other Nested If Configurations

You can use nested If statements in a variety of forms. Assume, for example, that the admissions policy for a different school is as follows: If an applying student has a GPA greater than 3.5 and an SAT score greater than 1100, then that student is granted admission. If an applying student has a GPA greater than 3.5 but an SAT score of 1100 or lower, the student is advised to retake the SAT exam. If an applying student has a GPA of 3.5 or lower, the student is denied admission. The nested If statement in Figure 5-45 solves this logic problem.

```
154        If decGPA > 3.5D Then
155            If intSatScore > 1100 Then
156                lblAdmissionStatus.Text = "You have earned admission"
157            Else
158                lblAdmissionStatus.Text = "Retake the SAT exam"
159            End If
160        Else
161            lblAdmissionStatus.Text = "You have been denied admission"
162        End If
```

FIGURE 5-45

In Figure 5-45, if the GPA is greater than 3.5, then the first inner If statement on line 155 is executed to determine if the SAT score is greater than 1100. If so, the person has earned admission. If not, the person is advised to retake the SAT exam. If the GPA is not greater than 3.5, the student is denied admission. Notice that an If statement does not follow the Else keyword on line 160. An inner If statement need not follow both the If and the Else keywords.

Sometimes, after a condition is found to be true, a statement must be executed before the inner If statement is executed. For example, assume that if the GPA for a student is greater than 3.5, then the student should be informed that their GPA is acceptable for admission. The code in Figure 5-46 implements this condition.

```
164        If decGPA > 3.5D Then
165            lblGPAStatus.Text = "Your GPA is acceptable"
166            If intSatScore > 1100 Then
167                lblAdmissionStatus.Text = "You have earned admission"
168            Else
169                lblAdmissionStatus.Text = "Retake the SAT exam"
170            End If
171        Else
172            lblGPAStatus.Text = "Your GPA is not acceptable"
173            lblAdmissionStatus.Text = "You have been denied admission"
174        End If
```

FIGURE 5-46

In Figure 5-46 on the previous page, on line 165 the message "Your GPA is acceptable" is assigned to the Text property of the lblGPAStatus Label object prior to checking the SAT score. As you can see, after the first condition has been tested, one or more statements can be executed prior to executing the inner If statement. This holds true for the Else portion of the If statement as well.

Matching If, Else, and End If Entries

When you write a nested If statement, the inner If statement must be fully contained within the outer If statement. To accomplish this, you must ensure that each Else entry has a corresponding If entry, and an inner If statement must be terminated with an End If entry before either the Else entry or the End If entry for the outer If statement is encountered. If you code the statement incorrectly, one or more entries in the nested If statement will be identified with a blue squiggly line, indicating an error in the structure of the statement.

You also must place the correct statements with the correct If and Else statements within the nested If statement. For example, in Figure 5-47, the code is *incorrect* because the statement following the Else statements has been switched.

```
164          If decGPA > 3.5D Then
165              lblGPAStatus.Text = "Your GPA is acceptable"
166              If intSatScore > 1100 Then
167                  lblAdmissionStatus.Text = "You have earned admission"
168              Else
169                  lblAdmissionStatus.Text = "You have been denied admission"
170              End If
171          Else
172              lblGPAStatus Text = "Your GPA is not acceptable"          incorrect
173              lblAdmissionStatus.Text = "Retake the SAT exam"            statements
174          End If
```

FIGURE 5-47

You must be precise when placing the executing statements in the nested If statement. It is easy to miscode a nested If statement.

Nesting Three or More Levels of If Statements

If statements are not limited to two levels of nesting. Three or more levels can be included in a nested If statement. When this is done, however, the nested If statement can become more difficult to understand and code. If more than two levels are required to solve a logic problem, great care must be taken to ensure errors such as the one shown in Figure 5-47 do not occur.

Testing the Status of a RadioButton Object in Code

In the Wood Cabinet Estimate chapter project, which finds the cost of wood cabinets, the user selects one RadioButton in the GroupBox object to select the wood type. The code must check each RadioButton to determine if that RadioButton has been selected by the user. When the user selects a radio button, the Checked property for that button is changed from False to True. In addition, the Checked property for other RadioButton objects in the GroupBox object is set to False. This Checked property can be tested in an If statement to determine if the RadioButton object has been selected.

To test the status of the Checked Property for a RadioButton object, the general statement shown in Figure 5-48 can be written.

```
237        If radPine.Checked Then
238            Statement(s) to be executed if radio button is checked
239        End If
```

FIGURE 5-48

Notice in Figure 5-48 that the RadioButton property is not compared using a relational operator. Instead, when a property that can contain only True or False is tested, only the property must be specified in the If statement. When the property contains True, then the If statement is considered true, and when the property contains False, the If statement is considered false.

Testing RadioButtons with the If . . . Then . . . ElseIf Statement

When a program contains multiple RadioButton objects in a Panel object or a GroupBox object, only one of the radio buttons can be selected. The statement that can be used to check multiple radio buttons is the If . . . Then . . . ElseIf statement because once the checked radio button is detected, checking the remaining radio buttons is unnecessary.

In the Wood Cabinet Estimate application, the user will click one of three radio buttons (Pine, Oak, or Cherry) to select the type of wood to be used for cabinets. To use an If . . . Then . . . ElseIf statement to check the status of the radio buttons, the most likely choice should be checked first. By doing this, the fewest number of tests will have to be performed. Therefore, the first If statement should test the status of the Pine radio button (radPine). If the radPine button is checked, the Cost Per Foot should be set to the value in the decPineCost variable, which is 150.00. No further testing should be done (see Figure 5-49 on the next page).

```
31              If radPine.Checked Then
32                  decCostPerFoot = decPineCost
33              ElseIf radOak.Checked Then
34                  decCostPerFoot = decOakCost
35              ElseIf radCherry.Checked Then
36                  decCostPerFoot = decCherryCost
37              End If
```

FIGURE 5-49

If the radPine button is not checked, then the radOak button should be tested. If it is checked, the Cost Per Foot should be set to the value in the decOakCost variable (200.00) and no further testing should be done. If the radOak button is not checked, then the radCherry button should be tested. If the other two buttons are not checked, then the radCherry button must be checked because one of the three must be checked. The Cost Per Foot will be set to the value in the decCherryCost variable (350.00).

As you learned earlier, during design time you can set the Checked property to True for the most frequently selected RadioButton to save the user from having to select the most common choice. In the Wood Cabinet Estimate program, after the Cost Per Linear Foot has been determined and the Cost Estimate has been calculated, the user can click the Clear button to clear the Linear Feet text box, clear the Cost Estimate, and reset the radio buttons so that the Pine button is selected. The code to reset the radio buttons is shown in Figure 5-50.

```
62          radPine.Checked = True
63          radOak.Checked = False
64          radCherry.Checked = False
```

FIGURE 5-50

In Figure 5-50, the Checked property for the radPine RadioButton object is set to True using the same method you have seen in previous chapters for setting an object property. Similarly, the Checked property for the other two RadioButton objects is set to False. As a result of these statements, the Pine radio button will be selected in the user interface, and the Oak and Cherry radio buttons will not be selected.

Block-Level Scope

In Chapter 4 you learned that the scope of a variable is defined by where it is declared within a program. For example, if a variable is declared within an event handler, then only code within that event handler can reference the variable. Code in one event handler within a program cannot reference a variable declared in another event handler.

Within an event handler, an If . . . Then . . . Else statement (the code beginning with the If keyword and ending with the corresponding Else keyword, or the code beginning with the Else keyword and ending with the End If keyword) is considered a block of code. Variables can be declared within the block of code. When this occurs, the variable can be referenced only within the block of code where it is declared. For example, variables defined within an If . . . Then block of code fall out of scope (cannot be referenced) outside that block of code. To illustrate this concept, the code in Figure 5-51 shows a variable, intYears, declared within an If . . . Then block of code.

```
11          If intAge < 18 Then
12              Dim intYears As Integer
13              intYears = 18 - intAge
14              lblMessage.Text = "You can vote in " & intYears & " years(s)."
15          Else
16              lblMessage.Text = "You can vote!"
17          End If
```

FIGURE 5-51

In Figure 5-51, on line 12 the variable intYears is declared as an Integer variable. On line 13, the variable is used in an arithmetic statement to receive the result of the calculation, 18 – intAge, which determines the number of years less than 18 that is stored in intAge. The result in intYears is concatenated with literals in the statement on line 14. The intYears variable can be referenced in any statements between the If keyword and the Else keyword. It cannot be referenced anywhere else in the program. Note that it cannot be referenced even in the Else portion of the If statement. When a statement referencing the intYears variable is written outside the area between the If keyword and the Else keyword, a compilation error will occur and the program will not be able to be compiled and executed.

Although the scope of the intYears variable in Figure 5-51 is between the If keyword on line 11 and the Else keyword on line 15, you should realize that the variable itself perseveres during the execution of the event handler procedure. Therefore, if the If statement in Figure 5-51 is executed a second time, the value in the intYears variable will be the same as when the If statement was completed the first time. To avoid unexpected results when the If statement is executed the second time, you should initialize block variables at the beginning of the block. In Figure 5-51, the statement on line 13 sets the value in the intYears variable immediately after the variable is declared, which is good programming technique.

Using Logical Operators

The If statements you have seen thus far test a single condition. In many cases, more than one condition must be true or one of several conditions must be true in order for the statements in the Then portion of the If . . . Then . . . Else statement to be executed. When more than one condition is included in an If . . . Then . . . Else statement, the conditions are called a **compound condition**. For example, consider the following business traveling rule: "If the flight costs less than $300.00 and the hotel is less than $120.00 per night, the business trip is approved." In this case, both conditions (flight less than $300.00 *and* hotel less than $120.00 per night) must be true in order for the trip to approved. If either condition is not true, then the business trip is not approved.

To create an If statement that processes the business traveling rule, you must use a **logical operator**. The most common set of logical operators are listed in Figure 5-52.

Logical Operator	Meaning
And	All conditions tested in the If statement must be true
Or	One condition tested in the If statement must be true
Not	Negates a condition

FIGURE 5-52

For the business traveling rule specified previously, you should use the And logical operator.

Using the And Logical Operator

The **And logical operator** allows you to combine two or more conditions into a compound condition that can be tested with an If statement. If any of the conditions stated in the compound condition is false, the compound condition is considered false and the statements following the Else portion of the If statement will be executed. The code in Figure 5-53 uses the And logical operator to implement the business traveling rule.

```
137        If decFlightCost < 300D And decHotelCost < 120D Then
138            lblTripMessage.Text = "Your business trip is approved"
139        Else
140            lblTripMessage.Text = "Your business trip is denied"
141        End If
```

FIGURE 5-53

In Figure 5-53, both conditions in the compound condition (flight cost less than 300 and hotel cost less than 120) must be true in order for the business trip to be approved. If one of the conditions is false, then the compound condition is considered false and the If statement would return a false indication. For example, if the flight cost is 300 or more, the trip will not be approved regardless of the hotel cost. Similarly, if the hotel cost is 120 or more, the trip will not be approved regardless of the flight cost. This process is illustrated in the diagram in Figure 5-54 on the next page.

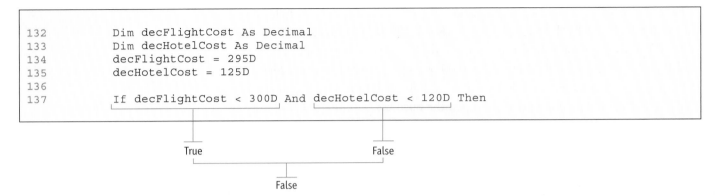

```
132          Dim decFlightCost As Decimal
133          Dim decHotelCost As Decimal
134          decFlightCost = 295D
135          decHotelCost = 125D
136
137          If decFlightCost < 300D And decHotelCost < 120D Then
```

FIGURE 5-54

In Figure 5-54, the flight cost is 295, so it is less than 300 and the first part of the compound condition is true. Following the And logical operator, the hotel cost (125) is not less than 120. Therefore, the second part of the compound condition is false. With the And logical operator, when either condition is false, the If statement considers the compound condition to be false. The result of the If statement in Figure 5-54 is that the compound condition is considered to be false.

Using the Or Logical Operator

When the **Or logical operator** is used to connect two or more conditions, the compound condition is true if any tested condition is true. Even if four conditional statements are included in the compound condition, if one conditional statement in the compound condition is true, the entire statement is considered true.

As an example, assume a college has an acceptance policy that states each student must either have a minimum of a 3.5 grade point average (GPA) or at least a 1080 score on the SAT college entrance exam to be accepted for enrollment. If the student meets one or both conditions, the student would be accepted. The If statement in Figure 5-55, which uses the Or logical operator, will solve this problem.

```
147          If decGPA >= 3.5D Or intSATScore >= 1080 Then
148              lblAcceptance.Text = "You have been accepted"
149          Else
150              lblAcceptance.Text = "You are not accepted"
151          End If
```

FIGURE 5-55

In Figure 5-55 if the GPA is 3.2, but the SAT score is 1130, the compound condition would be considered true because at least one of these conditions (SAT >= 1080) is true (Figure 5-56 on the next page).

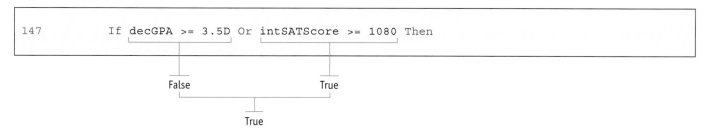

FIGURE 5-56

Using the Not Logical Operator

The **Not logical operator** allows you to state conditions that are best expressed in a negative way. In essence, the Not logical operator reverses the logical value of a condition on which it operates. For example, if a shoe store sells shoe sizes under size 14 from their showroom but requires special orders for larger sizes, the code could use the Not logical operator as shown in Figure 5-57 to negate the condition in the statement.

```
155        If Not decShoeSize >= 14 Then
156            lblOrderPolicy.Text = "Showroom shoe style available"
157        Else
158            lblOrderPolicy.Text = "Special order needed"
159        End If
```

FIGURE 5-57

The statement in Figure 5-57 works, but the use of the Not logical operator makes the If statement somewhat difficult to understand. Generally, a statement that avoids the Not logical operator is more easily understood. For example, the code in Figure 5-58 accomplishes the same task as the code in Figure 5-57, but is easier to understand.

```
162        If decShoeSize < 14 Then
163            lblOrderPolicy.Text = "Showroom shoe style available"
164        Else
165            lblOrderPolicy.Text = "Special order needed"
166        End If
```

FIGURE 5-58

IN THE REAL WORLD

Many developers avoid using the Not logical operator because it makes the code harder to understand. By removing the Not logical operator and reversing the relational operator, the statement becomes clearer.

Other Logical Operators

The Visual Basic programming language provides three other lesser used logical operators. These are shown in the table in Figure 5-59.

Logical Operator	Meaning
Xor	When one condition in the compound condition is true, but not both, the compound condition is true
AndAlso	As soon as a condition is found to be false, no further conditions are tested and the compound condition is false
OrElse	As soon as a condition is found to be true, no further conditions are tested and the compound condition is true

FIGURE 5-59

Order of Operations for Logical Operators

You can combine more than one logical operator in the same If . . . Then statement. In an If statement, arithmetic operators are evaluated first, relational operators are evaluated next, and logical operators are evaluated last. The order of operations for logical operators is shown in Figure 5-60.

Logical Operator	Order
Not	Highest Precedence
And, AndAlso	Next Precedence
Or, OrElse, Xor	Last Precedence

FIGURE 5-60

In most cases, if a developer uses multiple relational or logical operators in an If statement, the order of precedence should be established through the use of parentheses in order to clarify the sequence of evaluation. As in arithmetic expressions, conditional expressions within parentheses are evaluated before conditional expressions outside parentheses.

Select Case Statement

In some programming applications, different operations can occur based upon the value in a single field. For example, in Figure 5-61 on the next page, the user enters the number of the day in the week and the program displays the name of the day. The program must evaluate the number of the day value and display the correct name of the day.

FIGURE 5-61

In Figure 5-61, if the number of the day is 1, then the value Monday should be displayed. If the number of the day is 2, then Tuesday should be displayed, and so on. If the number of the day is 6 or 7, then the value Weekend should be displayed. If the user does not enter a value of 1 through 7, the user should be told to enter a value between 1 and 7.

To solve this problem, a series of If . . . Then . . . ElseIf statements could be used. An easier and clearer way to solve the problem, however, is to use the Select Case statement.

When using a Select Case statement, the value in a single field, such as the day number, is evaluated and a different action, such as displaying the name of the day, is taken based on the value in the field.

A general example of the Select Case statement is shown in Figure 5-62.

The coding for the Determine Day of Week application is shown in Figure 5-63 on the next page.

```
168        Select Case Test Expression
169            Case First Expression
170                Statement(s) for First Case
171            Case Second Expression
172                Statement(s) for Second Case
173            Case Third Expression
174                Statement(s) for Third Case
175            Case Else
176                Statement(s) for when the Case Conditions do not match the
177                    test expressions above
178        End Select
```

FIGURE 5-62

```
13          Select Case intDayNumber
14              Case 1
15                  lblDayOfWeek.Text = "Monday"
16              Case 2
17                  lblDayOfWeek.Text = "Tuesday"
18              Case 3
19                  lblDayOfWeek.Text = "Wednesday"
20              Case 4
21                  lblDayOfWeek.Text = "Thursday"
22              Case 5
23                  lblDayOfWeek.Text = "Friday"
24              Case 6
25                  lblDayOfWeek.Text = "Weekend"
26              Case 7
27                  lblDayOfWeek.Text = "Weekend"
28              Case Else
29                  lblDayOfWeek.Text = "Enter 1 through 7"
30          End Select
```

FIGURE 5-63

The Select Case statement begins with the Select Case command. The test expression entry is used to specify the value or variable that contains the value to be tested in the Select Case statement. In Figure 5-63, the variable is intDayNumber. So, when the Select Case statement is executed, each of the cases will be compared to the value in the intDayNumber variable.

Each Case statement specifies the value for which the test expression is checked. For example, the first Case statement on line 14 in Figure 5-63 specifies the value 1. If the value in the variable intDayNumber is equal to 1, the statement(s) following the first Case statement up to the second Case statement (line 16) are executed. In Figure 5-63, the assignment statement on line 15 that sets the Text property of the lblDayOfWeek to Monday is executed if the value in intDayNumber is equal to 1. More than one statement can follow a Case statement.

If the expression following the first Case statement is not true, then the next Case statement is evaluated. In Figure 5-63, the Case statement on line 16 checks if the value in intDayNumber is equal to 2. If so, the Text property of the lblDayOfWeek is set to Tuesday. This process continues through the remainder of the Case statements.

The Case Else statement on line 28 is an optional entry that includes all conditions not specifically tested for in the other Case statements. In Figure 5-63, if the value in the intDayNumber variable is not equal to 1 through 7, then the statement following the Case Else statement is executed. While not required, good programming practice dictates that the Case Else statement should be used so that all cases are accounted for and the program performs a specific action regardless of the value found in the test expression.

The End Select statement is required to end the Select Case statement. When you enter the Select Case statement in Visual Studio 2010, IntelliSense automatically includes the End Select statement.

Select Case Test Expressions

The example in Figure 5-63 on the previous page used an integer as the test expression value, but any data type can be used in the test expression. For example, the test expression in Figure 5-64 uses the Text property of the txtStudentMajor TextBox object as a string value.

```
217        Select Case Me.txtStudentMajor.Text
218            Case "Accounting"
219                lblDepartment.Text = "Business"
220            Case "Marketing"
221                lblDepartment.Text = "Business"
222            Case "Electrical Engineering"
223                lblDepartment.Text = "Engineering"
224            Case "Biochemistry"
225                lblDepartment.Text = "Chemistry"
226            Case "Shakespearean Literature"
227                lblDepartment.Text = "English"
228            Case "Web Design and E-Commerce"
229                lblDepartment.Text = "CIS"
230            Case Else
231                lblDepartment.Text = "Other"
232        End Select
```

FIGURE 5-64

In Figure 5-64, the Select Case statement is used to test the value in the Text property of the txtStudentMajor TextBox object and move the corresponding department name to the Text property of the lblDepartment object. The Case statements specify the values to be tested in the text box. The use of a string for the Select Case statement works in the same manner as other data types.

Using Relational Operators in a Select Case Statement

You can use relational operators in a Select Case statement. You must, however, use the keyword Is with the relational operator. For example, in Figure 5-41 on page 320, an If . . . Then . . . ElseIf statement was used to determine the shipping cost. That same processing could be accomplished using a Select Case statement, as shown in Figure 5-65.

HEADS UP

If you forget to type the Is keyword in the Case Is statement, Visual Studio will insert it for you.

```
191        Select Case decOrderAmount
192            Case Is > 500D
193                decShippingCost = 30D
194            Case Is > 400D
195                decShippingCost = 25D
196            Case Is > 200D
197                decShippingCost = 20D
198            Case Is > 0D
199                decShippingCost = 15D
200            Case Else
201                decShippingCost = 0D
202        End Select
203
```

FIGURE 5-65

Using Ranges in Select Case Statements

Another way to specify values in a Select Case statement is to use ranges. In Figure 5-66, the Case statements illustrate testing for six different conditions.

```
224         Select Case intGradeLevel
225             Case 1 To 3
226                 lblGradeLevelExam.Text = "Early elementary"
227             Case 4 To 6
228                 lblGradeLevelExam.Text = "Late elementary"
229             Case 7 To 8
230                 lblGradeLevelExam.Text = "Middle school"
231             Case 9 To 10
232                 lblGradeLevelExam.Text = "Early high school"
233             Case 11
234                 lblGradeLevelExam.Text = "Late high school"
235             Case 12
236                 lblGradeLevelExam.Text = "Final exam"
237             Case Else
238                 lblGradeLevelExam.Text = "Invalid grade level"
239         End Select
```

FIGURE 5-66

As you can see, a range of values in a Case statement is specified by stating the beginning value, the word To, and then the ending value in the range. The Case statements will test the value in the intGradeLevel variable, and the appropriate statements will be executed.

You also can write Case statements with more than one distinct value being tested. In Figure 5-67, the Case statement tests the individual values of 1, 3, 8, 11, and 17 against the value specified in the intDepartmentNumber variable.

```
230         Select Case intDepartmentNumber
231             Case 1, 3, 8, 11, 17
232
```

FIGURE 5-67

Notice in Figure 5-67 that each value in the Case statement is separated by a comma.

The code in Figure 5-68 shows a mixture of the two techniques, using both commas and a To statement.

```
234         Select Case intDepartmentNumber
235             Case 2, 4, 7, 12 To 16, 22
```

FIGURE 5-68

Selecting Which Decision Structure to Use

In some instances, you might be faced with determining if you should use the Select Case statement or the If . . . Then . . . ElseIf statement to solve a problem. Generally, the Select Case statement is most useful when more than two or three values must be tested for a given variable. For example, in Figure 5-64 on page 335, six different values are checked in the Text property of the txtStudentMajor TextBox object. This is a perfect example of the use of the Select Case statement.

The If . . . Then . . . ElseIf statement is more flexible because more than one variable can be used in the comparison, and compound conditions with the And, Or, and Not logical operators can be used.

Code Snippets

Visual Basic includes a code library of almost five hundred pieces of code, called IntelliSense **code snippets**, that you can insert into an application. Each snippet consists of a complete programming task such as an If . . . Then . . . Else decision structure, sending an e-mail message, or drawing a circle. Inserting these commonly used pieces of code is an effective way to enhance productivity. You also can create your own snippets and add them to the library.

In addition to inserting snippets in your program, you can display a code snippet to ensure you understand the syntax and requirements for a given type of statement. To display and insert a code snippet for the If . . . Then . . . Else statement, you can complete the following steps:

STEP 1   Right-click the line in the code editing window where you want to insert the snippet.

Visual Studio displays a shortcut menu (Figure 5-69). It is important to right-click in the code editing window in the exact location where you want the code snippet to appear. If you right-click outside this location, the shortcut menu might list choices that are customized to that area of code and not include the code snippet for which you were searching. In addition, if you click in the wrong place, the snippet will be positioned in the incorrect location in your program.

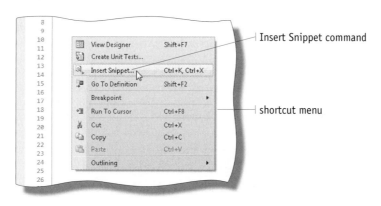

FIGURE 5-69

STEP 2   Click Insert Snippet on the shortcut menu.

Visual Studio displays a menu of folders containing snippets (Figure 5-70). The code snippets in each folder correspond to their folder titles.

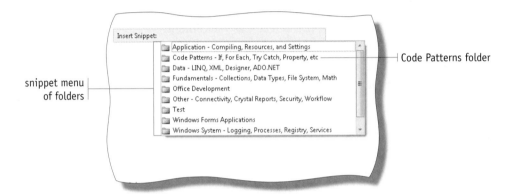

FIGURE 5-70

STEP 3   Double-click the folder Code Patterns - If, For Each, Try Catch, Property, etc, which contains commonly used code such as the If . . . Then . . . Else statement.

Visual Studio displays a menu of folders for code patterns (Figure 5-71).

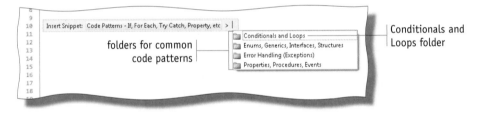

FIGURE 5-71

STEP 4   Double-click the Conditionals and Loops folder because an If . . . Then . . . Else statement is a conditional statement.

Visual Studio displays the list of Conditionals and Loops code snippets (Figure 5-72). Some of these statements will be unfamiliar until you complete Chapter 6, but you can see that the list of code snippets includes a number of different types of If statements.

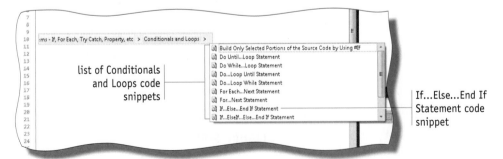

FIGURE 5-72

STEP 5 Double-click the If . . . Else . . . End If Statement code snippet.

The If . . . Else . . . End If Statement code snippet is inserted into the code on the line selected in step 1 (Figure 5-73). The highlighted text must be replaced by the condition(s) to be tested in the If statement. The code to be executed when the condition is true and the code to be executed when the condition is false must be added.

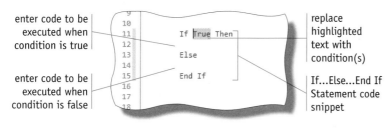

FIGURE 5-73

ONLINE REINFORCEMENT

To view a video of the process in the previous steps, visit scsite.com/vb2010/ch5 and then select Figure 5-69.

You must modify the code snippet shown in Figure 5-73 in order for the code to work properly. You may find that modifying the code in the snippet, particularly in a complicated code snippet, is more work than using IntelliSense to enter the statement.

Code snippets are also helpful for learning or reviewing the format and syntax of a statement. For example, if you wanted to review the syntax of an If . . . Else If . . . Else . . . End If statement, you could insert the statement into the code editing window and examine it. You could then either click the Undo button to remove the statement or you could comment out the snippet code and keep it for your review. In many cases of checking syntax, reviewing a snippet is faster and clearer than consulting Visual Basic help.

Validating Data

Since the first days of computers, the phrase "garbage in, garbage out" has described the fact that allowing incorrect input data into a program produces incorrect output. Developers should anticipate that users will enter invalid data. Therefore, they must write code that will prevent the invalid data from being used in the program to produce invalid output.

For example, in the Wood Cabinet Estimate chapter project, the user is asked to enter the number of linear feet for the wood cabinets. If the user enters a negative number, a letter, or even leaves the text box blank, the program should inform the user of the input error and allow the user to reenter a proper value. If the program attempts to process invalid data, unexpected errors can occur, which is not the way a program should respond to invalid input data.

To properly check the linear feet value entered by the user, two checks must be performed. First, the program must check the value to ensure it is numeric. Second, the numeric value entered by the user must be checked to ensure it is greater than zero. These checks are explained in the following section.

Testing Input to Determine If the Value Is Numeric

In the Wood Cabinet Estimate program, if no check is performed on the input data and the user accidentally enters a nonnumeric character such as an "a" or fails to enter a value at all, the program will fail when Visual Basic attempts to convert that value to a number. An exception (error) screen will open and the program will be terminated. Therefore, the program must check the value entered by the user to ensure it is numeric. In addition, if the user enters a nonnumeric value, the program should inform the user of the error and request a valid numeric value.

The Visual Basic **IsNumeric function** can check the input value to determine if the value can be converted into a numeric value such as an Integer or Decimal data type. If so, it returns a True Boolean value. If the value is not recognized as a numeric value, the IsNumeric function returns a False Boolean value.

For example, the IsNumeric function can check the value in the Text property of the Linear Feet text box. If the user enters a letter such as "a" in the text box, the IsNumeric function would return a False Boolean value because the letter "a" is not numeric.

Because the IsNumeric function returns a Boolean value (True or False), it can be placed within an If statement as the condition to be tested. If the returned value is True, the condition in the If statement is considered true. If the returned value is False, the condition in the If statement is considered false. The code in Figure 5-74 uses an If statement to determine if the Text property of the txtLinearFeet TextBox object is numeric.

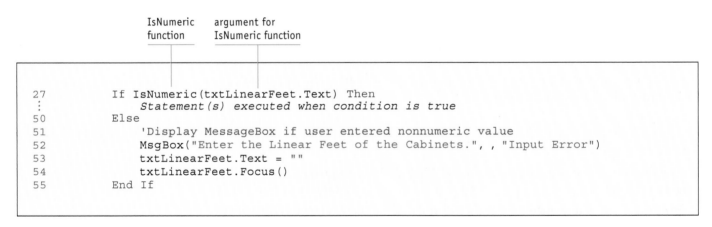

```
               IsNumeric       argument for
               function        IsNumeric function

27             If IsNumeric(txtLinearFeet.Text) Then
  ⋮                Statement(s) executed when condition is true
50             Else
51                 'Display MessageBox if user entered nonnumeric value
52                 MsgBox("Enter the Linear Feet of the Cabinets.", , "Input Error")
53                 txtLinearFeet.Text = ""
54                 txtLinearFeet.Focus()
55             End If
```

FIGURE 5-74

In Figure 5-74, the If statement on line 27 calls the IsNumeric function. The Text property of the txtLinearFeet TextBox object is the argument for the IsNumeric function. As a result of this specification, the IsNumeric function will analyze the data in the Text property of the txtLinearFeet TextBox object. If the data can be converted to a numeric data type, then the function will return a Boolean value of True. If the data cannot be converted to a numeric data type, the function will return a Boolean value of False.

Once the function has returned a Boolean value, the If statement tests the Boolean value. If it is true, which means the value in the Text property of the

txtLinearFeet TextBox object is numeric, the appropriate statements are executed. If
the condition is false, meaning the value is not numeric, the statements on lines 51–55
are executed. The statement on line 52 displays a message box telling the user to
enter the linear feet of the cabinet (see Figure 5-2 on page 293). The caption of the
message box is "Input Error". The statement on line 53 clears the Text property. The
statement on line 54 sets the focus on the text box so the user can reenter the value.

Checking for a Positive Number

If the condition in Figure 5-74 on the previous page is true, the value in the Text
property must be converted to a Decimal data type. Then, the program checks to ensure
the value entered is greater than zero. These statements are shown in Figure 5-75.

```
27          If IsNumeric(txtLinearFeet.Text) Then
28              decLinearFeet = Convert.ToDecimal(txtLinearFeet.Text)
29
30              ' Is linear feet greater than zero
31              If decLinearFeet > 0 Then
                  Statement(s) executed when condition is true
33              Else
34                  ' Display error message if user entered a negative value
35                  MsgBox("You entered " & decLinearFeet.ToString() &
36                      ". Enter a Number Greater Than Zero.", , "Input Error")
37                  txtLinearFeet.Text = ""
38                  txtLinearFeet.Focus()
39              End If
40          Else
41              ' Display error message if user entered a nonnumeric value
42              MsgBox("Enter the Linear Feet of the Cabinets.", , "Input Error")
43              txtLinearFeet.Text = ""
44              txtLinearFeet.Focus()
45          End If
```

FIGURE 5-75

When the value in the Text property is numeric, it is converted to a decimal value
(line 28). On line 31, the decimal value is compared to zero. If it is greater than zero,
then the processing for a true statement is executed. If the value is not greater than
zero, a message box is displayed informing the user an invalid entry was made (see
Figure 5-29 on page 311). The user then can enter a valid value.

The process of validating input data is fundamental to programming when using
a graphical user interface. A well-designed program must ensure the user enters
valid data.

Program Design

As you have learned, the requirements document identifies the purpose of the program being developed; the application title; the procedures to be followed when using the program; any equations and calculations required in the program; any conditions within the program that must be tested; notes and restrictions that must be followed by the program; and any other comments that would be helpful to understanding the problem. The requirements document for the Wood Cabinet Estimate application is shown in Figure 5-76. The Use Case Definition document is shown in Figure 5-77 on the next page.

REQUIREMENTS DOCUMENT

Date submitted: January 29, 2014

Application title: Wood Cabinet Estimate

Purpose: This application calculates the estimated cost of wood cabinetry for a job bid.

Program Procedures: The user should enter the linear footage of cabinets needed and select the type of wood. The estimated cost for the cabinet job will be displayed.

Algorithms, Processing, and Conditions:
1. The user must be able to enter the number of linear feet of cabinetry.
2. The user must be able to select one of three wood types: pine, oak, or cherry.
3. The user can initiate the calculation and display the cost estimate for the wood cabinets.
4. The application computes the cost estimate of the cabinets based on the number of linear feet and the cost of the wood. Pine costs $150 per linear foot of cabinets, oak costs $200 per linear foot, and cherry costs $350 per linear foot.
5. The estimate calculation is: linear feet $\times$ cost per linear foot
6. The cost estimate is displayed in currency format.
7. The user should be able to clear the linear feet entered, reset the wood type to pine, and clear the cost estimate.

Notes and Restrictions:
1. If the user enters a nonnumeric value for the linear feet or if the TextBox object is empty, the user should be advised and asked for a valid entry.
2. If the user enters a negative number for the linear feet, the user should be advised and asked for a valid entry.

Comments:
1. The title of the Windows Form should be Wood Cabinet Estimate.

FIGURE 5-76

USE CASE DEFINITION

1. The window opens and displays the title, Estimate, a text box requesting the number of linear feet for the cabinets, radio buttons to select the wood type, and two buttons labeled Calculate and Clear.
2. The user enters the linear feet and selects one of the wood types.
3. The user clicks the Calculate button.
4. The user will be warned if a nonnumeric value is entered, the text box is left empty, or a negative number is entered.
5. The program displays the cost estimate for the cabinetry job.
6. The user clicks the Clear button to clear the Linear Feet text box, set the wood choice to Pine, and erase the cost estimate.
7. The user clicks the Close button to terminate the application.

FIGURE 5-77

Event Planning Document

You will recall that the event planning document consists of a table that specifies an object in the user interface that will cause an event, the action taken by the user to trigger the event, and the event processing that must occur. The event planning document for the Wood Cabinet Estimate program is shown in Figure 5-78.

EVENT PLANNING DOCUMENT

Program Name: Wood Cabinet Estimate	Developer: Corinne Hoisington	Object: frmWoodCabinets	Date: January 29, 2014
OBJECT	EVENT TRIGGER	EVENT PROCESSING	

btnCalculate	Click	Ensure data entered is numeric
		Display error message if data is not numeric
		   or text box is empty
		Convert data entered to numeric
		Ensure data entered is greater than zero
		Display error message if data is not greater
		   than zero
		Assign wood cost per foot based on type of
		   wood selection
		Calculate cost (linear feet × cost per foot)
		Display cost	

btnClear	Click	Clear input text box Clear cost estimate Set the Pine radio button to checked Clear the Oak radio button Clear the Cherry radio button Set focus on input text box	
frmWoodCabinets	Load	Set focus on input text box Clear the placement zeros for cost	

FIGURE 5-78

Design and Code the Program

After the events and the tasks within the events have been identified, the developer is ready to create the program. As you have learned, creating the program means designing the user interface and then entering Visual Basic statements to accomplish the tasks specified on the event planning document. As the developer enters the code, she also will implement the logic to carry out the required processing.

NOTE TO THE LEARNER

As you will recall, in the following activity you should complete the tasks within the specified steps. Each task is accompanied by a Hint Screen. The Hint Screen indicates where in the Visual Studio window you should perform the activity and reminds you of the method to use to create the user interface or enter code. If you need further help completing the step, refer to the figure number identified by the term ref: in the step.

Guided Program Development

To design the user interface for the Wood Cabinet Estimate program and enter the code required to process each event in the program, complete the steps on the following pages.

Guided Program Development

Phase 1: Design the Form

1

- **Create a Windows Application** Open Visual Studio using the Start button on the Windows taskbar and the All Programs submenu. Create a new Visual Basic Windows Application project by completing the following: Click the New Project button on the Standard toolbar; select and expand Visual Basic in the left pane; select Windows Application; name the project Wood Cabinet Estimate in the Name text box; then click the OK button in the New Project dialog box.

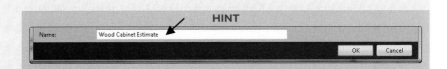

- **Name the Form** In the Solution Explorer pane, right-click Form1.vb and then click Rename. Type `frmWoodCabinets.vb`, and then press the ENTER key. Click the Yes button to automatically change the form (Name) in the Properties window.

- **Change the Size Property** In the Properties window, change the Size property to 318,518.

- **Change the BackColor Property** In the Properties window, change the BackColor property to Burly Wood.

- **Change the Title on the Title Bar** To change the title on the title bar, click the form, scroll down the Properties window until the Text property is displayed, double-click in the right column of the Text property, type Wood Cabinet Estimate, and then press the ENTER key.

(continues)

● **Add a Heading Title** Drag the first label onto the form and name the label lblHeading. Set the Text property for the Label object to Wood Cabinet Cost. Set the font to Goudy Old Style, Bold, Size 20. Position the label horizontally in the center of the form.

● **Add a Label** Drag the second label onto the frmWoodCabinets Form object and name the label lblLinearFeet. Set the Text property for the Label object to Linear Feet:. Set the font to Goudy Old Style, Bold, Size 14. Position the label to resemble Figure 5-79.

● **Add a TextBox Object** Drag a TextBox object onto the form. Using snap lines, align the top of the TextBox object with the top of the Label object. Name the TextBox object txtFeet. Change the TextAlign property to Center. Change the font to Goudy Old Style, Bold, Size 14. Reduce the width of the TextBox object to closely resemble Figure 5-79. Center the Label object and the TextBox object horizontally in the frmWoodCabinets Form object.

A title Label object is displayed on the first line of the form. A Label object and TextBox object occupy the second line of the frmWoodCabinets Form object (Figure 5-79). They are centered horizontally in the form.

RESULT OF STEP I

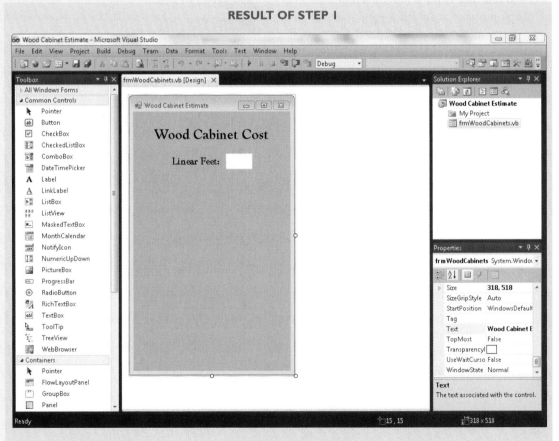

FIGURE 5-79

2

● **Add a GroupBox** Drag a GroupBox object onto the frmWoodCabinets Form object. Name the GroupBox grpWoodType. Change the Text property to Wood Type. Set the Size of the GroupBox object to 125,100. Change the Back-Color of the GroupBox object to White. Center the GroupBox object horizontally in the frmWoodCabinets Form object, and change the font to Goudy Old Style, Regular, Size 12 *(ref: Figure 5-4)*.

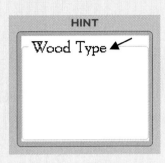
HINT

● **Add Radio Buttons** Place three RadioButton objects on the GroupBox object. Name the first RadioButton radPine and change its Text property to Pine. Name the second RadioButton radOak and change its Text property to Oak. Name the third RadioButton radCherry and change its Text property to Cherry. Select the three RadioButtons and change the font to Goudy Old Style, Regular, Size 12 *(ref: Figure 5-7)*.

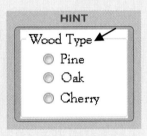
HINT

● **Set Radio Button Properties** Click the radPine RadioButton object and change its Checked property from False to True. Pine is the wood most commonly used by this cabinetmaker *(ref: Figure 5-11)*.

HINT

(continues)

The group box and radio buttons are included on the frmWoodCabinets Form object (Figure 5-80). The radPine radio button is selected because it is the most widely used wood type.

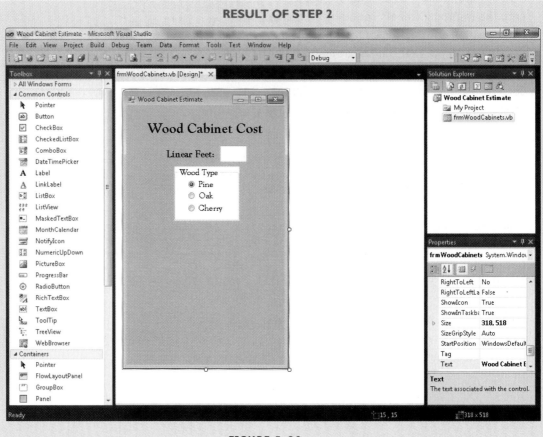

RESULT OF STEP 2

FIGURE 5-80

3

• **Add Estimate and Cost Labels** Drag two more Label objects below the GroupBox object. Align these labels by their tops using snap lines. Name the first label lblCost, change its Text property to Cost Estimate:, and resize the Label object to view the text. Name the second label lblCostEstimate and set its Text property to $0000.00. These placement zeros allow you to view the Label object when it is not selected. The placement zeros will be cleared using code when the form is loaded. Change the font for both Label objects to Goudy Old Style, Bold, Size 14. Horizontally center the labels as a unit on the frmWoodCabinets Form object.

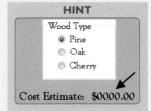

HINT

● **Add Calculate and Clear Buttons** Drag two Button objects onto the form. Align the tops of the Button objects using snap lines. Name the first Button object on the left btnCalculate and change its Text property to Calculate. Name the second Button object on the right btnClear and change its Text property to Clear. Change the font for these two buttons to Goudy Old Style, Regular, Size 12. Change the size of each button to 100,30. Change the BackColor property for each button to White.

● **Add a Picture to the Windows Form** Download the Cabinets.jpg picture from http://scsite.com/vb2010/ch5/images. Drag a PictureBox object to the bottom of the Windows Form. Name the picture picCabinets. Change the Size property of the PictureBox object to 310,175. Change the SizeMode property to StretchImage.

The user interface is complete (Figure 5-81).

RESULT OF STEP 3

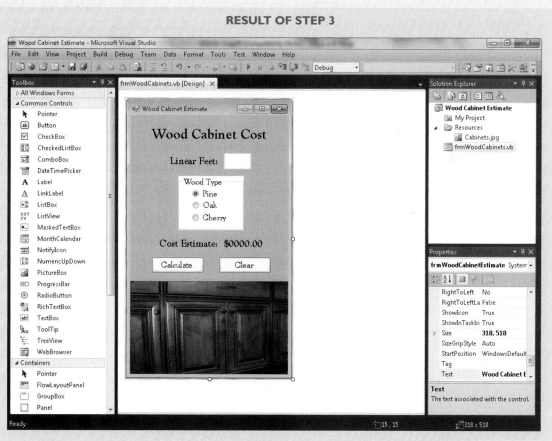

FIGURE 5-81

(continues)

Phase 2: Code the Application

4

● **Code the Comments** Double-click the btnCalculate Button object on the frmWoodCabinets Form object to open the code editing window and create the btnCalculate_Click event handler. Close the Toolbox. Click in front of the first words, Public Class frmWoodCabinetEstimate, and press the ENTER key to create a blank line. Insert the first four standard comments. Insert the Option Strict On command at the beginning of the code to turn on strict type checking.

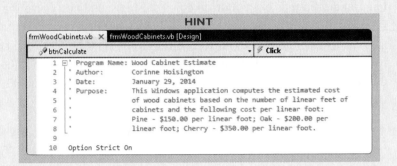

HINT

```
   frmWoodCabinets.vb × frmWoodCabinets.vb [Design]
   btnCalculate                                              Click
    1  ' Program Name: Wood Cabinet Estimate
    2  ' Author:       Corinne Hoisington
    3  ' Date:         January 29, 2014
    4  ' Purpose:      This Windows application computes the estimated cost
    5  '               of wood cabinets based on the number of linear feet of
    6  '               cabinets and the following cost per linear foot:
    7  '               Pine - $150.00 per linear foot; Oak - $200.00 per
    8  '               linear foot; Cherry - $350.00 per linear foot.
    9
   10  Option Strict On
```

● **Comment the btnCalculate_Click Event Handler** Enter a comment to describe the purpose of the btnCalculate_Click event.

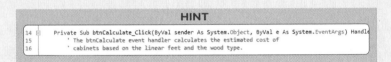

HINT

```
   14  Private Sub btnCalculate_Click(ByVal sender As System.Object, ByVal e As System.EventArgs) Handle
   15      ' The btnCalculate event handler calculates the estimated cost of
   16      ' cabinets based on the linear feet and the wood type.
```

● **Declare and Initialize the Variables** This application requires six variables: 1) decFeet: Holds the estimated linear footage of the cabinets. 2) decCostPerFoot: Holds the cost per linear foot based on the wood type; 3) decCostEstimate: Is assigned the calculated final estimated cost; 4) decPineCost: Is assigned the value 150.00; 5) decOakCost: Is assigned the value 200.00; 6) decCherryCost: Is assigned the value 350.00. Declare and initialize these six variables.

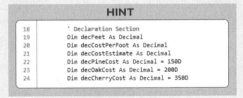

HINT

```
   18      ' Declaration Section
   19      Dim decFeet As Decimal
   20      Dim decCostPerFoot As Decimal
   21      Dim decCostEstimate As Decimal
   22      Dim decPineCost As Decimal = 150D
   23      Dim decOakCost As Decimal = 200D
   24      Dim decCherryCost As Decimal = 350D
```

● **Write the If Statement to Test for Numeric Data** When the user clicks the Calculate button, the program must first ensure that the user entered a valid numeric value in the txtFeet TextBox object. If the user has entered a valid numeric value, the value must be converted from a string value into a decimal data type. Write the If statement and conversion statement required for this process *(ref: Figure 5-74)*.

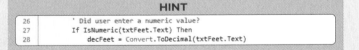

HINT

```
   26          ' Did user enter a numeric value?
   27          If IsNumeric(txtFeet.Text) Then
   28              decFeet = Convert.ToDecimal(txtFeet.Text)
```

● **Write the If Statement to Test for a Positive Number** If the value is numeric, then the converted numeric value must be checked to ensure it is a positive number. Write the If statement to check if the converted numeric value is greater than zero *(ref: Figure 5-75)*.

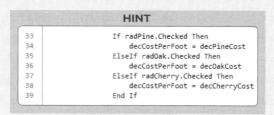

```
30        ' Is Linear Feet greater than zero
31        If decFeet > 0 Then
```

● **Write the If Statements to Determine Cost Per Linear Foot** When the value is greater than zero, the cost per linear foot is determined by checking the status of the RadioButton objects and placing the appropriate cost per linear foot in the decCostPerFoot variable. Using the If . . . Then . . . ElseIf structure, write the statements to identify the checked radio button and place the appropriate cost in the decCostPerFoot variable *(ref: Figure 5-49)*.

```
33            If radPine.Checked Then
34                decCostPerFoot = decPineCost
35            ElseIf radOak.Checked Then
36                decCostPerFoot = decOakCost
37            ElseIf radCherry.Checked Then
38                decCostPerFoot = decCherryCost
39            End If
```

● **Calculate and Display the Cost Estimate** The next step is to calculate the cost estimate by multiplying the value in the decCostPerFoot variable times the linear feet. Then you should display the cost estimate in the cost estimate label. Write the statements to calculate and display the cost estimate in the currency format.

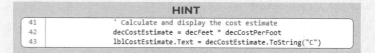

```
41            ' Calculate and display the cost estimate
42            decCostEstimate = decFeet * decCostPerFoot
43            lblCostEstimate.Text = decCostEstimate.ToString("C")
```

● **Display Message Box If Value Entered Is Not Greater Than Zero** After the processing is finished for the true portion of the If statements, the Else portion of the If statements must be written. Write the code to display the message box containing the error message when the value entered by the user is not greater than zero *(ref: Figure 5-24)*.

```
44        Else
45            ' Display error message if user entered a negative value
46            MsgBox("You entered " & decFeet.ToString() & ". Enter a Positive Number", , "Input Error")
47            txtFeet.Text = ""
48            txtFeet.Focus()
49        End If
```

(continues)

● **Display Error Message If Value Entered Is Not Numeric** Write the Else portion of the If statement if the value entered by the user is not numeric *(ref: Figure 5-24)*.

HINT
``` 50   Else 51   ' Display error message if user entered a nonnumeric value 52   MsgBox("Enter the Linear Feet of the Cabinets", , "Input Error") 53   txtFeet.Text = "" 54   txtFeet.Focus() 55   End If ```

The code for the click event of the Calculate button is completed (Figure 5-82).

RESULT OF STEP 4

```
1   ' Program Name: Wood Cabinet Estimate
2   ' Author:        Corinne Hoisington
3   ' Date:          January 29, 2014
4   ' Purpose:       This Windows application computes the estimated cost
5   '                of wood cabinets based on the number of linear feet of
6   '                cabinets and the following cost per linear foot:
7   '                Pine - $150.00 per linear foot; Oak - $200.00 per
8   '                linear foot; Cherry - $350.00 per linear foot.
9
10  Option Strict On
11
12  Public Class frmWoodCabinetEstimate
13
14      Private Sub btnCalculate_Click(ByVal sender As System.Object, ByVal e As System.EventArgs) Handles btnCalculate.Click
15          ' The btnCalculate event handler calculates the estimated cost of
16          ' cabinets based on the linear feet and the wood type.
17
18          ' Declaration Section
19          Dim decFeet As Decimal
20          Dim decCostPerFoot As Decimal
21          Dim decCostEstimate As Decimal
22          Dim decPineCost As Decimal = 150D
23          Dim decOakCost As Decimal = 200D
24          Dim decCherryCost As Decimal = 350D
25
26          ' Did user enter a numeric value?
27          If IsNumeric(txtFeet.Text) Then
28              decFeet = Convert.ToDecimal(txtFeet.Text)
29
30              ' Is Linear Feet greater than zero
31              If decFeet > 0 Then
32                  ' Determine cost per foot of wood
33                  If radPine.Checked Then
34                      decCostPerFoot = decPineCost
35                  ElseIf radOak.Checked Then
36                      decCostPerFoot = decOakCost
37                  ElseIf radCherry.Checked Then
38                      decCostPerFoot = decCherryCost
39                  End If
```

FIGURE 5-82 (continues)

```
40
41                     ' Calculate and display the cost estimate
42                     decCostEstimate = decFeet * decCostPerFoot
43                     lblCostEstimate.Text = decCostEstimate.ToString("C")
44                 Else
45                     ' Display error message if user entered a negative value
46                     MsgBox("You entered " & decFeet.ToString() & ". Enter a Positive Number", , "Input Error")
47                     txtFeet.Text = ""
48                     txtFeet.Focus()
49                 End If
50             Else
51                 ' Display error message if user entered a nonnumeric value
52                 MsgBox("Enter the Linear Feet of the Cabinets", , "Input Error")
53                 txtFeet.Text = ""
54                 txtFeet.Focus()
55             End If
56         End Sub
```

FIGURE 5-82 (continued)

5

● **Create the Clear Button Click Event Handler** The Clear Button click
event includes the following processing: 1) Clear the txtFeet Text
property; 2) Clear the lblCostEstimate Text property; 3) Set the radPine
Checked property to True; 4) Set the radOak and radCherry Checked
properties to False; 5) Set the focus in the txtFeet text box. To enter this
code, click the frmWoodCabinets.vb [Design] tab and then double-click
the Clear button. Using IntelliSense, enter the required code.

HINT

```
58     Private Sub btnClear_Click(ByVal sender As System.Object, ByVal e As System.EventArgs) Handles btnClear.Click
59         ' This event handler is executed when
60         ' the user clicks the Clear button. It
61         ' clears the Linear Feet text box and the
62         ' cost estimate label, resets the radio
63         ' buttons with Pine selected, and sets  the
64         ' focus to the Linear Feet text box.
65
66         txtFeet.Clear()
67         lblCostEstimate.Text = ""
68         radPine.Checked = True
69         radOak.Checked = False
70         radCherry.Checked = False
71         txtFeet.Focus()
72     End Sub
```

(continues)

● **Create the Form Load Event Handler** When the frmWoodCabinets Form object loads, the following processing should occur: 1) The focus is in the txtFeet text box; 2) The lblCostEstimate Text property is set to null. Click the frmWoodCabinets.vb [Design] tab to return to Design view and then double-click the form. Enter the code for the form load event handler.

```
                                          HINT
74  ⊟    Private Sub frmCabinetCost_Load(ByVal sender As System.Object, ByVal e As System.EventArgs) Handles MyBase.Load
75            ' This event handler is executed when
76            ' the form is loaded at the start of
77            ' the program. It sets the focus
78            ' to the Linear Feet text box and
79            ' clears the cost estimate label.
80
81            txtFeet.Focus()
82            lblCostEstimate.Text = ""
83       End Sub
```

6

● **Run the Application** After you have completed the code, you should run the application to ensure it works properly.

● **Test the Application** Test the application with the following data:
1) Linear feet: 25, wood type Oak; 2) Linear feet: 9, wood type Cherry;
3) Linear feet 100, wood type Pine; 4) Linear feet: Fifteen (use this word), wood type Cherry; 5) Linear feet: –21, wood type Oak; 6) Use other values to thoroughly test the program. After each test, click the Clear button before entering new data.

● **Close the Program** After testing the application, close the window by clicking the Close button (X) in the title bar of the window.

Code Listing

The complete code for the sample program is shown in Figure 5-83.

```vb
 1  ' Program Name: Wood Cabinet Estimate
 2  ' Author:       Corinne Hoisington
 3  ' Date:         January 29, 2014
 4  ' Purpose:      This Windows application computes the estimated cost
 5  '               of wood cabinets based on the number of linear feet of
 6  '               cabinets and the following cost per linear foot:
 7  '               Pine - $150.00 per linear foot; Oak - $200.00 per
 8  '               linear foot; Cherry - $350.00 per linear foot.
 9
10  Option Strict On
11
12  Public Class frmWoodCabinetEstimate
13
14      Private Sub btnCalculate_Click(ByVal sender As System.Object, ByVal e As System.EventArgs) Handles btnCalculate.Click
15          ' The btnCalculate event handler calculates the estimated cost of
16          ' cabinets based on the linear feet and the wood type.
17
18          ' Declaration Section
19          Dim decFeet As Decimal
20          Dim decCostPerFoot As Decimal
21          Dim decCostEstimate As Decimal
22          Dim decPineCost As Decimal = 150D
23          Dim decOakCost As Decimal = 200D
24          Dim decCherryCost As Decimal = 350D
25
26          ' Did user enter a numeric value?
27          If IsNumeric(txtFeet.Text) Then
28              decFeet = Convert.ToDecimal(txtFeet.Text)
29
30              ' Is Linear Feet greater than zero
31              If decFeet > 0 Then
32                  ' Determine cost per foot of wood
33                  If radPine.Checked Then
34                      decCostPerFoot = decPineCost
35                  ElseIf radOak.Checked Then
36                      decCostPerFoot = decOakCost
37                  ElseIf radCherry.Checked Then
38                      decCostPerFoot = decCherryCost
39                  End If
40
41                  ' Calculate and display the cost estimate
42                  decCostEstimate = decFeet * decCostPerFoot
43                  lblCostEstimate.Text = decCostEstimate.ToString("C")
44              Else
45                  ' Display error message if user entered a negative value
46                  MsgBox("You entered " & decFeet.ToString() & ". Enter a Positive Number", , "Input Error")
47                  txtFeet.Text = ""
48                  txtFeet.Focus()
49              End If
50          Else
51              ' Display error message if user entered a nonnumeric value
52              MsgBox("Enter the Linear Feet of the Cabinets", , "Input Error")
53              txtFeet.Text = ""
54              txtFeet.Focus()
55          End If
56      End Sub
57
```

FIGURE 5-83 (continues)

```
58  Private Sub btnClear_Click(ByVal sender As System.Object, ByVal e As System.EventArgs) Handles btnClear.Click
59      ' This event handler is executed when
60      ' the user clicks the Clear button. It
61      ' clears the Linear Feet text box and the
62      ' cost estimate label, resets the radio
63      ' buttons with Pine selected, and sets  the
64      ' focus to the Linear Feet text box.
65
66      txtFeet.Clear()
67      lblCostEstimate.Text = ""
68      radPine.Checked = True
69      radOak.Checked = False
70      radCherry.Checked = False
71      txtFeet.Focus()
72  End Sub
73
74  Private Sub frmCabinetCost_Load(ByVal sender As System.Object, ByVal e As System.EventArgs) Handles MyBase.Load
75      ' This event handler is executed when
76      ' the form is loaded at the start of
77      ' the program. It sets the focus
78      ' to the Linear Feet text box and
79      ' clears the cost estimate label.
80
81      txtFeet.Focus()
82      lblCostEstimate.Text = ""
83  End Sub
84
85  End Class
```

FIGURE 5-83 (continued)

Summary

In this chapter you have learned to make decisions based on the user's input.

The items listed in the table in Figure 5-84 on the next page include all the new Visual Studio and Visual Basic skills you have learned in this chapter.

Visual Basic Skills

Skill	Figure Number	Web Address for Video
Explore the Wood Cabinet Estimate	Figure 5-1	scsite.com/vb2010/ch5/figure5-1
Use a GroupBox object	Figure 5-4	scsite.com/vb2010/ch5/figure5-4
Add RadioButton objects	Figure 5-7	scsite.com/vb2010/ch5/figure5-7
Use Windows Application Container objects	Figure 5-14	
Display a Message Box	Figure 5-25	scsite.com/vb2010/ch5/figure5-25
Concatenate strings	Figure 5-29	
Code an If . . . Then statement	Figure 5-31	
Turn on Pretty Listing for indentation	Page 313	
Use relational operators	Figure 5-32	
Enter an If . . . Then statement	Figure 5-34	scsite.com/vb2010/ch5/figure5-34
Compare strings	Figure 5-37	
Code If . . . Then . . . Else statements	Figure 5-38	
Compare values using an arithmetic expression	Figure 5-40	
Code an If . . . Then . . . ElseIf statement	Figure 5-41	
Code a nested If statement	Figure 5-43	
Test the status of a RadioButton object in code	Figure 5-48	
Understand block-level scoping	Figure 5-51	
Code logical operators	Figure 5-52	
Code Select Case statements	Figure 5-62	
Insert code snippets	Figure 5-69	scsite.com/vb2010/ch5/figure5-69
Validate input data	Figure 5-74	

FIGURE 5-84

Learn It Online

Start your browser and visit scsite.com/vb2010/ch5. Follow the instructions in the exercises below.

1. **Chapter Reinforcement TF, MC, SA** Click one of the Chapter Reinforcement links for Multiple Choice, True/False, or Short Answer below the Learn It Online heading. Answer each question and submit to your instructor.

2. **Practice Test** Click the Practice Test link below Chapter 5. Answer each question, enter your first and last name at the bottom of the page, and then click the Grade Test button. When the graded practice test is displayed on your screen, submit the graded practice test to your instructor. Continue to take the practice test until you are satisfied with your score.

3. **Crossword Puzzle Challenge** Click the Crossword Puzzle Challenge link below the Learn It Online heading. Read the instructions, and then click the Continue button. Work the crossword puzzle. When you are finished, click the Submit button. When the crossword puzzle is redisplayed, submit it to your instructor.

Knowledge Check

1. Name the six relational operators and state the purpose of each operator.

2. Name six container objects.

3. Write an If...Then statement that tests if the value in the variable intTemp is between 32 and 95 degrees. If the number is in that range, set the Text property for the lblWarning Label object to "Normal Temperature".

4. Write an If...Then...Else statement that assigns 30 to a variable named intMinutes if strRoadway is equal to "Interstate". Otherwise, assign 60 to intMinutes.

5. List the three most common logical operators and explain their use.

6. Rewrite the following line of code without a Not logical operator but keeping the same logical processing:

```
If Not intHeight <= 75 Then
```

7. The intent of the following statement is to check if the radDormStudent RadioButton object is checked. What is the error in the statement? Rewrite the statement so it is correct.

```
If radDormStudent = Checked Then
```

8. The intent of following statement is to check if the value in the intGrade variable is less than 0 or greater than 100. What is the error in the statement? Rewrite the statement so it is correct.

```
If intGrade < 0 And intGrade > 100 Then
```

9. What is the most commonly used container object?

10. Fix this statement.

```
If decWage > 5.85 and < 15.25 Then
```

11. Why do most developers indent the code within a decision structure?

12. Write a statement that creates the dialog box shown in Figure 5-85 in a Windows application. Use a single numerical value to create the button and picture icon.

13. What is the difference between a Panel object and a GroupBox object?

14. What is the difference between the Or logical operator and the Xor logical operator?

FIGURE 5-85

15. Write a data validation statement that would check to ensure the value in the intAge variable is between 1 and 120. If the age is not valid, display an error message box stating that the age is not valid.

16. How many radio buttons in a group can be selected at one time?

17. Using the concatenation operator (&), write a statement that would create the compound word teahouse from the following two strings: strFirst = "tea" and strSecond= "house". Assign the compound word to the strCompound string variable.

18. Write a statement that would clear the radio button named radSurfBoard.

19. Write a Select Case statement using the fewest Case statements possible to display the number of days in each month. The user enters the number of the month, such as 8, which is converted to an integer and assigned to the intMonth variable. The Select Case statement should display a message box that states the number of days in the month, such as "31 Days".

20. Which logical operator has the highest precedence in the order of operations?

Debugging Exercises

1. Explain how the two statements shown in Figure 5-86 are evaluated.

```
If strResponse = "Red" AndAlso strAnswer = "Green" Then

    If strResponse = "Red" And strAnswer = "Green" Then
```

FIGURE 5-86

(continues)

2. Identify the error in the code shown in Figure 5-87 and explain how to correct the code.

```
If dblCommission >= 2500 Then
    Dim intBonus As Integer
    intBonus = 500
Else
    intBonus = 0
End If
```

FIGURE 5-87

3. The Select Case statement shown in Figure 5-88 contains one or more errors. Identify the error(s) and rewrite the statements correctly.

```
Select Case intNumberOfSeats
    Case > 5000
        strVenueType = "Stadium"
    Case > 2000
        strVenueType = "Amphitheater"
    Case > 1000
        strVenueType = "Auditorium"
    Case > 200
        strVenueType = "Theater"
    Case > 0
        strVenueType = "Club"
    Else Case
        strVenueType = "Error"
Select End
```

FIGURE 5-88

4. The Select Case statement shown in Figure 5-89 contains one or more errors. Identify the error(s) and rewrite the statements correctly.

```
Select Case charFlightCode
    Case 'F', 'A'
        lblFare.Text = 'First Class'
    Case 'B', 'Q'
        lblFare.Text = 'Business Class'
    Case 'Y', 'S', 'M'
        lblFare.Text = 'Full Fare Economy'
    Case 'K', 'C'
        lblFare.Text = 'Preferred Economy'
    Case 'U', 'J', 'P', 'G'
        lblFare.Text = 'Economy'
    Else
        lblFare.Text = 'Unknown'
End Select
```

FIGURE 5-89

5. The If . . . Then . . . Else statement shown in Figure 5-90 contains one or more errors. Identify the error(s) and rewrite the statements correctly.

```
If strShippingMethod = "Overnite" Then
    If strDeliveryTime = "Morning"
        decDeliveryCost = 29.00D
    Else
        decDeliveryCost = 24.00D
Else
    If strShippingMethod = "Two Days" Then
        decDeliveryCost = 14.00D
    Else
        decDeliveryCost = 4.00D
End If
```

FIGURE 5-90

Program Analysis

1. Write an If . . . Then . . . Else decision structure to compare the two numbers in the intPay1 and intPay2 variables. Display a message box stating intPay1 is greater than intPay2, or intPay1 is less than or equal to intPay2.

2. Write an If statement that displays the message box "Snow is possible" if the value in the variable decTemp is within the range 0 to 32.

3. Write an If . . . Then . . . Else statement that checks the value in the variable chrGender for the value M (Male) or F (Female) and assigns the information shown in Figure 5-91 to lblCollegeExpectation.Text based on the gender. If the variable chrGender contains a value other than M or F, assign the message "Invalid Gender" to lblCollegeExpectation.Text.

Gender	College Expectation
Male	75% plan to graduate from college
Female	85% plan to graduate from college

FIGURE 5-91

(continues)

4. Write a Select Case statement that tests the user's age in a variable named intAge and assigns the name of the favorite snack of that age group to the variable strSnack, according to the preferences shown in Figure 5-92.

Age	Favorite Snack
Under age 7	Yogurt
Age 7 to 12	Potato Chips
Age 13 to 18	Chocolate
Over Age 18	Gum

FIGURE 5-92

5. Rewrite the Select Case statement shown in Figure 5-93 as an If ... Then ... Else statement.

```
Select Case chrDepartment
    Case "B", "b"
        strDept = "Baby / Infant Clothing"
    Case "T", "t"
        strDept = "Technology"
End Select
```

FIGURE 5-93

6. Rewrite the If ... Then ... Else statement shown in Figure 5-94 as a Select Case statement.

```
If intGrade >= 9 And intGrade <= 12 Then
    lblSchool.Text = "High School"
ElseIf intGrade >= 7 Then
    lblSchool.Text = "Middle School"
ElseIf intGrade >= 1 Then
    lblSchool.Text = "Elementary School"
Else
    lblSchool.Text = "Invalid Grade"
End If
```

FIGURE 5-94

7. What is the output of the code shown in Figure 5-95 on the next page if the word Black is entered in the txtSkiSlope text box?

```
Select Case Me.txtSkiSlope.Text
    Case "Green"
        MsgBox("Beginner Slope")
    Case "Blue"
        MsgBox("Intermediate Slope")
    Case "Black"
        MsgBox("Expert Slope")
    Case Else
        MsgBox("Invalid Entry")
End Select
```

FIGURE 5-95

8. After the execution of the Select Case structure in Figure 5-96, what value will be found in the Text property of lblFemaleHeight if the user enters the number 74 into the txtEnterHeight text box? If the number 81 is entered? If the number 59 is entered?

```
Dim intHeightInches As Integer
intHeightInches = Convert.ToInt32(txtEnterHeight.Text)
Select Case intHeightInches
    Case Is < 61
        lblFemaleHeight.Text = "Petite"
    Case 61 To 69
        lblFemaleHeight.Text = "Average"
    Case 70 To 80
        lblFemaleHeight.Text = "Tall"
    Case 80 To 120
        lblFemaleHeight.Text = "Towering"
    Case Else
        lblFemaleHeight.Text = "Not Possible"
End Select
```

FIGURE 5-96

9. In each of the following examples, is the condition True or False?

a. "C" >= "C"

b. "G" >= "g"

c. "Amazed" < "Amaze"

d. "Cool" <> "cool"

e. "40" >= "Forty"

f. ("Paris" < "Barcelona") And ("Amsterdam" <= "Prague")

g. ("Ford" > "Chevrolet") Or ("Toyota" < "Honda")

h. 3 ^ 2 <= 3 * 4

i. Not ("CNN" >= "ABC")

j. Not ("Tim" > "Tom") And Not ("Great" <> "great")

Complete one or more of the following case programming assignments. Submit the program and materials you create to your instructor. The level of difficulty is indicated for each case programming assignment.

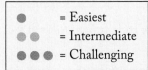

● = Easiest
●● = Intermediate
●●● = Challenging

1 ●

PARKING TICKET FINES

Design a Windows application and write the code that will execute according to the program requirements in Figure 5-97. The data to use is shown in Figure 5-98 on the next page. Before writing the code, create an event planning document for each event in the program, as shown in Figure 5-99 on the next page. The completed Form object and other objects in the user interface are shown in Figure 5-100 on the next page.

REQUIREMENTS DOCUMENT

Date submitted: May 6, 2013

Application title: Parking Ticket Fines

Purpose: This Windows application calculates a parking ticket fine.

Program Procedures: The user selects the type of parking violation and indicates if the owner of the vehicle is a repeat offender. The user then requests that the program calculate and display the parking ticket fine.

Algorithms, Processing, and Conditions:
1. The user selects the type of parking violation.
2. If the owner of the vehicle has been ticketed previously for a parking offense in the city, the fine is doubled.
3. The user must be able to indicate the owner is a repeat offender.
4. The fine is calculated based on the chart in Figure 5-98.
5. The user must be able to initiate the display of the parking ticket fine.
6. The user should be able to clear the type of violation indicator, the repeat offender indicator, and the ticket fine.

Notes and Restrictions: n/a

Comments:
1. Obtain an image for this program from scsite.com/vb2010/ch5/images. The image file name is Parking.

FIGURE 5-97

Case Programming Assignments

Parking Ticket Fines *(continued)*

Parking Violation	Fine
Expired Meter	$35
No Parking Zone	$75
Blocking Driveway	$150
Illegal Handicap Parking	$500

FIGURE 5-98

USE CASE DEFINITION

1. The Windows application window opens.
2. The user selects the type of parking offense.
3. The user selects whether the user is a repeat offender.
4. The user clicks the Display Fine button to display the parking ticket fine.
5. The user clears the input and the result by clicking the Clear button.
6. If desired, the user repeats the process.

FIGURE 5-99

FIGURE 5-100

2

AMUSEMENT PARK TICKETS

Design a Windows application and write the code that will execute according to the program requirements in Figure 5-101 and the Use Case Definition in Figure 5-102 on the next page. Before writing the code, create an event planning document for each event in the program. The completed Form object and other objects in the user interface are shown in Figure 5-103 on the next page.

REQUIREMENTS DOCUMENT

Date submitted: April 15, 2013

Application title: Amusement Park Tickets

Purpose: This Windows application calculates the cost of the amusement park tickets.

Program Procedures: The user should enter the number of single-day tickets for the amusement park. The park has a discount program for various club memberships. The user may use only one club membership. The user does not need to select a club membership. The park ticket costs $72 a day.

Algorithms, Processing, and Conditions:
1. The user enters the number of tickets.
2. The types of club memberships accepted are AAA (15% off full purchase cost), AARP (17.5% off full purchase cost), and Military ID (20% off full purchase price). The user can only select one type of membership.
3. The user must be able to initiate the calculation and display the total final cost of the tickets.
4. The user should be able to clear the number of tickets purchased, the types of membership, and the total cost.

Notes and Restrictions:
1. If a negative number is entered for tickets, the user should be advised and asked for a valid entry.
2. If a nonnumeric value is entered for the ticket number or if the input for the number of tickets is left blank, the user should be advised and asked for a valid entry.

Comments:
1. Obtain an image for this program from scsite.com/vb2010/ch5/images. The image file name is Amusement.

FIGURE 5-101

Amusement Park Tickets (continued)

USE CASE DEFINITION

1. The Windows application window opens.
2. The user enters the number of single-day tickets needed.
3. The user clicks the Display Cost button.
4. The program displays the total cost of the tickets after the discount is applied.
5. Using a MsgBox, the user is warned if a negative number is entered for the number of tickets.
6. Using the MsgBox, the user is warned if a nonnumeric value is entered for the number of tickets or if the value is left blank.
7. The user can clear the input and the results by clicking the Clear button.

FIGURE 5-102

FIGURE 5-103

3

PATIENT WEIGHT CONVERTER

Design a Windows application and write the code that will execute according to the program requirements in Figure 5-104 and the Use Case Definition in Figure 5-105 on the next page. Before writing the code, create an event planning document for each event in the program. The completed Form object and other objects in the user interface are shown in Figure 5-106 on the next page.

REQUIREMENTS DOCUMENT

Date submitted: May 11, 2013

Application title: Patient Weight Converter

Purpose: This Windows application converts the weight of the patient from pounds to kilograms and kilograms to pounds.

Program Procedures: The user enters the weight of the patient, selects the conversion type (pounds to kilograms or kilograms to pounds), and displays the converted weight of the patient.

Algorithms, Processing, and Conditions:
1. A user must be able to enter the weight of the patient in pounds or kilograms.
2. The user must be able to select the type of conversion: pounds to kilograms or kilograms to pounds.
3. The user must be able to initiate the weight conversion and the display of the patient's converted weight.
4. The conversion formulas are:
   kilograms = pounds / 2.2
   pounds = kilograms × 2.2
5. The user must be able to clear the entered weight, conversion choice, and results.

Notes and Restrictions:
1. If a nonnumeric value is entered or if the weight is left blank, the user should be advised and asked for a valid entry.
2. If a negative number is entered for the weight, the user should be advised and asked for a valid entry.
3. If the value entered is greater than 500 for the conversion from pounds to kilograms or greater than 225 for the conversion from kilograms to pounds, the user should be advised and asked for a valid entry.
4. The default conversion choice should be pounds to kilograms.
5. The converted weight should be displayed with one digit to the right of the decimal point.

Comments:
1. Obtain an image for this program from scsite.com/vb2010/ch5/images. The image file name is Scale.

FIGURE 5-104

Patient Weight Converter (continued)

USE CASE DEFINITION

1. The Windows application window opens.
2. The user enters the patient's weight.
3. The user selects the conversion type (pounds to kilograms or kilograms to pounds).
4. The user clicks the Display button to display the converted weight value.
5. The user clears the input and the result by clicking the Clear button.
6. If desired, the user repeats the process.

FIGURE 5-105

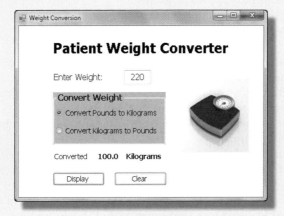

FIGURE 5-106

4 ●●
HEALTH CLUB MEMBERSHIP

Design a Windows application and write the code that will execute according to the program requirements in Figure 5-107. Before designing the user interface, create a Use Case definition. Before writing the code, create an event planning document for each event in the program.

REQUIREMENTS DOCUMENT

Date submitted: April 22, 2013

Application title: Health Club Membership

Purpose: This Windows application calculates the prepayment amount for a new member of a health club.

Program Procedures: The user should enter the name of the new member, the number of months the new user would like to prepay, and the type of membership. The health club prepayment cost will be computed and displayed for the entered number of months. The per month costs for the three types of membership are:

Single Membership	$38 per month
Family Membership	$58 per month
Senior Membership	$27 per month

Algorithms, Processing, and Conditions:
1. The user must enter the name of the new member, the type of membership, and the number of months the new member would like to prepay.
2. Based on the type of membership, the prepayment cost is calculated using the following formula: number of prepay months × cost per month.
3. The user must be able to initiate the calculation and display the prepay amount for the health club membership.
4. The user should be able to clear the name of the new member, the number of prepay months, the type of membership, and the prepay amount for the new member.

Notes and Restrictions:
1. If the user enters a nonnumeric value for the number of months, the user should be advised and asked for a valid entry.
2. If the user enters a negative number for the number of months or if the user leaves the number of months input area blank, the user should be advised and asked for a valid entry.
3. If the user leaves the input area for the user name blank, the user should be advised and asked for a valid entry.
4. The default membership type is single membership.

FIGURE 5-107

5 ●●
TWO-DAY PACKAGE SHIPPING

Design a Windows application and write the code that will execute according to the program requirements in Figure 5-108. Before designing the user interface, create a Use Case definition. Before writing the code, create an event planning document for each event in the program.

REQUIREMENTS DOCUMENT

Date submitted: May 6, 2013

Application title: Two-Day Package Shipping

Purpose: This Windows application calculates the cost of shipping a package with two-day delivery.

Program Procedures: The user enters the weight of the package (in pounds) and selects the destination of the package. The application will determine the cost of shipping. The destination of the package can be the continental U.S., Hawaii, or Alaska. If the package is going to Hawaii, a 20% surcharge is added to the shipping cost. If the package is going to Alaska, a 26% surcharge is added to the shipping cost.

Algorithms, Processing, and Conditions:
1. The user must be able to enter the number of pounds the package weighs and indicate that the package is being mailed to the continental U.S., Hawaii, or Alaska.
2. The shipping costs are calculated based on the rates in the table in Figure 5-109 on the next page. A 20% surcharge is added if the shipping destination is Hawaii. A 26% surcharge is added if the shipping destination is Alaska.
3. The user must be able to initiate the calculation and the display of the shipping cost.
4. The user must be able to clear the weight of the package and the shipping cost.

Notes and Restrictions:
1. If the entry for the shipping weight is blank or nonnumeric, the user should be advised and asked for a valid entry.
2. The maximum weight for a package is 30 pounds. If the weight is greater than 30 pounds, or if the value entered is not greater than zero, the user should be advised and asked for a valid entry.

FIGURE 5-108

(continues)

Case Programming Assignments

Two-Day Package Shipping *(continued)*

For Weight Not Over (Pounds)	2-Day Rate
2	$3.69
4	$4.86
6	$5.63
8	$5.98
10	$6.28
30	$15.72

FIGURE 5-109

6 ●●
PAYROLL CALCULATOR

Design a Windows application and write the code that will execute according to the program requirements in Figure 5-110. Before designing the user interface, create a Use Case definition. Before writing the code, create an event planning document for each event in the program.

REQUIREMENTS DOCUMENT

Date submitted:	May 11, 2013
Application title:	Payroll Calculator
Purpose:	This application calculates the payroll for employees of the Food For All local grocery store.
Program Procedures:	In a Windows application, the user enters the employee's name, hours worked, and pay per hour. If the employee works more than 40 hours per week, the grocery store pays time-and-a-half for overtime. The tax rate can be the single rate (18%) or at the family rate (15%). The application should compute and display the gross pay, the tax based on the single or family rate, and the net pay.
Algorithms, Processing, and Conditions:	1. The user must be able to enter the employee's name, hours worked, and pay per hour.
	2. The user must be able to indicate if the tax rate is at the single rate (18%) or the family rate (15%).
	3. The user must be able to initiate the calculation and the display of the gross pay, the tax amount based on the single or family rate, and the net pay.
	4. A Clear button will clear the user's input and final results.
Notes and Restrictions:	1. If the employee name, hours worked, or pay per hour are blank, the user should be advised and asked for a valid entry.
	2. If the hours worked or pay per hour are nonnumeric, the user should be advised and asked for a valid entry.
	3. The minimum value for hours worked is 5 hours. The maximum for hours worked is 60. If the user enters an hours worked value not within the range, the user should be advised and asked for a valid entry.
	4. The minimum pay per hour is $8.00. The maximum pay per hour is $40.00 per hour. If the user enters a pay per hour value not within the range, the user should be advised and asked for a valid entry.
	5. The user must be able to clear the employee's name, the hours worked, the pay per hour, and the pay information.

FIGURE 5-110

7 ●●●
TECHNOLOGY CONFERENCE REGISTRATION

Based on the case project shown in Figure 5-111, create a requirements document and a Use Case Definition document, and then design a Windows application. Before writing the code, create an event planning document for each event in the program.

It is important that developers update their skills by attending developers' conferences. The Dynamic International Management Consortium (DIMC) runs and manages the ADSE (Active Developers Skill Enhancement) Conference two times per year. To encourage companies to send multiple employees to the conference, the cost per attendee is determined based on the number of attending developers from a given company. The table below specifies the cost per attendee.

Number of Conference Registrations per Company	Cost per Attendee
1	$695
2-4	$545
5-8	$480
8 or more	$395

DIMC has requested that you develop a Windows application that can determine and display the total cost per company for developers attending the conference. DIMC has a conference policy that states if any member of a company has attended a previous DIMC conference, the company receives a 15% discount from the total cost of its employees who attend. The policy also states that no more than 16 people from a single company can attend the conference. DIMC has asked that you design the program so that the user must enter valid data.

FIGURE 5-111

Case Programming Assignments

8 ●●● CAR RENTAL

Based on the case project shown in Figure 5-112, create a requirements document and a Use Case Definition document, and then design a Windows application. Before writing the code, create an event planning document for each event in the program.

The Adventure Car Rental Company has asked that you create a Windows application for the rental of an adventure vehicle. The user selects the number of rental days, up to 7 days. The user also can select one of three types of vehicles. The types of vehicles and the cost per day for each vehicle is shown in the table below.

Vehicle Model	Cost per Day
Jeep Wrangler	$55.00
Jeep Grand Cherokee	$85.00
Land Rover	$125.00

The customer has a choice of filling the gas tank themselves at the end of their use, or prepaying for a full tank of gas ($52 total). If the vehicle will be driven by more than one driver, a multiple driver cost of $22 per day is added to the cost of the vehicle. Adventure has asked that the Windows application determine and display the total rental cost of the vehicle for the amount of time and the options chosen by the user. Adventure also has requested that you include all appropriate checking for invalid data entry by the user.

FIGURE 5-112

Case Programming Assignments

9 ●●● TAKE-OUT SANDWICHES

Based on the case project shown in Figure 5-113, create a requirements document and a Use Case Definition document, and then design a Windows application. Before writing the code, create an event planning document for each event in the program.

Your local gas station chain has a made-to-order sandwich station. The station has asked you to create a Windows application that allows the customer to enter their order on a flat screen computer. Create an application that allows the user to select one of five sandwich choices (create your own list) with prices displayed, three types of bread choices at no additional cost, and four condiment choices at no additional cost. The station has a loyalty program that deducts 5% of the cost of an order for every 10 points a customer has earned. Allow the user to enter their total number of loyalty points and compute the cost of their order. A customer cannot receive money back if their loyalty points exceed the full cost of their sandwich.

FIGURE 5-113

CHAPTER 6

Loop Structures

You will have mastered the material in this chapter when you can:

- Add a MenuStrip object

- Use the InputBox function

- Display data using the ListBox object

- Understand the use of counters and accumulators

- Understand the use of compound operators

- Repeat a process using a For…Next loop

- Repeat a process using a Do loop

- Avoid infinite loops

- Prime a loop

- Validate data

- Create a nested loop

- Select the best type of loop

- Debug using DataTips at breakpoints

- Publish a finished application using ClickOnce technology

Introduction

In Chapter 5, you learned about the decision structure, one of the major control structures used in computer programming. In this chapter you will learn another major structure called the **looping structure**, or the **iteration structure**.

A fundamental process in a computer program is to repeat a series of instructions either while a condition is true (or not true) or until a condition is true (or not true). For example, if a company is printing paychecks for its 5,000 employees, it can use the same set of instructions to print the check for each employee, varying only the name of the employee and amount paid for each check. This process would continue until all checks are printed. Unique check-printing instructions for each employee in the company are not required.

The process of repeating a set of instructions while a condition is true or until a condition is true is called **looping**, and when the program is executing those instructions, it is said to be in a loop. Another term for looping is **iteration**.

Chapter Project

The programming project in this chapter uses a loop to obtain input data and produce output information. A police department has requested a Windows application that determines the average speed for vehicles on a local highway. This application, called the Highway Radar Checkpoint application, computes the average speed for up to 10 vehicles that pass a checkpoint on a highway with a posted speed limit of 60 miles per hour (mph). The application uses a loop to request and display the speed for up to 10 vehicles. When the user has entered all vehicle speeds, the application displays the average speed of the vehicles (Figure 6-1).

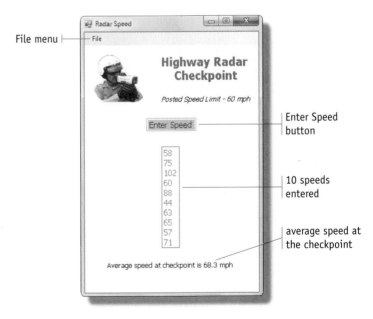

FIGURE 6-1

In Figure 6-1 on the previous page, the user entered the 10 vehicle speeds shown as a list. After the user entered the 10 speeds, the application calculated the average speed at the checkpoint.

When the Highway Radar Checkpoint application begins, the main window shows no speeds entered (Figure 6-2).

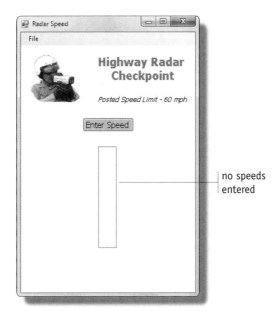

no speeds entered

FIGURE 6-2

When the user clicks the Enter Speed button, the Radar Speed dialog box shown in Figure 6-3 opens, allowing the user to enter the first vehicle's speed. This dialog box is called an **input box**.

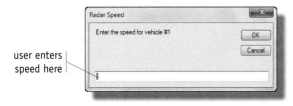

user enters speed here

FIGURE 6-3

ONLINE REINFORCEMENT

To view a video of program execution, visit scsite.com/ vb2010/ch6 and then select Figure 6-1.

After entering the first valid speed, the user clicks the OK button in the dialog box. The application lists the speed in the main window, and then displays the input box again, requesting the speed for the next vehicle. This process repeats for up to 10 vehicles. This repetitive process is implemented using a loop in the program and, when the user is entering vehicle speeds, the program is said to be in a loop. The loop is terminated when the user enters the speed for the tenth vehicle or clicks the Cancel button in the dialog box. After the loop is terminated, the Highway Radar Checkpoint application displays the average speed for the vehicles, as shown in Figure 6-1 on the previous page.

The Highway Radar Checkpoint application has several other features. In Figure 6-1 on page 378, you can see that a menu bar containing the File menu is displayed at the top of the window. The File menu contains the Clear command, which clears the list and the average speed; and the Exit command, which closes the window and terminates the application. In this chapter, you will learn to design and code a menu.

In addition, the application contains data editing features. For example, if a user enters a non-numeric or negative value for the vehicle speed, the user is asked for the speed of that vehicle again, until the entry is a reasonable value.

Finally, the application displays the average speed to one decimal place, such as 68.3 mph.

User Interface Design

The user interface for the Highway Radar Checkpoint application includes three new elements: a menu, the input box, and the list for the vehicle speeds. The menu and the list for vehicle speeds are objects placed on the Windows Form object. The input box is created through the use of a function call in the program code. Each of these items is explained in the following sections.

MenuStrip Object

A **menu bar** is a strip across the top of a window that contains one or more menu names. A **menu** is a group of commands, or items, presented in a list. In the sample program, a File menu is created in the application window (Figure 6-4).

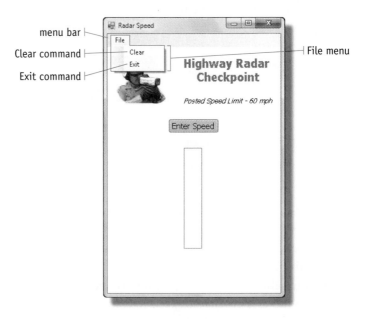

FIGURE 6-4

When the user clicks File on the menu bar during program execution, as shown in Figure 6-4 on the previous page, a menu appears with two commands: Clear and Exit. If the user clicks the Clear menu command, the entered speeds and the results are cleared. Clicking the Exit menu command closes the application. An advantage of a menu is that it conserves space instead of cluttering the form with objects such as buttons.

Using Visual Studio 2010, you can place menus at the top of a Windows Form using the MenuStrip object. To place a MenuStrip object on a Windows Form, you can complete the following steps:

STEP 1   With a Windows Form object open in the Visual Studio window, scroll in the Toolbox until the Menus & Toolbars category is visible. If the category is not open, click the expand icon (right-pointing triangle) next to the Menus & Toolbars category name. Drag the MenuStrip .NET component from the Menus & Toolbars category in the Toolbox to the Windows Form object.

The pointer changes when you place it over the Windows Form object (Figure 6-5).

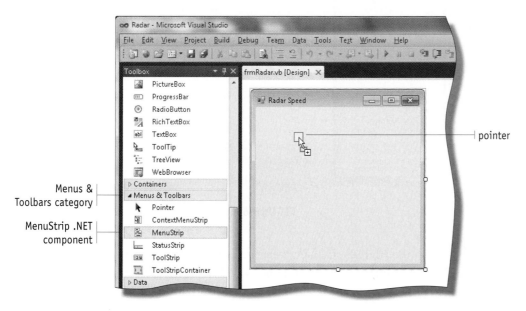

FIGURE 6-5

STEP 2 Release the mouse button.

Visual Studio places the MenuStrip object at the top of the form regardless of the location of the mouse pointer when you released the mouse button (Figure 6-6). The Component Tray, which is displayed below the form, organizes non-graphical Toolbox objects. It displays the MenuStrip1 object name.

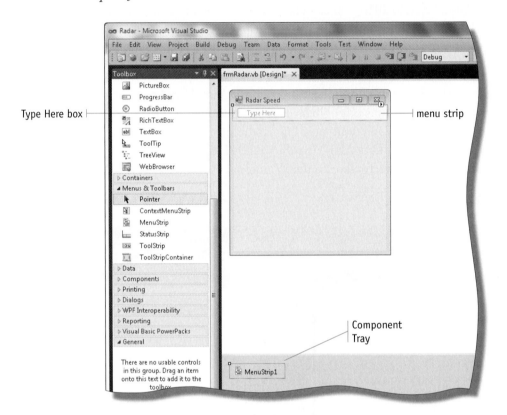

FIGURE 6-6

STEP 3 With the MenuStrip object selected, scroll in the Properties window until the (Name) property is visible. Change the MenuStrip object name to mnuHighwayRadarCheckpoint. (Note that the prefix for a MenuStrip object is mnu).

The name for the MenuStrip object is changed in the Properties window and in the Component Tray (Figure 6-7).

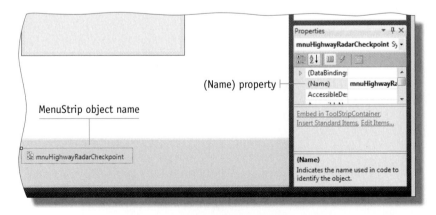

FIGURE 6-7

STEP 4   Click the Type Here box on the menu bar. Type &File to identify the File menu, and then press the ENTER key.

The menu name File is displayed in the upper-left corner of the MenuStrip object and new Type Here boxes are available to create other menu items (Figure 6-8). The ampersand (&) you entered preceding the F indicates that F is a hot key. A hot key provides a keyboard short-cut for opening the menu. Instead of clicking File to open the menu, the user can press and hold the ALT key and then press the designated hot key, such as ALT+F. After you enter the menu name, the character following the ampersand is underlined to indicate it is the hot key.

HEADS UP

Instead of typing the menu name on a MenuStrip object, you can choose to add a menu item, combo box, or text box to the menu bar. To do so, point to the Type Here box, click its list arrow, and then click MenuItem, ComboBox, or TextBox.

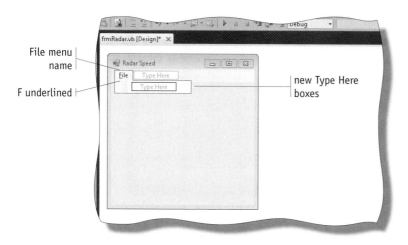

File menu name

F underlined

new Type Here boxes

FIGURE 6-8

STEP 5   Click File in the MenuStrip object to select it, scroll in the Properties window to the (Name) property, and then change the name to mnuFile.

The name of the File menu is displayed in the (Name) property in the Properties window (Figure 6-9).

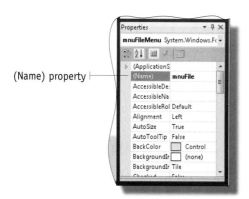

(Name) property

FIGURE 6-9

STEP 6 To add a menu item to the File menu, click the Type Here box below the File menu name. Type &Clear and then press ENTER to create a new menu item named Clear with C as the hot key.

The Clear menu item is displayed below the File menu (Figure 6-10). After you enter the item by pressing the ENTER key, the character following the ampersand is underlined to indicate it is the hot key.

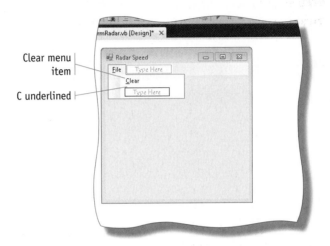

Clear menu item

C underlined

FIGURE 6-10

STEP 7 On the File menu, click Clear to select it, scroll in the Properties window until the (Name) property is visible, and then change the name to mnuClearItem.

The mnuClearItem name is displayed in the (Name) property in the Properties window (Figure 6-11).

(Name) property

FIGURE 6-11

The letter representing a hot key appears underlined in the menu name, as shown in Figure 6-10. The first letter often is used for the hot key, but not always. For example, in the chapter project, the File menu includes the Exit item (see Figure 6-4 on page 380). The hot key typically used for the Exit item is the letter x. When entering the Exit menu item on the File menu, the developer can type E&xit, which assigns the letter following the & (x) as the hot key.

When assigning hot keys, you should be aware that menu item hot keys are not case-sensitive. Therefore, you should not assign "T" to one menu item and "t" to another.

Event Handlers for Menu Items

As you are aware, the design of the user interface occurs before you write the code for event handlers. When you are ready to write code, however, you must write an event handler for each menu item because clicking a menu item or using its hot key triggers an event. Writing a menu item event handler is the same as writing an event handler for a button click.

To code the event handler for the Exit menu item, you can complete the following steps:

STEP 1 In Design view, double-click the Exit menu item to open the code editing window.

The code editing window is displayed and the insertion point is located within the Exit item click event handler (Figure 6-12). When the user clicks the Exit item on the File menu, the code in the event handler will be executed. Note in Figure 6-12 that the Toolbox is closed.

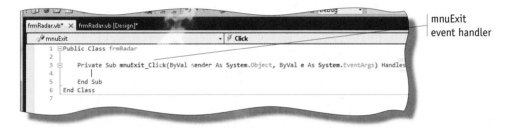

mnuExit
event handler

FIGURE 6-12

STEP 2 Using IntelliSense, enter the Close procedure call to close the window and terminate the application.

When executed, the Close procedure will close the window and terminate the program (Figure 6-13).

Close()
procedure

FIGURE 6-13

ONLINE REINFORCEMENT

To view a video of the process in the previous steps, visit scsite.com/vb2010/ch6 and then select Figure 6-12.

Standard Items for a Menu

Developers often customize the MenuStrip object for the specific needs of an application. In addition, Visual Basic 2010 contains an **Action Tag** that allows you to create a full standard menu bar commonly provided in Windows programs, with File, Edit, Tools, and Help menus. In Visual Basic 2010, an Action Tag (▶) appears in the upper-right corner of many objects, including a MenuStrip. Action Tags provide a way for you to specify a set of actions, called **smart actions**, for an object as you design a form. For example, to insert a full standard menu, you can complete the following steps:

STEP 1   With a new Windows Form object open, drag the MenuStrip .NET component onto the Windows Form object. Click the Action Tag on the MenuStrip object.

The MenuStrip Tasks menu opens (Figure 6-14).

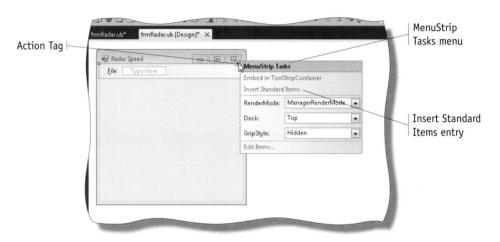

FIGURE 6-14

STEP 2   Click Insert Standard Items on the MenuStrip Tasks menu.

The MenuStrip object contains four menu names — File, Edit, Tools, and Help (Figure 6-15). These menus are the standard menus found on many Windows applications. Each menu contains the standard menu items normally found on the menus.

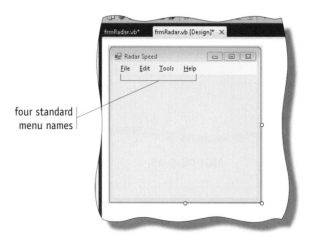

FIGURE 6-15

HEADS UP

In the new operating system, Windows 7, menus are de-emphasized as the focus switches to a more graphical layout such as the Ribbons used in Microsoft Office 2010, which uses more images for navigational control.

STEP 3   Click File on the menu bar to view the individual menu items and their associated icons on the File menu.

The standard File menu items (New, Open, Save, Save As, Print, Print Preview, and Exit) are displayed with their associated icons and shortcut keys (Figure 6-16). The other menus also contain standard items. You can code an event handler for each menu item by double-clicking the item.

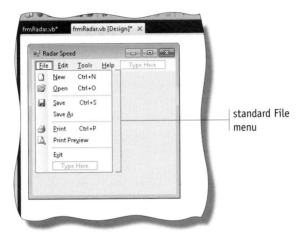

FIGURE 6-16

ONLINE REINFORCEMENT

To view a video of the process in the previous steps, visit scsite.com/vb2010/ch6 and then select Figure 6-14.

InputBox Function

To calculate the average vehicle speed, the Highway Radar Checkpoint application uses an InputBox object where users enter the speed for each vehicle. The InputBox object is a dialog box that prompts the user to enter a value. Similar to a MessageBox object, you code the InputBox function to specify when the InputBox object appears. The InputBox function displays a dialog box that consists of a message asking for input, an input area, a title, an OK button, and a Cancel button (see Figure 6-3 on page 379). When the user enters the text and clicks the OK button, the InputBox function returns this text as a string. If the user clicks the Cancel button, the function returns a null string (""). The code shown in Figure 6-17 demonstrates the syntax of the InputBox function:

General Format: InputBox Function

```
strVariableName = InputBox("Question to Prompt User", "Title Bar")
```

FIGURE 6-17

For example, the code in Figure 6-18 creates a dialog box that requests the user's age for a driver's license application. The string returned by the InputBox function is assigned to the strAge variable.

```
5      Dim strAge As String
6
7      strAge = InputBox("Please enter your age", "Driver's License Agency")
```

FIGURE 6-18

When the application is executed, the InputBox object in Figure 6-19 opens, requesting that the user enter her age. The InputBox function can be used to obtain input instead of a TextBox object.

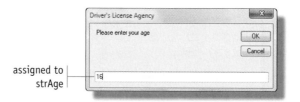

FIGURE 6-19

The InputBox object returns all entered data as a string, which then can be converted to the appropriate data type.

InputBox Object Default Value

The InputBox object can be assigned a default value. For example, if a college application for admission requests the student's home state and the college or university is located in Virginia, the most likely state, Virginia, can be the default value in the InputBox, as shown in Figure 6-20.

FIGURE 6-20

The code to produce this input box is shown in Figure 6-21.

```
9      Dim strState As String
10
11     strState = InputBox("Please enter the state in which you reside:", _
12         "College Application", "Virginia")
```

FIGURE 6-21

As you can see, the third argument for the InputBox function call is the default value that is placed in the input box. It must be a string value and follow the syntax shown in Figure 6-21 on the previous page.

InputBox Object for Highway Radar Checkpoint Application

The Highway Radar Checkpoint application uses an InputBox object that requests the speed of vehicles numbered 1–10, as shown in Figure 6-22.

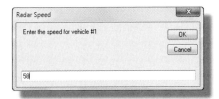

FIGURE 6-22

The code for the Radar Speed InputBox is shown in Figure 6-23. Notice that the prompt message for the user is assigned to the strInputBoxMessage variable, and the title bar text (Radar Speed) is assigned to the strInputBoxHeading variable.

```
15          Dim strVehicleSpeed As String
16          Dim strInputBoxMessage As String = "Enter the speed for vehicle #"
17          Dim strInputBoxHeading As String = "Radar Speed"
18          Dim intNumberOfEntries As Integer = 1
19
20          strVehicleSpeed = InputBox(strInputBoxMessage _
21              & intNumberOfEntries, strInputBoxHeading, " ")
```

FIGURE 6-23

The variable intNumberOfEntries identifies the vehicle number. It is included in the prompt message through the use of concatenation. The variable intNumberOfEntries is incremented later in the code so that it refers to the correct vehicle each time the InputBox function call is executed.

In Figure 6-23, the default value is specified as a space (" "). When the input box is displayed, a space will be selected in the input area. This space is required so that if a user clicks the OK button without entering any data, the InputBox will not return a null character (""), which indicates the user clicked the Cancel button. This normally is a good programming practice.

When the user clicks the Cancel button in an input box and the InputBox function returns a null character, the program can test for the null character to determine further processing.

HEADS UP

An InputBox object allows you to gather input without placing a TextBox for the requested value on the Windows Form object.

Displaying Data Using the ListBox Object

In the Highway Radar Checkpoint application, the user enters the speed of each vehicle into the InputBox object, and the program displays these speeds in a list box (see Figure 6-1 on page 378). To create such a list, you use the ListBox object provided in the Visual Basic Toolbox. A ListBox displays a group of values, called items, with one item per line. To add a ListBox object to a Windows Form object, you can complete the following steps:

STEP 1   Drag the ListBox object from the Toolbox to the Windows Form object where you want to place the ListBox object. When the pointer is in the correct location, release the left mouse button.

The ListBox object is placed on the form (Figure 6-24).

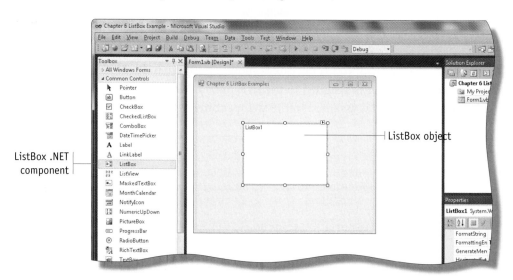

FIGURE 6-24

STEP 2   With the ListBox object selected, scroll in the Properties window to the (Name) property. Name the ListBox object `lstRadarSpeed`.

The name you entered is displayed in the (Name) property in the Properties window (Figure 6-25). Notice a ListBox object name begins with lst.

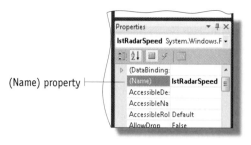

FIGURE 6-25

After placing a ListBox object on the Windows Form object, you can adjust the size as needed by dragging the size handles (see Figure 6-24 on the previous page). Be sure to resize the ListBox so that it is large enough to hold the application data. The ListBox object for the Highway Radar Checkpoint application is designed to be wide enough to hold three digits, and long enough to hold 10 numbers (Figure 6-26).

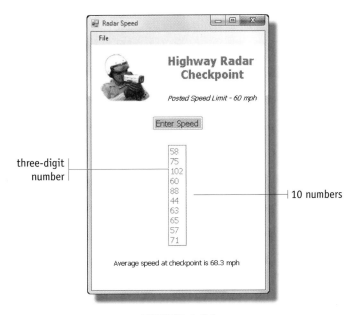

three-digit number   10 numbers

FIGURE 6-26

To display the speed of each vehicle in the list box, you must write code to add each item to the ListBox object. After an item is added, it is displayed in the list box. The general format of the statement to add an item to a ListBox object is shown in Figure 6-27.

General Format: Adding Items to a ListBox Object

```
lstListBoxName.Items.Add(Variable Name)
```

FIGURE 6-27

In Figure 6-27, the Add procedure will add the item contained in the variable identified by the Variable Name entry. The syntax for the statement must be followed precisely.

The code to add the vehicle speed to the lstRadarSpeed ListBox object and then display the speed of each vehicle (decVehicleSpeed) in the ListBox object is shown in Figure 6-28.

```
48        lstRadarSpeed.Items.Add(decVehicleSpeed)
```

FIGURE 6-28

If the number of items exceeds the number that can be displayed in the designated space of the ListBox object, a scroll bar automatically is added to the right side of the ListBox object as shown in Figure 6-29.

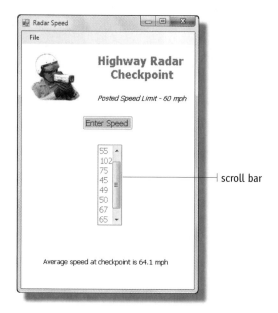

scroll bar

FIGURE 6-29

To clear the items in a ListBox object, the Clear method works as it does for the TextBox object. The syntax of the statement to clear the ListBox is shown in Figure 6-30.

General Format: Clear the ListBox Object

```
lstListBoxName.Items.Clear()
```

FIGURE 6-30

In the Highway Radar Checkpoint application, the user can select the Clear menu item to clear the form. The code in Figure 6-31 removes the items from the lstRadarSpeed ListBox.

```
87          lstRadarSpeed.Items.Clear()
```

FIGURE 6-31

Add Items During Design

The Highway Radar Checkpoint application allows the user to add items to the ListBox object during program execution, but you also can add items to a ListBox object while designing the form. Adding items to the ListBox object during the design phase allows the user to select an item from the ListBox object during execution. For example, in an application to select a favorite clothing store, you can add items to a ListBox object named lstStores during the form design by completing the following steps:

STEP 1   Assume the lstStores ListBox object already has been placed and named on the Windows Form object. Select the ListBox object on the Windows Form object and then click the Items property in the Properties window.

The Items property in the Properties window is selected. An ellipsis button appears to the right of the (Collection) entry (Figure 6-32).

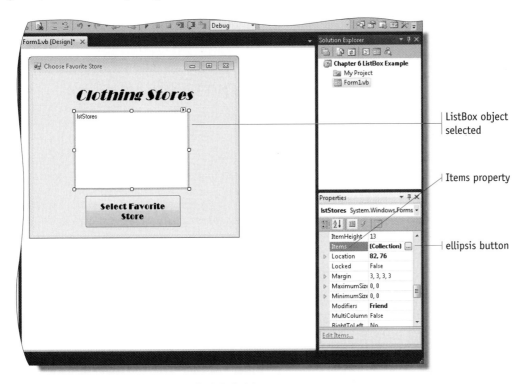

ListBox object selected

Items property

ellipsis button

FIGURE 6-32

STEP 2   Click the ellipsis button in the right column of the Items property.

The String Collection Editor window opens, allowing you to enter items that will be displayed in the ListBox object named lstStores (Figure 6-33).

String Collection
Editor window

enter items to
be placed in the
ListBox object

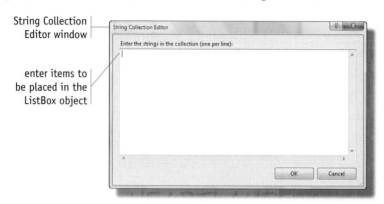

FIGURE 6-33

STEP 3   Click in the String Collection Editor window. Type the following items to represent popular retail stores, pressing ENTER at the end of each line:

```
Abercrombie & Fitch
Aeropostale
American Eagle
Express
Hollister
```

The items representing favorite retail stores appear in the String Collection Editor window on separate lines (Figure 6-34).

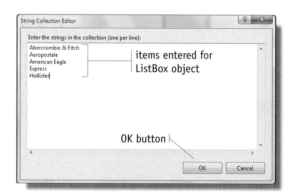

FIGURE 6-34

STEP 4   Click the OK button.

The Windows Form object displays the stores in the lstStores ListBox object (Figure 6–35). The user can select one of the items in the ListBox object during execution.

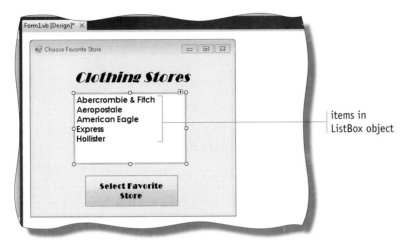

items in
ListBox object

FIGURE 6-35

Selected Item Property

The SelectedItem property identifies which item in the ListBox is selected. An assignment statement is used to assign that property to a variable, as shown in Figure 6-36.

General Format: Assign the Selected Item in a ListBox Object

```
strVariableName = lstListBoxName.SelectedItem
```

FIGURE 6-36

The actual code to show the user's selection of their favorite store from the List-Box object named lstStores in a message box is shown in Figure 6-37.

```
5          MsgBox("Your favorite store is "_
6          &lstStores.SelectedItem & ".")
```

FIGURE 6-37

Accumulators, Counters, and Compound Operators

In the Highway Radar Checkpoint application, after the user enters the speeds of up to 10 vehicles, the application calculates the average speed (see Figure 6-1 on page 378). The formula to calculate the average speed is: (total of all speeds entered) / (number of vehicles). For example, if the total of all the speeds entered is 683 and 10 vehicle speeds were entered, the average speed is 68.3 mph.

To calculate the average, the program must add the speed of each vehicle to a variable. The variable that contains an accumulated value such as the total of all the speeds is called an **accumulator**.

To compute the average speed, the program also must keep track of how many vehicle speeds the user has entered. The variable that is used to keep track of this value is called a **counter**. A counter always is incremented with a constant value. This value can be positive or negative. In the Highway Radar Checkpoint program, the counter is incremented by 1 each time the user enters a speed for a vehicle.

You can use one of two techniques when you need to add a value to a variable and update the value in the variable, as with an accumulator or a counter. The first technique is shown in Figure 6-38.

```
26        decTotalVehicleSpeed = decTotalVehicleSpeed + decVehicleSpeedEntered
27        intNumberOfEntries = intNumberOfEntries + 1
```

FIGURE 6-38

In Figure 6-38, on line 26 the value in the decTotalVehicleSpeed variable is added to the value in the decVehicleSpeedEntered variable and the result is stored in the decTotalVehicleSpeed variable. This statement has the effect of accumulating the vehicle speed values in the decTotalVehicleSpeed accumulator. Similarly, the number of entries counter is incremented by 1 by the statement on line 27. The effect is that the value in the number of entries counter is increased by 1 each time the statement is executed.

A second method for accomplishing this task is to use a shortcut mathematical operator called a **compound operator** that allows you to add, subtract, multiply, divide, use modulus or exponents, or concatenate strings, storing the result in the same variable. An assignment statement that includes a compound operator begins with the variable that will contain the accumulated value, such as an accumulator or a counter, followed by the compound operator. A compound operator consists of an arithmetic operator and an equal sign. The last element in the assignment statement is the variable or literal containing the value to be used in the calculation.

This means that an assignment statement using a compound operator such as:

```
intNumberOfEntries += 1
```

which is an assignment statement using a compound operator, is the same as:

```
intNumberOfEntries = intNumberOfEntries + 1
```

The += compound operator adds the value of the right operand to the value of the left operand and stores the result in the left operand's variable. Similarly, the statement:

```
decTotalVehicleSpeed += decVehicleSpeedEntered
```

is the same as:

```
decTotalVehicleSpeed = decTotalVehicleSpeed + decVehicleSpeedEntered
```

The table in Figure 6-39 shows an example of compound operators used in code. Assume that intResult = 24, decResult = 24, and strSample = "tree".

Operation	Example with Single Operators	Example with Compound Operator	Result
Addition	intResult = intResult + 1	intResult += 1	intResult = 25
Subtraction	intResult = intResult − 3	intResult −= 3	intResult = 21
Multiplication	intResult = intResult * 2	intResult *= 2	intResult = 48
Decimal Division	decResult = decResult / 5	decResult /= 5	decResult = 4.8
Integer Division	intResult = intResult \ 5	intResult \ =5	intResult = 4
Exponents	intResult = intResult ^ 2	intResult ^= 2	intResult = 576
Concatenate	strSample = strSample & "house"	strSample &= "house"	strSample = "treehouse"

FIGURE 6-39

HEADS UP

The compound operators +=, −=, *=, /=, \=, ^=, and &= run faster than their regular longer equation counterparts because the statement is more compact.

Compound operators often are used by developers in Visual Basic coding. The coding example in Figure 6-40 uses several compound operators and a MsgBox object. When the following code is executed, the result shown in the MsgBox object is "Final Result = 2".

```
30          Dim intTotal As Integer
31          intTotal = 7
32          intTotal += 6
33          intTotal *= 2
34          intTotal /= 13
35          MsgBox("Final Result = " & intTotal.ToString(), , "Compound Operators")
```

FIGURE 6-40

Compound operators also can be used to connect two strings using the concatenation operator (&). The code in Figure 6-41 creates the phrase, "To err is human!" in a MsgBox object by using compound operators to concatenate the strPhrase variable. Each compound operator joins another word to the end of the phrase assigned to the strPhrase variable.

```
30          Dim strPhrase As String
31          strPhrase = "To err"
32          strPhrase &= " is "
33          strPhrase &= "human!"
34          MsgBox(strPhrase, , "Compound Operators")
```

FIGURE 6-41

Using Loops to Perform Repetitive Tasks

In the Highway Radar Checkpoint application, the user enters up to 10 vehicle speeds using the InputBox function. The repetitive process of entering 10 vehicle speeds can be coded within a loop to simplify the task with fewer lines of code. Unlike If...Then statements that execute only once, loops repeat multiple times. Each repetition of the loop is called an **iteration**. An iteration is a single execution of a set of instructions that are to be repeated.

Loops are powerful structures used to repeat a section of code a certain number of times or until a particular condition is met. Visual Basic has two main types of loops: For...Next loops and Do loops.

Repeating a Process Using the For...Next Loop

You can use a For...Next loop when a section of code is to be executed an exact number of times. The syntax of a For...Next loop is shown in Figure 6-42.

General Format: For...Next loop

```
For Control Variable = Beginning Numeric Value To Ending Numeric Value

     ' Body of the Loop

Next
```

FIGURE 6-42

In Figure 6-42, the For...Next loop begins with the keyword For. Following this keyword is the control variable, which is the numeric variable that keeps track of the number of iterations the loop completes. To begin the loop, the For statement places the beginning numeric value in the control variable. The program then executes the code between the For and Next statements, which is called the body of the loop.

Upon reaching the Next statement, the program returns to the For statement and increments the value of the control variable. This process continues until the value in the control variable is greater than the ending numeric value. When this occurs, the statement(s) that follows the Next command are executed.

The first line of a For...Next loop that is supposed to execute four times is shown in Figure 6-43. The control value is a variable named intNumber.

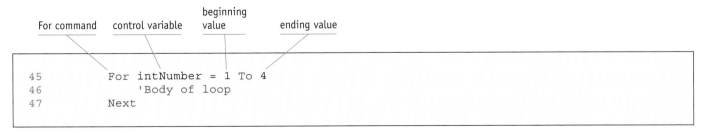

FIGURE 6-43

The first line in the For...Next loop in Figure 6-43 specifies that the control variable (intNumber) is assigned the value 1 because the literal 1 is the beginning value. Then the section of code between the For and Next statement, which is called the body of the loop, is executed. When the Next statement is encountered, control returns to the For statement where, by default, the value 1 is added to the control variable. The code in the body of the loop is executed again. This process continues until the value in the control value becomes greater than 4, which is the ending value. When this occurs, the statement(s) in the program that follow the Next command are executed. The table in Figure 6-44 illustrates this looping process.

Loop Iteration	Value of intNumber	Process
1	intNumber = 1	Executes the code inside the loop
2	intNumber = 2	Executes the code inside the loop
3	intNumber = 3	Executes the code inside the loop
4	intNumber = 4	Executes the code inside the loop
5 (exits the loop)	intNumber = 5	The control variable value exceeds the ending value, so the application exits the For...Next loop. This means the statement(s) following the Next command are executed.

FIGURE 6-44

Step Value in a For...Next Loop

A Step value is the value in a For...Next loop that is added to or subtracted from the beginning value on each iteration of the loop. If you do not include a Step value in the For statement, such as in Figure 6-43, by default the value in the control variable is incremented by 1 after each iteration of the loop.

You can include a Step value in a For statement. For example, in the For header statement in Figure 6-45, the Step value is 2. The control variable intNumber is set to the initial value of 1, and the lines of code in the body of the loop are executed. After the first iteration of the loop, the Step value is added to the control variable, changing the value in the control variable to 3 (1 + 2 = 3). The For loop will continue until the value in intNumber is greater than 99.

step value

```
49      For intNumber = 1 To 99 Step 2
50          ' Body of loop
51      Next
```

FIGURE 6-45

The Step value can be negative. If so, the value in the control variable is decreased on each iteration of the loop. To exit the loop, you must specify an ending value that is less than the beginning value. This is illustrated in Figure 6-46.

negative
Step value

```
55          For intCount = 25 To -10 Step -5
56              ' Body of loop
57          Next
```

FIGURE 6-46

In the first iteration of the For...Next loop header in Figure 6-46, the control variable value is 25. The value in the control variable intCount is decreased by 5 each time the loop repeats. This repetition will continue until the value in the intCount control variable is less than −10. Then the loop exits.

The control variable in a For...Next loop can be assigned decimal values as well. The For loop header in Figure 6-47 has a starting value of 3.1. The loop ends when the value in the control variable is greater than 4.5. The Step value is 0.1, which means the value in decNumber increments by 0.1 each pass through the loop.

decimal
Step value

```
61          For decNumber = 3.1 To 4.5 Step 0.1
62              ' Body of loop
63          Next
```

FIGURE 6-47

A For...Next loop also can include variables and mathematical expressions as shown in Figure 6-48.

```
69          For intNumber = intBegin To (intEnd * 2) Step intIncrement
70              'Body of loop
71          Next
```

FIGURE 6-48

In Figure 6-48, the control variable (intNumber) is initialized with the value in the intBegin variable. Each time the Next statement is encountered and control is returned to the For statement, the value in intNumber will be incremented by the value in the intIncrement variable. The loop will continue until the value in intNumber is greater than the product of the value in intEnd times 2.

Entering the For...Next Loop Code Using IntelliSense

To show the process for entering the For...Next loop code using IntelliSense, assume that an application is designed to show in a list box the population growth over the next six years for Alaska. Assume further that the current population of Alaska is 675,000 people and is expected to grow at 5% per year for the next six years. The code in Figure 6-49 will accomplish this processing.

```
4        Dim intAlaskaPopulation As Integer = 675000
5        Dim intYears As Integer
6
7        For intYears = 1 To 6
8            intAlaskaPopulation += (intAlaskaPopulation * 0.05)
9            lstGrowth.Items.Add("Year " & intYears & " Population " & intAlaskaPopulation)
10
11       Next
```

FIGURE 6-49

To use IntelliSense to enter the code shown in Figure 6-49, you can complete the following steps: (The following code assumes the lstGrowth ListBox object has been defined on the Windows Form object.)

STEP 1   In the code editing window, type `Dim intAlaskaPopulation As Integer = 675000` and then press the ENTER key. Type `Dim intYears As Integer` and then press the ENTER key two times. Type `for`, a space, and then an IntelliSense list opens.

The IntelliSense list shows all available entries (Figure 6-50).

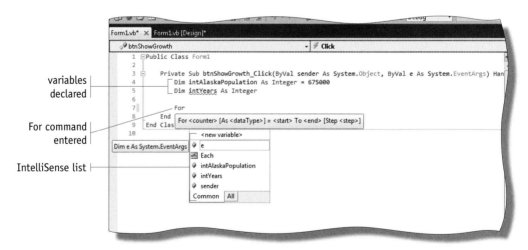

FIGURE 6-50

STEP 2 Type the first four letters of the intYears variable name (intY) to select intYears in the IntelliSense list. Type = 1 to 6 and press the ENTER key to specify the beginning value and ending value for the loop.

Visual Basic automatically inserts the Next statement in the code (Figure 6-51). For, To, and Next are blue to indicate they are keywords.

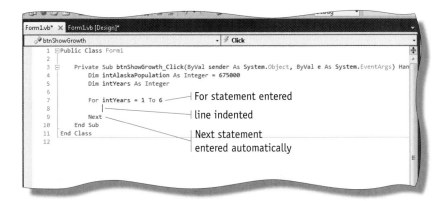

FIGURE 6-51

STEP 3 Use IntelliSense to select the appropriate variables. Enter the two new lines shown in Figure 6-52.

Each line of code automatically is indented between the For and Next statements (Figure 6-52).

FIGURE 6-52

STEP 4 Run the program to see the results of the loop.

The loop calculates and displays the Alaskan population growth for six years based on 5% growth per year (Figure 6-53).

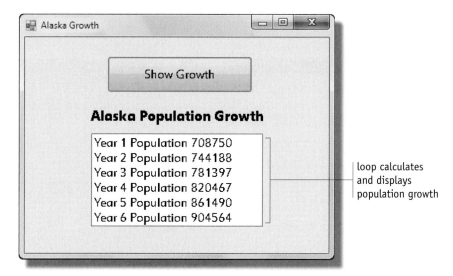

loop calculates and displays population growth

FIGURE 6-53

User Input and the For...Next Loop

The beginning, ending, and step values used in a For...Next loop can vary based on input from a user. For example, in Figure 6-54, the program displays the squared values of a range of numbers the user enters. The user enters the beginning (minimum) and ending (maximum) range of values, and then clicks the Calculate Values button to view the squares of the numbers in the range.

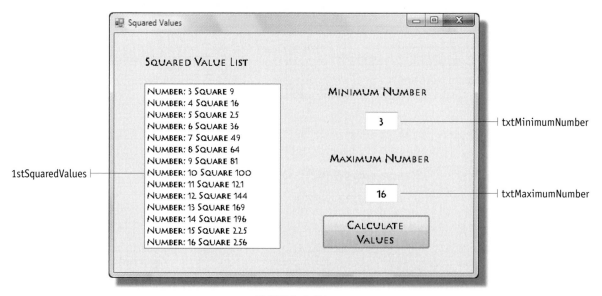

1stSquaredValues

txtMinimumNumber

txtMaximumNumber

FIGURE 6-54

The code for the Squared Values application in Figure 6-54 on the previous page is shown in Figure 6-55.

```
 5      Dim intCount As Integer
 6      Dim intBegin As Integer
 7      Dim intEnd As Integer
 8
 9      intBegin = Convert.ToInt32(txtMinimumNumber.Text)
10      intEnd = Convert.ToInt32(txtMaximumNumber.Text)
11
12      For intCount = intBegin To intEnd
13          lstSquaredValues.Items.Add("Number: " & intCount & " Squared Value: " & (intCount ^ 2))
14      Next
15
16      End Sub
```

FIGURE 6-55

In Figure 6-55, on line 9 the minimum value the user entered is converted to an integer and placed in the intBegin variable. Similarly, on line 10, the maximum value the user entered is converted to an integer and assigned to the intEnd variable. On line 12, the value in intBegin is used as the beginning value in the For...Next loop, and the value in intEnd is used as the ending value. As you can see, the number of iterations for the loop is determined by values the user entered.

Within the loop, the value in intCount, which begins with the value in intBegin and is incremented by the default value of one each time through the loop, is used as the number from which the squared value is calculated. As shown in Figure 6-54 on the previous page, this results in the squared values being calculated for all numbers beginning with the minimum number and ending with the maximum number.

Repeating a Process Using a Do Loop

A For...Next loop is used when a process is repeated an exact number of times. In many applications, however, a loop should be repeated until a certain condition changes. For example, in the Highway Radar Checkpoint application, the process of entering the speed of each vehicle is repeated 10 times or until the user stops entering the speed of the next vehicle by clicking the Cancel button. The loop in the Highway Radar Checkpoint application continues until one of two conditions becomes true — either the count of the speeds entered reaches 10 or the user clicks the Cancel button on the InputBox object.

In a **Do loop**, the body of the loop is executed while or until a condition is true or false. The Do loop uses a condition similar to an If...Then decision structure to determine whether it should continue looping. In this way, you can use a Do loop to execute a body of statements an indefinite number of times. In the Highway Radar Checkpoint application, the Do loop runs an indefinite number of times because the user can end the loop at any time by clicking the Cancel button.

Visual Basic 2010 provides two types of Do loops: the Do While loop and the Do Until loop. Both Do loops execute statements repeatedly until a specified condition becomes true or false. Each loop examines a condition to determine whether the condition is true. The **Do While loop** executes as long as the condition is true. It is stated as, "Do the loop processing while the condition is true."

The **Do Until loop** executes until the condition becomes true. It is stated as, "Do the loop processing until a condition is true."

Do loops are either top-controlled or bottom-controlled, depending on whether the condition is tested before the loop begins or after the body of the loop has executed one time. A **top-controlled loop** is tested before the loop is entered. The body of a top-controlled loop might not be executed at all because the condition being tested might be true before any processing in the loop occurs.

Bottom-controlled loops test the condition at the bottom of the loop, so the body of a bottom-controlled loop is executed at least once. Visual Basic provides top-controlled and bottom-controlled Do While and Do Until loops, meaning it can execute four types of Do loops.

Top-Controlled Do While Loops

You use a top-controlled Do While loop if you want the body of the loop to repeat as long as a condition remains true. Figure 6-56 shows the syntax of a top-controlled Do While loop.

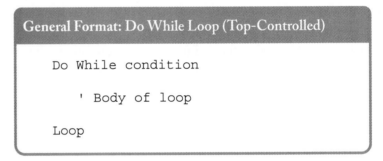

```
General Format: Do While Loop (Top-Controlled)

Do While condition

    ' Body of loop

Loop
```

FIGURE 6-56

A top-controlled Do While loop begins with the keywords, Do While. Next, the condition is specified. The condition is expressed using the same relational operators that are available with the If statements that you learned in Chapter 5. Any condition that can be specified in an If statement can be specified in a Do While condition. The condition can compare numeric values or string values.

The body of the loop contains the instructions that are executed as long as the condition is true. The Loop keyword indicates the end of the loop. It is inserted automatically when you enter the Do While loop header statement.

You must ensure that a statement within the body of the Do While loop will, at some point, cause the condition to change so the loop ends. For example, in the statement Do While strColor = "Red" the loop will continue to process as long as the value in the strColor variable remains Red. Based on the processing in the body of the loop, at some point the value in the strColor variable must be changed from Red. If not, the loop will not terminate. A loop that does not end is called an **infinite loop**.

The code in Figure 6-57 is an example of a top-controlled Do While loop. It continues to add 1 to the variable intScore while intScore is less than 5. It is considered a top-controlled loop because the condition is checked at the top of the loop.

```
17          Dim intScore As Integer = 0
18          Do While intScore < 5
19              intScore += 1
20          Loop
```

FIGURE 6-57

The loop in Figure 6-57 begins by testing whether intScore is less than 5. Because intScore starts with the value 0, the condition tested is true because 0 is less than 5. Next, the variable intScore is incremented by 1, and the loop repeats. The table in Figure 6-58 displays the values that are assigned to intScore each time the condition is checked in the code in Figure 6-57.

Loop Iteration	Value of intScore	Result of Condition Tested
1	intScore = 0	True
2	intScore = 1	True
3	intScore = 2	True
4	intScore = 3	True
5	intScore = 4	True
6	intScore = 5	False

FIGURE 6-58

The loop in Figure 6-57 is executed five times because intScore is less than 5 during five iterations of the loop. As shown in Figure 6-57, if the value in the variable intScore is 5 or greater when the Do While statement is first executed, the body of the loop never will be executed because the condition is not true prior to the first iteration of the loop.

Entering a Do Loop Using IntelliSense

To use IntelliSense to enter the Do While loop in Figure 6-57 on the previous page into the code editing window, you can complete the following steps:

STEP 1 In the code editing window, enter the intScore variable declaration and then press the ENTER key. Type Do While and a space, and then an IntelliSense list is displayed. Type ints to highlight intScore in the list.

The words Do While appear in blue because they are Visual Basic keywords (Figure 6-59). The IntelliSense list contains the valid entries and the intScore variable name is highlighted.

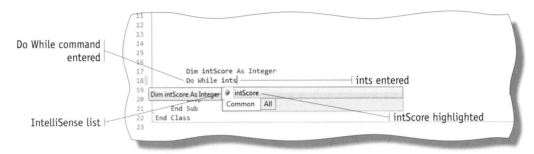

FIGURE 6-59

STEP 2 Type < 5 and then press the ENTER key.

Visual Basic automatically inserts the intScore variable name and the characters you typed (Figure 6-60). The keyword Loop also is inserted and the insertion point is located inside the loop, ready to enter the body of the loop.

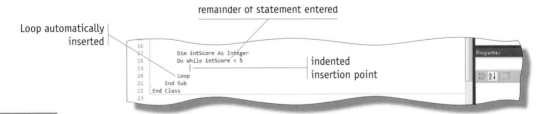

FIGURE 6-60

STEP 3 Type intS to highlight the intScore variable. Complete the statement by typing += 1 and then pressing the ENTER key. Press the DELETE key to delete the blank line.

The statement automatically is indented between the Do While and Loop statements (Figure 6-61). The intScore += 1 statement uses a compound operator to increment the intScore variable.

FIGURE 6-61

Bottom-Controlled Do While Loop

You can write a Do While loop where the condition is tested at the bottom of the loop. A bottom-controlled loop works the same way as the top-controlled Do While loop except that the body of the loop is executed before the condition is checked the first time, guaranteeing at least one iteration of a loop will be completed. The bottom-controlled Do While loop has the syntax shown in Figure 6-62.

```
General Format: Do While Loop (Bottom-Controlled)

Do

        ' Loop Body

Loop While condition
```

FIGURE 6-62

In the syntax shown in Figure 6-62, the word Do appears on its own line at the beginning of the loop. The loop body follows, and the Loop While statement is the last statement in the loop. The Loop While statement contains the condition that is tested to determine if the loop should be terminated. Because the While condition is in the last statement of the loop, the body of the loop is executed one time regardless of the status of the condition.

The code in Figure 6-63 is an example of a bottom-controlled Do While loop.

```
22          Dim intScore As Integer = 0
23          Do
24              intScore = intScore + 1
25          Loop While intScore < 5
```

FIGURE 6-63

The body of the Do loop in Figure 6-63 is executed one time before the condition in the Loop While statement is checked. The variable intScore begins with the initial value of 0 and is incremented in the body of the loop, changing the value to 1.

The condition is then tested and found to be true because 1 < 5. The loop repeats and the value of intScore increases, as shown in Figure 6-64.

Loop Iteration	Value of intScore at Start of the Loop	Value of intScore When Checked	Result of Condition Tested
1	intScore = 0	intScore = 1	True
2	intScore = 1	intScore = 2	True
3	intScore = 2	intScore = 3	True
4	intScore = 3	intScore = 4	True
5	intScore = 4	intScore = 5	False

FIGURE 6-64

The body of the loop in Figure 6-63 on the previous page is executed five times because intScore is less than 5 during five iterations of the loop.

Do Until Loops

A loop similar to a Do While loop is called a Do Until loop. The Do Until loop allows you to specify that an action repeats until a condition becomes true. When the condition in a Do Until loop becomes true, the loop ends.

Top-Controlled Do Until Loop

A Do Until loop can be both top-controlled and bottom-controlled. The syntax of the top-controlled Do Until loop is shown in Figure 6-65.

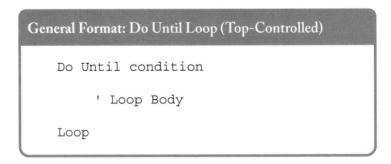

```
General Format: Do Until Loop (Top-Controlled)

    Do Until condition

        ' Loop Body

    Loop
```

FIGURE 6-65

A top-controlled Do Until loop begins with the keywords Do Until. Next, as with the Do While top-controlled loop, the condition is specified. The condition is expressed using the same relational operators that are available with If statements. Any condition that can be specified in an If statement can be specified in a Do Until condition. The condition can compare numeric values or string values.

The Do Until loop example shown in Figure 6-66 displays a parking meter application that computes the number of minutes a user can purchase based on the cost of 25 cents for each 15 minutes of parking. If the user only has 88 cents in pocket change, for example, the application computes how many minutes of parking time 88 cents will purchase.

```
4         Dim decAmount As Decimal = 0.88
5         Dim intQuarters As Integer = 0
6         Dim intTime As Integer = 15
7         Dim intParkingTime As Integer
8
9         Do Until decAmount < 0.25
10             intQuarters += 1
11             decAmount -= 0.25
12        Loop
13        intParkingTime = intQuarters * intTime
14        lblParkingTime.Text = "Parking Time: " &
15                            intParkingTime.ToString() & " minutes"
```

FIGURE 6-66

In the code example in Figure 6-66, the Do Until loop condition is checked before the body of the loop executes. The first time the condition is tested, the expression decAmount < 0.25 is false because the decAmount variable contains 0.88. The body of the loop is executed because the Do Until will be executed until the value in decAmount is less than 0.25. When the body of the loop is executed, it adds 1 to intQuarters to count the number of quarters the user has for the parking meter and 0.25 is subtracted from decAmount because a quarter is worth 25 cents. Because decAmount is first assigned the value 0.88, the loop executes three times (decAmount = 0.88, decAmount = 0.63, and decAmount = 0.38) and stops when decAmount becomes less than 0.25. The lblParkingTime Label object displays the text "Parking Time: 45 minutes".

Bottom-Controlled Do Until Loop

The last of the four Do loops is the bottom-controlled Do Until loop. This Do Until loop checks the condition after the body of the loop is executed. The loop continues until the condition becomes true. The syntax of the bottom-controlled Do Until loop is shown in Figure 6-67.

General Format: Do Until Loop (Bottom-Controlled)

```
Do

       ' Loop Body

Loop Until condition
```

FIGURE 6-67

As shown in Figure 6-67 on the previous page, the bottom-controlled Do Until loop begins with the word Do. The body of the loop is executed one time regardless of the condition being tested. The Loop Until statement checks the condition. The loop will be repeated until the condition is true.

User Input Loops

Do loops often are written to end the loop when a certain value is entered by the user, or the user performs a certain action such as clicking the Cancel button in an input box. The value or action is predefined by the developer. For example, the loop in Figure 6-68 continues until the user clicks the Cancel button in the input box. If the user clicks the Cancel button, the InputBox function returns a null string that is assigned to the strTestGrade variable. The Do Until statement tests the string. If it contains a null character, the loop is terminated. The Do Until loop accumulates the total of all the entered test scores until the user clicks the Cancel button.

```
40          Do Until strTestGrade = ""
41              strTestGrade = InputBox("Enter test grade", "Compute Average")
42              If IsNumeric(strTestGrade) Then
43                  decGrade = Convert.ToDecimal(strTestGrade)
44                  decTotal += decGrade
45              End If
46          Loop
```

FIGURE 6-68

Avoiding Infinite Loops

Recall that an **infinite loop** is a loop that never ends. It happens when the condition that will cause the end of a loop never occurs. If the loop does not end, it will continue to repeat until the program is interrupted. Figure 6-69 shows an example of an infinite loop.

```
22          Dim intProblem = 0
23          Do While intProblem <= 5
24              Box.Show("This loop will not end", "Infinite Loop")
25          Loop
```

FIGURE 6-69

The Do While loop in Figure 6-69 never ends because the value in the variable intProblem is never changed from its initial value of zero. Because the value in intProblem never exceeds 5, the condition in the Do While loop (intProblem <= 5) never becomes false. The processing in a loop eventually must change the condition being tested in the Do While loop so the loop will terminate. When working in Visual Basic 2010, you can interrupt an infinite loop by clicking the Stop Debugging button on the Standard toolbar.

Priming the Loop

As you have learned, a top-controlled loop tests a condition prior to beginning the loop. In most cases, the value that is tested in that condition must be set before the condition is tested the first time in the Do While or Do Until statement. Starting a loop with a preset value in the variable(s) tested in the condition is called **priming the loop**. You have seen this in previous examples, such as in Figure 6-66 on page 411 where the value in decAmount is set before the condition is tested the first time.

In some applications, such as the Highway Radar Checkpoint application, the loop is primed with a value the user enters or an action the user takes. You will recall that the user enters the speed for a vehicle (up to 10 vehicles) or clicks the Cancel button in the input box to terminate the input operation. Prior to executing the Do Until statement the first time in the Do Until loop that processes the data the user enters, the InputBox function must be executed to obtain an initial value. Then, the Do Until statement can test the action taken by the user (enter a value or click the Cancel button). The coding to implement this processing is shown in Figure 6-70.

```
31    Dim strCancelClicked As String = ""
32    Dim intMaxNumberOfEntries As Integer = 10
33    Dim intNumberOfEntries As Integer = 1
⋮
39    strVehicleSpeed = InputBox(strInputMessage & intNumberOfEntries, strInputHeading, " ")
40
41
42    Do Until intNumberOfEntries > intMaxNumberOfEntries Or strVehicleSpeed = strCancelClicked
43
⋮
50              intNumberOfEntries += 1
⋮
59        If intNumberOfEntries <= intMaxNumberOfEntries Then
60            strVehicleSpeed = InputBox(strInputMessage & intNumberOfEntries, strInputHeading, " ")
61
62        End If
63
64    Loop
```

FIGURE 6-70

In the Do Until loop shown in Figure 6-70, you can see that the Do Until statement on line 42 tests two conditions: is the value in the intNumberOfEntries variable greater than the value in the intMaxNumberOfEntries variable, or is the value in the strVehicleSpeed variable equal to the value in the strCancelClicked variable, which is a null character (see line 31). If either of these conditions is true, the body of the loop will not be executed.

The Do Until loop must have two primed variables — the intNumberOfEntries variable and the strVehicleSpeed variable. The intNumberOfEntries variable is initialized to the value 1 on line 33. The strVehicleSpeed variable is initialized by the InputBox function call on line 39. In this function call, either the user has entered a value or clicked the Cancel button. If the user clicked the Cancel button, the body of the loop should not be entered.

To continue the loop, the processing within the body of the loop eventually must change one of the conditions being tested in the Do Until statement or the loop never terminates. In the sample program, the conditions being tested are whether the user has entered 10 vehicle speeds or whether the user has clicked the Cancel button. Therefore, within the loop, the variable containing the number of vehicle speeds entered (intNumberOfEntries) must be incremented when the user enters a valid speed, and the user must be able to enter more speeds or click the Cancel button. On line 50 in Figure 6-70 on the previous page, the value in the intNumberOfEntries is incremented by 1 each time the user enters a valid value. In addition, the statement on line 60 displays an input box that allows the user to enter a new value or click the Cancel button as long as the number of valid entries is not greater than the maximum number of entries.

Validating Data

As you learned in Chapter 5, you must test the data a user enters to ensure it is accurate and that its use in other programming statements, such as converting string data to numeric data, will not cause a program exception. When using an input box, the data should be checked using the IsNumeric function and If statements as discussed in Chapter 5. If the data is not valid, the user must be notified of the error and an input box displayed to allow the user to enter valid data.

For example, if the user enters non-numeric data, the input box in Figure 6-71 should be displayed.

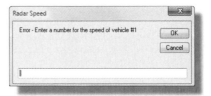

FIGURE 6-71

Similarly, if the user enters a negative number, the message in Figure 6-72 should be displayed in an input box.

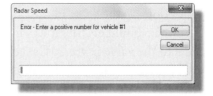

FIGURE 6-72

When error checking is performed within a loop and the user is asked to enter data through the use of an input box, the body of the loop must be executed each time the user enters data regardless of whether the data is valid or invalid. If the user enters valid data, then the data is processed according to the needs of the program.

If the user enters invalid data, an error message is displayed and the user is given the opportunity to enter valid data in the input box. The coding for the Highway Radar Checkpoint application that accomplishes these tasks is shown in Figure 6-73.

```
39        strVehicleSpeed = InputBox(strInputMessage & intNumberOfEntries, strInputHeading, " ")
40
41        Do Until intNumberOfEntries > intMaxNumberOfEntries Or strVehicleSpeed = strCancelClicked
42
43            If IsNumeric(strVehicleSpeed) Then
44                decVehicleSpeed = Convert.ToDecimal(strVehicleSpeed)
45                If decVehicleSpeed > 0 Then
46                    lstRadarSpeed.Items.Add(decVehicleSpeed)
47                    decTotalOfAllSpeeds += decVehicleSpeed
48                    intNumberOfEntries += 1
49                    strInputMessage = strNormalMessage
50                Else
51                    strInputMessage = strNegativeError
52                End If
53            Else
54                strInputMessage = strNonNumericError
55            End If
56
57            If intNumberOfEntries <= intMaxNumberOfEntries Then
58                strVehicleSpeed = InputBox(strInputMessage & intNumberOfEntries, strInputHeading, " ")
59            End If
60
61        Loop
62
```

FIGURE 6-73

In Figure 6-73, the loop is primed by the InputBox function call on line 39. The Do Until statement on line 41 checks the two conditions — if the value in the intNumberOfEntries counter is greater than the maximum number of entries, or the user clicks the Cancel button, then the body of the loop is not entered.

When the body of the loop is entered, the data the user entered is checked to verify it is numeric. If it is numeric, the value is converted to a Decimal data type and then is checked to ensure it is greater than zero (line 45). If it is greater than zero, it is added to the lstRadarSpeed ListBox object, the decTotalOfAllSpeeds accumulator is incremented by the speed the user entered, the intNumberOfEntries counter is incremented by 1, and the normal message is moved to the strInputMessage variable. This variable contains the message that is displayed in the input box (see line 39).

If the value the user entered is not greater than zero, the statement following the Else statement on line 50 moves the value in the strNegativeError variable to the strInputMessage variable so that the next time the InputBox function is called, the message will indicate an error, as shown in Figure 6-72 on page 414.

If the value the user entered was not numeric (as tested by the statement on line 43), the statement on line 54 moves the value in the strNonNumericError variable to the strInputMessage variable so the next time the InputBox function is called, the message will indicate a non-numeric error, as shown in Figure 6-71 on page 414.

On lines 57 and 58, as long as the number of entries is not greater than the maximum number of entries, the InputBox function is called. The message that is displayed in the input box depends on whether an error occurred. The Do Until statement on line 41 then is executed again and the process begins again.

Creating a Nested Loop

In the last chapter, you learned to nest If...Then...Else statements within each other. Loops also can be nested. You can place any type of loop within any other type of loop. Any loop can be placed within another loop under the following conditions: interior loops must be completely contained inside the outer loop and must have a different control variable. The example in Figure 6-74 uses a nested For loop to display a list of the weeks in the first quarter of the year (13 weeks) along with the day in each week. The outer For...Next loop counts from 1 to 13 for the 13 weeks, and the inner For...Next loop counts from 1 to 7 for the days in each of the 13 weeks.

```
6          Dim intOuterCount As Integer ' Counts the first 13 weeks in a quarter
7          Dim intInnerCount As Integer ' Counts the 7 days in a week
8          For intOuterCount = 1 To 13 ' For weeks in the 1st quarter of the year
9              For intInnerCount = 1 To 7 ' For the 7 days in a week
10                 lstDays.Items.Add("Week: " & intOuterCount.ToString() _
11                                   & " Day: " & intInnerCount.ToString())
12             Next
13         Next
```

FIGURE 6-74

The code in Figure 6-74 displays the output shown in Figure 6-75.

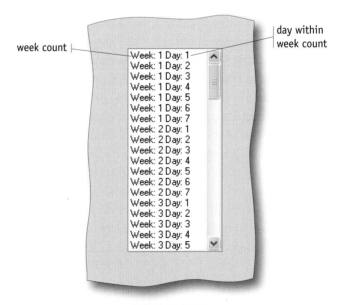

FIGURE 6-75

When writing a program, you might have to make a decision regarding which loop structure to use. For...Next loops are best when the number of repetitions is fixed. Do loops are best when the condition to enter or exit the loop needs to be re-evaluated continually. When deciding which loop to use, keep the following considerations in mind:

1. Use a Do loop if the number of repetitions is unknown and is based on a condition changing; a For...Next loop is best if the exact number of repetitions is fixed.
2. If a loop condition must be tested before the body of the loop is executed, use a top-controlled Do While or Do Until loop. If the instructions within a loop must be executed one time regardless of the status of a condition, use a bottom-controlled Do While or Do Until loop.
3. Use the keyword While if you want to continue execution of the loop while the condition is true. Use the keyword Until if you want to continue execution until the condition is true.

Using a DataTip with Breakpoints

As programs become longer and more complex, the likelihood of errors increases, and you need to carefully find and remove these errors. Resolving defects in code is called **debugging**. When you debug a program, you collect information and find out what is wrong with the code in the program. You then fix that code.

A good way to collect information is to pause the execution of the code where a possible error could occur. One way to pause execution is to use breakpoints. **Breakpoints** are stop points placed in the code to tell the Visual Studio 2010 debugger where and when to pause the execution of the application. During this pause, the program is in break mode. While in break mode, you can examine the values in all variables that are within the scope of execution through the use of **DataTips**. In the Highway Radar Checkpoint program, you can insert a breakpoint in the assignment statement that increments the decTotalOfAllSpeeds accumulator to view its value after each iteration of the loop as the user enters vehicle speeds. To set a breakpoint in your code and then check the data at the breakpoint using DataTips, you can complete the following steps:

STEP 1   With the program open in the code editing window, right-click line 47, which contains the code where you want to set a breakpoint, and then point to Breakpoint on the shortcut menu.

A shortcut menu opens that contains the Breakpoint command (Figure 6-76). The Breakpoint submenu contains the Insert Breakpoint command. Setting a breakpoint in line 47 means that the program will pause at that line during execution so that the values in variables within the scope of execution can be examined.

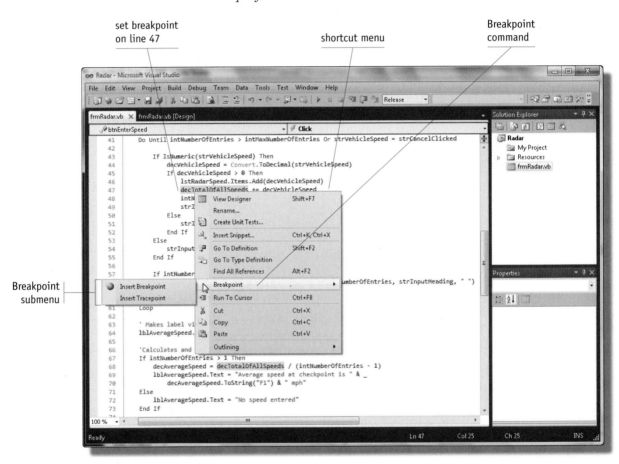

FIGURE 6-76

STEP 2 Click Insert Breakpoint on the submenu.

A breakpoint is set on line 47, which is the line inside the Do Until loop that adds the vehicle speed the user entered to the vehicle speed accumulator — decTotalOfAllSpeeds (Figure 6-77). The breakpoint is identified by the bullet to the left of the line numbers and the highlight on the code.

breakpoint set

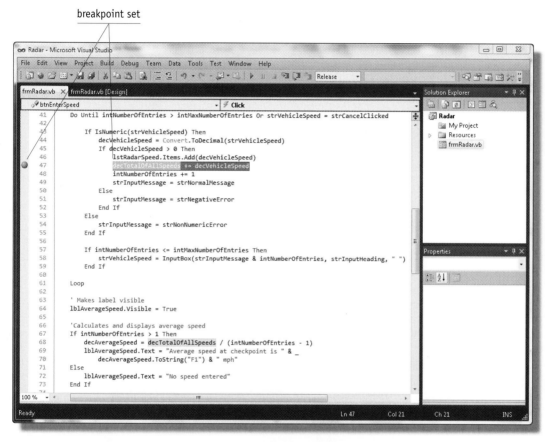

FIGURE 6-77

STEP 3 To run and test the program with the breakpoint, click the Start Debugging button on the Standard toolbar.

The program starts and the Radar Speed window opens (Figure 6–78).

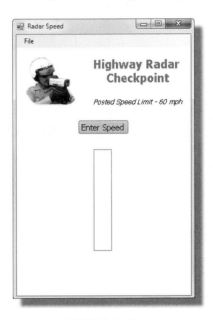

FIGURE 6-78

STEP 4 Click the Enter Speed button. Type 75 as the speed of the first vehicle.

The Radar Speed input box contains 75 as the speed of the first vehicle (Figure 6–79).

75 entered in Radar Speed input box

FIGURE 6-79

STEP 5 Click the OK button in the input box.

The program executes the lines of code in the event handler until reaching the breakpoint,
where it pauses execution on the accumulator line (Figure 6–80). The application is now in
break mode. Notice the breakpoint line is highlighted in yellow.

program execution
paused at breakpoint

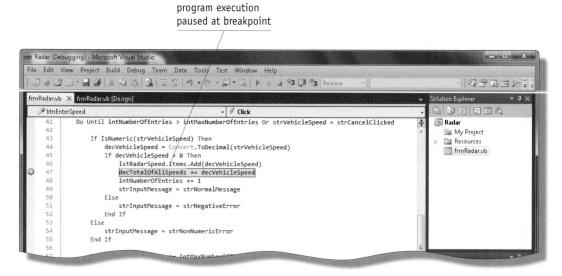

FIGURE 6-80

STEP 6 Point to the variable decVehicleSpeed on line 47.

A DataTip appears, displaying the value of the decVehicleSpeed variable at the time
program execution was paused (Figure 6–81). The value is 75 because that is the value the
user entered in Step 4. It is a decimal value (75D) because the value the user entered was
converted to a decimal value by the statement on line 44.

pointer points to
decTotalOfAllSpeeds
variable

DataTip displays the value
in the decVehicleSpeed
variable

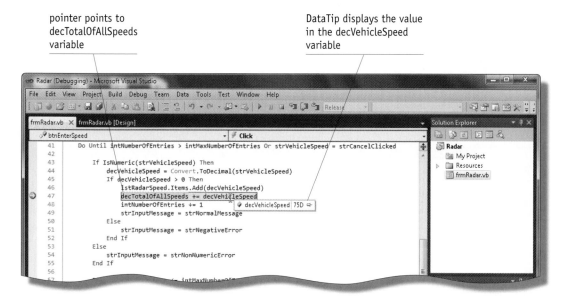

FIGURE 6-81

STEP 7 You can view the value in any other variable within execution scope by pointing to that variable. To illustrate, point to the variable decTotalOfAllSpeeds on line 47.

The value in the decTotalOfAllSpeeds variable is displayed (Figure 6-82). The value is zero, which means the assignment statement on line 47 has not yet been executed. When a breakpoint is set, the program pauses before executing the statement containing the breakpoint.

pointer points to
decTotalOfAllSpeeds
variable

DataTip displays the value in the
decTotalOfAllSpeeds variable

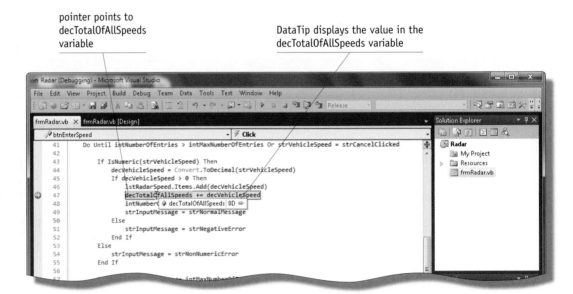

FIGURE 6-82

STEP 8 Continue the program by clicking the Continue button on the Standard toolbar. Notice that the Continue button is the same as the Start Debugging button.

The program continues by opening the next InputBox function where the user can enter the speed for the next vehicle. The program runs until it again reaches the breakpoint, where it pauses so you can point to any variable to view its present value in a DataTip (Figure 6-83).

program execution
paused again

Continue
button

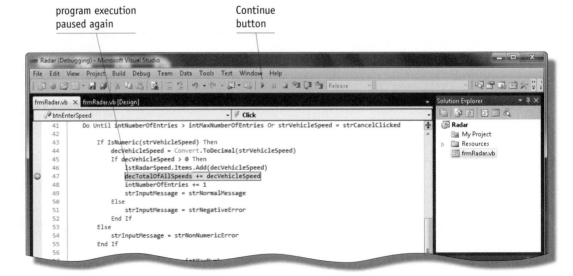

FIGURE 6-83

STEP 9 Point to the decTotalOfAllSpeeds variable.

The updated value in the decTotalOfAllSpeeds variable is shown (Figure 6-84). The value 75D is in the variable as a result of the processing in the first iteration of the loop. You also can examine the values in other variables by pointing to the variable name.

updated value
shown

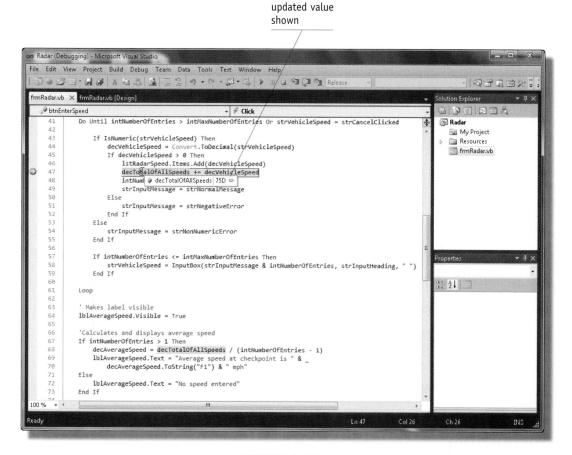

FIGURE 6-84

ONLINE REINFORCEMENT

To view a video of the process in the previous steps, visit scsite.com/vb2010/ch6 and then select Figure 6-76.

The preceding examples illustrated the use of one breakpoint, but you can include multiple breakpoints in a program if that will be useful. Sometimes, breakpoints before and after an instruction that you suspect is in error can pinpoint the problem.

To remove a breakpoint, you can complete the following steps:

STEP 1 Right-click the statement containing the breakpoint, and then point to Breakpoint on the shortcut menu.

The shortcut menu is displayed, the pointer is located on the Breakpoint entry, and the Breakpoint submenu is displayed (Figure 6-85). You can right-click the statement containing the breakpoint either when the program is running in Debugging mode or when the program is not running.

Delete Breakpoint command   shortcut menu

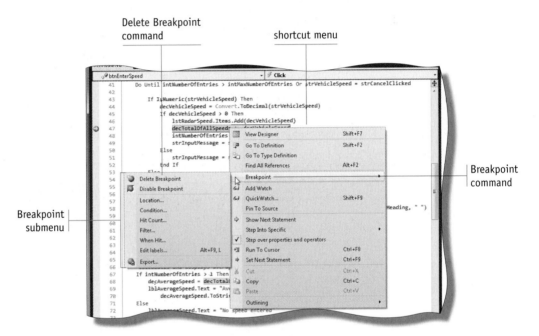

Breakpoint submenu

Breakpoint command

FIGURE 6-85

STEP 2 Click Delete Breakpoint on the Breakpoint submenu.
If the program is running in Debugging mode, the breakpoint is removed when you click the Continue button (Figure 6-86). If the program is not running, the breakpoint is removed immediately.

breakpoint is removed, but variable is highlighted

FIGURE 6-86

The use of breakpoints and DataTips allows you to examine any variables during the execution of the program. By moving step by step through the program, normally you will be able to identify any errors that might occur in the program.

Publishing an Application with ClickOnce Deployment

After an application is completely debugged and working properly, you can deploy the project. Deploying a project means placing an executable version of the program on your hard disk (which then can be placed on CD or DVD), on a Web server, or on a network server.

You probably have purchased software on a CD or DVD. To install the application on your computer, you insert the CD or DVD into your computer and then follow the setup instructions. The version of the program you receive on the CD or DVD is the deployed version of the program.

When programming using Visual Basic 2010, you can create a deployed program by using **ClickOnce Deployment**. The deployed version of the program you create can be installed and executed on any computer that has the .NET framework installed. The computer does not need Visual Studio 2010 installed to run the program.

To publish the Highway Radar Checkpoint program using ClickOnce Deployment, you can complete the following steps:

STEP 1   With the program open, click Build on the menu bar.

The Build menu is displayed (Figure 6-87).

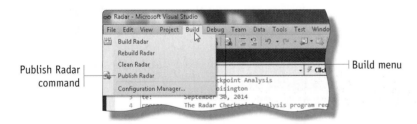

FIGURE 6-87

STEP 2 Click Publish Radar on the Build menu.

The Publish Wizard starts (Figure 6-88). The first Publish Wizard dialog box asks where you want to publish the application. The application can be published to a Web server, a network, or as a setup file on a hard disk or USB drive for burning on a CD or DVD. This dialog box includes publish\ as the default location, which you can change to a file location.

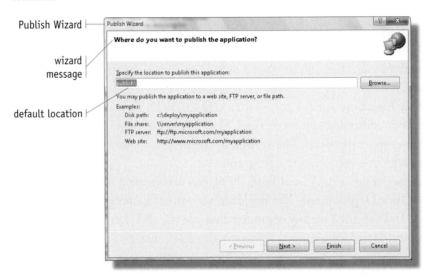

FIGURE 6-88

STEP 3 Change the default location from publish\ to a file location. To publish to a USB drive, type the drive letter. In this example, enter E: for a USB drive.

The Publish Wizard dialog box requests where the user intends to publish the application. The Radar application will be saved to the USB drive, which is drive E: in this example (Figure 6-89).

FIGURE 6-89

STEP 4   Click the Next button. If necessary, click the From a CD-ROM or
DVD-ROM radio button.

Visual Basic displays a Publish Wizard dialog box that asks, How will users install the application? (Figure 6-90). When the user will install the application from a CD or DVD, such as when you purchase software, you should select the CD or DVD option.

From a CD-ROM
or DVD-ROM
selected

FIGURE 6-90

STEP 5   Click the Next button. If necessary, click the The application will not
check for updates radio button.

The next Publish Wizard dialog box asks where will the application check for updates (Figure 6-91). You can select and enter a location, or indicate that the application will not check for updates. Generally, when an application will be deployed to a CD or DVD, the application will not check for updates. If the application is deployed to a Web server or network server, then it might check for updates before being executed on the user's computer.

application will
not check for
updates

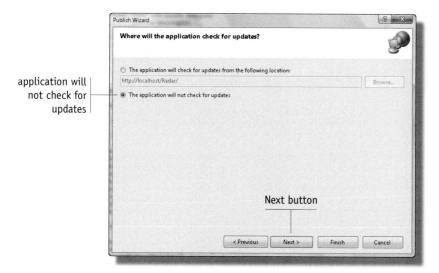

FIGURE 6-91

STEP 6 Click the Next button.

The Ready to Publish window is displayed (Figure 6-92). Notice the message in this window — when the program is installed on the user's machine, a shortcut for the program will be added to the Start menu, and the program can be deleted using the Add/Remove Programs function in the Control Panel.

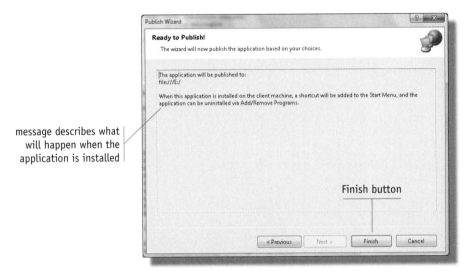

message describes what will happen when the application is installed

Finish button

FIGURE 6-92

STEP 7 Click the Finish button.

The Visual Basic window displays several messages indicating that the application is being published. The last message is "Publish succeeded" (Figure 6-93).

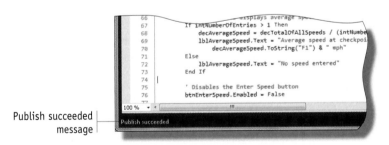

Publish succeeded message

FIGURE 6-93

STEP 8 To view the finished result, minimize the Visual Studio window, and then click Computer on the Windows 7 Start menu. Double-click the USB drive icon to view the published installation folder.

Installation files are placed on the USB drive (Figure 6-94). If all of these files are copied to a computer with the .NET framework, the program can be installed by double-clicking the setup file to begin the installation.

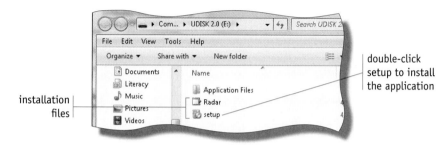

installation files

double-click setup to install the application

FIGURE 6-94

STEP 9 To install the application, double-click the setup file.

After double-clicking the setup file, the application installs on the local computer. During installation, Windows might display the Security Warning dialog box shown in Figure 6-95. This dialog box is intended to protect you from installing programs that might harm your computer. Because you know the source of this program, you can click the Install button to continue installing the program.

Security Warning dialog box

Install button

FIGURE 6-95

IN THE REAL WORLD

The installation files created by the ClickOnce Publishing Wizard can be burned to a CD or DVD and mass produced for a software release.

ONLINE REINFORCEMENT

To view a video of the process in the previous steps, visit scsite.com/vb2010/ch6 and then select Figure 6-87.

STEP 10 After installation, the program will run. To run the installed application again, click the Start button on the Windows taskbar. Point to All Programs, click Radar on the All Programs menu, and then click Radar on the Radar submenu.

Program Design

As you have learned, the requirements document identifies the purpose of the program being developed, the application title, the procedures to be followed when using the program, any equations and calculations required in the program, any conditions within the program that must be tested, notes and restrictions that must be followed by the program, and any other comments that would be helpful to understanding the problem. The requirements document for the Highway Radar Checkpoint application is shown in Figure 6-96.

REQUIREMENTS DOCUMENT

Date submitted: September 30, 2014

Application title: Highway Radar Checkpoint Application

Purpose: This application finds the average speed of vehicles on a highway with a posted speed limit of 60 mph.

Program Procedures: From a Windows application, the user enters the speed of up to 10 vehicles to compute the average speed on a highway with a posted speed limit of 60 mph.

Algorithms, Processing, and Conditions:
1. The user must be able to enter each of 10 vehicle's speeds after clicking the Enter Speed button.
2. Each speed is validated to confirm that the value is numeric and greater than zero.
3. Each vehicle speed is displayed in a ListBox object.
4. After the 10 speeds are entered or when the user clicks the Cancel button in an input box, the average speed is calculated and displayed.
5. A menu bar includes the File menu, which contains Clear and Exit items. The Clear menu item clears the result and the values representing vehicle speed. The Exit menu item closes the application.

Notes and Restrictions:
1. If a non-numeric or negative value is entered for the speed, the program should display an error message and ask the user to re-enter the value.
2. If the user clicks the Cancel button before entering any vehicle speeds, a message should indicate no speeds were entered. An average is not calculated when no speeds are entered.

Comments:
1. The picture shown in the window can be found on scsite.com/vb2010/ch6/images. The name of the picture is Radar.
2. The average speed should be formatted as a Decimal value with one decimal place.

FIGURE 6-96

The Use Case Definition shown in Figure 6-97 specifies the procedures the user will follow to use this application.

USE CASE DEFINITION

1. The Windows application opens, displaying the Highway Radar Checkpoint title, a ListBox object that will hold the numeric entries, and a Button object that allows the user to begin entering up to 10 vehicle speeds.
2. A menu bar displays the File menu, which has two menu items: Clear and Exit.
3. The user enters up to 10 values representing the vehicle speeds into an InputBox object.
4. The program asks the user for the vehicle speed again if a value is non-numeric or negative.
5. The user terminates data entry by entering 10 vehicle speeds or by clicking the Cancel button in the InputBox object.
6. The program calculates the average speed for the speeds that were entered.
7. The program displays the average vehicle speed in a Label object as a Decimal value with one decimal place.
8. The user can clear the input and the results by clicking the Clear menu item, and can then repeat steps 3 through 7.
9. The user clicks Exit on the File menu to close the application.

FIGURE 6-97

Event Planning Document

You will recall that the event planning document consists of a table that specifies an object in the user interface that will cause an event, the action taken by the user to trigger the event, and the event processing that must occur. The event planning document for the Highway Radar Checkpoint program is shown in Figure 6-98.

EVENT PLANNING DOCUMENT

Program Name: Highway Radar Checkpoint Application	Developer: Corinne Hoisington	Object: frmRadar	Date: September 30, 2014

OBJECT	EVENT TRIGGER	EVENT PROCESSING

btnEnterSpeed	Click	Display an InputBox object 10 times to obtain vehicle speeds or until the user clicks the Cancel button
		Check if strVehicleSpeed is numeric
		If vehicle speed is numeric, convert strVehicleSpeed to a decimal value
		If strVehicleSpeed is numeric, check if the value is positive
		If the vehicle speed is positive:
		    Display the vehicle speed in lstRadarSpeed
		    Accumulate the total of the speeds in decTotalOfAllSpeeds
		    Update the number of entries
		    Set the InputBox message to the normal message
		If the value entered is not numeric, display an error message in the input box
		If the value entered is not positive, display an error message in the input box
		After all speeds are entered, change the Visible property of lblAverageSpeed to true
		If one or more speeds were entered:
		    Calculate the average speed in decAverageSpeed
		    Display the average speed in lblAverageSpeed
		If no values were entered:
		    Display the text No Speed Entered
		Disable the btnEnterSpeed Button

mnuClear	Click	Clear lstRadarSpeed ListBox Change Visible property of lblAverageSpeed to False Enable btnEnterSpeed Button
mnuExit	Click	Exit the application

FIGURE 6-98

Design and Code the Program

After the events and tasks within the events have been identified, the developer is ready to create the program. As you have learned, creating the program means designing the user interface and then entering Visual Basic statements to accomplish the tasks specified on the event planning document. As the developer enters the code, she also will implement the logic to carry out the required processing.

Guided Program Development

To design the user interface for the Highway Radar Checkpoint program and enter the code required to process each event in the program, complete the steps on the following pages:

Guided Program Development

Phase 1: Design the Form

1

- **Create a Windows Application** Open Visual Studio and then close the Start page. Create a new Visual Basic Windows Forms Application project by clicking the New Project button on the Standard toolbar, selecting Visual Basic as the project type, selecting Windows Forms Application as the template, naming the project Radar in the Name text box, and then clicking the OK button in the New Project dialog box.

- **Display the Toolbox** Ensure the Toolbox is displayed in the Visual Studio window and the Common Controls are accessible.

- **Name the Windows Form Object** In the Solution Explorer window, right-click Form1.vb, click Rename, and then rename the form frmRadar.

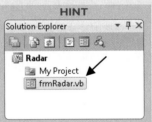

- **Change the Text on the Title Bar for the Windows Form Object** Change the title bar text of the Windows Form object to Radar Speed.

- **Change the Size of the Form Object** Resize the Form object by changing the Size property to 341, 509.

- **Add the MenuStrip Object** Drag a MenuStrip object from the Menus & Toolbars category of the Toolbox to the Windows Form object. The MenuStrip snaps into place below the title bar. Name the MenuStrip object mnuHighwayRadarCheckpoint in the Properties window. Click the Type Here box on the MenuStrip object, type &File, and then press the ENTER key. The ampersand creates a hot key for the letter F. Name the File menu item mnuFile (*ref: Figure 6-5*).

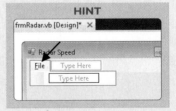

● **Add Menu Items** The next step is to add two menu items to the File menu. Click the Type Here box below the word File, and then enter &Clear. Name the Clear menu item mnuClearItem. Click the Type Here box below the Clear menu item, and then enter E&xit to make the "x" in Exit the hot key. Name the Exit menu item mnuExit (*ref: Figure 6-10*).

● **Add a PictureBox Object** Drag a PictureBox .NET component from the Toolbox to the left side of the Windows Form object. Name the PictureBox object picRadar. Change the Size property of the PictureBox object to 102, 89. Change the Location property of the PictureBox object to 13, 41.

● **Add the Title Label Object** Drag a Label .NET component onto the Windows Form object. Name the label lblTitle. Enter the text for this label as Highway Radar Checkpoint on two lines (Hint: Click the Text property list arrow in the Properties window to enter a label with multiple lines. Press the ENTER key to move to a new line.) Choose the font Tahoma, Bold font style, and 18-point size. Change the TextAlign property to MiddleCenter by clicking the TextAlign list arrow and then clicking the Center block. Change the Location property of the lblTitle Label object to 133,41.

● **Add the Posted Speed Label** Place a Label object below the lblTitle Label object. Name the second Label lblPostedSpeed. In the Text property, enter Posted Speed Limit – 60 mph. Change the Font property to Tahoma, Italic font style, and 10-point size. Align the bottom of the lblPostedSpeed Label object with the bottom of the picRadar PictureBox object. Align the center of the lblPostedSpeed label with the center of the lblTitle Label object.

(continues)

● **Add the Enter Speed Button Object** Drag a Button object onto the Windows Form object below the picture box and labels. Name the Button btnEnterSpeed. Change the text of the button to Enter Speed. Change the font to 11-point Tahoma. Resize the Button object to view the complete text. Horizontally center the button in the Windows Form object.

● **Add the ListBox Object for the Vehicle Speeds** To add the ListBox object that displays the vehicle speeds, drag a ListBox object onto the Windows Form object below the Button object. Name the ListBox lstRadarSpeed. Change the font for the text in the ListBox object to 11-point Tahoma. Resize the ListBox to the width of three characters because the top speed of a vehicle could reach speeds such as 102 mph. Lengthen the ListBox object to display 10 numbers. The Size property for the ListBox object in the sample program is 34, 184. Horizontally center the ListBox object in the Windows Form object (*ref: Figure 6-24*).

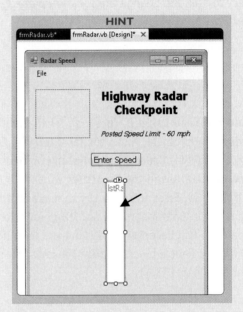

● **Add the Result Label** To add the label where the average speed message is displayed, drag a Label object onto the Windows Form object. Name the Label object lblAverageSpeed. Change the text to Average speed at checkpoint is X.XX mph. Change the font to Tahoma 10-point. Horizontally center the message in the Windows Form object.

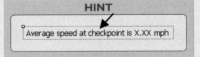

The user interface mockup is complete (Figure 6-99).

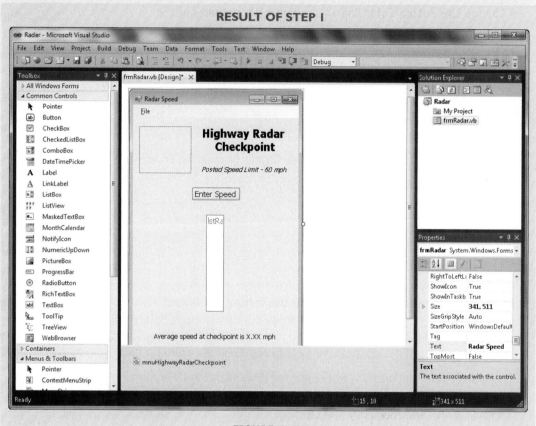

RESULT OF STEP I

FIGURE 6-99

Phase 2: Fine-Tune the User Interface

2

● **Change the BackColor Property of the Windows Form Object** Select the Windows Form object and then change its BackColor property to White on the Web tab.

● **Change the Color for the Title Label** Change the ForeColor property for the lblTitle Label object to SteelBlue on the Web tab.

(continues)

● **Change the Button Color** Change the BackColor property of the btnEnterSpeed Button object to LightSteelBlue.

● **Change the Font Color for the List Box Object** Change the ForeColor property of the lstRadarSpeed ListBox object to SteelBlue on the Web tab.

● **Insert and Size the Radar Image into the PictureBox Object** Visit scsite.com/vb2010/ch6/images and download the Radar image. Select the picRadar PictureBox object. In the Properties window, select the Image property and then click the ellipsis button in the right column. Import the Radar image from the location where you saved it. Click the OK button in the Select Resource dialog box. Select the SizeMode property, click the SizeMode arrow, and then click StretchImage.

● **Change the Visible Property for the Average Speed Label** Select the lblAverageSpeed Label object and change its Visible property to False because the Label object is not displayed until the average for the speeds entered is calculated.

HEADS UP

As you work on your program, do not forget to save it from time to time. You can save the work you have done by clicking the Save All button on the Standard toolbar.

● **Make the Enter Speed Button the Accept Button** Click the background of the Windows Form object to select it. In the Properties window, click the AcceptButton list arrow to display the buttons in the user interface. Click btnEnterSpeed in the list. During program execution, when the user presses the ENTER key, the event handler for btnEnterSpeed executes.

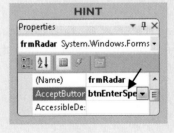

The user interface design is complete (Figure 6-100).

RESULT OF STEP 2

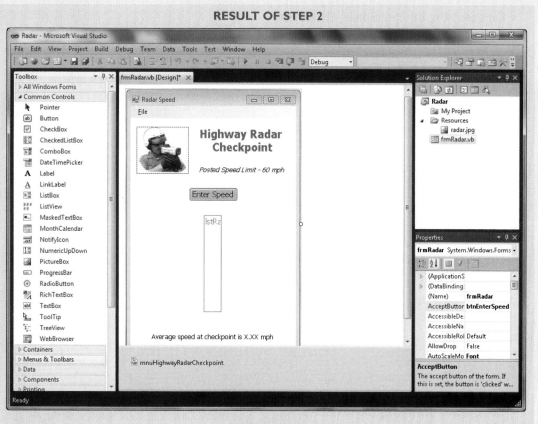

FIGURE 6-100

Phase 3: Code the Program

3

● **Enter the Comments for the Enter Speed Button Event Handler** Double-click the btnEnterSpeed Button object on the Windows Form object to open the button event handler. Insert the first four standard comments at the top of the code window. Insert the command Option Strict On at the beginning of the code to turn on strict type checking.

HINT

```
frmRadar.vb*  ×  frmRadar.vb [Design]*
btnEnterSpeed                        ▼  Click
1  ' Program Name: Radar Checkpoint Analysis
2  ' Author:       Corinne Hoisington
3  ' Date:         September 30, 2014
4  ' Purpose:      The Radar Checkpoint Analysis program requests
5  '               the speed from a highway radar checkpoint. It displays
6  '               each speed. After all speeds have been entered, it displays
7  '               the average speed for all vehicles.
8
9  Option Strict On
10
11  Public Class frmRadar
12
```

(continues)

● **Comment the btnEnterSpeed_Click Event Handler** Enter a comment to describe the purpose of the btnEnterSpeed_Click event handler.

HINT

```
13 ⊟      Private Sub btnEnterSpeed_Click(ByVal sender As System.Object, ByVal e As System.E
14              ' The btnEnterSpeed click event accepts and displays up to ten speeds
15              ' from the user, and then calculates and displays the average speed
```

● **Declare and Initialize the Variables to Calculate the Average Speed** Four variables are used to calculate the average speed (besides the vehicle count). These variables are: 1) strVehicleSpeed: Is assigned the value from the InputBox function call; 2) decVehicleSpeed: Is assigned the converted vehicle speed; 3) decAverageSpeed: Contains the calculated average speed; 4) decTotalOfAllSpeeds: The accumulator used to accumulate the total speeds entered by a user. Declare and initialize these four variables.

HINT

```
17          ' Declare and initialize variables
18
19          Dim strVehicleSpeed As String
20          Dim decVehicleSpeed As Decimal
21          Dim decAverageSpeed As Decimal
22          Dim decTotalOfAllSpeeds As Decimal = 0D
```

● **Declare and Initialize the Variables Used with the InputBox Function Call** Five variables contain messages used in the input box to obtain the vehicle speeds. These variables are: 1) strInputMessage: Is used in the function call to contain the message displayed in the input box; 2) strInputHeading: Contains the message displayed in the title bar of the input box; 3) strNormalMessage: The normal message that appears in the input box when no error has occurred; 4) strNonNumericError: The message that appears in the input box when the user has entered a non-numeric value; 5) strNegativeError: The message that appears in the input box when the user has entered zero or a negative number. Declare and initialize these five variables.

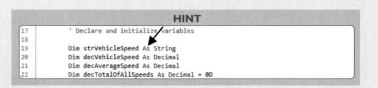

```
23          Dim strInputMessage As String = "Enter the speed for vehicle #"
24          Dim strInputHeading As String = "Radar Speed"
25          Dim strNormalMessage As String = "Enter the speed for vehicle #"
26          Dim strNonNumericError As String = "Error - Enter a number for the speed of vehicle #"
27          Dim strNegativeError As String = "Error - Enter a positive number for vehicle #"
28
```

● **Declare and Initialize Variables Used in the Loop Processing** Three variables are used for processing the loop in the program. These variables are: 1) strCancelClicked: This variable contains a null string. It is used to determine if the user clicked the Cancel button in the input box; 2) intMaxNumberOfEntries: Contains the maximum number of entries for vehicle speeds. Program requirements state the maximum number is 10; 3) intNumberOfEntries: The counter that counts the valid number of vehicle speeds entered by the user. This variable is used to determine when the maximum of entries has been made and to act as the divisor when calculating the average speed per vehicle.

HINT

```
29          'Declare and initialize loop variables
30
31          Dim strCancelClicked As String = ""
32          Dim intMaxNumberOfEntries As Integer = 10
33          Dim intNumberOfEntries As Integer = 1
34
```

● **Write Comments for the Do Until Loop and Write the Priming InputBox Function Call** You often can use comments to document a loop or other set of major processing statements. The comments here alert the reader to the role of the Do Until loop. The priming InputBox function call obtains the first vehicle speed, or allows the user to click the Cancel button. The normal message is displayed. The space at the end of the argument list places a space in the input box so if the user clicks the OK button without entering any data, it will not be treated the same as clicking the Cancel button (ref: Figure 6-70).

HINT

```
34
35          ' This loop allows the user to enter the speed of up to 10 vehicles.
36          ' The loop terminates when the user has entered 10 speeds or the user
37          ' clicks the Cancel button or the Close button in the InputBox
38
39          strVehicleSpeed = InputBox(strInputMessage & intNumberOfEntries, strInputHeading, " ")
40
```

● **Code the Do Until Loop** Because the application requests the speed of up to 10 vehicles, the Do Until loop should continue until 10 speeds are entered or until the user clicks the Cancel or Close Button in the input box. Enter the Do Until loop using IntelliSense (ref: Figure 6-59, Figure 6-65, Figure 6-70).

HINT

```
40
41          Do Until intNumberOfEntries > intMaxNumberOfEntries Or strVehicleSpeed = strCancelClicked
42
```

(continues)

● **Validate the Entry is a Number** The first process in the Do Until loop is to validate that the vehicle speed entered by the user is a numeric value. Enter the If...Then statement to test if the value in the strVehicleSpeed variable is numeric.

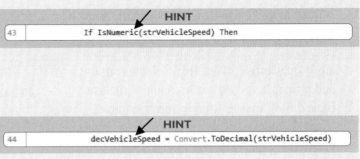

```
        HINT
43      If IsNumeric(strVehicleSpeed) Then
```

● **Convert the Value Entered from String to Decimal Data Type** If the user entered a numeric value, the next step is to convert the string value the user entered to a Decimal data type. Using IntelliSense, enter the code to convert the value in the strVehicleSpeed variable from String to Decimal data type and place the result in the decVehicleSpeed variable.

```
        HINT
44      decVehicleSpeed = Convert.ToDecimal(strVehicleSpeed)
```

● **Validate That the Entered Value is a Positive Number** After the value is converted, the program must validate that the number is positive. Write the If...Then statement to test whether the value in the decVehicleSpeed variable is greater than zero.

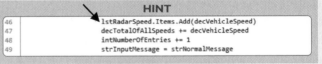

```
        HINT
45      If decVehicleSpeed > 0 Then
```

● **Perform the Processing When the User Enters a Valid Speed** After ensuring the speed entered by the user is valid, the next steps are to perform the processing for valid speeds. Four steps are required: 1) Add the speed as an item to the lstRadarSpeed ListBox object *(ref: Figure 6-28)*; 2) Add the speed the user entered to the decTotalOfAllSpeeds accumulator *(ref: Figure 6-38)*. The accumulated speed is used to calculate the average speed; 3) Increment the intNumberOfEntries counter by 1 because the user entered a valid speed *(ref: Figure 6-38)*. This value is used as the divisor to determine the average speed, and also as one of the indicators that the loop should be terminated; 4) Because the user entered a valid speed, the normal message should be displayed in the input box the next time the input box is displayed. Therefore, the normal message should be moved to the strInputMessage variable. Using IntelliSense, enter the code for these four activities.

```
        HINT
46      lstRadarSpeed.Items.Add(decVehicleSpeed)
47      decTotalOfAllSpeeds += decVehicleSpeed
48      intNumberOfEntries += 1
49      strInputMessage = strNormalMessage
```

● **Assign an Error Message if the User Entered a Negative Speed** If the user entered a negative speed, the next the input box that is displayed should show the negative number error message *(ref: Figure 6-73)*. Following the Else statement for the If statement that checks for a number greater than zero, enter the assignment statement that places the value in the strNegativeError variable in the strInputMessage variable.

```
50              Else
51                  strInputMessage = strNegativeError
52              End If
```

● **Assign an Error Message If the User Entered a Non-Numeric Speed** If the user entered a non-numeric speed, the next the input box that is displayed should show the non-numeric error message *(ref: Figure 6-73)*. Following the Else Statement for the If statement that checks for numeric data, enter the assignment statement that places the value in the strNonNumericError variable in the strInputMessage variable.

```
53              Else
54                  strInputMessage = strNonNumericError
55              End If
```

● **Code the InputBox Function Call** The first InputBox function call was placed before the Do Until loop to prime the loop. To continue the process after the first value is entered, another InputBox function is needed as the last statement inside the loop to request subsequent values. This statement should be executed only if the maximum number of entries has not been exceeded. So, an If structure is required to determine if the maximum number of entries has been reached. If not, the InputBox function call is executed *(ref: Figure 6-73)*.

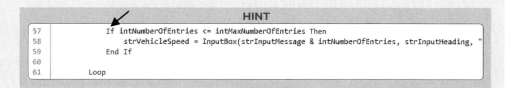

```
57          If intNumberOfEntries <= intMaxNumberOfEntries Then
58              strVehicleSpeed = InputBox(strInputMessage & intNumberOfEntries, strInputHeading, "
59          End If
60
61      Loop
```

(continues)

The coding for the variables and Do Until loop that processes the data in the program is complete (Figure 6-101). It is important that you examine the code in Figure 6-101 and understand the loop processing. The priming of the loop by both setting the value in the intNumberOfEntries value (line 33) and calling the InputBox function (line 39) is critical for proper execution of the loop. Increasing the loop counter when a valid entry is made (line 48) also is fundamental in the loop processing because testing this counter is one way the Do Until loop can be terminated. Also, using variables for messages instead literals in the actual code demonstrates how professional programs are coded. You should follow these examples in your programming.

RESULT OF STEP 3

```
18
19          Dim strVehicleSpeed As String
20          Dim decVehicleSpeed As Decimal
21          Dim decAverageSpeed As Decimal
22          Dim decTotalOfAllSpeeds As Decimal = 0D
23          Dim strInputMessage As String = "Enter the speed for vehicle #"
24          Dim strInputHeading As String = "Radar Speed"
25          Dim strNormalMessage As String = "Enter the speed for vehicle #"
26          Dim strNonNumericError As String = "Error - Enter a number for the speed of vehicle #"
27          Dim strNegativeError As String = "Error - Enter a positive number for vehicle #"
28
29          'Declare and initialize loop variables
30
31          Dim strCancelClicked As String = ""
32          Dim intMaxNumberOfEntries As Integer = 10
33          Dim intNumberOfEntries As Integer = 1
34
35          ' This loop allows the user to enter the speed of up to 10 vehicles.
36          ' The loop terminates when the user has entered 10 speeds or the user
37          ' clicks the Cancel button or the Close button in the InputBox
38
39          strVehicleSpeed = InputBox(strInputMessage & intNumberOfEntries, strInputHeading, " ")
40
41          Do Until intNumberOfEntries > intMaxNumberOfEntries Or strVehicleSpeed = strCancelClicked
42
43              If IsNumeric(strVehicleSpeed) Then
44                  decVehicleSpeed = Convert.ToDecimal(strVehicleSpeed)
45                  If decVehicleSpeed > 0 Then
46                      lstRadarSpeed.Items.Add(decVehicleSpeed)
47                      decTotalOfAllSpeeds += decVehicleSpeed
48                      intNumberOfEntries += 1
49                      strInputMessage = strNormalMessage
50                  Else
51                      strInputMessage = strNegativeError
52                  End If
53              Else
54                  strInputMessage = strNonNumericError
55              End If
```

FIGURE 6-101 (continues)

```
56
57              If intNumberOfEntries <= intMaxNumberOfEntries Then
58                  strVehicleSpeed = InputBox(strInputMessage & intNumberOfEntries, strInputHeading, " ")
59              End If
60
61          Loop
```

FIGURE 6-101 (continued)

4

● **Set the Result Label's Visible Property** When you finish the Do Until loop, you must complete three tasks to finish the Enter Speed button click event handler: 1) The label that will contain the average speed must be made visible; 2) The average speed must be calculated and displayed; 3) The Enter Speed button must be disabled. Using IntelliSense, write the code to make the lblAverageSpeed label visible.

```
                        HINT
63          ' Makes label visible
64          lblAverageSpeed.Visible = True
```

● **Calculate the Average Speed** To calculate the average of the speeds the user entered, the value in the decTotalOfAllSpeeds variable must be divided by the number of vehicles for which speeds were entered. At the end of the loop shown in Figure 6-101, the value in the intNumberOfEntries variable always will be one greater than the actual number of vehicles entered, so the total of all speeds must be divided by the value in the intNumberOfEntries less 1. This calculation should occur only if one or more vehicle speeds were entered, so an If statement must be used to check if the value in the intNumberOfEntries variable is greater than 1. If so, the average speed is calculated; if not, the "No speed entered" message should be displayed. Using IntelliSense, write the code to perform this processing.

```
                        HINT
66          'Calculates and displays average speed
67          If intNumberOfEntries > 1 Then
68              decAverageSpeed = decTotalOfAllSpeeds / (intNumberOfEntries - 1)
69              lblAverageSpeed.Text = "Average speed at checkpoint is " & _
70                  decAverageSpeed.ToString("F1") & " mph"
71          Else
72              lblAverageSpeed.Text = "No speed entered"
73          End If
```

(continues)

Guided Program Development *continued*

● **Change the Enter Speed Button Enabled Property to False** After the average speed is calculated and displayed, the Enabled property of the btnEnterSpeed button is set to False to dim the button. Using IntelliSense, write the code to accomplish this processing.

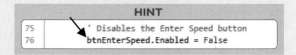

HINT	
75	' Disables the Enter Speed button
76	btnEnterSpeed.Enabled = False

The code for the btnEnterSpeed button click event handler is completed (Figure 6-102).

RESULT OF STEP 4

```
13    Private Sub btnEnterSpeed_Click(ByVal sender As System.Object, ByVal e As System.EventArgs) Handles btnEnterSpeed.Click
14        ' The btnEnterSpeed click event accepts and displays up to ten speeds
15        ' from the user, and then calculates and displays the average speed
16
17        ' Declare and initialize variables
18
19        Dim strVehicleSpeed As String
20        Dim decVehicleSpeed As Decimal
21        Dim decAverageSpeed As Decimal
22        Dim decTotalOfAllSpeeds As Decimal = 0D
23        Dim strInputMessage As String = "Enter the speed for vehicle #"
24        Dim strInputHeading As String = "Radar Speed"
25        Dim strNormalMessage As String = "Enter the speed for vehicle #"
26        Dim strNonNumericError As String = "Error - Enter a number for the speed of vehicle #"
27        Dim strNegativeError As String = "Error - Enter a positive number for vehicle #"
28
29        'Declare and initialize loop variables
30
31        Dim strCancelClicked As String = ""
32        Dim intMaxNumberOfEntries As Integer = 10
33        Dim intNumberOfEntries As Integer = 1
34
35        ' This loop allows the user to enter the speed of up to 10 vehicles.
36        ' The loop terminates when the user has entered 10 speeds or the user
37        ' clicks the Cancel button or the Close button in the InputBox
38
39        strVehicleSpeed = InputBox(strInputMessage & intNumberOfEntries, strInputHeading, " ")
40
41        Do Until intNumberOfEntries > intMaxNumberOfEntries Or strVehicleSpeed = strCancelClicked
42
43            If IsNumeric(strVehicleSpeed) Then
44                decVehicleSpeed = Convert.ToDecimal(strVehicleSpeed)
45                If decVehicleSpeed > 0 Then
46                    lstRadarSpeed.Items.Add(decVehicleSpeed)
47                    decTotalOfAllSpeeds += decVehicleSpeed
48                    intNumberOfEntries += 1
49                    strInputMessage = strNormalMessage
50                Else
51                    strInputMessage = strNegativeError
52                End If
53            Else
54                strInputMessage = strNonNumericError
55            End If
```

FIGURE 6-102 (continues)

```
56
57              If intNumberOfEntries <= intMaxNumberOfEntries Then
58                  strVehicleSpeed = InputBox(strInputMessage & intNumberOfEntries, strInputHeading, " ")
59              End If
60
61          Loop
62
63          ' Makes label visible
64          lblAverageSpeed.Visible = True
65
66          'Calculates and displays average speed
67          If intNumberOfEntries > 1 Then
68              decAverageSpeed = decTotalOfAllSpeeds / (intNumberOfEntries - 1)
69              lblAverageSpeed.Text = "Average speed at checkpoint is " & _
70                  decAverageSpeed.ToString("F1") & " mph"
71          Else
72              lblAverageSpeed.Text = "No speed entered"
73          End If
74
75          ' Disables the Enter Speed button
76          btnEnterSpeed.Enabled = False
77
78      End Sub
```

FIGURE 6-102 (continued)

(continues)

Guided Program Development *continued*

5

● **Run the Program** After coding a major section of the program, you should run the program to ensure it is working properly. Click the Start Debugging button on the Standard toolbar to run the Highway Radar Checkpoint program. Click the Enter Speed button and then enter a vehicle speed 10 times. Verify the speeds are displayed properly and the average speed is correct. Close the program by clicking the Close button. Run the program again, click the Enter Speed button, enter four vehicle speeds, enter a non-numeric speed, enter a speed that is less than zero, and then click the Cancel button in the input box. Ensure the speeds are displayed properly, the average speed is correct, and the error messages are displayed properly in the input box. Close the program. Run the program again, click the Enter Speed button, and then click the Cancel button in the input box. Ensure the no speed entered message is displayed. Close the program and then run it as many times as necessary to ensure the program is working properly. If the program does not run properly, consider setting a breakpoint and checking the values in the variables *(ref: Figure 6-76)*.

HINT

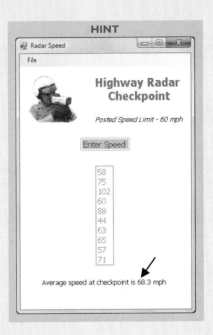

6

● **Enter the Code for the Clear Menu Item Click Event** Click the frmRadar.vb[Design]* tab in the code editing window to display the design window. Click File on the MenuStrip object, and then double-click the Clear menu item to open the Clear click event handler in the code editing window. The Clear click event handler must perform three tasks: 1) Clear the lstRadarSpeed list box; 2) Hide the average speed Label object; 3) Enable the Enter Speed Button object. Using IntelliSense, write the code for these three tasks.

HINT

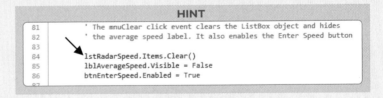

```
81          ' The mnuClear click event clears the ListBox object and hides
82          ' the average speed label. It also enables the Enter Speed button
83
84          lstRadarSpeed.Items.Clear()
85          lblAverageSpeed.Visible = False
86          btnEnterSpeed.Enabled = True
87
```

● **Enter the Code for the Exit Menu Item Click Event** Return to the design window. Double-click the Exit menu item. In the code window, enter a Close procedure call that will close the window and terminate the program.

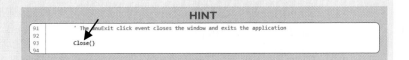

HINT

```
91        ' The mnuExit click event closes the window and exits the application
92
93        Close()
94
```

The code for the Clear menu item click event and the Exit menu item click event is completed (Figure 6-103). The program code for the program is done.

RESULT OF STEP 6

```
80  Private Sub mnuClear_Click(ByVal sender As System.Object, ByVal e As System.EventArgs) Handles mnuClearItem.Click
81        ' The mnuClear click event clears the ListBox object and hides
82        ' the average speed label. It also enables the Enter Speed button
83
84        lstRadarSpeed.Items.Clear()
85        lblAverageSpeed.Visible = False
86        btnEnterSpeed.Enabled = True
87
88  End Sub
89
90  Private Sub mnuExit_Click(ByVal sender As System.Object, ByVal e As System.EventArgs) Handles mnuExitItem.Click
91        ' The mnuExit click event closes the window and exits the application
92
93        Close()
94
95  End Sub
96
97  End Class
98
99
```

FIGURE 6-103

(continues)

7

● **Publish the Highway Radar Checkpoint Pro-gram Option** After completing the program, you can publish it using ClickOnce deployment so it can be installed on multiple computers. To open the Publish Wizard and begin the deployment process, click Build on the menu bar and then click Publish Radar on the Build menu *(ref: Figure 6-87)*.

● **Select the Publish File Location** The Publish Wizard dialog box asks where you want to pub-lish the application. Change the default location to the same file location that you used to save your Windows application by clicking the Browse button and then selecting the drive. For example, select the E: drive, a USB drive. After selecting the drive, click the Next button in the Publish Wizard dialog box *(ref: Figure 6-88)*.

● **Select How the Users Will Install the Appli-cation** In the next Publish Wizard dialog box, select the option that lets users install the ap-plication from a CD-ROM or DVD-ROM. Then, click the Next button *(ref: Figure 6-90)*.

● **Indicate the Application Will Not Check for Updates** Click the The application will not check for updates radio button to indicate no updates will be checked. This is the normal selection when programs are placed on CDs or DVDs. Then, click the Next button in the Publish Wizard dialog box *(ref: Figure 6-91)*.

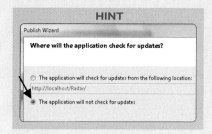

● **View the Summary Window** The Publish Wizard summary is displayed. Click the Finish button to publish the application *(ref: Figure 6-92)*.

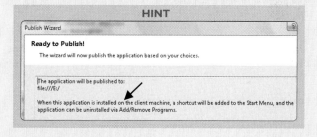

● **View the Installation Files** After the publishing succeeds, a folder is created with the installation files that could be placed on a CD, DVD, or other computer *(ref: Figure 6-94)*.

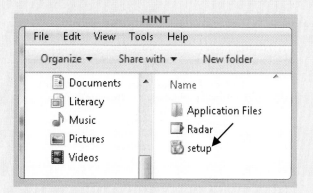

(continues)

Code Listing

The complete code for the sample program is shown in Figure 6-104.

```vb
1    ' Program Name: Radar Checkpoint Analysis
2    ' Author:        Corinne Hoisington
3    ' Date:          September 30, 2014
4    ' Purpose:       The Radar Checkpoint Analysis program requests
5    '                the speed from a highway radar checkpoint. It displays
6    '                each speed. After all speeds have been entered, it displays
7    '                the average speed for all vehicles.
8
9    Option Strict On
10
11   Public Class frmRadar
12
13       Private Sub btnEnterSpeed_Click(ByVal sender As System.Object, ByVal e As System.EventArgs) Handles btnEnterSpeed.Click
14           ' The btnEnterSpeed click event accepts and displays up to ten speeds
15           ' from the user, and then calculates and displays the average speed
16
17           ' Declare and initialize variables
18
19           Dim strVehicleSpeed As String
20           Dim decVehicleSpeed As Decimal
21           Dim decAverageSpeed As Decimal
22           Dim decTotalOfAllSpeeds As Decimal = 0D
23           Dim strInputMessage As String = "Enter the speed for vehicle #"
24           Dim strInputHeading As String = "Radar Speed"
25           Dim strNormalMessage As String = "Enter the speed for vehicle #"
26           Dim strNonNumericError As String = "Error - Enter a number for the speed of vehicle #"
27           Dim strNegativeError As String = "Error - Enter a positive number for vehicle #"
28
29           'Declare and initialize loop variables
30
31           Dim strCancelClicked As String = ""
32           Dim intMaxNumberOfEntries As Integer = 10
33           Dim intNumberOfEntries As Integer = 1
34
35           ' This loop allows the user to enter the speed of up to 10 vehicles.
36           ' The loop terminates when the user has entered 10 speeds or the user
37           ' clicks the Cancel button or the Close button in the InputBox
38
39           strVehicleSpeed = InputBox(strInputMessage & intNumberOfEntries, strInputHeading, " ")
40
41           Do Until intNumberOfEntries > intMaxNumberOfEntries Or strVehicleSpeed = strCancelClicked
42
43               If IsNumeric(strVehicleSpeed) Then
44                   decVehicleSpeed = Convert.ToDecimal(strVehicleSpeed)
45                   If decVehicleSpeed > 0 Then
46                       lstRadarSpeed.Items.Add(decVehicleSpeed)
47                       decTotalOfAllSpeeds += decVehicleSpeed
48                       intNumberOfEntries += 1
49                       strInputMessage = strNormalMessage
50                   Else
51                       strInputMessage = strNegativeError
52                   End If
53               Else
54                   strInputMessage = strNonNumericError
55               End If
56
57               If intNumberOfEntries <= intMaxNumberOfEntries Then
58                   strVehicleSpeed = InputBox(strInputMessage & intNumberOfEntries, strInputHeading, " ")
59               End If
60
61           Loop
62
63           ' Makes label visible
```

FIGURE 6-104 (continues)

```vb
64            lblAverageSpeed.Visible = True
65
66            'Calculates and displays average speed
67            If intNumberOfEntries > 1 Then
68                decAverageSpeed = decTotalOfAllSpeeds / (intNumberOfEntries - 1)
69                lblAverageSpeed.Text = "Average speed at checkpoint is " & _
70                    decAverageSpeed.ToString("F1") & " mph"
71            Else
72                lblAverageSpeed.Text = "No speed entered"
73            End If
74
75            ' Disables the Enter Speed button
76            btnEnterSpeed.Enabled = False
77
78        End Sub
79
80        Private Sub mnuClear_Click(ByVal sender As System.Object, ByVal e As System.EventArgs) Handles mnuClearItem.Click
81            ' The mnuClear click event clears the ListBox object and hides
82            ' the average speed label. It also enables the Enter Speed button
83
84            lstRadarSpeed.Items.Clear()
85            lblAverageSpeed.Visible = False
86            btnEnterSpeed.Enabled = True
87
88        End Sub
89
90        Private Sub mnuExit_Click(ByVal sender As System.Object, ByVal e As System.EventArgs) Handles mnuExitItem.Click
91            ' The mnuExit click event closes the window and exits the application
92
93            Close()
94
95        End Sub
96
97    End Class
98
99
```

FIGURE 6-104 (continued)

Summary

In this chapter you have learned to design and write code to implement loops and to create menus, list boxes, and an input box. The items listed in the following table include all the new Visual Studio and Visual Basic skills you have learned in this chapter.

Visual Basic Skills		
Skill	**Figure Number**	**Web Address for Video**
Place a MenuStrip object on the Windows Form object	Figure 6-5	scsite.com/vb2010/ch6/figure6-5
Code the Exit menu item event	Figure 6-12	scsite.com/vb2010/ch6/figure6-12
Insert a full standard menu	Figure 6-14	scsite.com/vb2010/ch6/figure6-14
Code the InputBox function	Figure 6-17	
Add a ListBox object	Figure 6-24	scsite.com/vb2010/ch6/figure6-24
Add an item to a ListBox object	Figure 6-27	
Add items to a ListBox object during design	Figure 6-32	scsite.com/vb2010/ch6/figure6-32
Assign a selected item from a ListBox object	Figure 6-36	
Write code using compound operators	Figure 6-39	
Write the code for a For...Next loop	Figure 6-42	
Use IntelliSense to enter the code for a For...Next loop	Figure 6-50	scsite.com/vb2010/ch6/figure6-50
Write code for a top-controlled Do While loop	Figure 6-56	
Use IntelliSense to code a Do While loop	Figure 6-59	scsite.com/vb2010/ch6/figure6-59
Write code for a bottom-controlled Do While loop	Figure 6-62	
Write code for a top-controlled Do Until loop	Figure 6-65	
Write code for a bottom-controlled Do Until loop	Figure 6-67	
Avoid infinite loops	Figure 6-69	
Prime a loop	Figure 6-70	
Validate data	Figure 6-73	
Create a nested loop	Figure 6-74	
Set a breakpoint and use a DataTip	Figure 6-76	scsite.com/vb2010/ch6/figure6-76
Publish an application with ClickOnce deployment	Figure 6-87	scsite.com/vb2010/ch6/figure6-87

FIGURE 6-105

Learn It Online

Start your browser and visit scsite.com/vb2010/ch6. Follow the instructions in the exercises below.

1. **Chapter Reinforcement TF, MC, SA** Click one of the Chapter Reinforcement links for Multiple Choice, True/False, or Short Answer below the Learn It Online heading. Answer each question and submit to your instructor.

2. **Practice Test** Click the Practice Test link below Chapter 6. Answer each question, enter your first and last name at the bottom of the page, and then click the Grade Test button. When the graded practice test is displayed on your screen, submit the graded practice test to your instructor. Continue to take the practice test until you are satisfied with your score.

3. **Crossword Puzzle Challenge** Click the Crossword Puzzle Challenge link below the Learn It Online heading. Read the instructions, and then click the Continue button. Work the crossword puzzle. When you are finished, click the Submit button. When the crossword puzzle is redisplayed, submit it to your instructor.

Knowledge Check

1. Write a statement that displays the default value of 12.50 in the input box shown in Figure 6-106 and assigns the return value from the InputBox function to a variable named strPayRate.

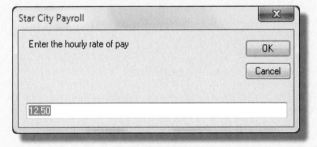

FIGURE 6-106

2. Write compound operators for the following equations:

   a. intTouchdown = intTouchdown + 6

   b. dblSquare = dblSquare ^ 2

   c. strFast = strFast & "Comet"

3. Write For...Next loops that calculate the sum of the following ranges and assign their sum to a variable named intSum:

   a. The first 100 numbers starting with number 1.

   b. The even numbers beginning at 10 and ending with 50.

   c. The numbers 20, 30, 40, 50, and 60.

(continues)

4. Find the errors in the following For...Next header statements:

   a. For intCounter = "1" To "19"

   b. For intNumber = 98 To 71 Step 2

   c. For intValue = 12 To 52 Step −4

   d. For strCount = −15 To 5 Step 5

5. Explain the purpose of placing an ampersand before or within a MenuStrip item.

6. Write the command to clear a ListBox object named lstBaseballPlayers.

7. Write a command to add your favorite sports team to a ListBox object named lstFavoriteTeam.

8. Using a compound operator, write an assignment statement to increment the value in intAmount by 7.

9. Using a compound operator, write an assignment statement to decrease the value in intCounter by 4.5.

10. Using a compound operator, write an assignment statement to increment the value in intQuantity by 10.

11. Write a top-controlled Do Until loop with an empty body that would continue until intValue is greater than 19.

12. Write a bottom-controlled Do While loop with an empty body that continues while the user enters "Yes" into the strContinue variable.

13. Write a Do While loop to validate that the user enters a non-zero integer into an input box for a variable named intDenominator.

14. Is the For...Next loop top-controlled or bottom-controlled?

15. Write the code for an infinite Do Until loop with the variable intInfinite.

16. Which loop should be used if you know the required number of times the loop will be executed?

17. What is the fewest number of times a top-controlled Do Until loop is executed?

18. Write a data validation Do loop to check that the variable intAge entered from an input box is between 1 and 115.

19. A loop inside another loop is called a _____ _____.

20. When you insert standard items in a MenuStrip object, what File menu items are automatically created by default?

Debugging Exercises

1. The loop shown in Figure 6-107 should repeat 10 times. If it will not repeat 10 times, change the code so it will.

```
7        For intRepeat = 20 To 10
8            MsgBox("The value is " & intRepeat.ToString("C0"))
9        Next
```

FIGURE 6-107

2. What output does the code shown in Figure 6-108 produce? How would you change the code to produce a list box containing the values 12-20?

```
15       intRate = 12
16       Do While intRate <= 10
17           lstDisplay.Items.Add(intRate)
18           intRate += 1
19       Loop
```

FIGURE 6-108

3. What is the output of the code shown in Figure 6-109?

```
5        Dim intAdd As Integer
6        Dim intOuterLoop As Integer
7        Dim intInnerLoop As Integer
8
9        intAdd = 0
10       For intOuterLoop = 1 To 8
11           For intInnerLoop = 3 To 7
12               intAdd += 1
13           Next
14       Next
         MsgBox.Show("The final value is " & intAdd.ToString())
```

FIGURE 6-109

(continues)

4. What is the output of the code shown in Figure 6-110?

```
33          Dim intValue As Integer
34
35          intValue = 2
36          Do While intValue <= 9
37              lstDisplay.Items.Add(intValue & " " & intValue ^ 3)
38              intValue += 2
39          Loop
```

FIGURE 6-110

5. Fix the errors in the loop shown in Figure 6-111.

```
41          Dim intStart As Integer = 8
42
43          Loop
44          intStart = +4
45          Do While intStart < 24
```

FIGURE 6-111

6. What is the output of the code shown in Figure 6-112?

```
53          intCount = 40
54          Do Until intCount < 26
55              intCount -= 2
56              lstCount.Items.Add(intCount)
57          Loop
```

FIGURE 6-112

7. Fix the errors in the code shown in Figure 6-113.

```
5           Dim decCost As Decimal = 3.5D
6
7           Do Until decCost > 10.5D
8               MsgBox("The cost is now " & decCost.ToString("F1"))
9               decCost -= 0.5
10          Loop
```

FIGURE 6-113

Debugging Exercises *continued*

8. In the example shown in Figure 6-114, you want the code to count the odd numbers from 1 to 99. What is missing?

```
66          Dim intOddNumber As Integer = 1
67
68          Do While intOddNumber <= 99
69              lstDisplay.Items.Add("Odd Numbers: " & intOddNumber.ToString())
70          Loop
```

FIGURE 6-114

Program Analysis

1. What is the value of lblResult after the code shown in Figure 6-115 is executed?

```
73          Dim intCounter As Integer = -20
74
75          Do While intCount < 25
76              intCount += 5
77              lblResult.Text &= intCount.ToString() & " "
78          Loop
```

FIGURE 6-115

2. What is the value of lblResult after the code shown in Figure 6-116 is executed?

```
80          Dim intCountIt As Integer
81
82          intCountIt = 6
83          Do
84              intCountIt += 3
85              lblResult.Text &= intCountIt.ToString() & " "
86          Loop Until intCountIt = 21
```

FIGURE 6-116

(continues)

3. Rewrite the top-controlled Do While loop shown in Figure 6-117 as a top-controlled Do Until loop.

```
88          Dim intQuantity As Integer
89
90          intQuantity = -5
91          Do While intQuantity < 30
92              intQuantity += 5
93          Loop
```

FIGURE 6-117

4. Convert the Do loop shown in Figure 6-118 to a For...Next loop:

```
95          Dim intIncrease As Integer
96
97          intIncrease = 10
98          Do While intIncrease < 40
99              lstDisplay.Items.Add(intIncrease)
100             intIncrease += 2
101         Loop
```

FIGURE 6-118

5. How many times will the inner statement inside the nested loop in Figure 6-119 be executed?

```
103         For intOuterLoop = 3 To 5
104             For intInnerLoop = 6 To 10
105                 lstDays.Items.Add("Value: " & intOuterLoop.ToString() & _
106                     " Count: " & intInnerLoop.ToString())
107             Next
108         Next
```

FIGURE 6-119

6. How many times will the loop in Figure 6-120 be executed?

```
110        Dim intQuantitySold As Integer
111        Dim decTax As Decimal
112
113        intQuantitySold = 1
114        Do Until intQuantitySold = 5
115            decTax = intQuantitySold * 0.07
116            lstDisplay.Items.Add("Tax Amount: " & decTax.ToString())
117            intQuantitySold += 1
118        Loop
```

FIGURE 6-120

7. Write a For...Next loop that adds the odd numbers 1 through 49 and assigns their sum to the variable intSum. The program should start with the lines shown in Figure 6-121 (use the following variables in your code).

```
120        Dim intLoopValue As Integer
121        Dim intStartvalue As Integer
122        Dim intEndvalue As Integer
123        Dim intSum As Integer
124
125        intStartvalue = 1
126        intEndvalue = 49
127        intSum = 0
```

FIGURE 6-121

Case Programming Assignments

Complete one or more of the following case programming assignments. Submit the program and materials you create to your instructor. The level of difficulty is indicated for each case programming assignment.

● = Easiest
●● = Intermediate
●●● = Challenging

1 ●

AVERAGE TEMPERATURE IN PARADISE

Design a Windows application and write the code that will execute according to the program requirements shown in Figure 6-122. Before writing the code, create an event planning document for each event in the program. The Use Case Definition document is shown in Figure 6-123 on the next page. The completed user interface is shown in Figure 6-124 on the next page.

REQUIREMENTS DOCUMENT

Date submitted: March 17, 2014

Application title: Hawaiian Average Temperature

Purpose: This Windows application is written for the Hawaiian Tourism Board with the task of calculating the yearly average temperature in the Hawaiian Islands for one year.

Program Procedures: In a Windows application, the user enters up to 12 average monthly temperatures to compute the annual average temperature in the Hawaiian islands.

Algorithms, Processing, and Conditions:
1. The user enters up to 12 monthly average temperatures for Hawaii in an InputBox object.
2. Each month's average temperature is displayed in a ListBox object.
3. After the 12 temperatures are entered, the average temperature is calculated and displayed.
4. A File menu contains a Clear and an Exit option. The Clear menu item clears the average and the 12 values representing the monthly temperatures. The Exit menu item closes the application.
5. If the user clicks the Cancel button before entering 12 values, compute the average for the number of months entered.
6. If the user clicks the Cancel button before entering any temperatures, display a message indicating the user did not enter a temperature.

Notes and Restrictions:
1. Non-numeric values should not be accepted.
2. Negative values should not be accepted.
3. The average temperature should be rounded to the nearest tenth.

Comments:
1. The application allows decimal entries.
2. Obtain the image from scsite.com/vb2010/ch6/images. Its name is Beach.

FIGURE 6-122

USE CASE DEFINITION

1. The Windows application opens, displaying the Hawaiian Tourism Board Average Temperature title, a ListBox object that displays the temperatures, an image, and a Button object that allows the user to begin entering the temperatures.
2. A menu bar displays the File menu, which has two menu items: Clear and Exit.
3. The user enters up to 12 values in an InputBox object, with each value representing an Hawaiian monthly average temperature.
4. The program asks the user for the temperature again if the value is a negative number or the entry is a non-numeric value.
5. The program displays the average temperature rounded to one decimal place.
6. The user can clear the input and the result by clicking the Clear menu item, and then can repeat steps 3-5. If the user clicks the Cancel button, the average for the values entered is calculated. If the user did not enter any values, the program displays an appropriate message.
7. The user clicks the Exit menu item to close the application.

FIGURE 6-123

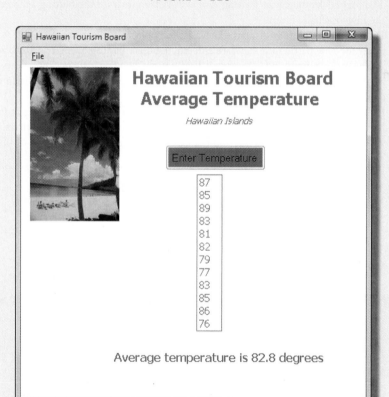

FIGURE 6-124

2 • BATTING AVERAGE

Design a Windows application and write the code that will execute according to the program requirements shown in Figure 6-125. Before writing the code, create an event planning document for each event in the program. The Use Case Definition document is shown in Figure 6-126 on the next page. The completed user interface is shown in Figure 6-127 on the next page.

REQUIREMENTS DOCUMENT

Date submitted:	July 31, 2014
Application title:	Little League Batting Average Windows Application
Purpose:	This Windows application finds the average batting average of the starting line-up of nine little league baseball players.
Program	In a Windows application, the user enters the present batting average of each of the nine starting line-up players to compute the team batting average.

Algorithms, Processing, and Conditions:

1. The user clicks the Enter Batting Averages button to enter the batting average for each of the nine baseball players.
2. Each batting average is displayed in a ListBox object.
3. After the nine batting averages are entered, the team batting average is displayed.
4. A File menu contains a Clear and an Exit option. The Clear menu item clears the team batting average and the nine individual batting averages. The Exit menu item closes the application.
5. If the user clicks the Cancel button after entering one but before entering nine players' batting averages, use the batting averages the user entered for the calculations.
6. If the user clicks the Cancel button before entering any batting averages, display an appropriate message.

Notes and Restrictions:

1. The result should go out three places past the decimal.
2. Non-numeric values should not be accepted.
3. Negative numbers should not be accepted.

Comments:

1. The application allows decimal entries.
2. Obtain the image from scsite.com/vb2010/ch6/images. Its name is Baseball.

FIGURE 6-125

USE CASE DEFINITION

1. The Windows application opens, displaying the little league team name as the title, a ListBox object that will display the batting averages, and a Button object that allows the user to enter the batting averages.
2. A menu bar displays the File menu, which has two menu items: Clear and Exit.
3. In an InputBox object, the user enters up to nine values, one at a time, representing the batting averages of the starting line-up of the team.
4. The program asks the user for the batting average again if the value is a negative or non-numeric number.
5. The program displays the team batting average out to 3 decimal places.
6. The user clicks the Clear menu item to clear the input and the result.
7. If the user clicks the Cancel button before entering nine batting averages, the program uses the batting averages entered for calculations. If the user entered no batting averages, an appropriate message is displayed.
8. The user clicks the Exit menu item to close the application.

FIGURE 6-126

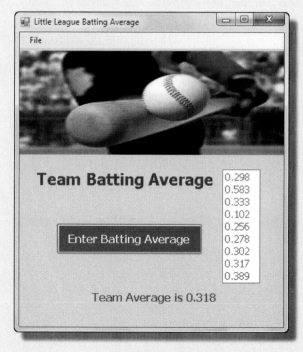

FIGURE 6-127

Case Programming Assignments *continued*

3 • FOOTBALL FEVER SCOREBOARD

Design a Windows application and write the code that will execute according to the program requirements shown in Figure 6-128. Before writing the code, create an event planning document for each event in the program. The Use Case Definition document is shown in Figure 6-129 on the next page. The completed user interface is shown in Figure 6-130 on the next page.

REQUIREMENTS DOCUMENT

Date submitted: November 3, 2014

Application title: Football Fever Scoreboard Windows Application

Purpose: This application calculates the points scored during a football game by one team.

Program Procedures: In a Windows application, the user enters each score one football team makes to display the team's score on the scoreboard.

Algorithms, Processing, and Conditions:

1. The user clicks the Enter Score button in an InputBox object to enter a score after the football team scores points in a game.
2. Each score and the running total is displayed in a ListBox.
3. After the user clicks the Cancel button in the InputBox object to end the game scoring, the total final score is displayed.
4. A File menu contains a Clear and an Exit option. The Clear menu item clears the result and the football scores. The Exit menu item closes the application.

Notes and Restrictions:

1. Non-numeric values should not be accepted.
2. A negative value should not be accepted.
3. Obtain the image from scsite.com/vb2010/ch6/images. Its name is Football.

Comments: n/a

FIGURE 6-128

USE CASE DEFINITION

1. The Windows application opens, displaying your favorite football team's name, scoreboard subtitle, a ListBox object that will display the football team scores throughout the game, and a Button object that allows the user to enter the scores.
2. A menu bar displays the File menu, which has two menu items: Clear and Exit.
3. In an InputBox object, the user enters points a football team scores.
4. The program asks the user for the score again if the value is a negative or non-numeric number.
5. The program displays the total score.
6. The program displays the final score when the user clicks the Cancel button in the input box.
7. The user clicks the Clear menu item to clear the input and the result.
8. The user clicks the Exit menu item to close the application.

FIGURE 6-129

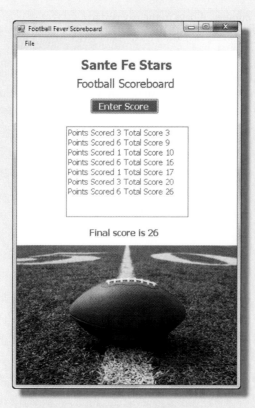

FIGURE 6-130

Case Programming Assignments *continued*

4 ●● DOUBLE YOUR PAY

Design a Windows application and write the code that will execute according to the program requirements shown in Figure 6-131. Before writing the code, create an event planning document for each event in the program. Create a Use Case Definition document for the application.

REQUIREMENTS DOCUMENT

Date submitted: June 21, 2014

Application title: Double Your Pay Windows Application

Purpose: This Windows application finds the amount of your pay if your pay is doubled each day, starting with a penny a day or a nickel a day. Instead of one month's salary, a boss offers her new employees a penny the first day and experienced employees a nickel the first day under the new pay system. Each day the pay will double.

Program Procedures: In a Windows application, the user enters the number of days in a pay period and the pay for the first day. The program calculates and displays the amount of pay for the pay period.

Algorithms, Processing, and Conditions:

1. The user enters the number of days in the pay period.
2. The user selects a RadioButton object to indicate the pay amount of the first day: a penny or a nickel.
3. After the user enters the number of days and pay for the first day, the total amount earned is calculated and displayed.
4. A File menu contains a Clear and an Exit option. The Clear menu item clears the result and the RadioButton objects. The Exit menu item closes the application.

Notes and Restrictions:

1. Non-numeric values should not be accepted.
2. Negative values should not be accepted.
3. The minimum number of days for the pay period is 19 days for the new employees and 16 days for the experienced employees. The maximum number of days in a pay period is 22 days.

Comments: n/a

FIGURE 6-131

5 ● ●

DISTANCE TRAVELED CALCULATOR

Design a Windows application and write the code that will execute according to the program requirements shown in Figure 6-132. Before writing the code, create an event planning document for each event in the program. Create a Use Case Definition document for the application.

REQUIREMENTS DOCUMENT

Date submitted: December 5, 2014

Application title: Vacation Distance Calculator Windows Application

Purpose: This application computes the number of miles traveled given the speed limit and the number of days traveled driving cross country.

Program Procedures: In a Windows application, the user enters the speed limit and the number of days you plan to travel cross country. You will enter the number of hours you would like to drive each of the days based on places you plan to visit as you drive and other factors. For example, the first day you plan to drive only 4 hours because you are driving after work. The application displays the distance that you are able to travel for the entire trip based on the speed limit and the hours driven.

Algorithms, Processing, and Conditions:
1. The application opens displaying a title. The user enters the speed limit and the number of days you plan to drive.
2. The user clicks the Distance button to request the number of hours you plan to drive each day. The result of the total number of miles you plan to drive over the entire trip will be displayed.
3. A File menu contains a Clear and an Exit option. The Clear menu item clears the result and the entered number of miles per hour and time traveled. The Exit menu item closes the application.

Notes and Restrictions:
1. Non-numeric values should not be accepted.
2. The number of hours for one day of travel should not exceed 20 hours.

Comments:
1. The application allows decimal entries.

FIGURE 6-132

6

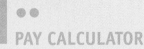

PAY CALCULATOR

Design a Windows application and write the code that will execute according to the program requirements shown in Figure 6-133. Before writing the code, create an event planning document for each event in the program. Create a Use Case Definition document for the application.

Requirements Document

Date submitted: August 23, 2014

Application title: The Next Decade Pay Calculator

Purpose: This Windows application computes the amount of money an employee earns over the next decade based on a raise, which is a percentage amount.

Program Procedures: In a Windows application, the user enters the present wage per hour and the raise percentage amount per year to compute the yearly pay over the next 10 years.

Algorithms, Processing, and Conditions:
1. The application opens displaying a title and requesting the amount of present pay per hour and the expected raise percentage per year.
2. When the Compute Future Pay button is clicked, the program calculates the yearly pay based on 40 hours per week and 52 weeks per year. The raise increases each amount after the first year.
3. The yearly amount of pay earned is displayed for the next 10 years.
4. A File menu contains a Clear and an Exit option. The Clear menu item clears the result. The Exit menu item closes the application.

Notes and Restrictions:
1. Non-numeric values should not be accepted.
2. Negative numbers should not be allowed.

Comments:
1. The application allows decimal entries.

FIGURE 6-133

Case Programming Assignments *continued*

7 ●●● FACTORIAL MATH

Create a requirements document and a Use Case Definition document, and design a Windows application based on the case project shown in Figure 6-134:

> Most calculators have an operation called a "factorial" which is shown on a calculator key as an exclamation point. For example 5! (5 factorial) multiplies 5 * 4 * 3 * 2 * 1 to calculate the result of 120. Using loops to compute the factorial, display the following factorials in a Listbox object:
>
> 1! 1
>
> 2! 2
>
> 3! 6
>
> 4! 24
>
> 5! 120
>
> 6! 720
>
> 7! 5040
>
> 8! 40320
>
> 9!

FIGURE 6-134

8 ● ● ●
GALAXY HOTEL

Create a requirements document and a Use Case Definition document, and design a Windows application based on the case project shown in Figure 6-135:

The Galaxy Hotel asks you to write a Windows application that computes the occupancy rate of the hotel. Occupancy rate is a percentage that is equal to the number of rooms sold divided by the total number of rooms available. The hotel has seven floors. The user should use an InputBox function to respond to two questions about each floor: How many rooms are occupied on that floor? How many rooms on the floor are vacant? Display which floor you are asking about in each question. Display how many rooms are occupied and vacant on each floor in a ListBox object. After the user has entered all the information, display the following results: the total number of rooms at the hotel, the number of occupied rooms, and the number of vacant rooms. Also display the occupancy rate as a percentage, such as 61%. Non-numeric values should not be accepted. Do not accept negative numbers. Publish the application after testing the application.

FIGURE 6-135

9 ● ● ●
BUYING A GAMING COMPUTER

Create a requirements document and a Use Case Definition document, and design a Windows application based on the case project shown in Figure 6-136:

The newest gaming computer costs $5000 for 31-inch screen, two 1 TB hard drives, a metallic case, and a blazing fast processor. Ten years ago, your grandmother gave you $2500. The money has been in a savings CD that earns compound interest of 7.5% per year. Write a Windows application that allows you to enter the amount in savings, the interest rate, and the number of years. Display a ListBox object with each year and the amount the entire account is worth at the end of that year. Determine whether you have saved enough money for the gaming computer. Non-numeric and negative values should not be accepted. Debug, and then publish the application. *Hint*: The formula for compound interest for one year is:

Amount = Principal * (1 + Rate). For 10 years of compound interest, this formula should be executed 10 times with the principal increasing to the new amount each year.

FIGURE 6-136

APPENDIX A

Unicode

The 256 characters and symbols that are represented by ASCII and EBCDIC codes are sufficient for English and western European languages (see Figure A-1), but do not provide enough characters for Asian and other languages that use different alphabets. Further compounding the problem is that many of these languages use symbols, called ideograms, to represent multiple words and ideas. One solution to the problem of accommodating universal alphabets is Unicode. Unicode is a 16-bit coding scheme that can represent all the world's current, classic, and historical languages in more than 65,000 characters and symbols. In Unicode, 30,000 codes are reserved for future use, such as ancient languages, and 6,000 codes are reserved for private use. Existing ASCII coded data is fully compatible with Unicode because the first 256 codes are the same. Unicode is implemented in several operating systems, including Windows 7, Windows Vista, Windows XP, Mac OS X, and Linux. To view a complete Unicode chart, see www.unicode.org.

UNICODE KEYBOARD CHARACTERS				
Decimal	**Hexadecimal**	**Octal**	**Binary**	**Character**
32	20	040	00100000	
33	21	041	00100001	!
34	22	042	00100010	"
35	23	043	00100010	#
36	24	044	00100100	$
37	25	045	00100101	%
38	26	046	00100110	&
39	27	047	00100111	'
40	28	050	00101000	(
41	29	051	00101001	)

FIGURE A-1 (continues)

Decimal	Hexadecimal	Octal	Binary	Character
42	2A	052	00101010	*
43	2B	053	00101011	+
44	2C	054	00101100	,
45	2D	055	00101101	-
46	2E	056	00101110	.
47	2F	057	00101111	/
48	30	060	00110000	0
49	31	061	00110001	1
50	32	062	00110010	2
51	33	063	00110011	3
52	34	064	00110100	4
53	35	065	00110101	5
54	36	066	00110110	6
55	37	067	00110111	7
56	38	070	00111000	8
57	39	071	00111001	9
58	3A	072	00111010	:
59	3B	073	00111011	;
60	3C	074	00111100	<
61	3D	075	00111101	=
62	3E	076	00111110	>
63	3F	077	00111111	?
64	40	100	01000000	@
65	41	101	01000001	A
66	42	102	01000010	B
67	43	103	01000011	C
68	44	104	01000100	D
69	45	105	01000101	E
70	46	106	01000110	F

FIGURE A-1 (continued)

Decimal	Hexadecimal	Octal	Binary	Character
71	47	107	01000111	G
72	48	110	01001000	H
73	49	111	01001001	I
74	4A	112	01001010	J
75	4B	113	01001011	K
76	4C	114	01001100	L
77	4D	115	01001101	M
78	4E	116	01001110	N
79	4F	117	01001111	O
80	50	120	01010000	P
81	51	121	01010001	Q
82	52	122	01010010	R
83	53	123	01010011	S
84	54	124	01010100	T
85	55	125	01010101	U
86	56	126	01010110	V
87	57	127	01010111	W
88	58	130	01011000	X
89	59	131	01011001	Y
90	5A	132	01011010	Z
91	5B	133	01011011	[
92	5C	134	01011100	\
93	5D	135	01011101	]
94	5E	136	01011110	^
95	5F	137	01011111	]
96	60	140	01100000	,
97	61	141	01100001	a
98	62	142	01100010	b

FIGURE A-1 (continues)

Decimal	Hexadecimal	Octal	Binary	Character
99	63	143	01100011	c
100	64	144	01100100	d
101	65	145	01100101	e
102	66	146	01100110	f
103	67	147	01100111	g
104	68	150	01101000	h
105	69	151	01101001	i
106	6A	152	01101010	j
107	6B	153	01101011	k
108	6C	154	01101100	l
109	6D	155	01101101	m
110	6E	156	01101110	n
111	6F	157	01101111	o
112	70	160	01110000	p
113	71	161	01110001	q
114	72	162	01110010	r
115	73	163	01110011	s
116	74	164	01110100	t
117	75	165	01110101	u
118	76	166	01110110	v
119	77	167	01110111	w
120	78	170	01111000	x
121	79	171	01111001	y
122	7A	172	01111010	z
123	7B	173	01111011	{
124	7C	174	01111100	|
125	7D	175	01111101	}
126	7E	176	01111110	~

FIGURE A-1 (continued)

The My Namespace

Rapid application development (RAD) uses a number of tools to help build graphical user interfaces that would normally take a large development effort. One of the Visual Basic RAD tool innovations introduced in the 2005 version and continued with the 2010 version is the **My** namespace. The My namespace provides a shortcut to several categories of information and functionality and is organized so that you can use IntelliSense to find code elements you use often. Microsoft created the My namespace to make it easier to execute common code patterns that you use when developing .NET applications. By providing a shortcut to the most commonly used .NET Framework Class Library classes and methods, the My namespace helps you retrieve settings and resources that your application requires.

The My namespace feature provides rapid access to the classes and methods through the My classes shown in the table in Figure B-1.

Object	Allows Access to
My.Application	The application information and its services such as name, version, log, and current directory.
My.Computer	The host computer and its resources, and services. My.Computer provides access to a number of very important resources including My.Computer.Network, My.Computer.FileSystem, and My.Computer.Printers.
My.Forms	All the forms in the current project.
My.Request	The current Web request.
My.Resources	The resource elements.
My.Response	The current Web response.
My.Settings	The configuration settings of the user and application level. This object enables great personalization without writing many lines of code.

FIGURE B-1 (continues)

Object	Allows Access to
My.User	The security context of the current authenticated user. The My.User object analyzes the user at runtime, which assists security issues.
My.WebServices	The XML Web services referenced by the current project. Consuming Web services is a necessary ability for modern Web applications.

FIGURE B-1 (continued)

Coding Examples

My is a wrapper that makes accessing the advanced features of .NET easier. For example, you can use the class **My.Application** to determine the version of the current application by using the line of code shown in Figure B-2. Figure B-3 shows the dialog box that displays the version number. You often need to know the latest version of the application to determine whether the application is in final form.

```
MsgBox(My.Application.Info.Version.ToString())
```

FIGURE B-2

FIGURE B-3

The **My.Application** class can also be used to display the current setting of the culture of a computer. Figure B-4 shows the code you can use to display the culture, which is the language that the computer has been assigned in the language settings. In Figure B-5, the culture is set to English – United States.

```
MsgBox(My.Application.Culture.ToString())
```

FIGURE B-4

FIGURE B-5

Another class called **My.Computer** can return information about the computer on which the application is deployed, as determined at run time. The My.Computer class provides properties for manipulating computer components such as audio, the clock, the keyboard, and the file system. The My.Computer class can play .wav files and system sounds using the Audio object. You can use the My.Computer.Audio.Play and My.Computer.Audio.PlaySystemSound methods to play .wav sound files and system sounds. The code shown in Figure B-6 plays a .wav file named beachmusic.wav.

```
My.Computer.Audio.Play("C:\beachmusic.wav")
```

FIGURE B-6

A .wav file can also be played in the background when a file named AudioPlayMode.Background is specified, as shown in Figure B-7.

```
My.Computer.Audio.Play("C:\blues.wav", _
            AudioPlayMode.Background)
```

FIGURE B-7

The My.Computer class can access the Clipboard and show what is temporarily stored in the system buffer. For example, if you copied the phrase, "Examples of the My.Computer class", the phrase would be stored in the Clipboard system buffer of the computer. Use the code shown in Figure B-8 to display the contents of the Clipboard in a dialog box as shown in Figure B-9.

```
MsgBox(My.Computer.Clipboard.GetText())
```

FIGURE B-8

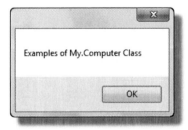

FIGURE B-9

The My.Computer class can access an object that provides properties for displaying the current local date and time according to the system clock by entering the code shown in B-10. Figure B-11 on the next page shows the dialog box that displays the system date and time.

```
MsgBox(My.Computer.Clock.LocalTime.ToString())
```

FIGURE B-10

FIGURE B-11

Another My.Computer class determines the current state of the keyboard, such as which keys are pressed, including the CAPS LOCK or NUM LOCK key. The code shown in Figure B-12 provides a true result if the CAPS LOCK key has been pressed. Figure B-13 shows the dialog box that displays the result.

```
MsgBox(My.Computer.Keyboard.CapsLock.ToString())
```

FIGURE B-12

FIGURE B-13

The My.Computer.Mouse class allows you to determine the state and hardware characteristics of the attached mouse, such as the number of buttons or whether the mouse has a wheel. The code shown in Figure B-14 determines if the mouse has a wheel, and Figure B-15 shows the dialog box that displays the result.

```
MsgBox(My.Computer.Mouse.WheelExists.ToString())
```

FIGURE B-14

FIGURE B-15

The My.Computer.Network class interacts with the network to which the computer is connected. For example, if the code in Figure B-16 is entered in the code window, the result would be true, as shown in Figure B-17 on the next page, if the computer is connected to an intranet or Internet network.

```
MsgBox(My.Computer.Network.IsAvailable.ToString())
```

FIGURE B-16

FIGURE B-17

You can use the My.Computer.Network class to ping another computer. Ping is a basic network function that allows you to verify a particular IP address exists and can accept requests. Ping is used diagnostically to ensure that a host computer you are trying to reach is operating. The code shown in Figure B-18 determines if the IP address is active, and the dialog box shown in Figure B-19 displays the result.

```
MsgBox(My.Computer.Network.Ping("71.2.41.1"))
```

FIGURE B-18

FIGURE B-19

The My.Computer.Screen object can be used to determine many properties of the screen connected to the computer system. You can determine the properties of each monitor attached to the computer system, including the name, the brightness of the screen, and the working area size. The number of bits per pixel can be determined by the code shown in Figure B-20. In a digitized image, the number of bits used to represent the brightness contained in each pixel is called bits per pixel. Bits per pixel is a term that represents the brightness of the screen resolution. Figure B-21 shows the result of the code.

```
MsgBox(My.Computer.Screen.BitsPerPixel.ToString())
```

FIGURE B-20

FIGURE B-21

The My.Computer.Screen class can also display the current resolution of the user screen, as shown in Figures B-22 and B-23 on the next page.

```
MsgBox(My.Computer.Screen.Bounds.Size.ToString())
```

FIGURE B-22

FIGURE B-23

Another class called **My.User** allows you to gather information about the current user. The code example in Figure B-24 shows how to use the **My.User.Name** property to view the user's login name. An application uses Windows authentication by default, so **My.User** returns the Windows information about the user who started the application, as shown in Figure B-25.

```
MsgBox(My.User.Name)
```

FIGURE B-24

FIGURE B-25

The My namespace also provides a simpler way of opening multiple forms in the same project by using the My.Forms object. If the project includes more than one form, the code shown in Figure B-26 opens a second form named Form2.

```
My.Forms.Form2.Show()
```

FIGURE B-26

Naming Conventions

The table in Figure C-1 displays the common data types used in Visual Basic 2010 with the recommended naming convention for the three-character prefix preceding variable names of the data type.

Data Type	Sample Value	Memory	Range of Values	Prefix
Integer	48	4 bytes	−2,147,483,648 to +2,147,483,647	int
Double	5.3452307	8 bytes	−1.79769313486232E308 to +1.79769313486232E308	dbl
Decimal	3.14519	16 bytes	Decimal values that may have up to 29 significant digits	dec
Char	'?' or 'C'	2 bytes	Single character	chr
String	"The Dow is up .03%"	Depends on number of character	Letters, numbers, symbols	str
Boolean	True or False	Typically 2 bytes; depends on implementing platform	True or False	bln

FIGURE C-1

The table in Figure C-2 displays the less common data types used in Visual Basic 2010 with the recommended naming convention for the three-character prefix preceding variable names of the data type.

Data Type	Sample Value	Memory	Range of Values	Prefix
Byte	7	1 byte	0 to 255	byt
Date	April 22, 2010	8 bytes	0:00:00 (midnight) on January 1, 0001 through 11:59:59 PM on December 31, 9999	dtm
Long	345,234,567	8 bytes	$-9,223,372,036,854,775,808$ to $+9,223,372,036,854,775,807$	lng
Object	Holds a reference	4 bytes (32-bit) 8 bytes (64-bit)	A memory address	obj
Short	16,567	2 bytes	$-32,786$ to $32,767$	shr
Single	234,654.1246	4 bytes	$-3.4028235E+38$ to $-1.401298E-45$ for negative values and $1.401298E-45$ to $3.4028235E+38$ for positive values	sng

FIGURE C-2

Form Object Naming Conventions

The table in Figure C-3 displays the prefix naming conventions for Form objects. The three-letter prefixes used before variables names are especially helpful when you use IntelliSense.

Object Type	Prefix	Object Type	Prefix
Button	btn	ListBox	lst
Calendar	cld	MenuStrip	mnu
CheckBox	chk	NumericUpDown	nud
ComboBox	cbo	PictureBox	pic
CompareValidator	cmv	RadioButton	rad
DataGrid	dgd	RangeValidator	rgv
DateTimePicker	dtp	RegularExpressionValidator	rev
DropDownList	ddl	RequiredFieldValidator	rfv
Form	frm	TextBox	txt
GroupBox	grp	ValidationSummary	vsm
Label	lbl		

FIGURE C-3

INDEX

A

AbortRetryIgnore message button type, 308

Accept button, 210–211, 264, 438

AcceptButton Button object, 438

AcceptButton property, 210–211, 264

Account Balance label, 7

Account Number text box, 7

accumulator, **396**

actions, undoing and redoing, 56

Action Tags, 204, **386**

ActiveX Data Objects. *See* ADO (ActiveX Data Objects)

addition, 234–235

addition arithmetic operator (+), **234–235**

Addition compound operator (+=), 397

Add procedure, 391

ADO (ActiveX Data Objects), 22

ADO.NET 4.0, 22–23

Align command, 63

alignment, **62**

Align submenu, 63, 90, 258

AndAlso logical operator, 332

And logical operator, **329–330**

applications, **5**

    database applications, **25**

    description of, 34

    device-specific, 25

    mobile applications, **25**

    Office applications, **25**

    programming languages and, 34

    Web site applications, **25**

    Windows applications, **25**

arguments, **229**

arithmetic expressions

    comparing to data types, 319

    literals, 234–235

    parentheses () and, 239

    variables, 234

arithmetic operations, 196, 232

    addition, 234–235

    arithmetic operators, **233**

    arithmetic results, 235

    assignment statement, 232

    Char variable, 223

    displaying numeric output data, 239–242

    division, 236–237

    exponentiation, 237–238

    hierarchy of operations, 238–239

    multiple, 238

    multiplication, 235

    number of positions after decimal point, 241–242

    numeric data types, **219–221**

    precision specifiers, **241–242**

    subtraction, 235

arithmetic operators, **233**

    addition arithmetic operator (+), **234–235**

    exponentiation arithmetic operator (^), 237–238

    integer division operator (\), 236–237

    MOD operator, 237

    multiplication operator (*), 235

    normal division operator (/), 236

    subtraction arithmetic operator (-), **235**

arithmetic results, 235

arithmetic statements and numeric variables, 228

ASCII codes, APP1

As keyword, 213, 215

ASP.NET 4.0, 23

    Web site applications, **25**

assignment statements, **133**, **214–220**

    arithmetic operations, 232

    assigning SelectedItem property to variable, 395

    compound operators, **396–398**

    equal sign (=) and, 214

    identifying variable to which value will be copied, 214

    IntelliSense and, 215–219

    literals, 222, **224**

    multiple arithmetic operations, 238

    property value, 133

    replacing procedure call, 230

    sequence of calculations, 238–239

    variable used before declaring, 227

Audio object, APP7

AudioPlayMode.Background file, APP7

Auto Hide button, **38**

Auto Hide mode, **38**

AutoSize property, 69, **123**

B

BackColor, 114–117
    Button objects, 160–161, 263
    darker and lighter colors, 116
    forms, 263
    palettes, 115
BackColor property, 160, 161, 263, 345, 437
BASIC (Beginner's All-purpose Symbolic Instructional Code)
    language, 19
beachmusic.wav file, APP7
Beginner's All-purpose Symbolic Instructional Code language.
    See BASIC (Beginner's All-purpose Symbolic Instructional
    Code) language
Bell Labs, 19
Bing Web site, 117
blnFullTimeStudent variable, 223
bln prefix, 223
block-level scope, 327–328
blue snap lines, **72–73**, 89
body of loop, 399–400
Boolean data type, 223
Boolean variables and bln prefix, 223
Both command, 88
bottom-controlled Do Until loops, 411–412
bottom-controlled Do While loops, 409–410
Bottoms command, 63
break mode, 417
Breakpoint command, 418, 424
breakpoints, **417**
    removing, 424–425
    running and testing program, 420
    setting, 418–423
Breakpoint submenu, 418, 424
btEnterSpeed Button object, 436
btnCalclulateCost Button object, 262
btnCalculate Button object, 349, 350
btnCalculate_Click event handler, 350
btnCalculateCost Button object, 211, 265
btnCalculateCost_Click event handler, 265, 266
btnClear Button object, 262, 349
btnDeluxeRoom Button object, 71, 90, 172
btnDeluxeRoom event handler, 173
btnEnterSpeed Button object, 438, 439, 446
btnEventSpeed_Click event handler, 440
btnExit Button object, 262
btnExitWindow Button object, 93, 166
btnExitWindow event handler, 175

btn prefix, 67
btnSelectRoom Button object, 127, 142
    disabling, 172
    Enabled property, 166, 174
btnStandardRoom Button object, 90, 172
btnStandardRoom_Click event handler, 138, 141, 158,
    168–169
btnStandardRoom event handler, 166
build errors message, **149–150**
Build menu, 425, 450
Button1 button, 66
Button class, 21
Button .NET component, 21, 70, 89, 93
Button objects, **65–66**, 81, 89, 93, 436
    aligning, 70–71
    AutoSize property, 69
    BackColor property, 160–161, 263
    btn prefix, 67
    disabled, **126–128**
    enabled, **126–128**
    Enabled property, 141–143
    moving, 69
    naming, 67, 71, 90
    resizing, 68–69, 71, 90
    text, 66, 67, 71
    Text property, 90
    triggering event, 158
    unselecting, 71
    vertically aligning, 72–73
buttons, 22, 65–66, 81, 262
    adding, 70–71
    aligning, 70–73
    centering, 262
    changing text and font style, 262
    clicking to trigger events, 244
    color, 438
    horizontally aligning, 70–71
    message box, 306–307
    resizing, 262
    spacing, 70, 262
    vertically aligning, 72–73
Byte data type, 223

C

C, 19
C++, 19, 20
Cabinets.jpg picture, 349

Calculate button click event handler, 305
Calculate button event handler, 247
Calculate Cost button, 248, 262
    as Accept button, 210–211, 264
Calculate Values button, 404
calculations and numeric data, 10
camel case, 36
Campus Parking Fees window, 13
Cancel button, 211
CancelButton property, 264
cascading style sheets, 23
Case Else statement, 334
case insensitivity, 19
Case statements, 334, 335
_cdecPricePerDownload class variable, 266
cdecPricePerDownload variable, 226, 232, 246–248
CenterImage option, **123**
Center in Form command, 54, 64, 86, 88
Center in Form submenu, 54, 65, 86, 88, 90, 256, 262
Centers command, 90
central processing unit. *See* CPU (central processing unit)
characters, 222–223, 316
Char data type, **222–223**
Char variable
    arithmetic operations, 223
    chr prefix, 222
Checked property, 300–301, 326
Choose Course Level GroupBox object, 303
Choose Semester GroupBox object, 303
chr prefix, 222
chrTopGrade Char variable, 222
classes, **21–22**, 25, **229**
    ADO.NET 4.0, 22
    ASP.NET 4.0, 23
    containing procedure, 229
    instance, **21**
    prebuilt, 22
    scope, 247–248
class libraries, **21–22**, 25
class variables, reverenced in more than one
    event handler, 266
Clear button, 242, 262
Clear Button event handler, 269
Clear Button object as Cancel button, 264
Clear command, 380, 381, 384, 435
Clear Menu Item Click event, 448
Clear method, 392

Clear procedure, 242
Click event, 139, 153
Click event handler, 130–131, 168
ClickOnce Deployment, **425–429**, 450
Clipboard
    accessing, APP7
    viewing system buffer, APP7
Close() procedure, 154–156, 175, 229, 385, 449
Close Project dialog box, 74
CLR (Common Language Runtime), **23–25**
code
    blue squiggly line, 153
    blue text for errors, 151
    comment statements, **143–148**
    continuing line of, 246
    correcting errors, 148–153
    events, 154
    executing exact number of times, 399–405
    preparation for entry, 211–212
    printing, 156–157
code editing window, 131, 175
    blank line, 167
    btnDeluxeRoom event handler, 173
    btnStandardRoom event handler, 166
    frmDigitalDownloads.vb [Design] tab, 269
    introductory comments, 167
    location of error, 150
    moving insertion point, 152
    positioning insertion point, 167
code library code snippets, **337–339**
Code Patterns - If, For Each, Try Catch, Property, etc.
    folder, 338
code snippets, **337–339**
coding programs, 159
coding statements, 131–132
color
    buttons, 438
    labels, 437
    list box, 438
    palettes, 115–116
color window, 115
comments
    code, 154
    event handler, 168–169, 173, 175
    green text, 145, 147, 149
    ignored by compiler, 144
    introductory, 146–148

preceding with apostrophe, 144, 145
same line, 145
without leading apostrophe, 148–149
comment statements, **143–148**
Common Language Runtime. *See* CLR (Common Language Runtime)
comparing
data types, 317–318
strings, 316–317
comparisons, 11
equal condition, 12–13
greater than condition, 15
less than condition, 14
compiler, comments ignored by, 144
components interaction, 3–4
Component Tray, 382
compound conditions, **329**
combining conditions, 329–330
connecting, 330–331
expressed negatively, 331
Not logical operator, **331**
Or logical operator, **330–331**
compound operators, **396–398**
computer hardware, **3**
computer programmers, **5**
computer programs, **2**, 3–4
computers, 2
arithmetic operations, 10–11
computer hardware, **3**
computer software, 3
CPU (central processing unit), **4**
data, **3–4**
human languages used by, APP6
information about, APP7
input, 10
pinging, APP9
properties for manipulating components, APP7
RAM (random access memory), **4**
computer software, **2**, 3
Concatenate compound operator (&=), 397
concatenation, **246–247**, 269
strings, 311
concatenation operator (&), **246**, 311, 398
Conditionals and Loops folder, 338
conditional statements, **312–341**
If...Then statements, 312–313
relational operators, 313–318

conditions
combining into compound condition, 329–330
multiple, 320
relational operators, 313
repeating instructions, 378
testing, 312, 320
true and false, 318–319
confirmation message
displaying, 172
Visible property, 165
console applications, 25
constants, 225–226, 246
constant variables, **226**
Const keyword, 226
container objects, 302–303
controlling objects, 61, 62
controls, **19**
Windows applications, 25
control structures
decision structures, **312**
looping structure, **378**
control variables, 400–401
Convert class, 230
converting data, 228–231
cost per download, 245–247
counters, **396**
c prefix, 226
CPU (central processing unit), **4**
Currency(C) format specifier, 241
currency format, 293
Custom palette, **115**

D

data, **3–4**
arithmetic operations, 196
checking for positive number, 341
checking validity, 293
converting, 228–231
displaying, 390–395
editing, 22–23
entering, 6
getting, 22
information, **4**
input data, **3**
masks, 205–208
output data, **4**
persistent, **4**

processing, **3**
RAM (random access memory), 10–11
saving, **4**, 16
storing, **4**, 9
testing input for numeric value, 340–341
TextBox object, 204
updating, 23
users entering, 197–208
validating, 339–341, 414–416
databases, **16**, 22–23
databases applications, **25**
DataTips, **417**, 421, 422, 424
data types
    automatically converting, 231
    Boolean data type, 223
    Byte data type, 223
    Char data type, **222–223**
    comparing, 317–319
    converting, 228–231
    Date data type, 223
    Decimal data type, **221**
    Double data type, **221**
    forced literal types, 225
    Integer data type, **220**
    literals, 224
    Long data type, 223
    naming conventions, APP11–APP12
    numeric, 219–221
    Object data type, 223
    omitting, 220
    preventing conversion, 231
    Short data type, 223
    Single data type, 223
    String data type, **213–214**
date, properties for displaying, APP7
Date data type, 223
dbl prefix, 221
dblTaxRate Double variable, 221
debugging, 248–250, **417**
decAmount variable, 411
decAverageSpeed variable, 440
decCherryCost variable, 327
decCostPerFoot variable, 351
decCosts variable, 235
decFootage variable, 311
Decimal data type, **221**, 246
    converting string value to, 442
    converting to String data type, 246–247

Decimal Division compound operator (\=), 397
decimal numbers, 221
Decimal numeric variable, 239
Decimal variables, 214, 221
decInternetTicketCost variable, 235
decision making and conditional statements, **312–341**
decision-making statements, 292
decision structures, **312**, 337
decNewProfit variable, 235
decNumericValue variable, 241
decOakCost variable, 327
decOldBalance variable, 238
decPineCost variable, 326–327
dec prefix, 221
decPrice variable, 234
decRevenue variable, 235
decTax variable, 234
decTemperature variable, 240
decTicketCost variable, 235
decTotalCostOfDownloads variable, 232–233, 266–267
decTotalOfAllSpeeds variable, 415, 417, 419, 422, 423, 440, 442, 445
decTotalPay variable, 234
decTotalVehicleSpeed variable, 396
decVehicleSpeed variable, 391, 421, 440, 442
decWithdrawals variable, 238, 319
default font, 51–53
Define Color window, 115
Delete Breakpoint command, 424
Delete command, 56
DELETE key, 55
Delphi, 20
Deluxe Room button, 71, 72, 81, 158
DeluxeRoom image, 162–163, 165
Deluxe Room image, 173
DeluxeRoom PictureBox object, 169, 173
deploying projects, 425–429
designing
    programs, 30
    user interface, 78–80
design principles, **79–80**
design window, 175, 269
Determine Day of Week program, 333–334
developers, **5**
    IntelliSense, 134
    understanding problem to be solved, 76
    writing procedures, 156
devices, input and output, 9

dialog boxes
    See also message box
    prompting for value, 387
Digital Downloads form, loading, 244–247
Digital Downloads program, 247
    arithmetic operations, 232
    Calculate Cost button, 196, 244, 248
    Clear button, 196, 242
    code listing, 271–272
    coding, 253, 265–270
    comments, 265
    event planning document, 252
    Exit button, 196
    form loading event handler, 244–247
    guided program development, 253–270
    numeric value for number of song downloads, 248–249
    Overflow Exception, **250**
    price per download, 246
    program design, 250–253
    requirements document, 251
    running, 268
    testing, 270
    use case definition, 252
    user interface, 196, 197–212
    user interface mockup, 254–262
Dim keyword, 213, 215
Dim statement, 216, 220, 221, 223
disabled, **126–128**
Display Account Balance button, 7, 8, 21
Display Tuition button, 13
Divide By Zero Exception, **250**
dividing by zero, 236, 250
division, 236–237
divisor, 236
Dockable mode, 38
documenting
    program, **75–76**
    program requirements, 76–78
Do loops, **405–410**, 417
    bottom-controlled, **406**
    top-controlled, 406
dot operator (period), 132, 133, 230
Double data type, **221**
Double variables, 221
Do Until keywords, 410
Do Until loops, **406**, 410–413, 416–417
    bottom-controlled, 411–412
    coding, 441, 444

    comments, 441
    priming InputBox function, 441
    top-controlled, 410–411
    validating data, 442
Do While keywords, 406, 408
Do While loops, **405**, 417
    bottom-controlled, 409–410
    infinite loops, **412**
    IntelliSense, 408
    top-controlled, 406–407
downloading
    calculating cost of, 267
    images, 117
Download Music title, 254

E

EBCDIC codes, APP1
ellipsis button, 51
Else keyword, 318–319, 321–324
enabled, **126–128**
Enabled property, **126–128**, 141–143, 166, 174, 446
End If keyword, 312–315, 318, 322
End Select statement, 334
End Sub statement, 131, 227
Enter Speed button, 438
Enter Speed button event handler, 439, 445
equal condition, 12–13
Equal to (=) relational operator, 313
Error List window, **150–153**
error messages, 303–304
    assigning, 443
errors
    correcting in code, 148–153
    Divide By Zero Exception, **250**
    Format Exception, 248–250
    Overflow Exception, **250**
event-driven programs, **5–8**, 20, 32, 129–130
event handlers, 153, 244
    class variables referenced in, 266
    click event, 130–131
    code, 327
    comments, 168–169, 173, 175
    If...Then...Else statements, 328
    menu items, 385
    program code, **130–131**
    variables referenced in multiple, 247
event planning document, **157–159**, 252

events, **6**, 129, **157**
  clicking button to trigger, 244
  entering code, 154
  GUI object triggering, 130
  list of tasks for, 158–159
  triggering, 6–8, 20, 158
Exit button, 262
Exit Button event handler, 269
Exit command, 380, 381, 384–385, 435
Exit Menu item Click event, 449
Exit Window button, 81, 153, 166, 172
Exit Window Button object, 93
Exit Window event handler, 154
exponentiation, 237–238
exponentiation arithmetic operator (^), 237–238
Exponents compound operator (^=), 397

F

File menu, 75, 156, 380, 381, 383
  adding commands to, 384, 435
  Exit command, 384
  hot keys, 434–435
  standard items, 387
Fixed(F) format specifier, 241
floating-point numbers, 221
FlowLayoutPanel container object, 302
focus, setting, 243–244
Focus procedure, 244
Font dialog box, 52–53, 85–86, 256, 262
Font property, **51**, 85, 201, 256, 260
fonts
  Label object, 85, 92, 258
  TextBox object, 260
font size, 51–53
font style, 51–53, 85
forced literal types, 225
ForeColor property, **115–116**, 437–438
For keyword, 399
For loops, nested, 416
Format, Center in Form command, 256, 262
Format, Make Equal command, 262
Format, Make Same Size command, 262
Format Exception, 248–250
Format menu, 54, 60–61, 63–64, 71, 86, 88, 90, 258
format specifiers
  ToString function, **240–241**
formatting numbers, 240

Form1 default text value, 42
form load event, 244, 247
Form Load event handler, 269
Form objects naming conventions, APP12
forms
  BackColor, 263
  Label object, 45–46
  naming, 345
  opening multiple, APP10
  resizing, 44–45
Form1.vb [Design] tabbed page, 37, 75
Form1.vb file, 40–41
For...Next loops, 399–405, 416
  control variable, 399–400
  IntelliSense, 402–404
  mathmatical expressions, 401
  Step value, 400–401
  user input and, 404–405
  variables, 401
fractional exponent, 238
frmDigitalDownloads class, 265
frmDigitalDownloads.vb [Design] tabbed page, 198
frmDigitalDownloads.vb file, 254
frmHotelRoomSelection form, 84
frmHotelRoomSelection.vb [Design] tab, 130, 175
frmHotelRoomSelection.vb file, 41
frmHotelRoomSelection.vb tab, 153
frmHotelRoomSelection.vb* tab, 131
frmHotelRoomSelection Windows Form object, 160
frm prefix, 40, 67
frmRadar form, 434
frmWoodCabinets Form object, 346
frmWoodCabinets.vb file, 345
Function procedures, **229–230**
functions, **229**

G

General(G) format specifier, 241
global variables, **228**
Google Web site, 117
graphical user interfaces. *See* GUIs (graphical user interfaces)
greater than condition, 15
Greater than or equal to (>=) relational operator, 313
Greater than (>) relational operator, 313
green text, 145, 147, 149

GroupBox object, 294, 347
    borders, 302
    grp prefix, 295
    (Name) property, 295, 296
    placing, 295–296
    resizing, 297
    Size property, 297
    Text property, 295
groups, associating items as, 294–297
grp prefix, 295
grpWoodType GroupBox object, 296, 347
GUI object triggering event, 130
GUIs (graphical user interfaces), **5–8**, 32
    alignment, **62**
    Button object, **65–66**
    buttons, 22
    controls, **19**
    designing, 78–80
    entering data, 6
    identifying object to trigger event, 158
    mock-up, 82, 112
    naming objects, 39–41
    .NET components, **18**
    objects, **19**, 80
    TextBox objects, **197–208**
    users, 79
    Windows Form object, 37

H

hardware, 3
heading label, 257
Highway Radar Checkpoint program, 378
    breakpoints, 417
    calculating average speed, 396
    closing, 448
    code listing, 452–453
    coding, 439–451
    comments, 439–440
    counter, 396
    designing and coding, 433
    designing form, 434–437
    displaying data, 390–395
    Do loop, 405
    event planning document, 432
    features, 379–380
    File menu, 380, 381
    fine-tuning user interface, 437–439

guided program development, 433–451
    InputBox object, 387, 389
    installation files, 451
    list box, 390–395
    priming the loop, 413
    program design, 430–433
    publishing, 425–429, 450–451
    requirements document, 430
    running, 448
    Use Case Definition, 431
    user interface design, 380–398
    validating data, 415
Horizontally command, 65, 86, 90
Horizontal Spacing submenu, 262
Hotel Room Selection label, 49
Hotel Room Selection program, 112–113
    Button objects trigger event, 158
    Deluxe Room button, 81
    event planning document, 157–159
    Exit Window button, 81
    guided program development, 82–94, 159–177
    heading, 81
    introductory comments, 167
    mock-up, 82–94
    program code, **129–157**
    requirements document, 80–81
    simple instructions, 81
    Standard Room button, 81
    Use Case Definition, 78, 80
    user interface design, 80–82
HotelRoomSelection project, 36
Hotel Room Selection window, 31
hot keys, 383–385, 434–435
HTML (Hypertext Markup Language) source
    code, 23, 25

I

icons and message box, 307–308
ideograms, APP1
IDEs (integrated development environments), **17**
If keyword, 312, 314, 318
If statements, 414
    cost per linear foot, 351
    nested, 322–325
    numeric data testing, 350
    positive number testing, 351
    RadioButton object testing, 326–327

If...Then...ElseIf statements, 320–321, 333, 337, 351
    testing RadioButton objects, 326–327
    trailing Else statements, 321
If...Then...Else statements, 318–319, 351
    code snippet for, **337–339**
    comparing to arithmetic expression, 319
    compound conditions, **329**
    event handlers, 328
    And logical operator, **329–330**
    logical operators, **329–337**
    Not logical operator, **331**
If...Then statements, 312–314, 442
    automatically indenting, 313
    comparing data types, 317–318
    comparing strings, 316–317
    keywords, 314–315
    relational operators, 313–315
Image property, **120**, 162, 264, 438
images
    adding to PictureBox object, 117–122
    copyrighted, 117
    determining size of, 118
    distortion, 118, 124
    downloading, 117
    importing into Resources folder, 120–122
    locating and saving, 117–119
    names, 118
    resizing, 123–124
    thumbnails, 118
    Web sites, 117
importing image into Resources folder, 120–122
infinite loops, **406**, **412**
information, **4**, 9–10
input, 10–11
    testing for numeric value, 340–341
input box, **379**
    assigning error messages, 443
    Cancel button, 389
InputBox function, 387, 412–413, 415–416, 422, 441, 444
    coding, 443
    string returned by, 388
    syntax, 387
InputBox object, 387, 388–389
input data, **3**
input devices, 9
Input Error warning dialog box, 293
Input Mask dialog box, 207–208

Insert Breakpoint command, 418–419
Insert Snippet command, 338
instance, **21**
instantiation, **21**
instructions, repeating, 378
Instructions Label object, 172
intAge variable, 314, 328
intAlaskaPopulation variable, 402
intBegin variable, 401, 405
intCount variable, 401, 405
intCreditHours variable, 220
intCubeArea variable, 237, 238
intDayNumber variable, 334
intDepartmentNumber variable, 336
Integer data type, **220**, 230
integer division, 236–237
Integer Division compound operator (\=), 397
integer division operator (\), 236–237
integers, 220
    converting values to, 267
Integer variables, 214, 220, **220**
IntelliSense, **134–139**
    allowable entries, 134–135, 137, 140, 142
    assignment statements, 215–219
    automatically indenting statements, 138
    code snippets, **337–339**
    Common tab, 137
    Do While loops, 408
    Enabled property, 141–143
    entering spaces, 136
    entering Visual Basic statements, 134–138
    formatting statement, 136
    For...Next loops, 402–404
    highlighting correct object name, 135
    highlighting entries in lists, 137
    identifying correct statement, 134–135
    list of allowable entries, 217
    message box, 308–310
    property name, 136
    reducing errors, 138
    speed, 138
    tips, 136
intEnd variable, 401, 405
intGradeLevel variable, 336
intHours variable, 237
intIncrement variable, 401
intLandPlotArea variable, 235

intLandPlotLength variable, 235

intLandPlotWidth variable, 235

intLengthOfCubeSide variable, 237, 238

intMaxNumberOfEntries variable, 413, 441

intMinutes variable, 237

intNumberOfEntries variable, 389, 413–415, 441–442, 444–445

intNumberOfSongs variable, 220, 230, 232, 266

intNumber variable, 399–400

int prefix, 220

intQuarters variable, 411

introductory comments, 146–148, 167

intScore variable, 407–409

intTotalNumberOfMinutes variable, 237

intYears variable, 328, 402–403

Is keyword, 335

IsNumeric function, **340–341**, 414

items, associating as group, 294–297

Items property, 393

iteration, **378**, **399**

iteration structure, **378**

J

Java, 20

K

keyboard

current state of, APP8

deleting objects, 55

L

Label .NET component, **45**, 85, 91, 255, 257

Label objects, **45–46**, 67, 81, 85, 91, 208–210, 255, 436

aligning, 209

automatically expanding, 49

center-aligning, 258

centering, 53–54, 92

changing text in, 48–50

default font, 51–53

fonts, 85, 92

font size, 51–53

font style, 51–53, 85

horizontally centering, 256

multiple lines, 50

naming, 47–48, 85, 91, 256, 258

positioning, 255

referencing by name, 48

resizing, 86

text, 258

Text property, 85, 92, 209–210, 239–240, 243, 245, 256, 346

labels, 208–210

centering, 53–54

clearing, 243

color, 437

default text, 46

fonts, 51–53, 258

font size, 51–53

font style, 51–53

multiple lines, 50

text, 261

lblAccountStatus Label object, 319

lblAverageSpeed Label object, 436, 438, 445

lblConfirmationMessage Label object, 92, 165

lblCostEstimate Label object, 348

lblCostHeading Label object, 245–247, 258

lblCost Label object, 348

lblDayOfWeek Label object, 334

lblDigitalDownloads Label object, 256, 258

lblGPAStatus Label object, 325

lblHeading Label object, 48, 85–86

lblInstructions Label object, 91

lblNumberOfDownloads Label object, 260

lblParkingTime Label object, 411

lblPostedSpeed Label object, 436

lbl prefix, 67

lblTemperature Label object, 240

lblTitle Label object, 435, 437

lblTotalCostLabel Label object, 261

lblTotalCostOfDownloads Label object, 209, 243, 261, 267, 269

lblVotingEligibility Label object, 314–315

less than condition, 14

Less than or equal to (<=) relational operator, 313

Less than (<) relational operator, 313

lifetime, **228**

Linear Feet TextBox object, 293

list box color, 438

ListBox object, 390–395, 436

adding items to, 391–392, 393–395

clearing items, 392

Forecolor property, 438

identifying object selected, 395

resizing, 391
scrollbar, 392
literals, 222, **224–225**
arithmetic expressions, 234–235
local variables, **227–228**
Location property, 435
logical operations, 11–16
equal condition, 12–13
greater than condition, 15
less than condition, 14
logical operators, **329–332**
AndAlso logical operator, 332
And logical operator, **329–330**
order of operations, 332
OrElse logical operator, 332
Xor logical operator, 332
Long data type, 223
looping, **378**
looping structure, **378**
Loop keyword, 406, 408
loops
body of, 399–400
bottom-controlled loops, **406**
Do loops, **405–410**
Do Until loops, **406**, 410–412
Do While loops, **405**
For...Next loops, 399–405
increasing counter, 444
indenting body, 403
nested, 416
performing repetitive tasks, 399–417
preset value in variable, 413–414
priming, **413–414**, 444
selecting type, 417
top-controlled loops, **406**, 408
user input, 412
validating data, 414–416
lstRadarSpeed ListBox object, 390–392, 415, 438, 442, 448
lstStores ListBox object, 393–395

M

main work area, **18**
Make Same Size command, 61, 71
Make Same Size submenu, 61–62, 71, 88, 262
MaskedTextBox .NET component, 206
Masked TextBox object, 204–208
MaskedTextBoxTasks list, 206–207

masks, 205–208
mathmatical expressions and For...Next loops, 401
menu bar, **18**, 33, **380–387**
menu items event handlers, 385
menus, **380–387**
MenuStrip .NET component, 381, 386
MenuStrip objects, 381–387, 434, 448
MenuStrip Tasks menu, 386
Message Box, 293
message box, 303
allowable arguments, 309
buttons, 306–307
captions, 305–306
displaying, 351
icons, 307–308
IntelliSense, 308–310
messages, 304–305
string concatenation, 311
string messages, 305
title bar, 305–306
MessageBox class, 304
MessageBox.Show command, 304
methods, 239
Microsoft Expression Web, 23
Microsoft Intermediate Language. *See* MSIL (Microsoft Intermediate Language)
Microsoft Office 2003, 25
Microsoft Office 2007, 25
Microsoft Office 2010, 25
Microsoft Visual Studio Professional 2010, 17
mnuClearItem MenuScript object, 384
mnuFile MenuScript object, 383
mnuHighwayRadarCheckpoint MenuScript object, 382, 434
mnu prefix, 382
mobile applications, **25**, 292
mobile devices, 25
mock-up file, 160
mock-ups, **79**, 81–82
MOD operator, 237
mouse state and hardware characteristics, APP8
MSDN Academic Alliance, 17
MsgBox command, 304, 305, 309
MsgBox object, 398
MsgBoxStyle, 308
MsgBoxStyle.AbortRetryIgnore argument, 310
MSIL (Microsoft Intermediate Language), **23–25**
MultiLine text boxes, 204–205

multiple arithmetic operations, 238
multiplication, 235
Multiplication compound operator (*=), 397
multiplication operator (*), 235
Music image, 264
My.Application class, **APP6**
My.Computer.Audio.Play method, APP7
My.Computer.Audio.PlaySystemSound method, APP7
My.Computer class, **APP7–APP8**
My.Computer.Mouse class, APP8
My.Computer.Network class, APP8–APP9
My.Computer.Screen class, APP9–APP10
My.Forms class, APP10
My namespace, **APP5**
    coding examples, APP6–APP10
    My.Application class, **APP6**
    My.Computer class, **APP7–APP8**
    My.Computer.Mouse class, APP8
    My.Computer.Network class, APP8–APP9
    My.Computer.Screen class, APP9–APP10
    My.Forms class, APP10
    My.User class, **APP10**
My.User class, **APP10**
My.User.Name property, **APP10**

N

Name property, 48
(Name) property, 47, 58, 85, 87–88, 90, 133, 200, 262, 296, 299, 382–384, 390
naming conventions, APP11–APP12
negative numbers, 221
negative speed error message, 443
nested For loops, 416
nested If statements, 322–325
nested loops, 416
.NET
    class library, 20–22
    CLR (Common Language Runtime), **23–25**
    technologies and products, 20
.NET components, **18**, **38**, 66
.NET Framework, **20**
    ADO.NET 4.0, 22–23
    ASP.NET 4.0, 23
    CLR (Common Language Runtime), **23–25**
    MSIL (Microsoft Intermediate Language), **23–25**
    .NET class library, 20–22

operating systems, 25
    RAD (rapid application development), 22
network interactions, APP8
New Project dialog box, 34–36, 254, 345, 434
Next statement, 399
nondecimal whole number, 220
non-numeric speed error message, 443
normal division, 235
Normal option, **123**
Not equal to (<>) relational operator, 313
Not logical operator, **331**
null characters, testing for, 389
null strings, 243, 387
Number(N) format specifier, 241
Number of Song Downloads Label object, 260
numbers, 221, 240
numeric data, 10
    displaying output, 239–242
    String data type, 239–240
    testing for, 350
numeric data types, **219–221**
numeric values
    comparing, 410–411
    converting to String value, 240–241
    testing input for, 340–341
    validating, 442
numeric variables, 228

O

Object data type, 223
objects, **19**, **21–22**, 39–41
    aligning, 70–73
    aligning text, 73
    arrangement, 80
    ASP.NET 4.0, 23
    capitalization, 133
    centering multiple horizontally, 64–65
    controlling, 61, 62
    deleting, 55–56
    [Design] tab, 51
    disabled, **126–128**
    enabled, **126–128**
    GUI (Graphical User Interface) and, 80
    moving, 69
    naming, 47–48, 133
    placing, 37

prefix, 40
properties, **19**
purpose, 80
same size, 60–62
selecting, 40
selecting multiple, 61
sizing handles, 40
smart actions, **386**
triggering event, 158
vertically aligning, 72–73
viewing properties, 39
visibility, 125–126
Office applications, **25**
Open dialog box, 121–122
operating systems
.NET Framework 4.0, 25
Visual Basic 2010 and, 32
Options command, 131
Options dialog box, 131
Option Strict On command, 231, 265, 350, 439
OrElse logical operator, 332
Or logical operator, **330–331**
output, 9–11
numeric data, 239–242
output data, **4**
output devices, 10
Overflow Exception, **250**

P

palettes, 115
Panel object, 302
PDLC (program development life cycle), **75–80**, 112
documenting program, **75–76**
processing objects, 75
program and system maintenance, **76**
program code, **75**
program processing objects design, 157–159
program requirements, 75–78
testing program, 75
user interface design, 75
Percent(P) format specifier, 241
persistent, **4**
Phone number input mask, 205–208
picCabinets Picture object, 349
picDeluxeRoom picture, 60
picDeluxeRoom Picture object, 138–141
picDownloadHeading Picture object, 255, 260, 264

pic prefix, 58, 67
picRadar PictureBox object, 435
picStandardRoom PictureBox object, 58, 120, 122, 132, 162, 164
PictureBox .NET component, 57, 60, 87–88, 255
PictureBox objects, **56–58**, 67, 81, 255, 349, 435, 438
adding, 60
adding images to, 117–122
aligning, 62–64, 90
centering, 64–65, 88
default size, 57
determining size of, 118
distance between, 88
horizontal alignment, 88
horizontally centering, 256
moving, 57
naming, 58, 60, 87–88, 255
pic prefix, 58
positioning, 255
resizing, 58–59, 87–88, 255
picture files, 349
pictures, 81, 164
pinging computers, APP9
positive numbers, 221
checking for, 341
testing for, 351
validating, 442
precision specifiers, **241–242**
presentation layer, **79**
prewritten procedures, 156
price per download, 246
priming the loop, **413–414**, 444
Print command, 156
Print dialog box, 156–157
printing
code, 156–157
user interface, 157
Private Sub statement, 131
procedure call statement, **155**
procedures, **154, 227–228**, 239
arguments, **229**
classes containing, 229
prewritten, 156
returning or not returning values, 229
usage, 228–231
writing, 156

processes, repeating, 405–410

processing, **3**, 11

    objects, 75, 157–159

program and system maintenance, **76**

program code, **75, 129–157**

program compilation, **23–25**

program development life cycle. *See* PDLC (program development life cycle)

programming languages, **5**, 19–20

    New Project window, 34

    programming rules, **17**

    syntax, **16**

    types of applications, 34

programming rules, **17**

program requirements, 75

    designing user interface, 78–80

    documenting, 76–78

    gathering, 76

    requirements document, **77**

    Use Case Definition, **78**

programs, 2–3, 3

    actions taken by, 78

    basic operations, 8–16

    break mode, 417

    breakpoints, **417**, 420

    checking for updates, 427

    closing, 129

    code for, 5

    coding, 159

    coding error, 149

    comments, 167

    comment statements, **143–148**

    common code, 21

    current version, APP6

    date comment line, 167

    debugging, 248–250, **417**

    designing, 30

    documenting, 75–76

    event-driven, **5–8**, 20, 32, 129–130

    general steps, 4

    input, 8–9

    installing, 427, 429

    introductory comments, 146–148, 167

    iterative development, 76

    logical operations, 11–16

    name of, 36, 147–148, 167

    output, 9–10

    pausing execution, **417**

    presentation layer, **79**

    program purpose comment lines, 167

    publishing, 425–429

    reusing, 21

    running, **128–129**

    saving, 16, 259, 438

    shortcut added to Start menu, 428

    terminating, 154–156

    testing, 75

    user interaction with, 7–8

    Windows authentication, APP10

    working together, 5

projects

    creation, 34–37

    deploying, 425–429

    listing recent, 75

    opening, 75

    opening multiple forms, APP10

    saving, 73

properties, **19, 39–40**, 133

Properties command, 118

Properties window, **19**, 48, 67, 118, 260, 263, 345, 382, 390, 438

    Alphabetical view, **39**

    Categorized view, **39**

    color window, 115

    displaying, 39

    ellipsis button, 51

    Web tabbed page, 115

publishing

    programs, 425–429

    to USB drive, 426

Publish Radar command, 426, 450

Publish Wizard, 426–429, 450

punctuation, 222–223

Pushpin icon, 38

R

Radar image, 438

Radar Speed dialog box, 379

Radar Speed InputBox object, 389, 420–421

radCherry button, 327

radCherry RadioButton object, 347

RadioButton objects, 293–294, 298–301, 326–327

    placing in container object, 303

    testing status in code, 326–327

radio buttons, 298–300
    Checked property, 326, 347
    grouping, 294
    naming, 299
    selecting, 300–301
radOak RadioButton object, 327, 347
radPine RadioButton object, 301, 326–327, 347
RAD (rapid application development), 22, APP5
RAD (rapid application development) tools, **32**
RAM (random access memory), **4**, 9–11
ranges and Select Case statements, 336
rapid application development. *See* RAD (rapid application development)
Ready to Publish Wizard window, 427
Recent Projects and Solutions command, 75
Redo button, 56
redoing actions, 56
red snap lines, **73**, 201
referencing variables, 227
relational operators, 313–318
    comparing strings, 316–317
    Select Case statements, 335
remainder, 237
Rename command, 40–41, 84
repeating processes, 405–410
repetitive tasks, 399–417
requirements document, **77**, 80–81
Reset Window button, 8
Resources folder, **117**, 264
    importing images into, 120–122
rounding numbers, 240
running programs, **128–129**

S

same line comments, 145
Save Picture As command, 119
Save Picture dialog box, 119
Save Project dialog box, 74
saving data, **4**
Scientific(E) format specifier, 241
scope
    block-level, 327–328
    classes, 247–248
scope of a variable, **227**, 247, 327
screen, APP9–APP10
security and ASP.NET 4.0, 23
Select Case statements, 332–337

SelectedItem property, 395
Select Resource dialog box, **121–122**, 162, 264, 438
Select Room button, 159, 166, 169, 174
Set Mask command, 206–207
shortcut menu, deleting objects, 56
Short data type, 223
Short date input mask, 205–208
Show procedure, 304, 307
Single data type, 223
SizeMode property, **123–124**, 264, 349, 438
Size property, **44–45**, 118, 345, 349, 436
smart actions, **386**
snap lines, **70**, 72–73
Social Security number input mask, 205–208
software, 2–3, 16
Solution Explorer, **18**, 39–41
sounds, playing, APP7
SplitContainer container object, 302
Squared Values application, 405
Standard Items command, 386
Standard Room button, 67, 72, 81, 139, 158–159
Standard Room Button object, 90, 130–131
StandardRoom image, 120–122, 174
StandardRoom.jpg file, 118, 119, 121
StandardRoom PictureBox object, 169
Standard toolbar, **18**, 33
    Continue button, 422
    New Project button, 34, 254, 345, 434
    Open File button, 75
    Redo button, 56
    Save All button, 74, 259
    Start Debugging button, 128–129, 149, 270, 310, 420, 448
    Stop Debugging button, 250
    Toolbox button, 37, 254
    Undo button, 56
Start Page, 33
statements
    allowable entries, 134
    automatic indentations, 138
    capitalization, 133
    correct entries, 132
    dot operator (period), 132, 133
    elements separated by space, 132
    equal sign and, 132–133, 133
    general format, 133
    identifying object containing property to set, 132

IntelliSense and, **134–138**
object name, 133
property name, 132–133
spaces, 136
Status bar, 45
Step value, 400–401
storing data, **4**
strAge variable, 388
StretchImage, 163
StretchImage option, **124**
strict type checking, 265, 439
String Collection Editor window, 394
string concatenation, 311
String data type, **213–214**, 230
concatenation, 246–247
numeric data, 239–240
string messages, 305
strings
comparing, 316–317
concatenating, 246–247
defining, 213
null length, 243
string values
comparing, 410–411
converting numeric value to, 240–241
converting to Decimal data type, 442
String variables, **213**
converting data type, 228–229
converting to integers, 267
defining, 215
str prefix, 213
strInputBoxMessage variable, 389
strInputHeading variable, 440
strInputMessage variable, 415, 440, 442
strNegativeError variable, 415, 440, 443
strNonNumericError variable, 415, 440, 443
strNormalMessage variable, 440
strNumberOfDownloads String variable, 217
strNumberOfSongs String variable, 214–219
strNumberOfSongs variable, 217, 225, 227, 229–230, 232, 266
strPhrase variable, 398
str prefix, 213, 216
strTestGrade variable, 412
strVehicleSpeed variable, 413, 440, 442
Sub procedure, 227, **229**
subtraction, 235

subtraction arithmetic operator (-), **235**
Subtraction compound operator (-=), 397
symbols, 222–223
syntax, **16**, **131–132**
system buffer, viewing, APP7
system clock, APP7
System palette, **115**

T

TabControl container object, 302
TableLayoutPanel container object, 302
tasks, repetitive, 399–417
testing input for numeric value, 340–341
text
aligning, 202–203
Button object, 66–67, 71
default font, 51–53
font size, 51–53
font style, 51–53
horizontally aligning, 201
Label object, 48–50, 258, 261
multiple lines, 50
title bar, 42–43
Windows Form object, 84
TextAlign property, 202, 261, 435
text boxes
clearing, 211
data format of value typed, 205–208
maximum and minimum sizes, 199
MultiLine, 204–205
TextBox .NET component, 198
TextBox objects, **197–208**, 260–261, 346
aligning text, 202–203
default size, 199
entering data, 204
focus, 243–244
multiple lines of text, 204–205
naming, 199, 200
positioning, 199–201
resizing, 199–201
txt prefix, 199
Text property, **42–43**, 48, 50, 67, 84–85, 90, 92, 200, 219, 239–240, 254, 262, 345
clearing, 242, 243
entering data into, 260
null length string, 243
Then keyword, 315, 318–319, 322–323

time, properties for displaying, APP7
title bar, **17**, 42–43, 74
ToInt32 procedure, 229, 250
Toolbox, **18**
    Auto Hide button, **38**
    Auto Hide mode, **38**
    Button .NET component, 70
    closing, 211–212, 265
    Common Controls category, 37, 46
    Containers category, 295, 302
    displaying, **37–38**, 254, 434
    Dockable mode, 38
    hidden, 38
    Label .NET component, 46, 85, 91, 255, 257
    MaskedTextBox .NET component, 206
    Menus & Toolbars category, 381, 434
    MenuStrip .NET component, 381
    .NET components, **38**, 66
    permanently displaying, 38
    PictureBox .NET component, 57, 60, 87–88, 435
    TextBox .NET component, 198
    visible, 83
Toolbox button, **37**
Tools menu, 131
top-controlled Do Until loops, 410–411
top-controlled Do While loops, 406–407
top-controlled loops, **406**, 408
ToString function, 239–241
ToString procedure, 246
trailing Else statements, 321
txtFeet TextBox object, 346, 350
txtLinearFeet TextBox object, 340–341
txtNumberOfDownloads TextBox object, 199, 200, 214, 218–219, 260, 267, 269
    focus, 244
txt prefix, 199
txtStudentMajor TextBox object, 335
type inference, 220

U

Undo button, 56
undoing actions, 56
Unicode, 222, APP1–APP4
    characters, 316
Until keyword, 417
USB drive, publishing to, 426

use case, **78**
Use Case Definition, **78**, 80, 252
user input and For...Next loops, 404–405
user input loops, 412
user interface
    Accept button, 210–211
    aligned objects, 54
    BackColor property, 263
    buttons, 81, 262
    designing, 32–75, 75, 78–80
    design principles, **79–80**
    Digital Downloads program, 197–212
    fine-tuning, 114–129
    Hotel Room Selection program, 80–82
    interacting, 79
    intuitive, 80
    items, 81
    mock-up, **79**, 81–94, 160
    pictures, 81
    printing, 157
    tools for user to make selections, 81
users
    entering data, 197–208
    information about, APP10

V

validating data, 293, 339–341, 414–416
values
    converting to integer, 267
    displaying group of, 390–395
    equal, 12–13
    greater than, 15
    greater than maximum value, 250
    less than, 14
    preventing automatic conversion, 231
variable dimension, 213
variables, **213**
    adding value to, 396
    arithmetic expressions, 234
    block of code and, 328
    classes and, 247–248
    class scope, 247–248
    coding, 444
    constants, 248
    converting data, 228–231
    declaring, 266, 350, 440–441
    defining, 213–214, 247–248

Dim keyword, 213
examining values, 417–425
For...Next loops, 401
global, **228**
initializing, 266, 350, 440–441
As keyword, 213
local, **227–228**
for messages, 444
multiple event handlers, 247
names, 213–214
prefixes, 224
referencing, 227
scope, 227–228, 247–248, 327
testing in Select Case statements, 334
value copied to, 214
values, 225
Virtual Studio 2010 window, 19
Visible property, **125–126**, 132, 136, 138–141, 164, 172, 174, 438
Visual Basic 2010, 16, 17, 19, 32
case insensitivity, 19
coding statements, 131–132
information about, 33
mobile applications, 25
syntax, **131–132**
writing programs, 17
Visual Basic code, 23
Visual Basic projects
opening, 75
saving, 73–74
Visual Basic solution, **18**
Visual Basic statements
allowable entries, 134
general format, 133
IntelliSense and, **134–138**
Visual Basic Web site, 25
Visual C#, 20
Visual F#, 20
Visual Studio 2010, **17**, **30**
automatically indenting statements, 138
closing, 74
opening, 32–33, 83
preparation for code entry, 211–212
programming languages, 19
splash screen, 33
versions, 17
Visual Studio 2010 window, 17–18, 37, 39

W

.wav files, APP7
Web applications, 23
Web palette, **115**
Web services, 25
Web Shots Web site, 117
Web site applications, **25**
Web sites, 23, 117
Web tabbed page, 115
While keyword, 417
windows
buttons, 70
centering multiple objects horizontally, 64–65
closing, 154–156
pictures in, 56–58
Windows 7
de-emphazing menus, 386
Visual Basic 2010, 32
Windows applications, **25**, 254, 434
container objects, 302–303
controls, 25
creation, 34–37, 345
Panel object, 302
Windows authentication, APP10
Windows Form object, 21, **37**, 67, 80
Accept button, 210–211
aligning objects, 62–64
Button objects, 65–66, 89
Cancel button, 211
changing title, 254
deleting objects, 55–56
frm prefix, 40
heading, 256
Label object, **45–46**, 53–54
Label objects, 208–210
moving objects on, 69
naming, 39–41, 84, 254, 434
PictureBox .NET component, 255
PictureBox object, 56–58
resizing, 44–45, 85, 255, 434
selecting, 114
text, 84
TextBox object, 198, 260
title bar text, 42–43, 434
Windows Forms Application, 35, 80
Windows Forms Application project, 83
Windows graphical user interface, 35

Windows projects types, 35
Windows Vista, 32
Windows XP, 32
Wood Cabinet Estimate program, 292–293
    Calculate and Clear buttons, 349
    Calculate button code, 352–353
    calculations, 293, 351
    Clear button click event handler, 353
    code listing, 355–356
    coding, 350–354
    comments, 350
    declaring and intializing variables, 350
    designing and coding, 344
    error message, 352
    estimate and cost labels, 348
    event planning document, 343
    Form Load event handler, 354
    guided program development, 344–354
    labels, 346
    message box, 303–310, 351
    picture files, 349
    program design, 342–344
    requirements document, 342
    running, 310, 354
    string concatenation, 311
    testing, 354
    testing status of RadioButton object in code, 326–327
    title bar, 345
    Use Case Definition document, 342–343
    user interface design, 294
work area, **37**
World Wide Web, locating and saving image from, 117–119

X

Xor logical operator, 332

Z

zero, dividing by, 236, 250
Zoom option, **123**

PHOTO CREDITS

Figure #	Credit
1.01a	© 2011 Jupiterimages Corporation
1.01b	© 2011 Jupiterimages Corporation
1.01c	© 2011 Jupiterimages Corporation
1.01d	PRNewsFoto/Donna Karan
1.01e	© iStockphoto/Fuat Kose
1.02a	Courtesy of Seagate Technology
1.02b	Courtesy of Lenovo
1.02c	© 2011 Jupiterimages Corporation
1.02d	Courtesy of Kingston Technology Company, Inc.
1.02e	Courtesy of Epson America, Inc.
1.02f	Courtesy of Umax Systems GmbH
1.02g	Courtesy of Umax Systems GmbH
1.03a	© 2011 Jupiterimages Corporation
1.03b	Courtesy of Umax Systems GmbH
1.03c	© 2011 Jupiterimages Corporation
1.03d	© 2011 Jupiterimages Corporation
1.03e	Courtesy of Umax Systems GmbH
1.03f	© 2011 Jupiterimages Corporation
1.03g	Courtesy of Kingston Technology Company, Inc.
1.03h	© 2011 Jupiterimages Corporation
1.03i	© 2011 Jupiterimages Corporation
1.03j	Courtesy of Epson America, Inc.
1.03k	Courtesy of Epson America, Inc.
1.04	Courtesy of Kingston Technology Company, Inc.
1.10a	© 2011 Jupiterimages Corporation
1.10b	Courtesy of Kingston Technology Company, Inc.
1.11	Courtesy of Kingston Technology Company, Inc.
1.12a	PRNewsFoto/WebMD Health Corp
1.12b	Image copyright 2010, Denise Kappa. Used under license from Shutterstock.com
1.12c	Courtesy of Epson America, Inc.
1.13	Courtesy of Kingston Technology Company, Inc.
1.22	Courtesy of Kingston Technology Company, Inc.
2.73	© 2011 Jupiterimages Corporation
3.84	Image copyright 2010, Denise Kappa. Used under license from Shutterstock.com
3.90	© 2011 Jupiterimages Corporation
3.93	© 2011 Jupiterimages Corporation
4.100	Image copyright 2010, byphoto. Used under license from Shutterstock.com
4.103	© 2011 Jupiterimages Corporation
4.106	Image copyright 2010, Scott Rothstein. Used under license from Shutterstock.com
5.03	Image copyright 2010, Christopher David Howells. Used under license from Shutterstock.com
5.100	Image copyright 2010, Svetlana Larina. Used under license from Shutterstock.com
5.103	Image copyright 2010, Marcio Jose Bastos Silva. Used under license from Shutterstock.com
5.106	Image copyright 2010, broeb. Used under license from Shutterstock.com
6.01	Courtesy of the Shawnee Police Department
6.124	© 2011 Jupiterimages Corporation
6.127	Image copyright 2010, Todd Taulman. Used under license from Shutterstock.com
6.130	Image copyright 2010, David Lee. Used under license from Shutterstock.com